黄土高原
古土壤S1的地理分异

——末次间冰期古气候重建置疑

汪海斌　冯兆东　/ 著

Geographic Differentiation of the Paleosol S1 in the Chinese Loess Plateau

Disputation on Paleoclimatic Reconstruction of the Last Interglacial

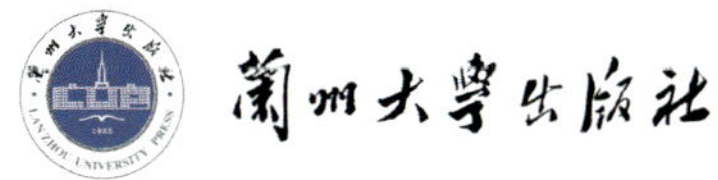

蘭州大學出版社

图书在版编目（CIP）数据

黄土高原古土壤S1的地理分异 : 末次间冰期古气候重建置疑 / 汪海斌, 冯兆东著. -- 兰州 : 兰州大学出版社, 2014.7
ISBN 978-7-311-04500-5

Ⅰ. ①黄… Ⅱ. ①汪… ②冯… Ⅲ. ①黄土高原—古气候—古土壤—研究 Ⅳ. ①P531

中国版本图书馆CIP数据核字(2014)第158341号

策划编辑 施援平 王曦莹
责任编辑 郝可伟 施援平
封面设计 管军伟

书　　名 黄土高原古土壤S1的地理分异
　　　　 ——末次间冰期古气候重建置疑
作　　者 汪海斌 冯兆东 著
出版发行 兰州大学出版社 (地址:兰州市天水南路222号 730000)
电　　话 0931-8912613(总编办公室) 0931-8617156(营销中心)
　　　　 0931-8914298(读者服务部)
网　　址 http://www.onbook.com.cn
电子信箱 press@lzu.edu.cn
印　　刷 甘肃兴方正彩色数码快印有限公司
开　　本 787 mm×1092 mm 1/16
印　　张 15.25(插页4)
字　　数 334千
版　　次 2014年10月第1版
印　　次 2014年10月第1次印刷
书　　号 ISBN 978-7-311-04500-5
定　　价 60.00元

(图书若有破损、缺页、掉页可随时与本社联系)

冯兆东

Feng Zhaodong

1955 年生于甘肃定西，现任中国科学院新疆生态与地理研究所特聘研究员（2012 年起）。1982 年获得兰州大学地理学硕士，1987 年获得美国 Vashington University 地质学硕士，1992 年获得美国 Kansas University 地理学博士；1992—1994 年在美国 Columbia University Lamont-Doherty 地球研究中心从事博士后研究工作。1982—1985 年任兰州大学地理系讲师；1994—1996 年任美国 Utah University 地理系助理教授，1996—2008 年任美国 Montclair State University 地球环境系助理教授、副教授、教授；2000 年被聘为教育部“长江学者奖励计划”特聘教授（兰州大学）。

汪海斌

Wang Haibin

1976 年生于浙江金华，生前任兰州大学西部资源与环境学院副教授。2001 年获得兰州大学地理学硕士学位；2005 年获得兰州大学地理学博士学位；2005—2008 年在北京师范大学资源学院从事博士后研究工作，2006 年在美国 Montclair State University 做访问学者。

主要从事黄土与气候变化研究，主讲自然地理学研究方法、专业外语等课程。曾主持自然科学面上基金项目 1 项，参加科技部“973”重大项目 1 项，参与自然科学基金重点项目 1 项；共发表 SCI、核心文章十余篇。2008—2011 年在兰州大学西部资源与环境学院先后任讲师和副教授。

前 言

这本书的立意是:批判地审视"基于黄土高原末次间冰期古土壤S1的高分辨率气候重建"。

虽然An（安芷生）和Porter（1997）关于末次间冰期冬季风存在千年尺度剧烈变化的报道是很有影响力的（见：An and Porter. Geology，1997，25（7）：603-606），但他们报道的黄土高原中部地区S1中表达气候剧烈变化的粉尘事件是值得怀疑的。他们重建的末次间冰期风尘气候序列存在两个主要问题：（1）黄土高原末次间冰期古土壤S1年代的可靠性问题；（2）气候代用指标的可靠性问题。

记得那是1998年12月的一个周末，我（冯兆东）在我当时任教的美国新泽西蒙特克莱尔州立大学（Montclair State University）办公室赶写NSF的基金申请书（关于蒙古高原全新世的），突然接到任教于美国路易安娜州立大学的廖淦标教授的电话，他问我有没有读过An和Porter1997发表于《Geology》的文章。在知道我没读过的情况下，廖淦标立即传真了一份给我。我十分认真地读了那篇文章，并激动地认为：在黄土高原中部和东部地区的S1中重建高分辨率气候事件是不大可能的。于是，我激情地撰写了关于中国黄土高原末次间冰期古土壤S1问题的NSF申请书（题目：Geographic Differentiation of the Last Interglacial Paleosol S1 in the Chinese Loess Plateau）。出乎意料的是：在我的关于蒙古高原全新世的NSF申请两次被毙的低迷情况下，我的关于中国黄土高原末次间冰期古土壤S1问题的NSF申请书于1999年竟然一举成功（批准号：NSF BCS-0078577）。2000年我开始在兰州大学做教育部"长江学者奖励计划特聘教授"，接着又从教育部获得了重点项目基金（批准号：MOE-2000-65）的支持，这些都给我深入研究黄土高原末次间冰期古土壤S1问题创造了良好的条件。

出版这本书的动机是：纪念本书的第一作者——汪海斌博士。

本书的核心是汪海斌的博士论文——《黄土高原末次间冰期古土壤S1的地理分异及其气候和年代学意义》。早在2008年，我和汪海斌博士就计划要将他的博士论文整理出版。可是万分痛惜的事发生在我们的计划实现之前：汪海斌博士于2011年

11月8日因车祸殉职于去昆仑山北麓采样的路上！汪海斌的去世给我们所有了解他的人留下了难以抹去的心理阴影。作为他的导师和朋友，我在这个阴影下痛苦地生活了两年有余。汪海斌博士去世的第二天，我和我的同事马玉贞教授在网上交流回忆汪海斌时，我们的归纳是：那么聪慧、那么勤奋、那么谦和、那么有前程的一个小伙子怎么说没就没了呢？他才35岁呀！汪海斌博士实际上是“中国黄土高原末次间冰期古土壤S1问题”项目的具体执行人。这个项目的顺利完成完全是他刻苦努力的结果，这个项目的顺利完成也将他造就成为一名同行信任的黄土地层与古土壤学者。“同行信任”是有据可查的：无论是从上海来的同行，还是从西宁来的同行，无论是从德国来的同行，还是从美国来的同行，他们都特意请汪海斌博士带他们去野外考察，帮他们描述黄土剖面。写到这里，汪海斌博士的许多往事浮现在我的眼前：我们多次一起去黄土高原野外考察的情景；我们多次一起去蒙古高原野外考察的情景；我们在离贝加尔湖不远的Gun Nuur湖畔玩扑克牌的情景；我们一起在兰州大学榆中校区萃英山顶放声狂吼的情景……

汪海斌博士有三个宝贵的品质是我这辈子忘不了的：诚实；勤奋；谦逊。第一，他的诚实。我和他频繁地打交道有十年之久，没有一件事让我对他有不信任的感觉。我和汪海斌之所以从师生关系演化为朋友关系是因为我们俩有共同的生活底线：从来不以不诚实的态度和别人打交道。第二，他的勤奋。他在做我的研究助手时，无论是实验分析，还是图件制作，他完成的速度总比我预期的速度要高出至少一倍。而且他总是让人放心，因为他的实验数据是经得起检验的，他做出来的图件是完美得无须再作任何修改的。第三，他的谦逊。许多人问过我：老冯，你的风格怎么可能带出这么谦逊的学生呢？他不卑不亢的谦逊很是讨人喜欢。他去世后有那么多的人来向他告别就足以说明这一点。

这本书的结论是：复杂的成壤过程往往使得S1高分辨率气候重建成为不可能。

我们的研究表明，沉积前黄土源区的风化程度控制着黄土粒度分布的第一级变化与次一级变化，这对粒度作为冬季风强度指标的正确性提出了强有力的挑战。至于磁化率，它确实主要受成壤因素的影响，但成壤过程并不是导致磁化率增强的必然条件。具有消磁作用的碳酸盐的聚集、导致磁性加强的淋溶过程、植物残体分解过程中产生的超细磁性颗粒以及对磁化率进行改造的氧化还原反应都属于成壤作用。因此，要作为夏季风强度的定量指标，磁化率信号必须被订正。从地理分异的角度看，在中国黄土高原西北边缘地带，与氧同位素亚阶段5a、5c和5e对应的三层古土壤（S1S1、S1S2、S1S3）和其中相间的与氧同位素亚阶段5b和5d对应的两层黄土（S1L1和S1L2）保存完整。向东南到黄土高原中部和东部，S1L1和S1L2被后期发育的土壤所吞并，三层古土壤部分地融合在一起，S1剖面是多次成壤事件的结果，而且古土壤伸入到了下伏的更老黄土（L2）。我们的研究结果证明：S1古土壤的形成年代与其母质的形成年代是不一致的。这警示我们：在进行高分辨率气候重建时，必须充分理解S1的土壤发生学和土壤地貌学意义。

致谢：

汪海斌的博士论文完成于2005年5月，在论文评审和答辩过程中得到了以下同行的学术指导：陈发虎教授、方小敏教授、郭正堂教授、潘保田教授、肖举乐教授、姚檀栋教授、郑洪波教授。

我自己也想借着这个机会感谢我的四位导师，因为是他们把我带到“黄土与第四纪气候研究”这条学术道路上的。首先，兰州大学的李吉均教授在我学术生涯的早期给予了我巨大的支持。第二，美国华盛顿大学的Stephen Porter教授耐心地让我完成了我的第二个硕士学位的学习。第三，美国堪萨斯大学的William Johnson教授以及他的同事们给予了我完整的“土壤发生学和土壤地貌学”方面的训练，也让我有机会深入地研究了美国大平原地区的黄土地层（我还在堪萨斯大学接受了完整的地理信息系统和遥感方面的训练）。第四，美国哥伦比亚大学的George Kukla教授的严谨的治学风格与Lamont-Doherty Earth Observatory的活跃的学术氛围让我彻底理解了：做科学研究既需要一丝不苟的严谨态度，也需要“宗教狂般”的追求精神。

本书的出版经费来自新疆生态与地理研究所提供的所长基金（时任所长是陈曦博士）。

冯兆东

2014年5月8日

于新疆生态与地理研究所

目 录

摘 要

An和Porter（Geology，1997，25（7）：603-606）报道了末次间冰期洛川地区2.5 m厚的S1记录了9次高粉尘事件，前6次可以同北大西洋V29.191深海钻孔记录的寒冷事件相比，后3次可与GRIP冰芯记录的强烈降温事件对照。然而，土壤发生过程的复杂性令年代上的对比并不可靠。为了考察S1土壤发生的复杂性，我们选择了黄土高原东、西两个断面对土壤形态、粒度、磁化率等进行观测或分析。结果表明：从黄土高原的西北端到东南端，由于粉尘的堆积速率呈递减趋势而成壤作用逐渐加强，造成了末次间冰期古土壤S1从3层土壤逐渐融合为一个单一的土壤剖面。具体地说，沿黄土高原西部S1的断面，在西北边缘，对应于MIS 5中3个暖的亚阶段（5a、5c、5e）的3层古土壤（S1S1、S1S2、S1S3）以及对应于MIS 5中两个冷的亚阶段（5b、5d）的两层黄土都完整地保存下来了（如兰州剖面和定西剖面）。向东南来到秦安剖面，S1L2受到后期的成壤改造而被S1S2吞并了。而且秦安剖面的S1S1、S1S2、S1S3的发育程度都比兰州剖面或定西剖面的高。继续向东南便是天水剖面，不仅S1L2而且S1L1皆为后期的土壤发育（S1S2，S1S1）所吞噬，故3个土壤（S1S1、S1S2、S1S3）部分地融合到一起。沿黄土高原的东部断面，环县剖面S1的土壤地层与定西剖面相似，3层古土壤嵌两层黄土的结构也被完整地保存了下来，而发育程度最高的S1S3伸入到了下伏的L2黄土。庆阳剖面和旬邑剖面是天水剖面的“压缩版”，即，S1L1、S1L2由于受到后期的成壤改造而分别成为S1S1、S1S2的组成部分；3个土壤（S1S1、S1S2、S1S3）完全地融合在一起，形成一个类似软土状的加积型土壤复合体。在东南端，宝鸡剖面和蓝田剖面的S1亦为经多次成壤（S1S1、S1S2、S1S3）作用形成的土壤复合体，并且呈现为单一的土壤剖面，Bt层发育得很好。从所有考察的剖面看，中值粒径和>63 μm粗颗粒组分可以相当好地确定古土壤S1岩性的上下界限，我们可以用此来估计S1古土壤的穿时性特征。土壤融合，土壤发生过程中的生物扰动、物质转化和迁移都使得黄土高原东南部的S1无法保存详细的、高分辨率的气候变化信息。

关键词：末次间冰期；气候变化；中国黄土高原；古土壤

Abstract

An and Porter (1997) reported nine high dust - influx events of millennial timescales recovered from the last interglacial paleosol S1 and correlated them to six cool events of millennial timescales in the North Atlantic. However, the complexity of soil forming processes may have made the chronological correlation with the North Atlantic records inadequate. To examine the complexity of the S1 formation, the S1 paleosol was traced laterally and identified based on the preserved characteristics observed in the field and analyzed in the laboratory. Our data show that from the northwest to the southeast, the S1 paleosol gradually converges from three distinctive soil profiles into a single welded profile because the net rate of loess accumulation was attenuated to the southeast and pedogenic development intensified southeastward during the last interglacial. Three soil - forming events within the S1 paleosol (S1S1, S1S2 and S1S3) separated by two loess units (S1L1 and S1L2) in the northwestern part of the Loess Plateau are stratigraphically coeval with a single soil profile in the southeastern margin of the Loess Plateau. In the southeast, the S1 paleosol developed into underlying older loess L2 (e.g., at the Lantian section). The three paleosols (S1S1, S1S2 and S1S3) are partially welded in the central part of the Chinese Loess Plateau (e.g., at the Tianshui section) where the lower portion of S1 paleosol developed in the underlying older loess unit L2. In the northwestern margin of the Chinese Loess Plateau (e.g., at the Lanzhou section), the preservation of the soil - loess sequence (S1S1, S1L1, S1S2, S1L2, S1S3) continuously documented the climatic events of the last interglacial. Our data also show that the magnetic signatures and particle - size information are more or less acceptable climatic proxies only for the northwestern sections where the degree of pedogenesis was lower and the rate of eolian influx was greater during the last interglacial. It appears that in all cases investigated, the median grain size and the coarse fraction (>63 μm) content define the upper and lower boundaries of the S1 paleosol reasonably well and can be used to estimate the time - transgressive nature of the S1 paleosol relative to its parent material. Soil welding, bioturbation and material translocation within the S1 soil profiles make it impossible to preserve the detailed and high - resolution information of climate changes in those S1 profiles in the southeastern part (including the central part) of the Chinese Loess Plateau.

Key Words: Last Interglacial; Climate Change; Chinese Loess Plateau; Paleosols

1 绪 论

国际地圈-生物圈计划（International Geosphere Biosphere Programme，简称IGBP）的总体目标是："阐明并理解调控整个地球系统的物理的、化学的以及生物的交互过程，阐明并理解这些过程影响之下的供养生命的独一无二的环境系统、正在该系统内发生的变化以及它在人类活动的影响下以何种方式发生变化……"人类活动对气候系统的影响自19世纪中叶以来日益增强，大量的观测数据和证据表明：地球正在变暖，伴随气候系统的其他变化，20世纪全球平均表面温度增加了0.6 ℃左右；20世纪全球的海平面上升了0.1～0.2 m；20世纪是过去千年最暖的一个世纪，20世纪90年代是过去千年最暖的一个年代。人类活动产生的温室气体和气溶胶改变了大气状况进而影响着气候系统。不过，我们到目前为止还不甚清楚温室效应的作用到底有多大、人为气溶胶的反馈究竟如何（Anderson等，2003；Houghton等，2001）。在这种背景下，理解地球系统的关键是要尽可能定量地理解并界定气候的自然变化过程，然后区分和评估叠加在其上的人为影响。而要理解气候变化的自然过程和自然驱动因子，我们必须超越非常有限的仪器记录到的、短暂的、深受人类活动影响的气候历史，向更早的时期寻求古气候变化记录（Bradley，2000）。

米兰柯维奇理论为我们揭示了地球气候400/100 ka（与偏心率相关，ka代表千年）、41 ka（与倾角相关）以及23/19 ka的变化周期（与岁差相关）（Berger，1988），而且揭示了65°N的夏季太阳辐射是控制全球冰量变化的因子，比较成功地解释了冰期—间冰期的转换（见图1.1）。但是，这个理论仍存在一些不完满的地方，而且它不能用于解释亚轨道尺度的气候变化事件，例如Heinrich事件、Dansgaard-Oscheger（D-O）事件和Younger Dryas（新仙女木）事件等。换言之，米兰柯维奇理论不能直接提供给我们关于未来千百年中气候变化趋势的清晰图景。人类目前正处在现代间冰期——全新世（对应于深海氧同位素1阶段，即MIS1），由于100 ka的主导周期在最近0.8 Ma表现强烈，0.8 Ma以来的间冰期都可以作为现代间冰期气候变化趋势的参比对象。部分气候模拟和气候记录显示，深海氧同位素11阶段（简称MIS11）的气候情形是全新世及未来气候的最佳参照物（Loutre和Berger，2003；Loutre，2003；EPICA community members，2004）。但是目前可靠的高分辨率的MIS11气候记录非常有限，更老的间冰期记录更是罕见。在这种情形下，距离现代间冰期最近的一次间冰期——末次间冰期是我们理解间冰期气候自然变化过程的最佳参比对象（Kukla，2000）。（注：Ka=千年；Ma=百万年前）

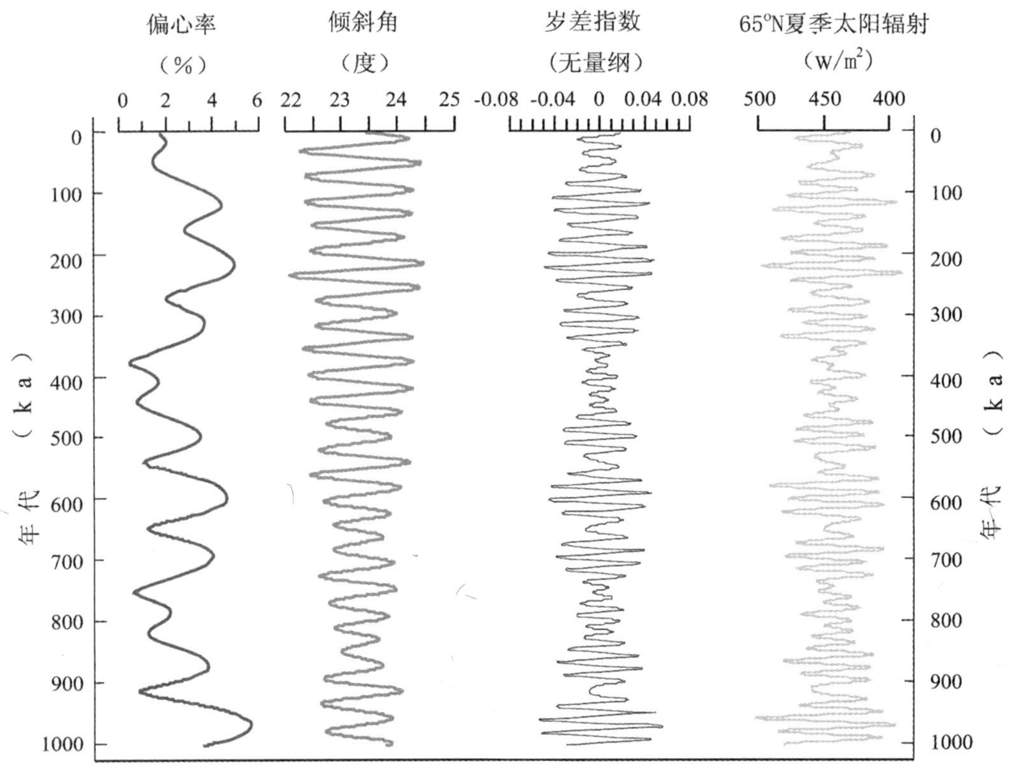

图1.1　100万年以来地球轨道参数以及北纬65°N夏季太阳辐射的变化

（数据来源于http://www1.ncdc.noaa.gov/pub/data/paleo/insolation/，由Berger（1988）提供）

1.1　末次间冰期气候不稳定性的国际争论

关于末次间冰期的定义，存在着两种意见：第一，末次间冰期对应于MIS 5e（Shackleton，1969）。在欧洲，MIS 5e对应于Eemian，年代大致相当于130～116 ka BP；在北美，MIS 5e对应于Sangamon土壤发育期。第二，整个MIS 5都属于末次间冰期（Bowen，1978）。在中国，通常将整个MIS 5称作末次间冰期，对应于黄土-古

土壤序列中的S1发生期（大约128～73 kaBP）。（注：kaBP=千年前）

首先，对末次冰期千年尺度（亚轨道尺度）的气候快速变化（Heinrich，1988；Broecker等，1992；Broecker，1994；Bond等，1992，1993，1995）的探讨几乎引领了20世纪整个90年代古气候研究的风尚。Andrews（1998）形象地说，自1992年始，研究Heinrich事件成了人人都在从事的“家庭手工业”，相关数据层出不穷。冰期内部的千百年尺度事件，在格陵兰冰芯中早已发现，Dansgaard等（1993）指出了冰芯中$\delta^{18}O$与粉尘含量的变化及其与欧洲湖泊记录的对应性。海洋和冰芯记录均显示，末次冰期（MIS 2－4：7.3～1.0 kaBP）发生了一系列准周期为5000～6000年的Heinrich事件，每两个相邻的Heinrich事件是一个逐渐升温的过程，被称为Bond旋回（Bond Cycles）。每个Bond旋回又包含准周期为1300～1500年的Dansgarrd-Oeschger（D－O）事件（Broecker,1994）。

1.1.1 末次间冰期气候不稳定的证据

GRIP members（1993）率先向末次间冰期的稳定观点提出挑战。从格陵兰Summit钻取的3000 m长的冰芯记录中的氧同位素（$\delta^{18}O$）以及粉尘Ca^{2+}浓度表明，MIS 5e中温度变化非常剧烈。MIS 5e中的3个暖阶段的$\delta^{18}O$平均值较全新世的平均值高出1.4‰，折算成温度差为2.1 ℃。Dansgaard等（1993）研究了GRIP冰芯记录的250 ka BP以来的气候变化，认为气候不稳定性贯穿了最近两个冰期旋回。这些结果和推论无疑增加了我们对全球变暖后果的忧虑。

格陵兰冰芯揭示出的“气候不稳定性”霎时激发了学者们对末次间冰期的特殊兴趣。由于北半球高纬度地区对气候的敏感性更高，科学家们首先在北半球的高纬度地区寻找末次间冰期内的气候突发事件。来自北大西洋的深海钻孔资料显示MIS 5e中期海水表面温度（SST）下降了2～3.5 ℃（Cortijo等，1994；Seidenkrantz等，1995；Fronval和Jansen，1996，1997；Cortijo等，1999，2000）。需要指出的是，总体说来，从海洋记录中检测到的气候快速变化事件持续的时间比从GRIP冰芯中检测到的要短些，在幅度上也不像GRIP冰芯中检测到的那么极端。来自欧洲内陆湖泊沉积的孢粉和磁化率记录显示，Eemian时期也存在着气候快速变化（Thouveny等，1994；Field等，1994）。最近，贝加尔湖地区的两个钻孔也记录到了Eemian中期的一次显著的降温事件（Karabanov等，2000；Prokopenko等，2002）。Heusser和Oppo（2003）报道了亚热带大西洋西岸（美国东南海岸）的ODP 1059大洋钻孔记录到了千年尺度的寒冷事件。

1.1.2 末次间冰期气候稳定的证据

尽管有如此多的记录显示了末次间冰期气候千年尺度的快速变化，可是争论与分歧也始终存在（Kukla，2000）。距离GRIP Summit以西28 km处的GISP2冰芯记录显示，GRIP记录到的MIS 5e内的突然变化在这里一概不见（Taylor等，1993；Grootes等，1993）。通过与南极洲东方站冰芯中的甲烷和$\delta^{18}O$等指标的对比，Chappellaz等（1997）推测，GRIP和GISP2冰芯的底部曾经发生过扰动。最新的被认为是北半球第一个详细记录了Eemian后期和末次冰期早期气候且未受扰动的冰芯——NGRIP冰芯的$\delta^{18}O$记录表明，MIS 5e中期（123 ka BP）的气候是稳定的（NGRIP members，2004）。这个结果对末次冰期气候不稳定的先前推论（GRIP members，1993）产生了严重的冲击。南极的Vostok冰芯（Petit等，1999）和Dome C冰芯（EPICA community members，2004）也表明，MIS 5e内部没有发生气候突变。南极另外一个冰穹（Taylor）的$\delta^{18}O$记录也佐证，MIS 5e的气候是稳定的（Grootes等，2001）。

来自北大西洋的另外的一些证据表明，MIS 5e北大西洋深层水和（或）表层水均没有剧烈的变化（McManus等，1994，1999；Adkins等，1997；Oppo等，1997；Rasmussen等，1999；Matthiessen和Knies，2001；Tzedakis等，2003）。气候模拟的结果显示末次间冰期北大西洋的温盐环流仅衰减了5%，这种轻微的变化不足以对北半球高纬度地区的热量平衡造成任何显著的影响（Crucifix和Loutre，2002）。在欧洲内陆，更多的证据表明，Eemian时期的气候是稳定的。这些记录包括希腊西北部（Frogley等，1999；Tzedakis等，2002）和德国中部的孢粉记录（Böettger等，2000），法国Ribains玛尔湖泊记录（Rioual等，2001；Shemesh等，2001）以及地中海西部的钻孔记录（ODP-977A）（Martrat等，2004）。对于法国La Grandle Pile与德国Bispingen和Gröbern湖泊的孢粉数据，Kühl和Litt（2003）使用不同于孢粉转换函数的概率密度函数重建了Eemian时期的温度变化，结果显示温度变化平缓。美国西部Carp湖过去125 ka的孢粉记录也表明，末次间冰期气候没有表现出强烈的波动（Whitlock和Bartlein，1997）。

1.1.3 千年尺度气候变化的驱动机制的两个假说

除了对末次间冰期的气候情形有争议外，科学家对气候突变的驱动机制也未取得一致的意见。目前，存在两种不同的设想：第一，大洋温盐环流状态的转换（Brocker，1994）。由于大量的淡水输入到北大西洋的北部，温盐环流因此而关闭。

温盐环流关闭的信号通过海洋内部的机制（相对迟缓地）传播到其他地区。这种观点的支持者主要来自古气候学家和搞模拟的海洋学家。该驱动的缺陷在于缺乏引起快速、剧烈、广泛的气候效应的链条。第二，热带海洋的ENSO活动（Cane，1998）。这一假说主要是由大气物理学家和年代际气候变化研究者倡导的。支持者认为，热带的对流系统是构成地球气候系统的控制性要素，ENSO确实解决了困扰基于海洋无法解释的遥相关问题，但是，还没有足够的证据表明地球热带海洋-大气耦合系统存在多种分立的调节模式。也就是说，除非考虑海洋的调节作用，目前还缺乏证据表明大气可以在一个状态稳定几百年。在高纬度气候波动传播、气候系统内部反馈放大作用及气候变化南北半球耦合方面，亚洲季风区的水汽、粉尘变化可能是被忽视的重要因子（冯兆东等，2000）。

1.2 中国黄土高原末次间冰期古土壤S1的研究现状与问题

1.2.1 中国黄土研究历史简述

从第四纪科学的角度出发，黄土研究有几大被广泛关注的焦点：（1）黄土的来源问题，包括黄土的搬运动力和源区；（2）黄土的地层；（3）黄土记录的古气候和古环境信号。

1.2.1.1 中国黄土的来源

Lyell可能是对黄土（loess）最早开展科学研究的地质学家。根据欧洲莱茵河流域和美国密西西比河流域的黄土研究，Lyell（1834，1847）提出了黄土的“水成说”。自称为“孤独旅人”的冯·李希霍芬基于自己在中国的多年考察和对沙尘暴的亲身经历提出了黄土的“风成说”（Von Richthofen，1882）。刘东生和他的团队从20世纪60年代开始，通过对黄土高原大范围、多学科的研究，进一步完善、发展了黄土的风成说（刘东生，1964，1965，1985）。张德二（1984）对历史时期降尘文献的过滤和对现代降尘的研究为黄土风成说提供了天气过程依据。Pye（1987）为中国黄土高原大致为西北到东南的砂黄土（中值粒径Md介于30 μm和16 μm之间）—典型黄土（15 μm<Md<25 μm）—黏黄土（Md<15 μm）的带状分布提供了有益的风动力学解释。张小曳等（1991，1994a，1994b，1996a，1996b）对现代粉尘的研究为黄土的风成说提供了地球化学证据。近年来对黄土-古土壤的地球化学分析表明，黄土是高度混合的物质，为黄土的风力搬运说再添力证（Jahn等，2001）。

冯·李希霍芬还认为，中国北部的沙漠是黄土的来源地。这一观点得到了众多学者的认同（刘东生，1964，1965，1985；Pye和Zhou，1989；Derbyshire等，1998；张小曳等，1996a；Sun等，2000，2001）。之后的研究对它有一定的修正。刘东生（1985）认为，不仅中国北部的沙漠和戈壁是中国黄土高原黄土的来源地，而且西北内陆盆地（塔里木盆地和柴达木盆地）也是其来源地，并且认为蒙古—西伯利亚高压、西风带、气旋活动、夏季风都是黄土堆积过程的参与者。Bowler等（1987）也认为柴达木盆地是重要的黄土源区，Liu等（1994）也认为塔里木盆地是黄土高原黄土的源区之一。Derbyshire（1998）等认为，青藏高原北部祁连山沿河西走廊分布巨大冲积扇为黄土高原西部地区提供了主要的粉砂来源。Wright（2001）认为，中国黄土的粉砂物质的最初起源包括了冻融风化、盐风化、冰川研磨等等。在粉砂最终被搬运沉积到黄土高原之前，上述过程产生的未分选的物质经坡积过程、冰川搬运、冰川融水沉积、冲积—洪积过程在干河道、冲积扇或冰水沉积平原沉积下来，期间颗粒可能进一步地被风化。其中一部分很细的物质（<20 μm，见Pye，1987）随高空气流被长距离地运移，主要在太平洋上空开始降落；另一部分较细的物质（20～70 μm，见Pye，1987）则被中短距离地悬移，在黄土高原沉积下来；较粗的颗粒（>70 μm，见Pye，1987）经历多次的跃移—沉积过程在中国和蒙古的沙漠中沉积下来。这个概念模式显示，蒙古—中国的岩漠、戈壁（砾漠）、沙漠、天山、阿尔泰山、祁连山是粉砂物质的“最终”来源地。Wright的观点得到了孙继敏的认可，但是孙继敏认为昆仑山、天山、阿尔泰山等高山的地貌过程产生的粉砂大多贡献于当地的黄土堆积，尽管有细物质可以飙升至山体的高度之上，但这些物质却被西风急流携带至很远的下游地区，对黄土高原的贡献很小。孙继敏认为，蒙古的戈壁和中国北方的戈壁、沙漠（包括巴丹吉林沙漠、腾格里沙漠、乌兰布和沙漠、库布齐沙漠、毛乌素沙漠）才是黄土高原的主要物质来源区（孙继敏，2004；Sun，2002a，2002b）。换言之，西风带对黄土高原的黄土沉积贡献不大，西伯利亚冷空气爆发后形成的蒙古反气旋或者自蒙古南下的单独活动冷锋是黄土高原最主要的粉尘搬运者。

1.2.1.2 中国黄土的地层

德日进和杨钟健（1930）对中国的黄土地层和古生物学作了开创性的研究，他们将中国的黄土划分为马兰黄土和红色土，红色土又可分为A、B、C三层。1961年刘东生和张宗祜在波兰举办的第六届国际第四纪大会（INQUA VI）上提交了第一个关于中国黄土-古土壤地层详细的报告（Liu和Chang，1961），提出了上更新统马兰黄土、中更新统离石黄土、早更新统午城黄土岩石地层命名规则。后来，刘东生（1985）将离石黄土再分为离石黄土上部和离石黄土下部，并在马兰黄土上部增加了全新世黄土。他还采纳了将古土壤层视为独立的地层单位（如S1、S2……S32）的建议（卢演俦和安芷生，1979）。刘东生的这项总结基本成了以后黄土地层划分的标准（Kukla和An，1989；陈发虎和张维信，1993）。丁仲礼等引入了土壤地层单位的概念：由一个或多个土壤发生层所组成、其发育程度与当地全新世土壤相当或更高、能指示当时地带性气候条件的、在空间上可以追索的三维埋藏地质体。他们指出，完整的中国黄土地层至少包含了37个土壤地层单元（Ding等，1993）。

中国磁性地层学研究始于李华梅等（1974）在山西午城和安芷生等（1977）在陕西洛川剖面的工作。Heller和Liu（1982）在洛川剖面建立了首个完整的黄土磁性地层，并将2.4 Ma（M/G，松山和高斯分界线）作为中国黄土沉积的起始年代。B/M（布容正极性期—松山反极性期）的界线为0.73 Ma，对应于L8的下部。贾拉米洛正极性事件发生在0.90～0.97 Ma，对应于L11与L13上部之间。奥都维正极性事件发生在1.67～1.87 Ma，对应于WS3。Heller和Liu的工作得到了Kukla等在西峰剖面研究结果的佐证，同时Kukla还用极性转换点的年龄作为控制点设计了磁化率年龄模式（Kukla和An，1989）。磁性地层的建立解决了时间标尺的问题，为区域间的气候对比提供了可能性，客观上加速了中国黄土的古气候研究。

1.2.1.3 中国黄土高原古气候和古环境研究

洛川剖面磁化率曲线同深海岩芯V28-239的氧同位素曲线（指示全球冰量）良好的相似性意味着中国的黄土是很好的气候记录者并且具有全球气候意义（Heller和Liu，1986），这项工作一方面提升了中国黄土研究的学术地位，另一方面引发了黄土气候研究的热潮。磁化率的环境意义进一步被认为可指示粉尘源区和堆积区植被覆盖度（Kukla和An，1989）或者成壤强度（Zhou等，1990；Maher等，1988，1991），不论是植被覆盖度还是成壤强度都受控于夏季风带来的降水。安芷生进而提出将磁化率作为反映夏季风强度的指标（安芷生等，1990；An等，1991a，1991b）。同时，An等（1990）强调了冬季风对黄土搬运的重要性，并仿照Rea等（1988）对北太平洋的亚洲内陆风尘的研究工作，将中值粒径作为反映冬季风强度的指标，将粉尘通量（=容重×沉积速率）作为风场（频度和强度）的指标，并认为这两个指标也可反映粉尘源区的干旱化程度。丁仲礼等（1991）也认为冬季风是黄土物质的主要搬运者，他们将<2 μm/>10 μm的值作为2.5 Ma以来冬季风强度的指标。对于使用什么样的粒度指标作为冬季风的标志在有关研究者中间是有争议的（Xiao等，1995；鹿化煜等，1997，1998；汪海斌等，2001）。夏季风和冬季风的标志“破译”颇有“里程碑”的意义。

安芷生和他的团队建立了末次冰期旋回黄土高原东亚冬季风的变迁序列和夏季风锋面的时空分布框架（An等，1991a，1991b；安芷生等，1990；安芷生等，

1994；孙东怀等，1995；Lu和Sun，2000；Xiao等，1995，1999a，1999b；Porter和An，1995；An和Porter，1997），他们还获得了末次冰期和末次间冰期东亚季风的不稳定性的证据，并将不稳定性归因于西风环流的调整（Porter和An，1995；An和Porter，1997）。An（2000）就古季风变迁机制进行了系统的讨论，认为北半球高纬度地区的冷空气活动、南半球的越赤道气流和ENSO活动影响着东亚季风气候的变率。Xiao等（1995）认为石英颗粒粒径是更好的冬季风指标，因为其沉积受到的风化改造很小。Xiao和An（1999a）揭示了第四纪以来东亚季风发生了三次大的调整，时间分别为：2.5 Ma，1.2～1.1 Ma和550～450 ka，这些调整与太阳辐射的变化和青藏高原的隆升过程有关。Lu等（2000）检测出了L9和L15记录到的冬季风变化的1450年的主导周期，并认为暖期的冬季风相对稳定。

丁仲礼和他的团队系统地研究了黄土与红黏土地层及年代框架（Ding等，1992，1994，1998a，1998b，1998c，1999a，1999b，1999c），获得了一系列表征古气候变迁的记录，并分析了古气候记录的周期性、相位特征以及与全球气候变化的关系，提出了全球冰量在第四纪时期的变化对东亚古气候变化的控制作用的概念模型（丁仲礼等，1991，1996；丁仲礼和余志伟，1995；丁仲礼和刘东生，1998；Ding等，2000，2002）。他们还在证明黄土高原第三纪红黏土为风成成因上做了较系统的工作（Ding等，1998b，1998c，2001），并对黄土沉积与沙漠演变之关系做了探索性的研究（Ding等，1999b）。

郭正堂和他的团队对第四纪黄土-古土壤序列中沉积-成壤过程相互作用的历史进行了较为系统的研究（Guo和Fedoroff，1991；Guo和Liu，1993；Guo等，1996），发展了新的古环境替代指标Fed/Fet（游离铁与总铁含量的比值），并在季风环境演化的“非轨道”行为研究中取得进展。他们进而建立了全球独有的中新世陆相风尘环境变迁序列，将中国风尘堆积起始年代推到2200万年前，在“非行星风系型”亚洲内陆荒漠、季风环境形成演化及其与青藏高原隆升的关系上取得了新的进展（Guo等，2002）。

陈骏和他的团队一直很重视使用地球化学指标来研究黄土-古土壤的风化问题，创建了多种夏季风指标（黄土Rb/Sr值和酸不溶物Fe/Mg值，$^{87}Sr/^{86}Sr$比值，白度指数，赤铁矿、针铁矿含量等）和新的冬季风指标（Zr/Rb值）（陈骏等，1996，1998；刘连文等，2001；陈旸等，2003；Chen等，1999，2002），这些指标与冬季风或夏季风的机制联系明确，对更加全面地认识东亚季风活动规律和东亚古环境演变历史起到了重要作用。

吕厚远和吴乃琴等强调使用生物化石（如植物硅酸体、蜗牛等）来研究黄土高原的古气候变化（吕厚远等，1996，1999；吴乃琴等，2000，2004）。

陈发虎等系统地研究了陇西黄土高原的黄土地层，建立了陇西黄土高原区域黄土-古土壤标准序列（陈发虎和张维信，1993），发现了我国末次冰期冬夏季风均存在快速变化的特点，并提出了我国冰期和间冰期气候变化的受控机制不同的观点（Chen等，1997，1999，2000，2003）。

方小敏等探讨了中国黄土高原黄土沉积与青藏高原隆升的关系，他们还对末次间冰期以来的气候变化给予了颇多的关注。他们很早就指出，末次冰期夏季风存在千年尺度的变化，他们还提出，末次间冰期夏季风是不稳定的（方小敏等，1996；Fang等，1999a，1999b，1999c）。

冯兆东等从土壤发生学的角度出发，对广泛应用的夏季风代用指标（磁化率）的可靠性进行了系统的检验和有力的挑战（Feng，1995；Feng和Chen，1999；Feng等，2004a，2004b）。

限于篇幅，这里无法一一列出每个人的研究。

1.2.2 中国黄土高原末次间冰期古土壤（S1）记录的气候变化

格陵兰冰芯亚轨道尺度的气候快速变化（GRIP members，1993；Dansgaard，1993）引起了研究中国黄土的学者们的注意，Porter和An（1995）提出，洛川地区末次冰期的黄土L1中记录到了千年尺度的Heinrich事件，这个发现得到了来自黄土高原其他地区记录的不断支持（郭正堂等，1996；Guo等，1996；Chen等，1997；丁仲礼等，1996；Ding等，1998a；Fang等，1999b）。不久，An和Porter（1997）还指出，末次间冰期冬季风同样存在千年尺度的剧烈变化。他们认为，粗石英颗粒含量记录了洛川地区2.5 m厚的S1（即末次间冰期古土壤）记录了9次高粉尘事件，前6次（MIS 5a－5d内）可以同北大西洋V29-191深海钻孔记录到的寒冷事件（McManus等，1994）相比，后3次（MIS 5e内）可与GRIP冰芯记录的强烈降温事件对照（见图1.2）。方小敏等（1996）指出，黄土高原西部兰州的两个剖面和临夏北塬剖面的$CaCO_3$含量、粗细颗粒比（>16 μm/<4 μm）、磁化率都记录到了末次间冰期的千年尺度的气候变化，方小敏等的后续工作进一步表明，兰州九州台剖面超顺磁颗粒浓度在5e时段内的变化也表现出三峰二谷之势，与GRIP冰芯$\delta^{18}O$有“极好”的对应关系（Fang等，1999a）。但是，黄土高原西部的S1（厚6～8 m）都没有记录到MIS 5e可与GRIP冰芯相比的冬季风突发事件（Chen等，1999，2000，2003；Ding等，1999a；丁仲礼等，1996），黄土—沙漠边界地带的S1也没有显示出季风—沙漠系统的不稳定性（Ding等，1999b；Wu等，2002）。在黄土高原中部的长武剖面中Fed/Fet指示夏季风在典型的末次间冰期（5e）也比较稳定（郭正堂等，1999）。

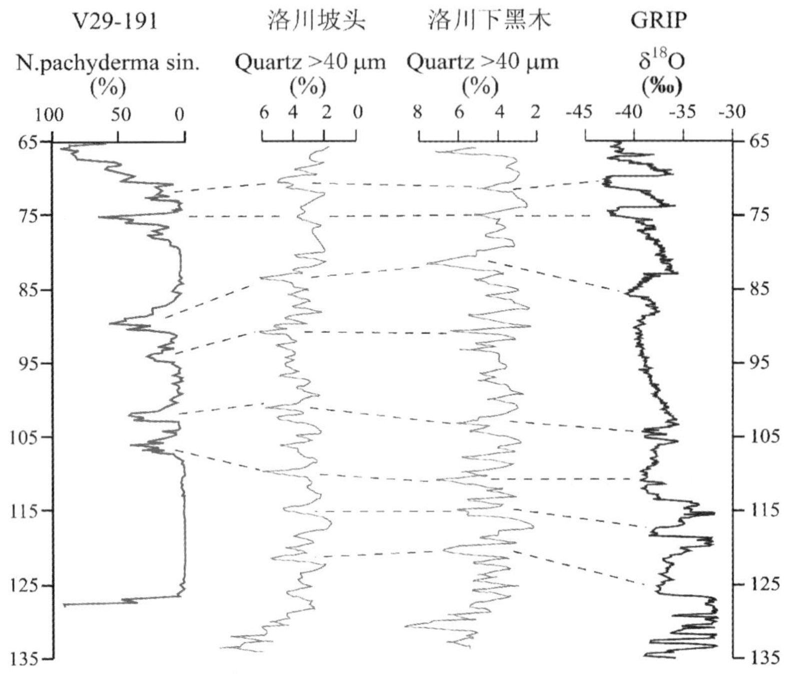

图1.2　洛川地区两个剖面的粗石英颗粒含量与北大西洋V29-191 N.pachyderma sin.含量以及格陵兰GRIP冰芯$\delta^{18}O$的对比（An and Porter，1997）

1.2.3 中国黄土高原末次间冰期高分辨率气候重建的主要问题

An和Porter（1997）报道的黄土高原中部地区表达气候剧烈变化的粉尘事件是值得怀疑的，他们重建的末次间冰期气候序列存在两个主要问题：（1）黄土高原末次间冰期古土壤S1年代的可靠性；（2）气候代用指标的可靠性。

1.2.3.1 末次间冰期古土壤S1年代的精确性和可靠性问题

1.2.3.1.1　测年技术的局限性

年代的可靠性问题首先受制于测年技术，由于末次间冰期远远超出^{14}C测年的下限，目前针对古土壤S1测年较理想的是采用释光测年，包括热释光（Thermoluminescence，简称TL）和光释光（Optical Stimulated Luminescence，简称OSL）。尽管轨道调谐得到的时间标尺以及一些热释光测年数据表明，中国黄土高原的末次间冰期古土壤大概形成于70～130 ka，对应于深海氧同位素的第五阶段（即MIS 5），但是TL或OSL年代存在许多不确定性（Oches等，1998；李秉成，1998；李虎侯，2000）。比如，释光测年下限受到矿物存在的陷阱电子的稳定性、释光信号的衰退和饱和程度以及环境剂量的大小等诸多因素的影响。目前就释光测年的下限有多种意见（李虎侯，2000），普遍认为，当材料的年龄超过10万年时，由于释光信号接近饱和，测量的准确性会大大下降（赵晖博士，2005，私人交流），因此，释光测年的误差较大，通常在±10%（13万年的误差就是1.3万年）。因此，释光测年技术尚达不到建立可靠的地质年代标尺的要求。

1.2.3.1.2 土壤发生过程的复杂性

既然释光测年仅能提供粗略的年代框架，那么，详细的年代序列的建立必须依赖年代模式和地层对比。通常，S1年代序列的建立先依据轨道调谐的办法确定基点（年龄控制点），然后采用三次样点函数内插（Ding等，1994；Lu等，1999），或者采用粒度模型（Porter和An，1995；鹿化煜等，1999）、磁化率模型（Kukla和An，1989）计算S1的年代序列。S1的年代通常用轨道调谐的办法调至73～128 ka BP，也就是说S1形成历时达55 000年（Kukla和An，1989）。然而，即便S1确实发生在这段时间，洛川地区S1底部的母质或至少部分母质沉积时间早于128 ka BP的可能性仍无法被排除（Feng等，2004a，2004b）。也就是说，土壤发生过程的复杂性被规避了。

传统的土壤发生学认为，一个土壤的发育是时间和四个环境要素（母质、地形、生物、气候）的函数（Jenny，1941），即

$$S=f(cl, o, r, p, t, \cdots) \quad (1)$$

其中S代表土壤特性，cl代表气候，o代表生物，r代表地形，p代表母质，t代表时间；此外还有其他一些次要的和非特定的因素也影响土壤发育。该函数向我们传达的含义是：在四个环境因子的影响之下，随着时间的推移，土壤发育的方向总是从简单向复杂（如，土壤剖面中层次的分异和土纲的分化，见图1.3），直至“成熟”的稳定状态为止。所谓的稳定状态是指土壤发育到某个阶段，能量流持续输入土壤系统，各种反应持续进行，但土壤的理化性质不发生改变或者改变的速度几乎不能被观测到。Birkeland（1999）给出了三个表征土壤特性的因素达到稳定状态的时间顺序（图1.4）。如图1.4，我们可以看到土壤的各个成分到达稳定状态的顺序依次为有机碳、碳酸盐、黏粒，t时刻可以被认为是整个土壤剖面达到了稳定状态。Yaalon（1975）对一些土纲获得稳定状态所需的时间进行了研究，研究的结果如图1.5所示。

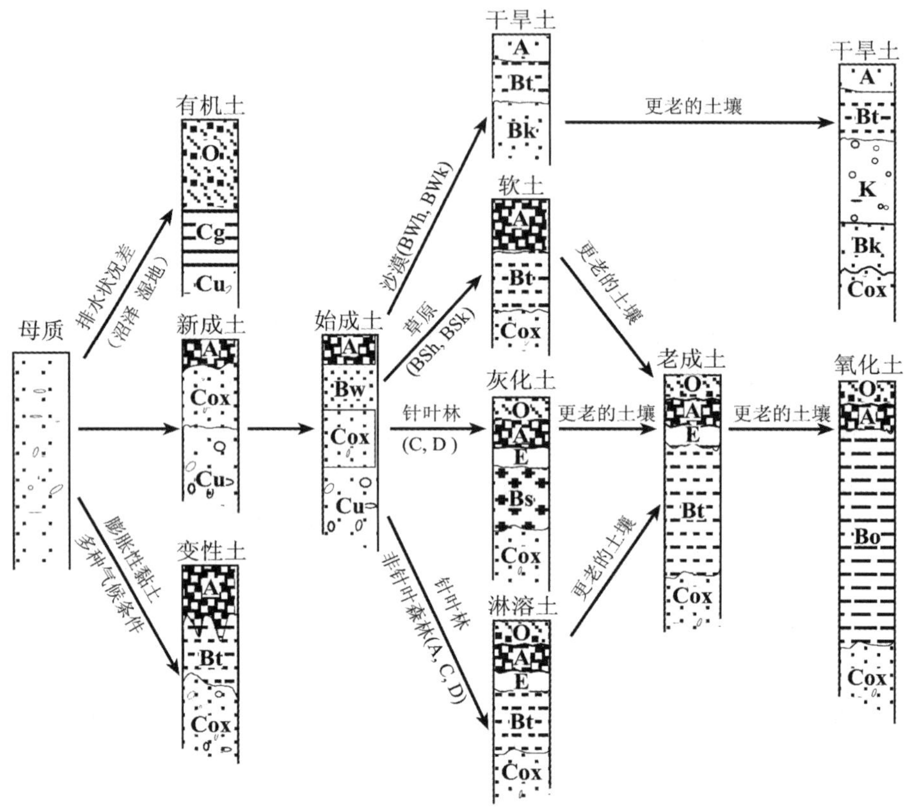

O层:堆积于表层的有机质层

A层:位于O层之下,以矿物质为主,同时富含有机质,使颜色发黑

E层:浅灰色亚表层,由针叶残积物分解产生的有机酸将色素淋洗出该层,黏粒、铁、铝皆有损失,而砂粒和粉砂聚集

Bw层:年轻的B层,由于轻微的氧化作用而略泛红色,但没有黏粒的聚集

Bs层:无定形有机质和倍半氧化物(如Al_2O_3,Fe_2O_3)的复合体

Bk层:浅色的B层,碳酸盐包裹矿物颗粒表面所致

Bt层:成熟的B层,由于氧化作用变红,且黏粒聚集

Bo层:深红色,经强烈的风化和淋溶作用,残余倍半氧化物非常丰富,通常发生在热带气候条件下的非常老的土壤中

Cox层:A或B层之下的经过氧化作用的C层

K层:类似Bk层,但由于极富碳酸盐而发白

Cg层:经潜育化的亚表层,有蓝色、灰色和绿色的斑纹,是还原条件下的产物

Cu层:未经风化的母质

(括号中的A:热带;C:温暖带;D:冷温带;BS:草原气候;BW:沙漠气候;h:炎热;k:寒冷)

图1.3 土壤发生进程模式图(自Dennis I. Netoff,1997;转引自Birkeland,1999)

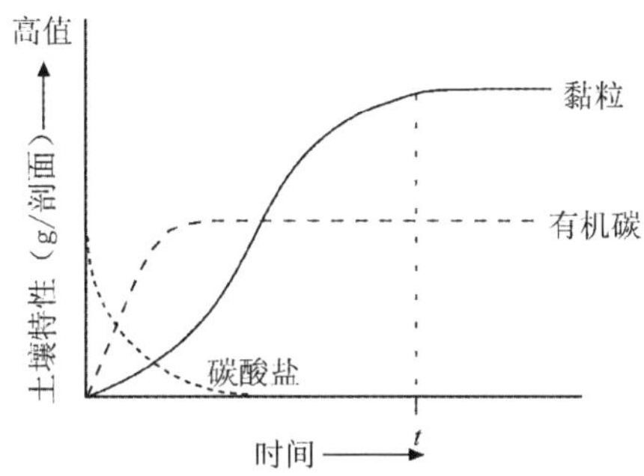

图 1.4　几个土壤特性随时间变化的示意图(自 Birkeland,1999)

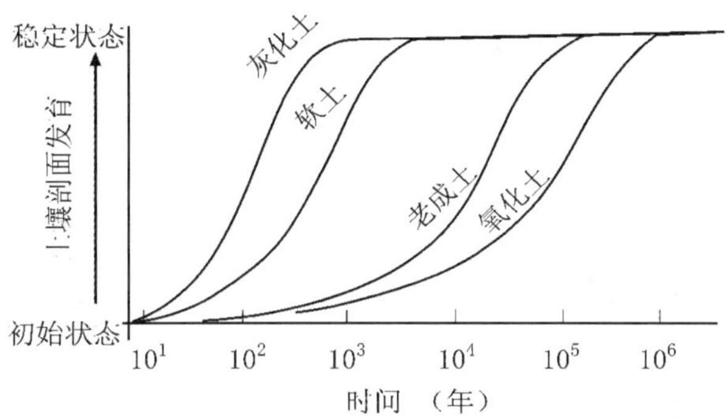

图 1.5　某些土壤达到稳定状态所需的时间(自 Yaalon,1975)

随着土壤学研究成果的积累，特别是土壤地貌学研究的进展（Birkeland, 1999)，土壤学家开始意识到土壤发育进程并不一定是土层增厚和发生层垂直分异增大的单向过程，比如，一个土壤的厚度是加积作用、侵蚀作用、土壤加深（或土壤向下发育）等过程综合作用的结果（Buol 等，1980)。Johnson 和 Watson-Stegner（1987）系统地提出了土壤发生的两个模式（见图 1.6)：渐进式（Progressvie）和逆退式（Regressive)，即

$$S=f(P, R) \tag{2}$$

P 代表渐进式过程，指使土壤剖面的分异度增加的过程（Horizonational Pathway)；R 代表逆退式过程，指使土壤剖面单一化的过程（Haploidizational Pathway)。

Phillips（1993）进一步提出随时间变化的土壤发育模型：

$$S_t=S_{t-1}+\Delta P-\Delta R \tag{3}$$

S_t 为 t 时段内的土壤发育强度，它依赖于前一时段（$t-1$）内土壤发育的强度（S_{t-1}）与 $t-1$ 之后的渐进式成壤改造（ΔP）和逆退式作用（ΔR)。

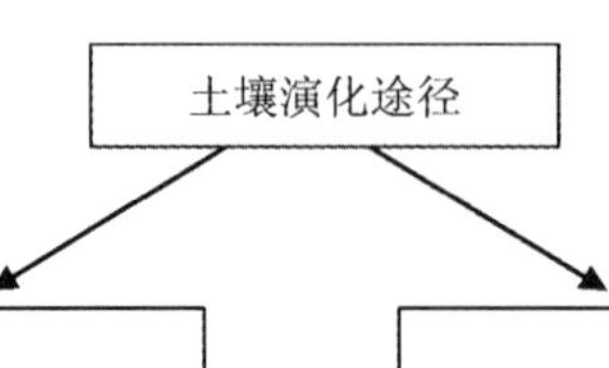

渐进式过程

层次分异：使剖面趋异的过程（剖面分异的各个方面），物质或能量增加、搬运、迁移、转化，内在反馈和土壤趋异。

土壤向上发育：成壤化改造少量坡面物质或风尘的加积。

土壤向下发育：土壤的底界伸向新鲜未经风化的下伏物质。

逆退式过程

层次简化：使剖面趋同变单一化的过程（剖面“复原”的各个方面），物质或能量增加、移除、迁移、转化、黑化，营养元素的生物循环、富集，内在反馈和土壤趋同。

延缓土壤向上发育的过程或效应：由于大量坡面物质或风尘的加积致使土壤发育受阻或延缓。

侵蚀作用：各种侵蚀事件，包括风蚀、片蚀、溶出、陷穴等。

图1.6　土壤演化的两条路径及其组成要素(Johnson and Watson-Stegner，1987)

在中国的黄土高原地区，土壤发育显然也存在渐进式过程和逆退式过程（朱显谟，1983），黄土高原的土壤发育可以简单地视为成壤改造（*P*）与粉尘加积和侵蚀过程（*R*）之间的平衡，如果忽略侵蚀过程，土壤发育更是可以简化为成壤改造与粉尘加积之间的平衡（见图1.7）。

土壤发生学认为，时间对土壤发育来说有两层含义：首先，时间代表从母质开始沉积的那一刻起土壤所经历的时段；第二，时间还意味着地表的稳定性（Foth，1978）。如果土壤发育的时段地表是相对稳定的，即成壤速率远远大于粉尘加积速率，那么土壤就向下发育（见图1.8）。在这种情况下，土壤母质的形成时间要早于土壤开始发育的时间。如果土壤发育的时段粉尘不断地加积，且两者的速率是相当的（如图1.7中*A*、*B*曲线的交点），那么土壤就持续地向上增长，并发育出A层（见图1.8），土壤年龄可以被认为等同于母质的年龄。可是，土壤的发育程度却不能反映当时的气候和植被条件，换言之，加积型土壤是不能达到与气候和植被之间的平衡的（Almond等，1999；Birkeland，1999）。Arduino等（1986）对意大利北部土壤形成与时间关系的研究表明，淋溶土（Alfisol）形成的年龄为3～7.3 ka，始成土（Inceptisol）为1.3～3 ka，新成土（Entisol）为0.1 ka～1.3 ka。Busacca（1987）对美国加利福尼亚土壤进行的研究表明，新成土（Entisol）形成的时间少于3 ka，软土（Mollisol）为3～29 ka，老成土（Ultisol）为0.5～3.2 Ma。末次间冰期，在黄土高原的东南部（包括黄土高原中部）地区，55 ka对黄土高原东部地区来说完全足够

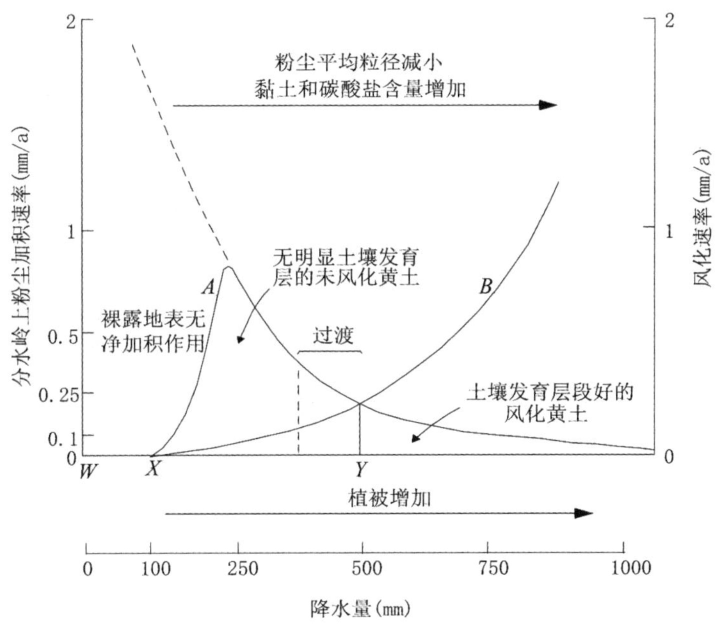

曲线A表示粉尘传输路线上各点粉尘的加积速率。在沙漠粉尘源区W至降水足以使捕捉粉尘的植被生长区X之间为极干旱带，几乎无粉尘堆积。当捕捉粉尘的植被出现在源区附近时，曲线A的虚线外延部分表示所期望的粉尘加积速率。在这些条件下，粉尘加积速率随离源区距离增加而有规律地下降。粉尘的平均粒径亦随之变小，而黏土矿物和碳酸盐含量却增加。曲线B表示随着离沙漠源区距离和降水量增加，沉积粉尘的风化速率(以淋溶深度mm/a表示)亦随之增加。当离源区距离大于Y点时，风化速率就超过粉尘加积速率，黄土沉积物将表现出明显的风化和成壤层段的证据。无论是粉尘加积速率的变化还是降水量的变化都会使Y点移动。若Y点多次来回移动，那么，会产生黄土与土壤层交替出现。

图1.7 黄土高原成壤改造速率与粉尘堆积速率的空间变化趋势示意图

(据Pye和Tsoar，1987)

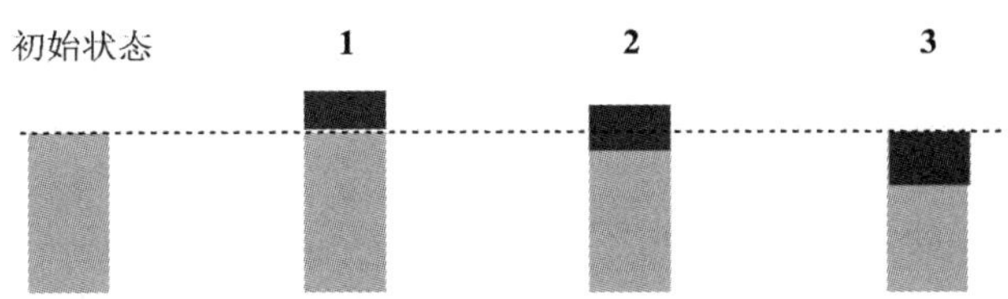

1 成壤速率<加积速率，地表持续增高，加积型土壤

2 成壤速率>加积速率，地表次稳定，土壤部分深入母质

3 成壤速率>>加积速率，地表稳定，土壤完全在原先沉积的母质上发育

母质 土壤 ------- 假想的等时地表

(注意，此处的母质是一个相对的概念，而且土壤发育程度也未必相同)

图1.8 依赖于成壤改造速率与风尘堆积速率差别的三种土壤发育模式图

发育一个带B的较成熟的软土。实际上，黄土高原东南部地区S1普遍是复合古土壤（Wang，1997）。位于著名的洛川剖面南部50 km处的黄陵S1剖面就是由三个相互叠加的B层组成的。毫无疑问，S1的发育至少部分是以倒数第二次冰期沉积的物质为母质的，这意味着S1的年龄要老于轨道调谐获得的年龄。

黄土高原西部地区S1的三次成壤事件是可以截然分开的（Chen等，2000；Feng等，2004a，2004b），可是，在黄土高原的东部地区，S1中潜在的三个亚土壤层通常无法区分。其原因是粉尘加积速率低，因而地表相对稳定，较强的成壤作用使得下一期的土壤与上一期的土壤发生了融合（Soil welding）。土壤融合是指“在母岩或沉积物表层的成壤作用使得该土壤的理化性质和其他印记伸入到一个更老的形成于另外的母岩或沉积物上的埋藏土壤，从而导致两个土壤的融合”（美国土壤学会网站：http://www.sssa.org）。可以设想，$t-1$时段形成的土壤，后来又经历t时段的进一步改造，根据物理和化学特性来重建的气候变化同时具有两个时段的印记，即，这样的土壤是有历史重叠的，在高分辨率的气候重建方面也就缺乏价值（Vreeken，1975）。

如果还考虑到土壤侵蚀问题，那么年代就变得更加不确定。目前关于古气候侵蚀事件的研究工作仅在黄土高原中部和东部地区开展。有学者认为侵蚀多发生在干湿过渡期，即S1向L1过渡的时期或L2向S1过渡的时期（唐克丽等，1991；贺秀斌，1999；周杰等，1998）；也有学者认为气候侵蚀发生在湿润期（邓成龙和袁宝印，2001；Porter和An，2005），也就是整个末次间冰期。不管何时发生侵蚀，它对土壤发生的干扰都不可忽视。如果将土壤侵蚀效应叠加到土壤向下发育之上，S1底部的年龄可能远比我们原先想象的要老。土壤侵蚀造成的另外一个问题是可能使得我们错误估计保存下来的土壤的发育历时。

遗憾的是，过去所做的气候重建工作，特别是所谓的高分辨率的气候重建，土壤发生过程对年代的影响被彻底地规避了。

1.2.3.2 气候指标的精确性

S1研究中的第二个问题就是气候指标的问题。在An和Porter的报道中，粗石英颗粒用作冬季风的指标。An和Porter还特别强调石英颗粒作为冬季风指标的可靠性，其理由是后期的成壤改造作用对它的影响很小。事实上，在特定的环境下，比如，在盐（Goudie等，1979）和有机酸（Bennet等，1991；Dixon等，1984）的参与下，即使最具抗风化能力的石英也会发生化学溶解。在干旱—半干旱区，有证据表明，石英颗粒内部细微的风化作用对<50 μm的颗粒的形成有贡献（Pope，1995，1997）。不容置疑，较细的颗粒可能是较暖的时期由较弱的冬季风带来的，可是，我们不能排除较细的颗粒同时也是暖湿时期在森林或森林—草原

景观下经有机酸作用而加速风化的产物。实际上，Guo等（1999）已证实，在暖湿的末次间冰期，黄土颗粒是被有效地风化了的。因此，我们有必要检验冬季风替代指标的可靠性。

至于磁化率，如前面提到的，它受到多种因素的影响。沉积成因或成壤作用被用于解释磁化率在古土壤层增高的原因。有学者还提出了折中意见：中国黄土高原的磁化率是成壤作用和母质继承两种过程彼此竞争的结果（Feng，1996；Fine等，1993，1995；Verosub等，1993，1994）。可是就成壤过程而言，它并不必然地导致磁化率的增强。具有消磁作用的碳酸盐的聚集（Heller和Liu，1986）、导致磁性加强的淋溶过程（Anderson和Hallet，1996）、植物残体分解过程中产生的超细磁性颗粒（Meng等，1997）以及对磁化率进行改造的氧化还原反应（Feng等，1995，1999；Feng，1996，1997，2001；Liu等，1999）都属于成壤作用。因此，要作为夏季风强度的定量指标，磁化率信号必须被订正。

还有，在干旱和半干旱地区，土壤碳酸钙的聚集与淋溶过程很可能成为高分辨率古气候重建的“麻烦制造者”。Retallack（1994）收集了世界各地317个土壤剖面碳酸钙的资料，得到降水（P/mm）与碳酸钙淀积深度（D/cm）的关系是：

$$P=139.6-6.388D-0.01303D^2 \tag{4}$$

赵景波（2000）根据中国14种不同类型的土壤碳酸钙的资料，通过回归分析得到二者的关系（为统一P、D的指代意义，作者对原公式作了转化）是：

$$P=-3.05\,D+168.5 \tag{5}$$

注意，D以负值的形式表示。如果$CaCO_3$淋溶深度为50 cm，根据公式（4）和（5），可以计算需要的P分别为426.4 mm和321 mm。

Gile等（1966，1981）曾对美国新墨西哥州南部的土壤钙积层的形成进行了系统的研究。他们区分了碳酸盐聚积的两种发生序列和四个发育阶段。一种序列发生在砾质物质中，另一种序列发生在非砾质、砂质或壤质物质中。发育阶段是按碳酸盐聚积物的形态类型确定的，主要反映碳酸盐的发育程度和聚积特性，但不完全反映发生年代。在Ⅰ、Ⅱ、Ⅲ阶段，两种序列中碳酸盐聚积物的形态类型明显不同，但发育到Ⅳ阶段后，均在硬结堵塞层的上部形成片状亚层，在形态上会聚为同一类型。Machette（1985）在Gile等的工作基础上，又添加了两个发育阶段（见表1.1）。换句话说，碳酸钙在土壤剖面中分布可能既是气候的函数又是时间的函数。

表1.1　两种发生序列中$CaCO_3$不同聚积阶段的形态

<table>
<tr><th>阶段</th><th>砾质土壤</th><th>非砾质土壤</th></tr>
<tr><td>Ⅰ</td><td>砾石表面有薄而不连续的碳酸盐包膜；有一些丝状物；基质可以近乎石灰岩；碳酸盐含量约为4%</td><td>有少许丝状碳酸盐或包膜附着在砂粒上；$CaCO_3$含量<10%</td></tr>
<tr><td>Ⅰ⁺</td><td>砾石表面有许多或者全部是薄且连续的包膜</td><td>丝状碳酸盐较多</td></tr>
<tr><td>Ⅱ</td><td>连续的碳酸盐包被；有少许或一些碎屑胶结在一起；基质松散，由于所含碳酸盐增多而有些发白</td><td>少量结核；结核之间的基质略微发白(15%～50%的面积)，碳酸盐呈丝状或细脉状；一些基质可能不含碳酸钙；土壤中总的碳酸盐含量为10%～15%</td></tr>
<tr><td>Ⅱ⁺</td><td>与阶段Ⅱ相同，但基质中的碳酸钙更多</td><td>结核量中等，50%～90%的基质是白色的，碳酸盐含量为15%以上</td></tr>
<tr><td colspan="3">垒结连续，碳酸盐含量高</td></tr>
<tr><td>Ⅲ</td><td>发生层中50%～90%为K垒结，碳酸盐连续充填；颜色较白；富含碳酸盐的层次通常在上部；$CaCO_3$含量为20%～25%</td><td>有许多结核；大量的碳酸盐包被于颗粒表面，发生层的90%是白色的；富含碳酸盐的层次通常在上部；$CaCO_3$含量约为20%</td></tr>
<tr><td>Ⅲ⁺</td><td>大多数碎屑有厚的碳酸盐包膜；基质颗粒为碳酸盐连续包被或者孔隙中填满碳酸盐；或多或少低连续硬结在一起；$CaCO_3$含量>40%</td><td>大多数颗粒为碳酸盐包被；大多数孔隙填满碳酸盐；$CaCO_3$含量>40%</td></tr>
<tr><td colspan="3">部分或完全硬结</td></tr>
<tr><td>Ⅳ</td><td colspan="2">K层顶部几乎为纯的硬结碳酸盐(75%～90%的$CaCO_3$)，由于碳酸盐不显著的片状淀积而形成一个不显著的板状结构；K层其他部分的碳酸盐含量也高达50%～75%</td></tr>
<tr><td>Ⅴ</td><td colspan="2">薄片状或板状结构发育；有初步的角砾化，并且形成豆石状
(多层碳酸盐包裹于颗粒外部)</td></tr>
<tr><td>Ⅵ</td><td>角砾化并重胶结，豆石状较普遍</td><td></td></tr>
</table>

总之，土壤的发生过程对土壤绝对年龄和气候指标都存在着影响，对试图利用古土壤重建高分辨率气候和环境的科学家来说，必须重视土壤发生过程。

1.3　选题依据和研究思路

理想的野外条件（如，S1的侧向可追踪性）和成熟的实验室技术让我们深信，成功地识别古土壤S1的地理分异是可能的。首先，多层土壤（或S1土壤复合体）在相同的景观条件下应当可以横向追踪（Ruhe等，1955；Ruhe，1967；Ruhe和Olson，1980；Valentine和Dalraymple，1976）。也就是说，在多层土壤完全融合成一个土壤剖面之前，黄土高原西北部S1的3个土壤层（对应于MIS 5e、MIS 5c和MIS 5a）应当可以向东南追踪。其次，如果后来的土壤形成事件没有完全改造先前形成的土壤，则先前的土壤特征可以从土壤层的野外识别和实验室的分析资料中得到辨认（Hallberg等，1978；Ruhe和Olson，1980）。如果土壤是加积型的话，情况更是如此，因为地表母质（风尘沉积）新的增长至少可以使先前形成的土壤的底部免受后来成壤过程的影响。第三，不论是确认土壤形成过程，还是辨认部分融合的土壤复合体中的多层土壤，土壤微形态分析都是最可靠的方法之一（Birkeland，1999；Boardman，1985；Mack等，1993；Ruhe和Olson，1980；Stoops和Eswaran，1986；Valentine和Dalrymple，1976）。

1.3.1 选题依据

对黄土高原末次间冰期古土壤S1地理分异进行研究的意义在于：

1.3.1.1 末次间冰期的关键性

末次间冰期（即MIS 5）是我们理解间冰期自然过程的最佳对象之一（Rind和Overpeck，1993）。可是对于MIS 5时期的气候，不论是在国际还是在国内都存在两种相反的意见，需要更多的末次间冰期记录来考证气候稳定与否。

1.3.1.2 对气候突变的假说进行检验

目前有两种驱动机制用于解释气候快速波动：一是起源于北大西洋的大洋温盐环流的重组（Broecker，1994；Bond和Lotti，1995）；二是热带太平洋地区的海气耦合作用——ENSO（Cane，1998）。为了检验这两个理论或者为了证实或证伪这两个被提议的气候突变的源区（北大西洋与热带太平洋），不同区域的记录是必需的。

1.3.1.3 东亚季风的重要性

黄土高原处在东亚夏季风和冬季风交相作用的“三角地带”（Li等，1988）。解决东亚季风的演化及其动力机制问题在全球变化研究中具有十分重要的意义，这是因为：

（1）东亚冬季风的强度为西伯利亚高压的强弱和位置所控制，而第四纪时期的西伯利亚高压又受到高纬度地区的冰期条件（如冰盖大小、植被条件）的制约。现代气候研究还表明，西伯利亚高压与北大西洋涛动（NAO）和北太平洋涛动（NPO）具有耦合关系（Gong等，2001）；

（2）东亚夏季风来自低纬度海洋，低纬度海洋ENSO活动引发的感热和潜热的变化又制约着夏季风的盛衰（Webster和Yang，1992）；

（3）冬季风和夏季风均与越赤道气流相联系，它们极可能是南北半球间能量交换的载体，黄土高原正好处在能量交换的通道上。

1.3.1.4 强化对土壤发生过程的复杂性与古气候重建关系的认识

对第四纪地质与土壤发生关系研究（Catt，1986）已经导出一个土壤学的分支学科——土壤地貌学（McFadden和Kneupfer，1990；Birkeland，1999）。陆景冈（1997）将其称作土壤地质学（Geopedology）。有不少学者已经对中国黄土高原沉积-成壤环境给予了关注（Kemp等，1997；Feng等，1999，2004a，2004b）。可是更多的研究者有意或无意地忽视了土壤发生过程的复杂性，本研究试图借助多方面的分析手段更加全面地诠释黄土高原S1的土壤发生过程以及这些过程在气候重建方面的意义。

1.3.2 研究目标

本研究着重研究末次间冰期古土壤S1（128～73 ka）沿着黄土高原西北—东南大断面上的空间变化。本研究将对中国黄土高原与北半球高纬度地区的气候突发事件的对比（An和Porter，1997）进行检验；并对典型的土壤地理学问题给予关注，以确定沿此断面的S1的母质沉积与土壤形成的同时性问题；综合考虑各种影响因子，对作为夏季风强度指标的磁化率进行了校正；对作为冬季风强度指标的石英粒径也将得到仔细的检验。得到校正和检验的指标最终用于重建季风历史。

1.3.3 研究思路

我们使用了以下研究方法和手段：

1.3.3.1 建立S1的地层和年代

（1）选取若干剖面进行野外考察，确立土壤地层。

（2）野外选取若干剖面对S1的底界和顶界样品进行实验室的红外激发释光测年

（IRSL）。

（3）沿东南—西北断面比较母质的IRSL测年结果和S1土壤的理论年龄（128～73 kaBP）的差别。

1.3.3.2 研究土壤形态学

（1）描述土壤层的宏观形态，以追踪多次土壤形成事件的历史并关注土壤剖面内的黏土和碳酸盐迁移以及土壤质地/土壤结构。

（2）调查土壤物像：如，碳酸盐特征、无定形的物质迁移、颗粒垒结、排泄物的特征、氧化壳与黏粒包膜、有机体或植物标识等。主要目的是确定土壤形成的环境、详细阐述土壤形成与风尘沉积的关系以及发掘土壤复合体剖面中多次土壤发生事件的记录。

1.3.3.3 恢复风化成壤的细节

（1）用淋溶指数（$CaO+K_2O+Na_2O$）/Al_2O_3和还原指数（FeO/Fe_2O_3）以及风化指数（游离铁与全铁含量之比，Fed/Fet）重建淋溶、还原和风化历史。

（2）建立模型：磁化率（SI）是多个因子的函数。即SI=f（氧化还原相关的成壤转化，淋溶强度，碳酸盐含量，碎屑贡献）。

（3）以成壤/风化强度的测量结果（物理的和化学的）和观测结果（形态学）检验模型，再重建成壤/风化作用的历史并对其进行解译。

1.3.3.4 改进冬季风的重建

（1）分析全样粒度（>40 μm），建立该代用指标的时间序列。

（2）分析粒度分布特征形成的主导因素。

参考文献

安芷生，Kukla G，Porter S C，等. 最近13万年黄土高原季风的变迁的磁化率证据. 科学通报，1990 (7): 529-532.

安芷生，孙东怀，张小曳，等. 最近130 ka洛川黄土堆积序列与格陵兰冰芯记录. 科学通报，1994，39 (24): 2254-2256.

安芷生，王俊达，李华梅. 洛川黄土剖面的古地磁研究. 地球化学，1977 (4): 239-249.

安芷生，王俊达，李华梅. 洛川黄土剖面的古地磁研究. 地球化学，1990 (4): 239-249.

陈骏，安芷生，汪永进，等. 最近800 ka洛川黄土剖面中Rb/Sr分布和古季风变迁. 中国科学（D辑），1998，28 (6): 498–504.
陈发虎，张维信. 甘青地区的黄土地层学与第四纪冰川问题. 北京：科学出版社，1993.
陈骏，仇刚，鹿化煜，等. 最近130 ka黄土高原夏季风变迁的Rb和Sr地球化学证据. 科学通报，1996，41 (21): 1963–1966.
陈旸，陈骏，刘连文，等. 最近13万年来黄土高原Rb/Sr记录与夏季风时空变迁. 中国科学（D辑），2003，33 (6): 513–519.
德日进，杨钟健. 山西西部陕西北部蓬蒂纪后黄土期前之地层观察. 地质学报，1930，甲种第8号: 1–19.
邓成龙，袁宝印. 末次间冰期以来黄河中游黄土高原沟谷侵蚀–堆积过程初探. 地理学报，2001，56 (1): 92–98.
丁仲礼，刘东生. 晚更新世东亚古季风变化动力机制的概念模型. 科学通报，1998，43 (2): 122–132.
丁仲礼，任剑璋，刘东生，等. 晚更新世季风–沙漠系统千年尺度的不规则变化及其机制问题. 中国科学（D辑），1996，26 (5): 385–391.
丁仲礼，余志伟. 第四纪时期东亚季风变化的动力机制. 第四纪研究，1995，1: 63–74.
丁仲礼，余志伟，刘东生. 中国黄土研究新进展（三）：时间标尺. 第四纪研究，1991，4: 336–348.
方小敏，戴雪荣，李吉均，等. 亚洲季风演化的突发性与不稳定性——以末次间冰期土壤发生为例. 中国科学（D辑），1996，26 (2) : 154–160.
冯兆东，陈发虎，张虎才，等. 末次冰期—末次间冰期蒙古高原与黄土高原对全球变化的重要贡献. 中国沙漠，2000，20 (2): 171–177.
郭正堂，刘东生，吴乃琴，等. 最后两个冰期黄土中记录的Heinrich型气候节拍. 第四纪研究，1996，1: 21–29.
郭正堂，彭淑贞，魏兰英，等. 22万年以来东亚夏季风的千年尺度变化及其在不同时期的差异. 第四纪研究，1999，4: 299–305.
贺秀斌. 20万年来黄土剖面土壤发生学特征与侵蚀环境演变. 土壤侵蚀与水土保持学报，1999，5 (2): 92–95.
李秉成. 黄土热释光测年问题. 西安工程学院学报，1998，20 (4): 41–44.
李虎侯. 光释光断代. 核电子学与探测技术，2000，20 (3): 217–228.
李华梅，安芷生，王俊达. 午城黄土剖面古地磁研究的初步结果. 地球化学，1974(2): 93–104.
刘东生. 黄河中游黄土. 北京：科学出版社，1964.
刘东生. 中国的黄土堆积. 北京：科学出版社，1965.
刘东生. 黄土与环境. 北京：科学出版社，1985.
刘连文，陈骏，王洪涛，等. 一个不受风力分选作用影响的化学风化指标: 黄土酸不溶物中Fe/Mg值. 科学通报，2001，46 (7): 578-582.

卢演俦，安芷生. 约70万年以来黄土高原自然环境变化系列探讨. 科学通报，1979，24: 221-224.

陆景冈. 土壤地质学. 北京：地质出版社，1997.

鹿化煜，安芷生. 洛川黄土粒度组成的古气候意义. 科学通报，1997，42 (1): 66-69.

鹿化煜，安芷生. 黄土高原黄土粒度组成的古气候意义. 中国科学（D辑），1998，28 (3): 278-283.

鹿化煜，Huissteden K V，安芷生，等. 早、中更新世东亚冬季风强度的快速变化. 海洋地质与第四纪地质，1999，19 (2): 75-83.

吕厚远，刘东生，吴乃琴，等. 末次间冰期以来黄土高原南部植被演替的植物硅酸体记录. 第四纪研究，1999，4: 336-349.

吕厚远，吴乃琴，刘东生，等. 150 ka来宝鸡黄土植物硅酸体组合季节性气候变化. 中国科学（D辑），1996，26 (2): 131-136.

孙东怀，周杰，蒋复初，等. 末次间冰期黄土高原夏季风气候的初步研究. 科学通报，1995，40 (20): 1873-1875.

孙继敏. 中国黄土的物质来源及其粉尘的产生机制与搬运过程. 第四纪研究，2004，24 (2): 175-183.

唐克丽，张平仓，王斌科. 土壤侵蚀与第四纪生态环境演变. 第四纪研究，1991，4: 300-309.

汪海斌，陈发虎，张家武. 黄土高原西部地区黄土粒度的环境指示意义. 中国沙漠，2001，22 (1): 21-26.

吴乃琴，Rousseau D D，刘东生. 110 ka来洛川黄土地层中蜗牛化石记录与环境因子分析. 中国科学（D辑），2004，26 (5): 405-410.

吴乃琴，Rousseau D D，刘秀平. 25万年来黄土蜗牛的生态演替对地球轨道变化的响应. 中国科学（D辑），2000，45 (4): 765-770.

张德二. 我国历史时期以来降尘的天气气候学初步分析. 中国科学（B辑），1984，3: 278-288.

张小曳，安芷生，刘东生，等.中国北部和西北部三次尘暴的研究——矿物气溶胶中微量元素源区特征及在大气搬运过程中的变化.科学通报，1991，19: 1487-1490.

张小曳，安芷生，张光宇，等.中国内陆大气颗粒物的搬运、沉积及反映的气候变化——Ⅱ. 黄土高原中部晚第四纪大气矿物气溶胶沉积. 中国科学（B辑），1994a，24 (12): 1315-1322.

张小曳，安芷生，张光宇，等.中国内陆大气颗粒物的搬运、沉积及反映的气候变化——Ⅰ. 现代大气气溶胶.中国科学（B辑），1994b，24 (11): 1206-1215.

张小曳，沈至宝，张光宇，等. 青藏高原远源西风粉尘与黄土沉积. 中国科学（D辑），

1996a，25 (2): 147–153.

张小曳，张光宇，朱光华，等. 中国源区粉尘的元素示踪. 中国科学（D辑），1996b，26 (5): 423–430.

赵景波. 风化淋滤带地质新理论——$CaCO_3$ 淀积深度理论. 沉积学报，2000，18 (1): 29–35.

周杰，张信宝，陈惠中，等. 130 ka BP前后黄土高原东部地区的气候侵蚀事件. 中国沙漠，1998，18 (2): 105–109.

朱显谟. 论原始土壤的成土过程.中国科学（B辑），1983，10：919–925.

Adkins J F, Boyle E A, Keigwin L, et al. Variability of the North Atlantic thermohaline circulation during the last interglacial period. Nature, 1997, 390: 154–156.

Almond P C, Tonkin P J. Pedogenesis by upbuilding in an extreme leaching and weathering environment, and slow loess accretion, south Westland, New Zealand. Geoderma, 1999, 92: 1–36.

An Z S. The history and variability of the East Asian paleomonsoon climate. Quaternary Science Reviews, 2000, 19: 171–187.

An Z S, Kukla G, Porter S C, et al. Magnetic susceptibility evidence of monsoon variation on the Loess Plateau of central China during the last 130, 000 years. Quaternary Research, 1991a, 36: 29–36.

An Z S, Kukla G, Porter S C, et al. Late Quaternary dust flow on the Chinese Loess Plateau. Catena, 1991b, 18: 125–133.

An Z S, Liu T S, Lu Y C, et al. The long - term paleomonsoon variation recorded by the loess - paleosol sequence in central China. Quaternary International, 1990, 7–8: 91–95.

An Z S, Porter S C. Millennial - scale climatic oscillations during the last interglaciation in central China. Geology, 1997, 25 (7): 603–606.

Anderson R S, Hallet B. Simulating magnetic susceptibility profiles in loess as an aid in quantifying rates of dust deposition and pedogenic development. Quaternary Research, 1996, 45: 1–16.

Anderson T L, Charlson R J, Schwartz S E, et al. Climate forcing by aerosols — a hazy picture. Science, 2003, 300: 1103–1104.

Andrews J T. Abrupt changes (Heinrich events) in late Quaternary North Atlantic marine environments: a history and review of data and concepts. Journal of Quaternary Science, 1998, 13 (1): 3–16.

Arduino E, Barberis E, Ajmone M F, et al. Iron oxides and clay minerals within profiles as indicators of soil age in northern Italy. Geoderma, 1986, 37: 45–55.

Bennet P C, Siegal D I, Hill B M, et al. Fate of silicate minerals in a peat bog. Geology, 1991,

19: 328–331.

Berger A. Milankovitch theory and climate. Reviews of Geophysics, 1988, 26: 624–657.

Birkeland. Soils and Geomorphology. 3rd ed. Oxford: Oxford University Press, 1999.

Boardman J. Comparison of soils in Midwestern United States and Western Europe with the interglacial record. Quaternary Research, 1985, 23: 62–75.

Böettger T, Junge F W, Litt T. Stable climatic conditions in central Germany during the last interglacial. Journal of Quaternary Science, 2000, 15 (5): 469–473.

Bond G, Broecker W S, Johnsen S, et al. Correlations between climate records from North Atlantic sediments and Greenland ice. Nature, 1993, 365: 143–147.

Bond G, Heinrich H, Broecker W S, et al. Evidence for massive discharges of icebergs into the North Atlantic ocean during the last glacial period. Nature, 1992, 360: 245–249.

Bond G C, Lotti R. Iceberg discharges into the North Atlantic on millennial time scales during the last glaciation. Science, 1995, 267: 1005–1009.

Bowen D Q. Quaternary Geology. Pergamon: Oxford Press, 1978.

Bowler J M, Chen K Z, Yuan B Y. Systematic variations in loess source areas: Evidence from Qaidam and Qinghai basins, western China // Liu T S. Aspects of Loess Research. Beijing: China Ocean Press, 1987: 39–51.

Bradley R S. Past global changes and their significance for the future. Quaternary Science Reviews, 2000, 19: 391–402.

Broecker W S. Massive iceberg discharges as triggers for global climate change. Nature, 1994, 372: 421–424.

Broecker W S, Bond G, McManus J, et al. Origin of the Northern Atlantic' s Heinrich events. Climatic Dynamics, 1992, 6: 265–273.

Broecker W S, Denton G H. The role of ocean - atmosphere reorganizations in glacial cycles. Geochimica at Cosmochimica Acta, 1989, 53: 2465–2501.

Buol S W, Hole F D, McCracken R J. Soil Genesis and Classification. 2nd ed. Ames: Iowa State University Press, 1980.

Busacca A J. Pedogenesis of a chronosequence in the Sacramento Valley, California, USA. I: Application of a soil development index. Geoderma, 1987, 41: 123–148.

Cane M A. A Role for the Tropic Pacific. Science, 1998, 282: 59–61.

Catt J A. Soils and Quaternary Geology: A handbook for Field Scientists. Oxford: Clarendon Press, 1986.

Catt J A. The agricultural importance of loess. Earth–Science Reviews, 2001, 54: 213–229.

Chappellaz J A, Brook E, Blunier T, et al. CH_4 and $\delta^{18}O$ of O_2 records from Antarctic and Greenland ice: A clue for stratigraphic disturbance in the bottom part of the Greenland Ice

Core Project and the Greenland Ice Sheet Project 2 ice cores. Journal of Geophysical Research, 1997, 102: 26547–26557.

Chen F H, Bloemendal J, Feng Z D, et al. East Asian monsoon variations during the last interglacial: evidence from the northwestern margin of the Chinese Loess Plateau. Quaternary Science Reviews, 1999, 18 (8–9): 1127–1135.

Chen F H, Bloemendal J, Wang J M, et al. High - resolution multiproxy climate records from Chinese loess: evidence for rapid climatic changes over the last 75 kyr. Palaeogeography, Palaeoclimatology, Palaeoecology, 1997, 130: 323–335.

Chen F H, Feng Z D, Zhang J W. Loess particle size data indicative of stable winter monsoons during the last interglacial in the western part of the Chinese Loess Plateau. Catena, 2000, 39 (4): 112–121.

Chen F H, Qiang M R, Feng Z D, et al. Stable East Asian monsoon climate during the Last Interglacial (Eemian) indicated by paleosol S1 in the western part of the Chinese Loess Plateau. Global and Planetary Change, 2003, 36 (3): 171–179.

Chen J, An Z S, Head J. Variation of Rb/Sr ratios in the loess - paleosol sequences of central China during the last 130, 000 years and their implications for monsoon paleoclimatology. Quaternary Research, 1999, 51: 215–219.

Chen J, Ji J F, Balsam W, et al. Characterization of the Chinese loess - paleosol stratigraphy by whiteness measurement. Palaeogeography, Palaeoclimatology, Palaeoecology, 2002, 183: 287–297.

Cortijo E, Duplessy J C, Labeyrie L, et al. Eemian cooling in the Norwegian Sea and North Atlantic Ocean preceding continental ice-sheet growth. Nature, 1994, 372: 446–449.

Cortijo E, Labeyrie L, Elliot M, et al. Rapid climatic variability of the North Atlantic Ocean and global climate: a focus of the IMAGES program. Quaternary Science Reviews, 2000, 19: 227–241.

Cortijo E, Lehman S, Keigwin L, et al. Changes in meridional temperature and salinity gradients in the North Atlantic Ocean (30°–72°N) during the last interglacial period. Paleoceanography, 1999, 14 (1): 23–33.

Crucifix M, Loutre F. Transient simulations over the last interglacial period (126–115 kyr BP): feedback and forcing analysis. Climate dynamics, 2002, 19: 417 –433.

Dansgaard W, Johnsen S J, Clausen H B, et al. Evidence for general instability of past climate from a 250-kyr ice-core record. Nature, 1993, 364: 218–220.

Derbyshire E, Meng X M, Kemp R A. Provenance, transport and characteristics of modern aeolian dust in eastern Gansu Province, China, and interpretation of the Quaternary loess record. Journal of Arid Environments, 1998, 39: 497–516.

Ding Z L, Derbyshire E, Yang S L, et al. Stacked 2.6 Ma grain size record from the Chinese loess based on five sections and correlation with the deep - sea $\delta^{18}O$ record. Paleoceanography, 2002, 17 (3): 1–21.

Ding Z L, Ren J Z, Yang S L, et al. Climate instability during the penultimate glaciation: evidence from two high-resolution loess records, China. Journal of Geophysical Research, 1999a, 104 (89): 20, 123–130, 132.

Ding Z L, Rutter N W, Han J T, et al. A coupled environmental system formed at about 2.5 Ma over eastern Asia. Palaeogeography, Palaeoclimatology, Palaeoecology, 1992, 94: 223–242.

Ding Z L, Rutter N W, Liu T S. Pedostratigraphy of Chinese loess deposits and climatic cycles in the last 2.5 Ma. Catena, 1993, 20: 73–91.

Ding Z L, Rutter N W, Liu T S, et al. Correlation of Dansgaard– Oscheger cycles between Greenland ice and Chinese loess. Paleoclimates, 1998a, 2: 281–291.

Ding Z L, Rutter N W, Sun J M, et al. Rearrangement of atmospheric circulation at about 2.6 Ma over northern China: evidence from grain size records of loess - paleosol and red clay sequences. Quaternary Science Reviews, 2000, 19: 547–558.

Ding Z L, Sun J M, Liu T S, et al. Wind-blown origin of the Pliocene red clay formation in the Chinese Loess Plateau. Earth and Planetary Science Letters, 1998b, 161: 135–143.

Ding Z L, Sun J M, Rutter N W, et al. Changes in sand content of loess deposits along a north-south transect of the Chinese Loess Plateau and the implications for desert variations. Quaternary Research, 1999b, 52: 56–62.

Ding Z L, Sun J M, Yang S L, et al. Geochemistry of the Pliocene red clay formation in the Chinese Loess Plateau and implications for its origin, source provenance and paleoclimate change. Geochimica et Cosmochimica Acta, 2001, 65 (6): 901–913.

Ding Z L, Sun J M, Yang S L, et al. Preliminary Magnetostratigraphy of a thick aeolian red clay-loess sequence at Lingtai, the Chinese Loess Plateau. Geophysical Research Letters, 1998c, 25: 1225–1228.

Ding Z L, Xiong S F, Sun J M, et al. Pedostratigraphy and paleomagnetism of a about 7.0 Ma eolian loess-red clay sequence at Lingtai, the Loess Plateau, north-central China and the implications for paleomonsoon evolution. Paleogeography, Palaeoclimatology, Palaeoceology, 1999c, 152: 49–66.

Ding Z L, Yu Z W, Rutter N W, et al. Towards an orbital time scale for Chinese loess deposits. Quaternary Science Reviews, 1994, 13: 39–70.

Dixon J C, Thorn C E, Darmody R G. Chemical weathering processes on the Vantage Peak Nunatak, Juneau Icefield, Southern Alaska. Physical Geography, 1984, 5: 111–131.

EPICA community members. Eight glacial cycles from an Antarctic ice core. Nature, 2004, 429:

623–628.

Fang X M, Li J J, Banerjee S K, et al. Millennial - scale climatic change during the last interglacial period: superparamagnetic sediment proxy from paleosol S1, the western Chinese Loess Plateau. Geophysical Research Letters, 1999a, 26 (16): 2485–2488.

Fang X M, Li J J, Van der voo R. Rock magnetic and grain size evidence for intensified Asian atmospheric circulation since 800,000 years BP related to Tibetan uplift. Earth and Planetary Science Letters, 1999b, 165: 129–144.

Fang X M, Ono Y, Fukusawa H, et al. Asian summer monsoon instability during the past 60,000 years: magnetic susceptibility and pedogenic evidence from the western Chinese Loess Plateau. Earth and Planetary Science Letters, 1999c, 168: 219–232.

Feng Z D. Climatic implications of magnetic susceptibility and ^{10}Be flux in Chinese loess. Catena, 1996, 27: 143–147.

Feng Z D. Geochemical characteristics of a loess - soil sequence in central Kansas, USA. Soil Science Society of American Journal, 1997, 61: 534–541.

Feng Z D. Gobi dynamics in the Northern Mongolian Plateau during the past 20,000 yr: preliminary results. Quaternary International, 2001, 76/77: 77–83.

Feng Z D, Chen F H. Problems of magnetic susceptibility signature as the summer monsoon proxy in Chinese loess sequences. International Symposium on Paleosols and Climate Change, Chinese Science Bulletin, 1999, 44 (suppl. 1): 97–104.

Feng Z D, Johnson W C. Factors affecting the magnetic susceptibility of a loess - soil sequence, Barton County, Kansas, USA. Catena, 1995, 24: 25–37.

Feng Z D, Wang H B, Olson C G. Pedogenic factors affecting magnetic susceptibility of the last interglacial paleosol S1 in the Chinese Loess Plateau. Earth Surface Processes and Landforms, 2004a, 29: 1389–1402.

Feng Z D, Wang H B, Olson C G, et al. Chronological discord between the last interglacial paleosol (S1) and its parent material in the Chinese Loess Plateau. Quaternary International, 2004b, 117: 17–26.

Field C R, Behrenfeld M J, Randerson J T, et al. Primary production of the biosphere: integrating terrestrial and oceanic components. Science, 1998, 281: 237–240.

Field M H, Huntley B, Müller H. Eemian climate fluctuations observed in a European pollen record. Nature, 1994, 371: 779–783.

Fine P, Singer M J, Verosub K L, et al. New evidence for the origin of ferrimagnetic minerals in loess from China. Soil Science Society of American Journal, 1993, 57: 1537–1542.

Fine P, Verosub K L, Singer M L. Pedogenic and lithogenic contribution to the magnetic susceptibility record of the Chinese loess - paleosol sequence. Geophysical Journal of

International, 1995, 122: 97–107.

Foth H D. Fundamentals of soil science. 6th ed. New York: John Wiley & Sons Inc, 1978.

Frogley M R, Tzedakis P C, Heaton T H E. Climate variability in Northwest Greece during the last interglacial. Science, 1999, 285: 1886–1889.

Fronval T, Jansen E. Rapid changes in ocean circulation and heat flux in the Nordic seas during the last interglacial period. Nature, 1996, 383: 806–810.

Fronval T, Jansen E. Eemian and early Weichselian (140–60 ka) paleoceanography and paleoclimate in the Nordic sea with comparisons to Holocene conditions. Paleoceanography, 1997, 12 (3): 443–462.

Gile L H, Hawley J W, Grossman R B. Soils and geomorphology in the Basin and Range area of southern New Mexico — Guidebook to the desert project. New Mexico Bur. Mines and Mineral Resources Mem, 1981, 39: 222.

Gile L H, Peterson F F, Grossman R B. Morphological and genetic sequences of carbonate accumulation in the desert soils. Soil Science, 1966, 101: 347–360.

Gong D Y, Wang S W, Zhu J H. East Asian winter monsoon and Arctic oscillation. Geophysical Research Letters, 2001, 28: 2073–2076.

Goudie A S, Cooke R U, Doornkamp J C. The formation of silt from quartz dune sand by salt weathering processes in deserts. Journal of Arid Environments, 1979, 2: 105–112.

GRIP Members. Climate instability during the last interglacial period recorded in the GRIP ice core. Nature, 1993, 364: 203–207.

Grootes P M, Steig E J, Stuiver M, et al. The Taylor Dome Antarctic ^{18}O record and globally synchronous changes in climate. Quaternary Research, 2001, 56: 289–298.

Grootes P M, Stuiver M, White J W C, et al. Comparison of oxygen isotope records from the GISP2 and GRIP Greenland ice cores. Nature, 1993, 366: 552–554.

Guo Z T, Fedoroff N. Paleoclimatic and stratigraphic implications of the S1 paleosol in the loess sequence in China // Liu T S. Loess, Environment and Global Change. Beijing: Science Press, 1991: 187–198.

Guo Z T, Liu T S. Paleosols as evidence of difference of climates between Holocene and the last interglacial. Quaternary Sciences, 1993, 1: 41–55.

Guo Z T, Liu T S, Guiot J, et al. High frequency pulses of east asia monsoon climate in the last two glaciations: link with the North Atlantic. Climate Dynamics, 1996, 12: 701–709.

Guo Z T, Peng S Z, Wei L Y, et al. Weathering Signals of Millennial - scale Oscillations of the East - Asian Summer Monsoon over the Last 220 ka.Chinese Science Bulletin, 1999, 44 (Suppl.): 20–25.

Guo Z T, Ruddiman W F, Hao Q Z, et al. Onset of Asian desertification by 22 Myr ago inferred from loess deposits in China. Nature, 2002, 416: 159–163.

Hallberg G R, Wollenhaupt N C, Miller G A. A century of soil development in spoil derived from loess in Iowa. Soil Science Society of America Journal, 1978, 42: 339–343.

Heinrich H. Origin and consequences of cyclic ice rafting in the northeast Atlantic Ocean during the past 130, 000 years. Quaternary Science Reviews, 1988, 29: 143–152.

Heller F, Liu T S. Magnetostratigraphical dating of loess deposits in China. Nature, 1982, 300: 431–433.

Heller F, Liu T S. Paleoclimatic and sedimentary history from magnetic susceptibility of loess in China. Geophysical Research Letters, 1986, 13 (11): 1169–1172.

Heusser L, Oppo D. Millennial - and orbital - scale climate variability in southeastern United States and in subtropical Atlantic during MIS 5: evidence from pollen and isotope from ODP site 1059. Earth and Planetary Science Letters, 2003, 214: 483–490.

Houghton J T, Ding Y, Griggs D J, et al. Climate Change 2001: The Scientific Basis. Cambridge: Cambridge University Press, 2001.

Jahn B, Gallet S, Han J M. Geochemistry of the Xining, Xifeng and Jixian sections, the Loess Plateau of China: eolian dust provenance and paleosol evolution during the last 140 ka. Chemical Geology, 2001, 178: 71–94.

Jenny H. Factors of soil formation: a system of quantitative pedology. New York: McGraw–Hill, 1941.

Johnson D L, Watson–Stegner D. Evolution model of pedogenesis. Soil Science, 1987, 143: 349–366.

Karabanov E B, Prokopenko A A, Williams D F, et al. Evidence for mid - Eemian cooling in continental climatic record from Lake Baikal. Journal of Paleolimnology, 2000, 23: 365–371.

Kemp R A, Derbyshire E, Meng X M. Micromorphological variation of the S1 paleosol across northwest China. Catena, 1997, 31: 77–90.

Kühl N, Litt T. Quantitative time series reconstruction of Eemian temperature at three European sites using pollen data. Veget Hist Archaeobot, 2003, 12: 205–214.

Kukla G. The last interglacial. Science, 2000, 287: 987–988.

Kukla G, An Z S. Loess stratigraphy in central China. Palaeogeography, Palaeoclimatology, Palaeoecology, 1989, 72: 203–225.

Kukla G, Bender M L, Beaulieu J, et al. Last interglacial climates. Quaternary Research, 2002, 58: 2–13.

Kukla G, Heller F, Liu X M, et al. Pleistocene climate in China dated by magnetic susceptibility. Geology, 1988, 16: 811–814.

Li J J, Feng Z D, Tang L Y. Late Quaternary monsoon patterns on the Loess Plateau of China. Earth Surface Processes and Landforms, 1988, 13: 125–135.

Liu C Q, Masuda A, Okada A, et al. Isotopic geochemistry of Quaternary deposits from the arid lands in northern China. Earth Planetary Science Letters, 1994, 127: 25–38.

Liu T S, Chang T H. The "Huangtu" (loess) of China. Proceedings of the 6th International Congress of Quaternary. Warsaw: 1961, vol. IV: Symposium on Loess: 503–524.

Liu X M, Hesse P, Rolph T, et al. Properties of magnetic mineralogy of Alaskan loess: evidence for pedogenesis. Quaternary International, 1999, 62: 93–102.

Loutre M F. Clues from MIS 11 to predict the future climate — a modeling point of view. Earth and Planetary Science Letters, 2003, 212: 213–224.

Loutre M F, Berger A. Marine Isotope Stage 11 as an analogue for the present interglacial. Global and Planetary Change, 2003, 36(3), 209–217.

Lu H Y, Huissteden K V, Zhou J, et al. Variability of East Asian winter monsoon in Quaternary climatic extremes in North China. Quaternary Research, 2000, 54: 321–327.

Lu H Y, Liu X D, Zhang F Q, et al. Astronomical calibration of loess - paleosol deposits at Luochuan, central Chinese Loess Plateau. Palaeogeography, Palaeoclimatology, Palaeoecology, 1999, 154: 237–246.

Lu H Y, Sun D H. Pathways of dust input to the Chinese Loess Plateau during the last glacial and interglacial periods. Catena, 2000, 40: 251–261.

Lyell C. Observations on the loamy deposit called "loess" of the basin of the Rhine (Excerpts). Edinburgh New Phil Journal, 1834, 17: 110–113, 118–120.

Lyell C. On the delta and alluvial deposits of the Mississippi and other points in the geology of North America, observed in years 1845, 1846. American Journal Science, 1847, 3 (2): 34–37.

Machette M N. Calcic soils of the southwestern United States. Geological Society of America, Spec Pap, 1985, 203: 1–21.

Mack G H, James W C, Monger H C. Classification of paleosols. Geological Society of America Bulletin, 1993, 105: 129–136.

Maher B A, Taylor R M. Formation of ultrafine - grained magnetite in soils. Nature, 1988, 336: 368–370.

Maher B A, Thompson R. Mineral magnetic record of the Chinese loess and Paleosols. Geology, 1991, 19 (1): 3–6.

Martrat B, Grimalt J O, Lopez–Martinez C, et al. Abrupt temperature changes in the western Mediterranean during the last and penultimate glacial and interglacial periods. Science, 2004, 306: 1762–1765.

Matthiessen J, Knies J. Dinoflagellate cyst evidence for warm interglacial conditions at the northern Barents Sea margin during marine oxygen isotope stage 5. Journal of Quaternary Science, 2001, 16 (7): 727–737.

McFadden L D, Kneupfer P L K. Soil geomorphology: the linkage of pedology with supperficial processes. Geomorphology, 1990, 3: 197–205.

McManus J F, Bond G C, Broecker W, et al. High - resolution climate records from the North Atlantic during the last interglacial, Nature, 1994, 371: 326–329.

McManus J F, Oppo D W, Cullen J L. A 0.5 - million - year record of millennial - scale climate variability in the North Atlantic. Science, 1999, 283: 971–975.

Meng X M, Debershire E, Kemp R A. Origin of the magnetic susceptibility signal in Chinese loess. Quaternary Science Reviews, 1997, 16: 833–839.

North Greenland Ice Core Project members. High - resolution record of Northern Hemisphere climate extending into the last interglacial period. Nature, 2004, 431: 147–151.

Oches E A, Banerjee S K, Soheid P A, et al. High-resolution proxies of climate variability in the Alaska loess record // Busacca A J. International Symposium on Dust Aerosols, Loess Soil and Global Change. Pullman, WA: Washington State University' s CAHE MISC0190, 1998: 167–170.

Oppo D W, Horowitz M, Lehman S J. Marine core evidence for reduced deep water production during Termination Ⅱ followed by a relatively stable substage 5e (Eemian). Paleoceanography, 1997, 12 (1): 51–63.

Petit J R, Jouzel J, Raynaud D, et al. Climate and atmospheric history of the past 420, 000 years from the Vostok ice core, Antarctica. Nature, 1999, 399: 429–436.

Phillips J D. Progressive and regressive pedogenesis and complex soil evolution. Quaternary Research, 1993, 40 (2): 169–176.

Pope G A. Internal weathering of quartz grains. Physical Geography, 1995, 16: 315–338.

Pope G A. Issues of scale in quartz weathering. Fort Worth: Association of American Geographers 93rd Annual Meeting, 1997: 211.

Porter S C, An Z S. Correlation between climate events in the North Atlantic and China during the last glaciation. Nature, 1995, 375: 305–308.

Porter S C, An Z S. Episodic gullying and paleomonsoon cycles on the Chinese Loess Plateau. Quaternary Research, 2005, 6(2): 232–241.

Prokopenko A A, Karabanov E B, Williams D F, et al. The stability and the abrupt ending of the last interglaciation in southeastern Siberia. Quaternary Research, 2002, 58: 56–59.

Pye K. Aeolian dust and dust deposits. London: Academic Press, 1987.

Pye K,Tsoar H. The mechanics and geological implications of dust transport and deposition in deserts, with particular reference to loess formation and dune sand diagnosis in the northern Negev, Journal of Arid Environments, 1987, 2004(58): 559–574.

Pye K, Zhou L P. Late Pleistocene and Holocene eolian dust deposition in North China and the Northwest Pacific Ocean. Palaeogeography, Palaeoclimatology, Palaeoecology, 1989, 73: 11–23.

Rasmussen T L, Balbon E, Thomsen E, et al. Climate records and changes in deep outflow from the Norwegian Sea 150–55 ka. Terra Nova, 1999, 11: 61–66.

Rea D K, Leinen M. Asian aridity and the zonal westerlies: late Pleistocene and Holocene record of eolian deposition in the Northwest Pacific Ocean. Palaeogeography, Palaeoclimatology, Palaeoecology, 1988, 66: 1–8.

Retallack G J. The environmental factor approach to the interpretation of paleosols. Soil Science Society of America, Spec. Publ. 1994, 33: 31–64.

Rind D, Overpeck J. Hypothesized causes of decade - to - century - scale climate variability: climate results. Quaternary Science Reviews, 1993, 12: 357–374.

Rioual P, Andrieu–Ponel V, Rietti–Shati M, et al. High - resolution record of climate stability in France during the last interglacial period. Nature, 2001, 413: 293–296.

Ruhe R V. Geomorphic surfaces and surficial deposits in sounthern New Mexico. State Bureau of Mines and Mineral Resources, 1967, Mem. 18.

Ruhe R V, Olson C G. Soil welding. Soil Science, 1980, 130 (3): 132–139.

Ruhe R V, Prill R C, Piecken F F. Profile characteristics of some loess - derived soils and soil aeration. Soil Science Society of America Journal, 1955, 19: 345–348.

Seidenkrantz M S, Kristensen P H, Knudsen K L. Marine evidence for climatic instability during the last interglacial in shelf records from NW Europe. Journal of Quaternary Sciences, 1995, 10 (1): 77–82.

Shackleton N J. The last interglacial in the marine and terrestrial records. Proceedings of Royal Society B: Biological Sciences, 1969, 174: 135–154.

Shemesh A, Rietti–Shati M, Rioual P, et al. An oxygen isotope record of lacustrine opal from European Maar indicates climatic stability during the last interglacial. Geophysical Research Letters, 2001, 28 (12): 2305–2308.

Stoops G, Eswarn H. Soil Micromorphology. New York: A Hutchinson Ross Publication, 1986.

Sun J M. Source regions and formation of the Loess sediments on the high mountain regions of Northwestern China. Quaternary Research, 2002a, 58: 341–351.

Sun J M. Provenance of less material and formation of loess deposits on the Chinese Loess Plateau. Earth and Planetary Science Letters, 2002b, 203: 845–859.

Sun J M, Liu T S, Le Z F. Sources of heavy dust fall in Beijing, China on April 16, 1998. Geophysical Research Letters, 2000, 27: 2105–2108.

Sun J M, Zhang M Y, Liu T S. Spatial and temporal characteristics of dust storms in China and its surrounding regions, 1960—1999: Relations to source area and climate. Journal of Geophysical Research (D-series), 2001, 106: 10325-10334.

Taylor K C, Hammer C U, Alley R B, et al. Electrical conductivity measurements from the GISP2 and GRIP Greenland ice cores. Nature, 1993, 366: 549-552.

Thompson R, Oldfield F. Environmental Magnetism. London: Allen & Unwin, 1986.

Thouveny N, Beaulieu J L, Bonifay E, et al. Climate variations in Europe over the past 140 ka deduced from rock magnetism. Nature, 1994, 371: 503-506.

Tzedakis P C, Frogley M R, Heaton T H E. Duration of last interglacial conditions in Northwest Greece. Quaternary Research, 2002, 58: 53-55.

Tzedakis P C, McManus J F, Hooghiemstra H, et al. Comparison of changes in vegetation in northeast Greece with records of climate variability on orbital and suborbital frequencies over the last 450, 000 years. Earth and Planetary Science Letters, 2003, 212: 197-212.

Valentine K W G, Dalrymple J B. Quaternary buried paleosols: a critical review. Quaternary Research, 1976, 6: 209-222.

Verosub L K, Fine P, Singer M J, et al. Pedogenesis and paleoclimate: interpretation of the magnetic susceptibility record of Chinese loess - paleosol sequences. Geology, 1993, 21: 1011-1014.

Verosub L K, Fine P, Singer M J, et al. Reply to the comments on "Pedogenesis and paleoclimate" : interpretation of the magnetic susceptibility record of Chinese loess - paleosol sequences. Geology, 1994, 22: 859-860.

Von Richthofen F. On the mode of origin of loess. Geological Magazine, 1882, 9: 293-305.

Vreeken W J. Principal kinds of chronosequence and their significance in soil history. Journal of Soil Science, 1975, 26: 378-394.

Wang H, Ambrose S H, Liu C L J, et al. Paleosol stable isotope evidence for early Hominid Occupation of East Asian Temperate environments. Quaternary Research, 1997, 48: 228-238.

Webster P J, Yang S. Monsoon and ENSO: Selectively Interactive Systems. Quarterly Journal Royal Meteorology Society, 1992, 118: 877-926.

Whitlock C, Bartlein P J. Vegetation and climate change in northwest America during the past 125 kyr. Nature, 1997, 388: 57-61.

Wright J S. "Desert" loess versus "glacial" loess: Quartz silt formation, source areas and sediment pathways in the formation of loess deposits. Geomorphology, 2001, 36: 231-256.

Wu G J, Pan B T, Guan Q Y, et al. Loess record of climatic changes during MIS 5 in the Hexi Corridor northwest China. Quaternary International, 2002, 97/98: 167-172.

Xiao J L, An Z S. Three large shifts in East Asian monsoon circulation indicated by loess - paleosol sequences in China and late Cenozoic deposits in Japan. Palaeogeography, Palaeoclimatology, Palaeoecology, 1999a, 154: 179–189.

Xiao J L, An Z S, Liu T S, et al. East Asia monsoon variation during the last 130, 000 years: evidence from the Loess Plateau of Central China and lake Biwa of Japan. Quaternary Science Reviews, 1999b, 18: 147–157.

Xiao J L, Porter S C, An Z S, et al. Grain Size of Quartz as an Indicator of Winter Monsoon Strength on the Loess Plateau of Central China during the Last 130, 000 Yr. Quaternary Research, 1995, 43: 22–29.

Yaalon D H. Conceptual models in pedogenesis: Can soil - forming functions be solved? Geoderma, 1975, 14: 189–205.

Zhou L P, Oldfield F, Wintle A G, et al. Partly pedogenic origin of magnetic variations in Chinese loess. Nature, 1990, 346: 737–739.

2　野外采样策略和实验方法

2.1　中国黄土高原现代自然背景及野外采样策略

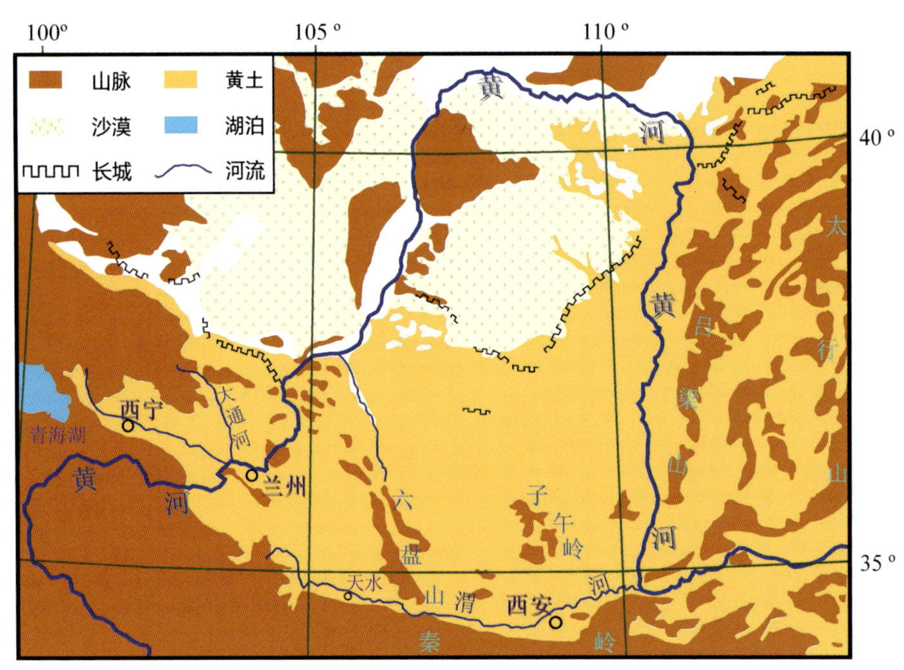

图2.1　黄土高原示意图

黄土和黄土状岩石在中国的分布很广，自东向西主要分布在黑龙江、吉林、辽宁、内蒙古、山东、河北、河南、山西、陕西、甘肃、青海、新疆等地，在中国南方的江苏、湖北和四川等地也有分布，总计面积达63万平方千米（刘东生，1965）。我们所指的黄土高原是从地貌单元的角度来划分的，也就是说它与东面的华北平原、西面的青藏高原、南面的秦岭山地、北面的鄂尔多斯高原在地貌类型上截然不同，是以黄土地貌为主体的高原，大体位于北纬33°43′—40°16′，东经100°45′—114°33′，面积达44万平方千米（刘东生，1985；马乃喜，1987；裴新富，1991）。塬、梁和峁是黄土高原地貌的基本类型，此外，黄土高原地区分布有岩石山地和断陷盆地或地堑谷地（罗来兴，1980）。塬是一种地形平坦（坡度<1°）的高地，高地的边缘为沟谷侵蚀。黄土高原上较大的塬包括白草塬、董志塬（或西峰塬）以及洛川塬等。梁、峁是一种地面起伏稍大的两侧为沟谷侵蚀的丘陵地。根据地质地貌条件，黄土高原可分为东部地区、中部地区、西部地区：太行山至吕梁山之间为黄土高原的东部地区，俗称山西高原；吕梁山至六盘山之间为黄土高原的中部地区，是典型的黄土高原；六盘山以西为黄土高原的西部地区，通称陇西黄土高原（见图2.1）。另外一种简单的分法是以六盘山为界将黄土高原分为东、西两部分。本研究采用二分法。

由于冬季风和夏季风的交互作用，现代黄土高原的气候–植被带的空间分布存在大致东南—西北的梯度。从气候区划来说，由南向北，黄土高原可分为南温带亚湿润大区、南温带亚干旱大区以及中温带亚干旱大区（西北师范学院地理系.地图出版社，1984）。具体来说，如图2.2.a所示，在黄土高原的东南部年均温最高，如，蓝田的年均温达到了12.5 ℃，向西（经度减小）和向北（纬度增高）年均温逐渐降低，如兰州的年均温为9.8 ℃，环县的年均温为8.6 ℃。在年均温沿经向纬向变化的同时，地形要素对气温的影响较大，例如，西部的定西地区海拔较高，达1897.5 m，所以年均温下降幅度较大（参见表2.1）。降水量从西北到东南逐渐增加的趋势比较显

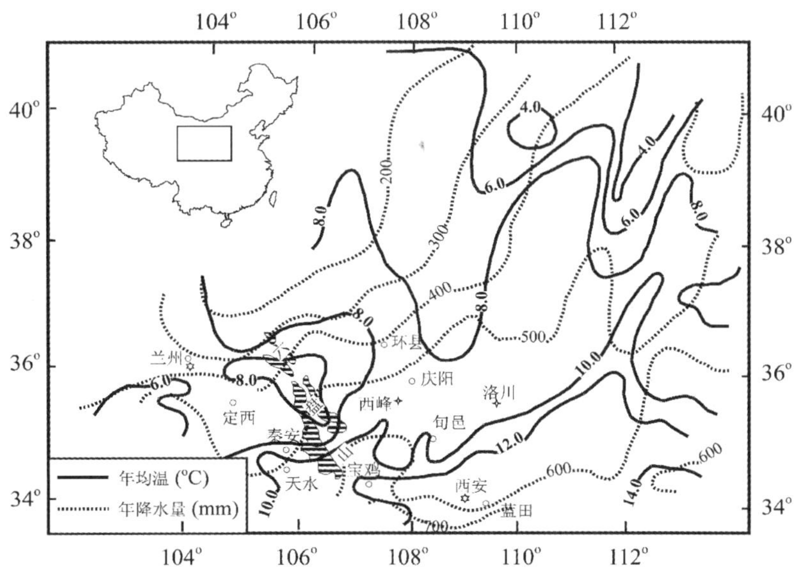

图 2.2.a　黄土高原地区年平均气温和年降水量分布图

（据钱林清主编《黄土高原气候》P31、P55页的图改绘）

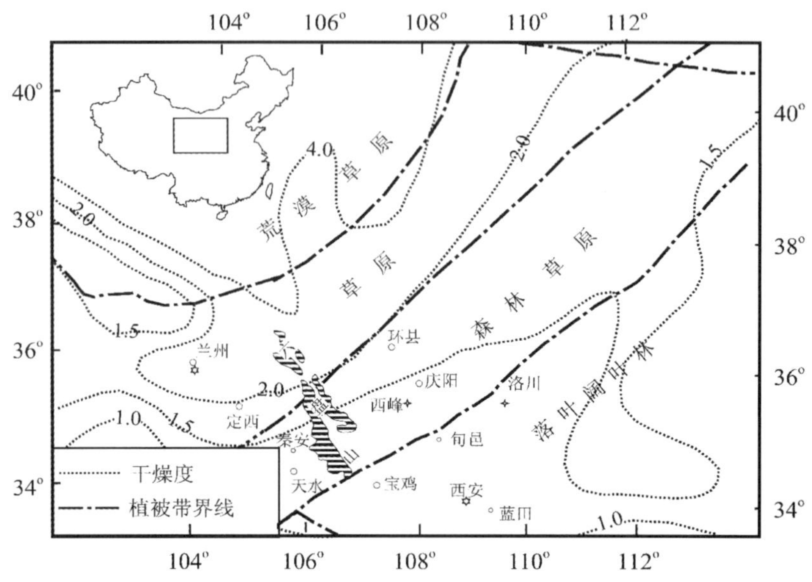

图 2.2.b　黄土高原地区干燥度和植被带分布图

（据《中国自然地理图集》P64、P89页的图改绘）

著，降水量南北相差在500 mm以上。大部分地区的降水以降雨的形式出现，降雪较少。降水多集中在夏季的6、7、8月份，夏季降水占全年的45%～55%，且以暴雨为多。降水量的季节分配有利于植物在夏季合成有机物，有利于微生物对土壤有机质的分解，但对土壤腐殖质的积累是不利的。年均温和降水量一方面制约着植被的分布，另一方面还控制着本区土壤风化的强度（朱显谟，1989）。如图2.2.b所示，干燥度（潜在蒸发量与年降水量之比）从东南到西北逐渐增大，且干燥度的等值线在西北部更加密集。植被带的分布也呈现由东南到西北逐渐变化的趋势，黄土高原在我国的植被区划中地跨草原、森林草原和落叶阔叶林三个植被带，镶嵌于荒漠草原带和常绿阔叶林带之间。

注意到现代气候、植被分布的梯度，我们在黄土高原的东、西部各选了一个断面来考察、探讨末次间冰期古土壤S1的地理分异。东部有5个剖面被选为研究对象，自北而南依次为环县城东塬剖面、庆阳雷家岘剖面、旬邑剖面、宝鸡宝陵剖面和蓝田剖面。我们在黄土高原西部选择了4个剖面作为研究点，从西北到东南分别是兰州九州台剖面、定西李家坪剖面、秦安剖面、天水李家塬剖面（见图2.2.a和2.2.b）。剖面的具体地理位置和相关的气候参数见表2.1。地形是影响土壤发育的重要因素，此外，据张信宝和周杰（1996）对黄土高原东部地区（六盘山以东）的研究，塬地或残塬与梁峁地貌对侵蚀的抵抗程度有很大差别。因此，除了气候-生物梯度是剖面选择的主要依据外，对剖面选择我们还注意了地形的统一性原则，上述

9个剖面大都位于地形比较相似的台地或塬地。

在9个剖面上绝大部分样品是以2 cm间隔连续采集的，蓝田剖面底部50 cm和环县剖面顶部100 cm的样品按10 cm间隔采样，样品采集涵盖L1（末次冰期的黄土）的底部、整个S1、L2（倒数第二次冰期）的顶部。这些样品用于实验室的粒度、磁化率和碳酸盐含量以及化学元素分析。兰州剖面总厚13 m，采样650个；定西剖面总厚6 m，获得样品300个；秦安剖面总厚4.8 m，样品数量为240个；天水剖面总厚5 m，样品总数计250个；宝鸡剖面总厚5 m，取得样品250个，但部分样品遗失；蓝田剖面总厚5.5 m，取样255个；旬邑剖面总厚3.8 m，样品采集数量为170个；庆阳剖面总厚3.9 m，采集样品190个；环县剖面总厚6.5 m，采集样品305个。我们还在定西剖面、天水剖面、蓝田剖面、庆阳剖面、环县剖面S1的顶部和底部采集了块状释光样品，为避免太阳照射，样品采集在微光条件下（夜晚）进行。另外，我们还在上述9个剖面上采集土壤微形态的小块样品，每个剖面大约采集了40个。

表2.1 采样点的地理位置与气候条件

地　点	纬度	经度	海拔(m)	年均温(℃)	降水量(mm)
兰州	36°03′	103°53′	2066.0	9.8	311.7
定西	35°35′	104°37′	1897.5	6.4	413.9
秦安	34°52′	105°40′	1225.8	10.5	474.2
天水	34°34′	105°46′	1141.7	10.7	540.2
宝鸡	34°25′	107°06′	—	12.9	679.0
蓝田	34°10′	109°19′	800.0	12.5	668.0
旬邑	35°07′	108°19′	—	9.0	606.0
庆阳	35°55′	107°49′	1421.0	8.3	561.5
环县	36°38′	107°07′	1256.0	8.6	407.3

（注：年平均气温和降水量为1961—1990年30年的平均值，由于统计年限和统计的年代不一致，可能与图2.2.a有出入。）

2.2 常用气候代用指标以及释光年龄的实验室测量

2.2.1 粒度前处理与测量

对沉积物来说，粒度是指示动力状况的良好指标（任明达和王乃梁，1981）。第四纪以来，沉积的黄土主要是风力搬运的结果，而风动力又主要是近地表的冬季风。因此，黄土的粒度大小至少可以部分地指示冬季风强盛与否。需要注意的是，源区物质的粗细和距离源区的远近、搬运过程中颗粒间的撞击、沉积后的就地风化和细颗粒的迁移等对粒度的分布都有影响（Feng和Chen，1999；Ding等，1999；Pye，1987；Feng等，2004a，2004b；季峻峰等，1999；Birkeland，1999）。

目前，沉积学上对粒级的划分方法有两大类（见表2.2）。一种是采用真数，即以毫米（mm）或微米（μm）为单位来表示颗粒的直径（Wentworth，1922）；另一种是采用粒径的对数值来表示（Krumbein，1934），即

$$\Phi=-\log_2 d \tag{1}$$

式中的d是颗粒直径（μm）。

土壤学中对粒级的划分又有另外的标准，而且国家间的标准也不尽相同，例如对黏粒的上限有的定为1 μm，多数定为2 μm；对粉砂的上限有的定为20 μm，多数定为50 μm（黄昌勇，2000）。

本研究中采用温德华的标准，即以2 μm、63 μm分别作为黏粒、粉砂的粒径上限。

粒度样品的实验室处理与鹿化煜等（1997）的方法相同，即以浓度为10%的过氧化氢（H_2O_2）去除有机质，以浓度为10%的盐酸（HCl）去除碳酸盐（主要为$CaCO_3$），反应完全后将烧杯注满蒸馏水并静置24小时，抽去烧杯中上层的液体，然后加入10 ml 5%的六偏磷酸钠作为分散剂在超声波振荡仪内超声振荡7分钟左右以达到充分分散的效果，最后用英国Malvern公司制造的MasterSizer 2000型激光粒度仪进行粒度分析。MasterSizer2000型粒度仪测量精度高，测量的重复性好，误差在1%以内。

表2.2 **温德华粒级划分方法**

粒级名称	粒级界限(mm)	粒级界限(μm)	粒级界限(F)
漂石	>256	256 000	<-8
卵石	64～256	64 000～256 000	-8～-6

续表 2.2

粒级名称		粒级界限(mm)	粒级界限(μm)	粒级界限(F)
砾石		2～64	2000～64 000	-6～-1
砂	极粗砂	1～2	1000～2000	-1～0
	粗砂	0.5～1	500～1000	0～1
	中砂	0.25～0.5	250～500	1～2
	细砂	0.125～0.25	125～250	2～3
	极细砂	0.0625～0.125	63～125	3～4
粉砂	粗粉砂	0.031～0.0625	31～63	4～5
	中粉砂	0.0156～0.031	15.6～31	5～6
	细粉砂	0.0078～0.0156	7.8～15.6	6～7
	极细粉砂	0.002～0.0078	2～7.8	7～9
黏粒		<0.002	<2	>9

（据 Wentworth，1922，黏粒的上限被改为 2 μm；转引自任明达和王乃梁，1981）

2.2.2 磁化率实验室测量

磁化率（Magnetic susceptibility），又称初始磁化率或低频磁化率，是物质在外磁场中受感应产生的磁化强度 M 与外加磁场 H 的比值，即：

$$\kappa = M/H \tag{2}$$

κ 为容积磁化率（无量纲），M 为磁化强度（特斯拉，T），H 为外磁场强度（安培/米，A/m）。在环境磁学中，常用质量磁化率（Mass magnetic susceptibility，χ）反映物质的磁化难易程度和亚铁磁性矿物粗略含量，它与 κ 的换算关系是：

$$\chi = \kappa/\rho \tag{3}$$

ρ 为物质的密度（kg/m^3），质量磁化率的国际单位为 $10^{-6}\ m^3 \cdot kg^{-1}$，出于习惯，黄土-古土壤中常用 $10^{-8}\ m^3 \cdot kg^{-1}$ 或 $10^{-7}\ m^3 \cdot kg^{-1}$。

频率磁化率（frequency-dependent susceptibility，χ_{fd}）是指样品在低频（0.47 kHz）磁场和高频（4.7 kHz）磁场中磁化率值的相对差异，即

$$\chi_{fd}(\%) = \frac{(\chi_{lf} - \chi_{hf}) \times 100}{\chi_{lf}} \tag{4}$$

式中 χ_{lf} 表示低频磁化率（质量磁化率）、χ_{hf} 表示高频磁化率。由于稳定单畴向超顺磁性颗粒过渡的磁性颗粒具有磁黏滞性，所以它对高频（10 kHz）磁化无反应，结果是 $\chi_{hf} < \chi_{lf}$。因此，频率磁化率反映了样品中超顺磁性颗粒的存在和相对含量

(Zhou等，1990)。

测量前先在电子天平上称出样品质量 W（g），然后在安静的室内环境下使用Bartington MS2型磁化率仪对样品的磁化率进行测量，具体的仪器操作和测定见Dearing（1999）。所有样品都测量了低频（0.47 kHz）磁化率和高频（4.7 kHz）磁化率。每个样品均测量3次，若以 R 表示得到的最初结果，则最终的低频磁化率或高频磁化率（χ）结果为：

$$\chi=\frac{\sum_{i=1}^{3}R_i}{3\times W} \tag{5}$$

频率磁化率根据公式（4）计算获得。

2.2.3 碳酸钙含量的测定

碳酸盐是黄土物质的重要组成部分，其主要形式为 $CaCO_3$。钙积是干旱区和半干旱区重要的成土过程，主要指碳酸盐在土壤剖面中的溶解、移动并淀积为钙积层的成土作用。$CaCO_3$ 在土壤中的移动有随重力水向下淋溶和随毛细管水的季节性向上移动两种形式。这个过程的实质是 $CaCO_3$ 和 $Ca(HCO_3)_2$ 之间的动态平衡：

$$CaCO_3+H_2O+CO_2 \rightleftharpoons Ca(HCO_3)_2 \tag{6}$$

这个动态平衡主要受控于植物或微生物的呼吸作用和植物残体的分解作用以及降水的供给。具体地说，植物根系、微生物的呼吸作用和植物残体的分解作用将提升土壤中的 CO_2 分压，平衡向着生成 $Ca(HCO_3)_2$ 的方向推移，Ca^{2+} 和 HCO_3^- 随土壤水分向下迁移，由于向下渗透的水分逐渐减少或者由于蒸腾散发过程引起水分的流失，平衡向着生成 $CaCO_3$ 的方向发展。这样，$CaCO_3$ 在一定深度发生淀积。研究表明，降水量与 $CaCO_3$ 的淀积深度有较好的线性关系（Jenny，1941；Arkley，1963；Retallack，1994；Caudill等，1996；Royer，1999；赵景波，2000）。因此，$CaCO_3$ 的淀积深度通常作为恢复古降水的依据（赵锦慧等，2004）。

实验室里 $CaCO_3$ 含量的测量是在江苏海安石油仪器厂生产的GMY-3型岩石碳酸盐含量测定仪上完成的。原理是气量法（Machette，1986），理论依据是理想气体状态方程：

$$pV=nRT \tag{7}$$

$CaCO_3$ 含量的计算公式为：

$$c(\%)=\frac{p\times V\times 100}{R\times T\times W}\times 100\% \tag{8}$$

其中，p 为压强（帕斯卡，Pa），V 为气体体积（立方米，m^3），n 为物质的量（摩尔，mol），*R*为摩尔气体常数（8.3145 J・mol^{-1}・K^{-1}），*T*为温度（K），*c*为$CaCO_3$的百分含量，*W*为样品质量（g）。

2.2.4 氧化铁全量和游离铁含量的测量

铁在地壳中的丰度约为5%，根据文启忠等（1996）的报道，中国黄土高原马兰黄土中铁的丰度为2.93%左右。马兰黄土中99.8%以上的铁为硅酸盐矿物铁和游离铁（刁桂仪和文启忠，1999）。土壤学中，游离铁一般指的是铁的氧化物或氢氧化物，可以用连二亚硫酸钠（Dithionite）－柠檬酸钠（Citrate）－碳酸氢钠（Bicarbonate）（三者合起来简称为DCB或CBD）提取。游离铁（Fed）包括无定形铁（又称“活性”氧化铁，FeO）和晶形铁，无定形铁是指用酸性草酸铵所提取的铁。游离铁对土壤的着色有着重要的贡献，野外的土壤颜色可以直观地告诉我们土壤发育的强弱。游离氧化铁还是土壤黏粒的重要组成部分，它部分继承自母质，多数来自层状硅酸盐矿物晶格中铁的氧化和释放，因此土壤游离铁的含量或铁的游离度反映土壤的风化程度（陈家坊，1981）。游离度是游离铁与铁（通常以Fe_2O_3表示）的总量的比值（Fed/Fet），在黄土高原古气候研究中它已成为夏季风的替代指标（Guo等，1996）。

全铁或游离铁的测量采用原子吸收光谱法，其原理是利用铁空心阴极灯发出的铁的特征谱线的辐射，通过含铁试样产生原子蒸气时，被蒸气中铁元素的基态原子所吸收，由辐射特征谱线光被减弱的程度来测定试样中铁元素的含量。先称取5 g左右样品研磨至200目以下，分别用酸溶法提取全铁（McKeague，1976），用DCB提取游离铁（Mehra和Jackson，1960），然后在中国科学院地质和地球物理研究所的WFD-Y2型原子吸收光谱仪上测定（比色波长为248.3 nm）。游离铁和全铁的分析精度分别为11%和0.4%。

2.2.5 其他化学元素的测量

土壤发生的实质是各种化学元素的重新组合和迁移（陈家坊，1990）。表生作用过程中化学元素的迁移、富集是元素对环境条件变化响应的表现。20世纪80年代以后，中国黄土地球化学的研究开始强调化学风化、气候代用指标的元素地球化学分析以及对黄土物质来源的进一步调查。这期间，土壤学中一些非常成熟的土壤风化强度指标，如，

- 硅铝率（SiO_2/Al_2O_3）、
- 硅钛比（SiO_2/TiO_2）、

• 硅铝铁率［$SiO_2/(Al_2O_3+Fe_2O_3)$］、

• 淋溶指数［$(Na_2O+K_2O+CaO)/Al_2O_3$或$(Na_2O+K_2O+CaO+MgO)/Al_2O_3$］、

• 风化指数μ值（淋溶层K_2O/Na_2O与母质层K_2O/Na_2O的比值）等

被引入了黄土-古土壤研究（Liu等，1995；文启忠等，1995）。同时还根据各种元素在剖面中的富集特征，将元素（或氧化物）间的比值作为风化强度的指标，例如MgO/Al_2O_3、F/Cl、Fe/Al、Rb/Sr、Zr/Sr、Fe/Mg（余素华等，1994；刘玉兰等，1981；程燕等，2003；陈骏等，1996；刘连文等，2001，2002）。

在实验室里对定西、天水、蓝田3个剖面的样品测量了元素浓度。测量前将烘干后的样品研磨至200目（75 μm）以下，然后称取4 g左右的样品倒入压样孔的中央，周围加入适量的硼酸，加压至30 t/m^{2}并维持20 s左右，将样品压制成直径约4 cm、厚约8 mm的圆饼。压制好的样品在Panalytical Magix PW2403型X荧光仪测量元素的浓度（ppm）。该仪器可以测量三十多种元素（P、Ti、V、Cr、Mn、Co、Ni、Cu、Zn、Ga、As、Br、Rb、Sr、Y、Zr、Nb、Mo、Ba、La、Ce、Pb、Th、Hf、Bi、Si、Fe、Al、Mg、Ca、K、Na），同一样品的测量标准差为2%左右。

2.2.6 土壤薄片的制作和观察

1938年奥地利的土壤学家库比纳（W. L. Kubiëna）发表了《Micropedology》一书，标志着土壤微形态学的建立。土壤微形态学是利用显微技术或超显微技术观察鉴定未扰动土壤样品或风化壳样品的物质组成、时空关联的一门土壤分支学科，其目的是寻求土壤及其具体物像（specific features）形成和转化所涉及的过程（Stoops，2003）。土壤微形态描述的重要性在于（黄瑞采，1990）：

（1）土壤的各种特性，无论是在一个石英黏粒、结构排列单位上还是特定过程产生的土壤物像的水平上，都可以得到详细的记录；

（2）重建土壤中已经发生的或正在发生的过程；

（3）提供通用的或专用的土壤分类的基础；

（4）可以用于比较土纲、亚纲或土类；

（5）佐证其他方法分析所得的结果，以作为矿物学、化学和物理学分析选择的参考。

Bronger、Kemp、郭正堂等学者较为重视使用土壤微形态的方法研究中国的黄土-古土壤序列，并取得了不少的研究成果（Bronger，1989；郭正堂等，1994，1996；Kemp等，1995，1996，1997，2001；Kemp，1995，1998，1999）。他们的研究表明，土壤微形态对于揭示沉积-成壤环境非常有效。

实验室里对野外采集的非扰动定向样品采用甲基丙烯酸甲酯与偶氮二乙丁氰的混

合液（比例为50 mL：5 g）经浴热反应固化（贺秀斌，1998），然后磨成直径30 mm的薄片。所有土壤薄片的制作都是在中国地震局地质所完成的。土壤薄片制作完成后，在偏光显微镜下观察其中的土壤物像。

2.2.7 年代测量

我们对其中6个剖面（兰州、定西、天水、蓝田、庆阳、环县）的样品进行了光释光年龄测定。9个样品是在英国牛津大学年代实验室完成的，释光样品的制作流程和测量过程参照Bailey等（2003）以及Murray和Wintle（2000）；5个样品是在美国沙漠研究所完成的，样品的制作流程和测量过程参照Aitken等（1998）。

参考文献

陈家坊. 土壤胶体中的氧化物. 土壤通报，1981，2: 44–49.

陈家坊. 土壤发生中的化学过程. 北京：科学出版社，1990：1–25.

陈骏，仇刚，鹿化煜，等. 最近130 ka黄土高原夏季风变迁的Rb和Sr地球化学证据. 科学通报，1996，41 (21): 1963–1966.

程燕，张小曳，鹿化煜，等. 最近140 ka以来黄土元素地球化学演化及其古气候意义. 海洋地质与第四纪地质，2003，23 (3): 103–108.

刁桂仪，文启忠. 黄土中铁的形态分布及其组合特征研究. 海洋地质与第四纪地质，1999，19 (3): 75–82.

郭正堂，刘东生，安芷生. 渭南黄土沉积中15万年来的古土壤及其形成时的古环境. 第四纪研究，1994，3: 256–269.

郭正堂，Fedoroff N，刘东生. 130 ka来黄土–古土壤序列的典型微形态特征与古气候事件. 中国科学（D辑），1996，26 (5): 392–398.

贺秀斌. 土壤薄片的甲基丙烯酸甲酯固结方法. 土壤通报，1998,29 (2) : 封三.

黄昌勇. 土壤学. 北京：中国农业出版社，2000.

黄瑞采. 土壤微形态学: 发展及应用. 北京：高等教育出版社，1990.

季峻峰，陈骏，刘连文，等. 洛川黄土中绿泥石的化学风化与磁化率增强. 自然科学进展，1999，9 (7): 619–623.

刘东生. 中国的黄土堆积. 北京：科学出版社，1965.

刘东生. 黄土与环境. 北京：科学出版社，1985.

刘连文，陈骏，王洪涛，等. 一个不受风力分选作用影响的化学风化指标: 黄土酸不溶物中Fe/Mg值. 科学通报，2001，46 (7): 578-582.

刘连文，陈骏，陈旸，等. 最近130 ka以来黄土中Zr/Rb值变化及其对冬季风的指示意义. 科学通报，2002，47 (9): 702-706.

刘玉兰，文启忠，陈庆沐. 陕西洛川黄土剖面中F/Cl比值——反映古气候的一种地球化学标志. 地球化学，1981，4: 388-391.

鹿化煜，安芷生. 洛川黄土粒度组成的古气候意义. 科学通报，1997，42 (1): 66-69.

罗来兴. 黄土地貌 // 中国科学院《中国自然地理》编辑委员会. 中国自然地理. 北京: 科学出版社，1980: 167-182.

马乃喜. 黄土高原的界线问题 // 西北大学地理系黄土高原地理研究室编. 黄土高原地理研究. 西安：陕西人民出版社,1987.

裴新富. 关于黄土高原范围问题. 中国水土保持，1991,12: 37-42.

钱林清. 黄土高原气候. 北京：气象出版社，1991.

任明达，王乃梁. 现代沉积环境概论. 北京：科学出版社，1981.

文启忠，刁桂仪，贾蓉芬，等. 黄土剖面古气候变化的地球化学记录. 第四纪研究，1995，3: 223-231.

文启忠，刁桂仪，潘景瑜，等. 黄土高原黄土的平均化学成分与地壳克拉克值的类比. 土壤学报，1996，33(3): 225-231.

西北师范学院地理系. 中国自然地理图集. 北京：地图出版社，1984.

余素华，文启忠，张士三，等. 中国西北地区晚第四纪黄土中镁铝地球化学与古气候意义. 沉积学报，1994，12 (1): 112-116.

张信宝，周杰. 晚更新世以来黄渤海海侵与黄土高原地貌区域分异. 中国沙漠，1996，16 (4): 411-416.

赵锦慧，李东平，鹿化煜，等. 中国北方四剖面$CaCO_3$含量变化及其反映的古降水量. 海洋地质与第四纪地质，2004，24 (3): 117-122.

赵景波. 风化淋滤带地质新理论——$CaCO_3$ 淀积深度理论. 沉积学报，2000，18 (1): 29-35.

朱显谟. 黄土高原土壤与农业. 北京：农业出版社，1989.

Aitken M J. Introduction to Optical Dating. Oxford：Oxford University Press, 1998.

Arkley R J. Calculation of carbonate and water movement in soil from climatic data. Soil Science, 1963, 96: 239-248.

Bailey R M, Stokes S, Bray H. Inductively - Coupled Plasma Mass Spectrometry (ICP-MS) for dose rate determination: some guidelines for sample preparation and analysis. Ancient TL, 2003, 21(1): 11-15.

Birkeland. Soils and Geomorphology. 3rd ed. Oxford: Oxford University Press, 1999.

Bronger A. Micromorphology and genesis of paleosols in the Luochuan loess section, China:

pedostratigraphic and environmental implications. Geoderma, 1989, 45: 123–143.

Caudill M R, Driese S G, Mora C I. Preservation of a paleo - Vertisol and an estimate of Late Mississippian paleoprecipitation. Journal of Sedimentary Research, 1996, 66: 58–70.

Dearing J A. Environmental magnetic susceptibility, using the Bartington MS2 system. 2nd ed. England: Chi Publishing, 1999.

Ding Z L, Sun J M, Rutter N W, et al. Changes in sand content of loess deposits along a north - south transect of the Chinese Loess Plateau and the implications for desert variations. Quaternary Research, 1999, 52: 56–62.

Feng Z D, Chen F H. Problems of magnetic susceptibility signature as the summer monsoon proxy in Chinese loess sequences. Chinese Science Bulletin, 1999, 44 (suppl. 1): 97–104.

Feng Z D, Wang H B, Olson C G. Pedogenic factors affecting magnetic susceptibility of the last interglacial paleosol S1 in the Chinese Loess Plateau. Earth Surface Processes and Landforms, 2004a, 29: 1389–1402.

Feng Z D, Wang H B, Olson C G, et al. Chronological discord between the last interglacial paleosol (S1) and its parent material in the Chinese Loess Plateau. Quaternary International, 2004b, 117: 17–26.

Guo Z T, Liu T, Guiot J, et al. High frequency pulses of east Asian monsoon climate in the last two glaciations: link with the North Atlantic. Climate Dynamics, 1996, 12: 701–709.

Jenny H. Calcium in the soil: Ⅲ. Pedologic relations. Soil Science Society of America Proceedings, 1941, 6: 27–35.

Kemp R A. Distribution and genesis of calcitic pedofeatures within a rapidly aggrading loess - paleosol sequence in China. Geoderma, 1995, 65: 303–316.

Kemp R A. Role of micromorphology in paleopedological research. Quaternary International, 1998, 51/52: 133–141.

Kemp R A. Micromorphology of loess - paleosol sequences: a record of paleoenvironmental change. Catena, 1999, 35: 179–196.

Kemp R A, Derbyshire E, Meng X M, et al. Pedosedimentary reconstruction of a thick loess - paleosol sequence near Lanzhou in north - central China. Quaternary Research, 1995, 43: 30–45.

Kemp R A, Derbyshire E, Chen F H. Pedosedimentary development and paleoenvironmental significance of the S1 paleosol on the northeastern margin of the Qinghai - Tibetan Plateau. Journal of Quaternary Science, 1996, 11: 95–106.

Kemp R A, Derbyshire E, Meng X M. Micromorphological variation of the S1 paleosol across northwest China. Catena, 1997, 31: 77–90.

Kemp R A, Derbyshire E, Meng X M. A high - resolution micromorphological record of changing landscapes and climates on the western Loess Plateau of China during oxygen isotope stage 5. Palaeogeography, Palaeoclimatology, Palaeoecology, 2001, 170: 157–169.

Krumbein W C. Size Frequency Distribution of Sediments. Journal of Sedimentary Petrology, 1934, 4: 65–77.

Liu T S, Guo Z T, Liu J Q, et al. Variation of eastern Asian monsoon over the last 140 000 years. Bulletin Societ Geologique France, 1995, 166: 221–229.

Machette M. Calcium and magnesium carbonates // Singer M J, Janitzky P. Field and Laboratory Procedures used in a Soil Chronosequence Study. US Geological Survey Bulletin 1648. US Government Printing Office: Washington, DC, 1986: 30–33.

McKeague J A. Manual on soil sampling and methods of analysis. Toronto: Canadian Society of Soil Science, 1976.

Mehra O, Jackson M L. Iron oxide removal from soil and clay by a dithionite - citrate system buffered with sodium bicarbonate. Clay and Clay Minerals, 1960, 7:317–327.

Murray A S, Wintle A G. Luminescence dating of quartz using an improved single - aliquot regenerative-dose protocol. Radiation Measurements, 2000, 32(1): 57–73.

Pye K. Aeolian dust and dust deposits. London: Academic Press, 1987.

Retallack G J. The environmental factor approach to the interpretation of paleosols // Amundson R. Factors of soil formation: A fiftieth anniversary retrospective. Soil Science Society of America Special Publication, 1994, 33: 31–64.

Royer D L. Depth to pedogenic carbonate horizon as a paleoprecipitation indicator. Geology, 1999, 27 (12): 1123–1126.

Stoops G. Guidelines for analysis and description of soil and regolith thin sections. Madison: Soil Society of America Inc., 2003.

Wentworth C K. A scale of grade and class terms for clastic sediments. Journal of Geology, 1922, 30: 377–392.

Zhou L P, Oldfield F, Wintle A G, et al. Partly pedogenic origin of magnetic variations in Chinese loess. Nature, 1990, 346: 737–739.

3　末次间冰期古土壤S1的岩石地层、土壤地层以及年代学

3.1　岩石地层和土壤地层的划分说明

岩石地层学就是通过地层的岩性特征（颜色、粒度分布、矿物、化学成分、层理构造）和作为沉积条件证据的古生物特征来描述地层。岩石地层学不考虑年龄、作为年龄证据的化石和沉积后的改造作用以及地层单元在地表发生时的地貌。地层单元的上下界线是根据岩性的急剧变化来划定的。

土壤地层的基本定义是：由一个或多个土壤发生层所组成、在空间上可以追索的三维埋藏岩石体。土壤通常是独立于形成它的沉积物（母质）的，Ding 等（1993）强调中国的古土壤还应满足另外两个条件：（1）发育程度同当地全新世土壤相当或更高；（2）能指示当时的地带性气候条件。

中国黄土的岩石地层在第一级划分为黄土组，包括全新世黄土组、马兰黄土组、离石黄土组、午城黄土组。在第二级的岩石地层划分为我们所熟悉的黄土-古土壤序列。黄土高原东部和西部二级黄土地层划分标准是不太一样的：黄土高原东部的黄土地层以黄土层顶部首次出现的次生碳酸盐或锰结核层作为界线，黄土高原以西的黄土主要是根据颜色及物质组成变化来划分的（刘东生，1985；张宗祜等，1989；陈发虎和张维信，1993）。多数研究表明，粒度在黄土和古土壤之间有较大的反差（Feng 等，2004a，2004b；Ding 等，1993），考虑到黄土的主要组成物质是粉砂（4～9 μm，2～63 μm），本文选取>63 μm 作为二级岩性地层划分的重要参考。进一步的划分则是以土壤发生层次为依据，如：S1S1、S1L1、S1L2、S1S2、S1S3。

土壤地层划分的依据是土壤发生层次的界线，土壤地层的上界为土壤发生层的最上部，下界为土壤发生层最低的物理界线。土壤通常是独立于形成它的沉积物（母质）的，因此它可以穿越两个以上的岩石地层。换句话说，土壤地层与岩性地

层未必是重合的。当然，如果土壤母质的沉积与土壤发生是同时的（加积型土壤），那么土壤就需要根据岩石地层和土壤地层共同来确定（Catt，1986）。地层学规定土壤地层的单位仅有一个（Geosol），Morrison（1993）建议实际应用中对复合型土壤可再分出成壤段（Pedomembers）。黄土高原的末次间冰期古土壤S1为复合型土壤（Composite soil，Compound soil，Pedocomplex），Morrison的建议是非常符合实际的。根据一些历久不变的土壤特性，如土壤发生层次、垒结、根孔和虫孔、饱和盐基等，Nettleton等（2000）将古土壤划分为11个土纲：古有机土、古灰化土、古始成土、古火山灰土、古氧化土、古变性土、古老成土、古干旱土、古软土、古盐化土和其他古土壤。我们将借鉴这一规则，同时参照美国土壤分类的标准（Soil Survey Staff，2003），对野外观察到的土壤进行分类，不过，我们在每个古土壤的分类名称前略去“古”字。土壤层次的划分则参照土壤学中的土壤发生层术语（例如，Birkeland，1999；黄昌勇，2000）。

3.2 各个剖面的岩石地层和土壤地层

以下给出对9个剖面的岩石地层和土壤地层的描述（土壤层的代号请见图1.3），并且对定西、天水、蓝田、庆阳、环县等5个剖面进行了释光测年。

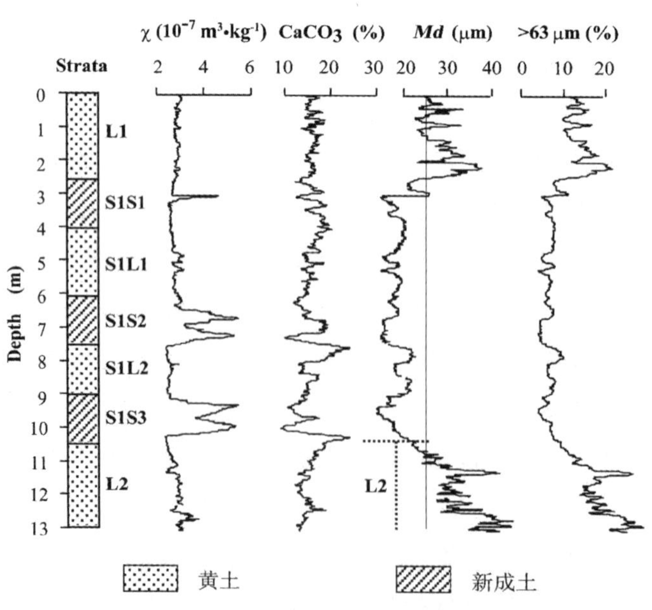

图3.1 兰州剖面的地层示意图和磁化率、$CaCO_3$含量、粒度曲线

3.2.1　兰州剖面

兰州剖面位于兰州市黄河以北的九州台。陈发虎和张维信（1993）曾对九州台剖面做过细致的研究工作，不过S1的深度与探井剖面S1的深度（方小敏等，1996）有很大的出入。经过对九州台南坡和北坡多处挖掘考察并通过水平测量尺自上而下地测量，我们确定南坡约37 m深度处为S1的底部，北坡约40 m深度处为S1的底部，这个深度和探井的深度比较接近。九州台剖面的S1厚约8 m，由3个新成土（Entisol）夹2个黄土层构成（见图3.1）。关于剖面的详细描述见表3.1。从图3.1可以看到，S1中$CaCO_3$含量（平均为15.8%）与上覆黄土L1和下伏黄土L2的$CaCO_3$含量（平均值分别为16.0%、15.0%）没有显著差别，不过，S1复合古土壤中$CaCO_3$含量的波动幅度比黄土层中的要大得多，意味着碳酸盐在S1发生了较清晰的迁移作用（淋溶和淀积）。这里需要提醒，表3.1中的地层单元被认为是与深海氧同位素阶段相对应的。即，L1=MIS 2—4；S1S1=MIS 5a；S1L1=MIS 5d；S1S2=MIS 5c；SIL2=MIS 5b；S1S3=MIS 5e。

表3.1　兰州剖面野外特征描述

地层	深度	描述
L1	0～2.7 m	颜色：10YR 5/4（湿）、10YR 6/3（干），颗粒粗，粉砂质，松散，均质结构。
S1S1	2.7～3.7 m	颜色：10YR 4/3（湿）、10YR 6/3（干），颗粒粗，粉砂质，易碎，有少量残存根须。
S1L1	3.7～6.0 m	颜色：10YR 5/4（湿）、10YR 6/3（干），颗粒粗，粉砂质，松散，均质结构。
S1S2	6.0～7.8 m	颜色：10YR 4/4（湿）、10YR 6/4（干），颗粒粗，紧实，微弱的次棱块状结构，有少量根孔。
S1L2	7.8～8.9 m	颜色：10YR 5/4（湿）、10YR 6/4（干），颗粒粗，稍紧实，均质结构。
S1S3	8.9～10.7 m	颜色：10YR 4/3（湿）、10YR 6/4（干），次棱块状结构，粉壤质，用水沾湿时可搓出黏粒条。
L2	10.7～13.0 m	颜色：10YR 5/4（湿）、10YR 6/3（干），颗粒粗，松散，均质结构。

3.2.2　定西剖面

定西剖面位于定西市安定区西南2 km处的李家坪。我们在山路边的直立崖上发现S1。定西剖面的S1厚5 m，也是由3层土壤（即S1S3、S1S2、S1S1）和2个黄土层（即S1L2和S1L1）构成（见图3.2）。上2层土壤为新成土（Entisol），底部土壤属软土（Mollisol），由A层和Bk层组成。剖面的详细描述见表3.2。S1顶部、中部和底部的测年结果分别是：58.46±6.9 ka、109.19±9.31 ka、119±10.09 ka。

粒团或粉砂团粒。Bt层以下为过渡层BC，Ck为碳酸钙的淀积层（见图3.6），野外测量显示5 m上下有厚达20～30 cm的碳酸钙结核层。结核的直径可达5 cm以上。如果将BC层和Ck层也归入S1，那么整个土壤的厚度达到5 m。同其他剖面比起来，蓝田剖面的S1颜色偏红，看上去更像淋溶土（Alfisol）或老成土（Ultisol）。由于土壤的颜色比照是后来在白鹿塬一剖面上进行的，这里我们仅提供颜色范围供参考：7.5YR 4/6～5YR 3/4（湿），7.5YR 6/6～5YR 5/4（干）。蓝田剖面S1的释光年龄有两个：顶部年龄为111.45±9.76 ka，底部（3.5 m处）年龄为136.57±9.40 ka。

3.2.7 旬邑剖面

旬邑剖面处于与洛川剖面相似的生物-气候带上。S1由A层、Bt层和Bk层组成（见图3.7），属于软土。A层厚约0.65 m，次棱块状结构，结构体表面有粉状或丝状碳酸钙。Bt厚约1.55 m，棱块状结构，结构体表面裹有淀积黏粒胶膜和碳酸钙胶膜。Bk层厚约1 m，底部出现碳酸钙结核。此剖面没有进行颜色描述。

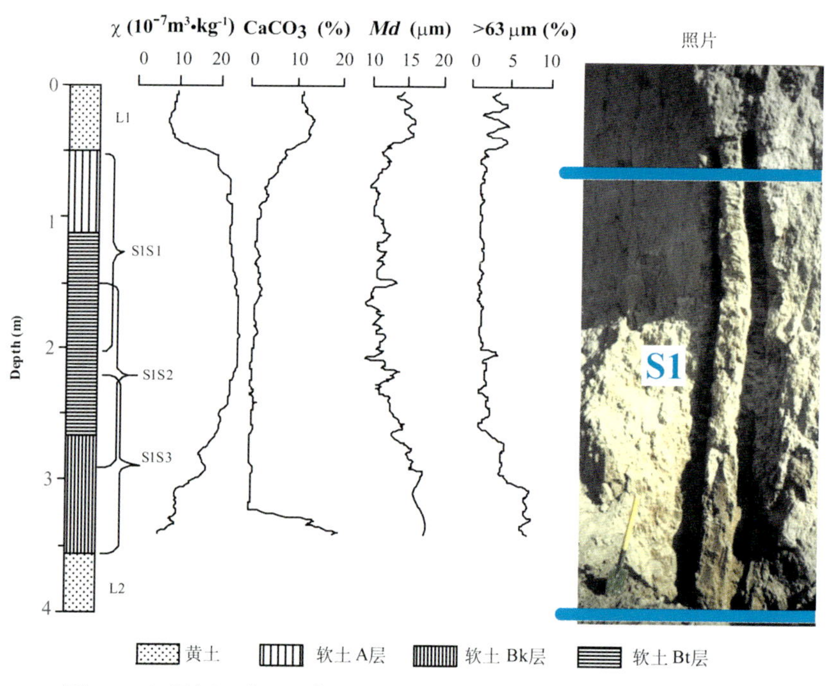

图 3.7 旬邑剖面地层示意图、磁化率、$CaCO_3$含量、粒度曲线以及照片

3.2.8 庆阳剖面

庆阳剖面位于西峰镇和庆城县城之间的雷家岘加油站内，地处西峰塬的边缘地带，它与洛川剖面处于相同的生物-气候带上。由于路面拓宽，我们可以观察到S1

顺地形变化的情形：加油站内S1古土壤的上下界线比较平整，但距离剖面约200 m处，S1的界线开始缓慢起伏，而且沿着下坡路S1逐渐尖灭。这种情况表明当时的地面是一个边坡。庆阳剖面S1由A层、Bt层和Bk层组成（见图3.8），属于软土，土壤剖面的特征与旬邑剖面几乎一样。我们对该剖面S1也进行了光释光测年，结果是顶部为59.70±4.60 ka，中部为55.00±7.40 ka，底部为124.00±17.00 ka。

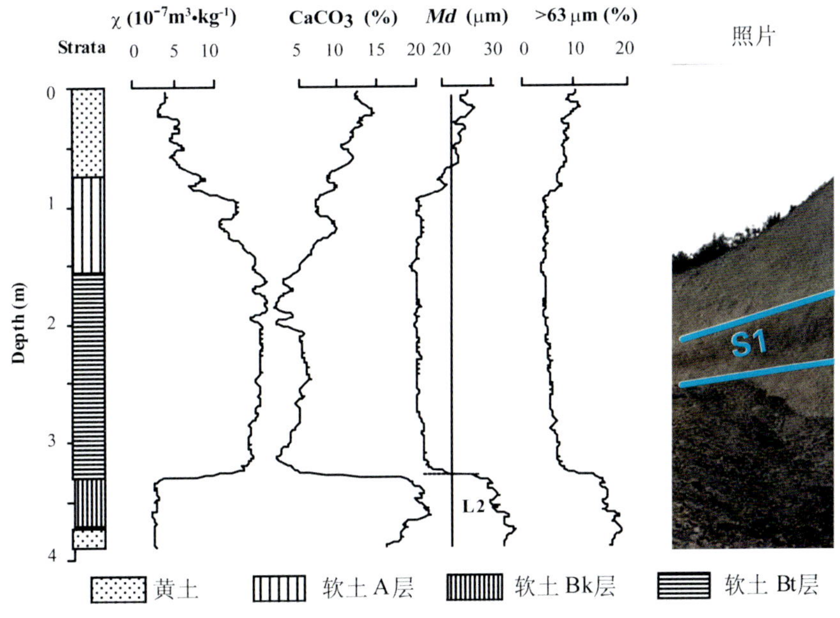

图3.8　庆阳剖面地层示意图、磁化率、$CaCO_3$含量、粒度曲线以及照片

表3.4　庆阳剖面野外特征描述

地层	深度	描述
L1	0～0.75 m	颜色：10YR 4/4（湿）、10YR 5/4（干）；颗粒较粗，均质结构；有少量细小的植物根系、丝状碳酸钙。
S1	0.75～1.6 m	0.75～1.4 m颜色：10YR 4/3（湿）、10YR 5/4（干）；下部（1.4 m～1.6 m）颜色过渡为7.5YR 4/4（湿）、7.5YR 5/4（干）。有少量的虫孔和较多的植物根系，孔隙中充填有碳酸钙。较小的次棱块状结构，易碎。
	1.6～3.3 m	颜色：7.5YR 3/4（湿）、7.5YR 5/4（干）；轻黏壤质，次棱块状结构；裂隙中充填有黏粒胶膜和丝状碳酸钙；偶有小的结核（2 mm）。
	3.3～3.9 m	颜色：10YR 5/4（湿）、10YR 7/2（干）；次棱块状结构，有少量的根孔和虫孔；3.7 m处出现碳酸钙的大结核。
L2	3.9～4.0 m	颜色：10YR 4/4（湿）、10YR 6/4（干）。

3.2.9　环县剖面

环县剖面位于环县城东塬中庄村的一条沟谷中。野外观察发现环县剖面的土壤地层与定西剖面的比较相似，由3层土壤和2个黄土层构成。S1S1和S1S2为新成土，底部的S1S3的发育程度最好，属于软土，由A层和Bk层组成（见图3.9）。但是，与定西剖面不同的是，环县剖面S1的下部有碳酸钙的结核。该剖面的S1有3个IRSL/OSL测年数据：70.95±7.41 ka（顶部）、75.04±6.22 ka（中部）、132.00±15.00 ka（底部）。

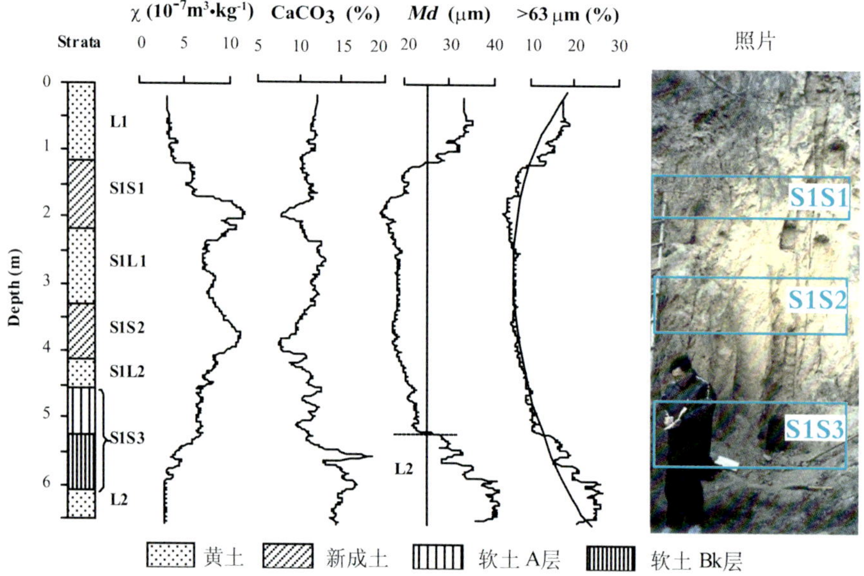

图3.9 环县剖面地层示意图、磁化率、$CaCO_3$含量、粒度曲线以及照片

表3.5 环县剖面野外特征描述

地层	深度	描述
L1	0～1.15 m	颜色:10YR 4/3(湿)、10YR 6/3(干),颗粒粗,粉砂质,松散,均质结构。
S1S1	1.15～2.2 m	颜色:10YR 4/3(湿)、10YR 6/3(干),颗粒粗,稍紧实,粉砂质,有少量根孔和虫孔。
S1L1	2.2～3.3 m	颜色:10YR 4/3(湿)、10YR 6/4(干),较小的次棱块状结构,虫孔较少,可见粉状碳酸钙。
S1S2	3.3～4.1 m	颜色:10YR 4/3(湿)、10YR 6/3(干),颗粒粗,紧实,中等的次棱块状结构,有少量根孔。
S1L2	4.1～4.55 m	颜色:10YR 4/3(湿)、10YR 6/4(干),颗粒粗,稍紧实,均质结构。
S1S3	4.55～5.25 m	上部:颜色:10YR 4/4(湿)、10YR 6/3(干),紧实,次棱块状结构。
	5.25～6.1 m	下部:颜色:10YR 5/4(湿)、10YR 6/4(干),粉砂质,次棱块状结构过渡为均质结构,5.7～5.8 m散布有碳酸钙结核。
L2	6.1～6.5 m	颜色:10YR 5/4(湿)、10YR 6/3(干),颗粒粗,粉砂质,松散,均质结构。

野外的土壤形态学特征表明S1的层次在黄土高原的西北和北部是分异的，即，S1可以分出3个层（S1S1、S1S2、S1S3），例如兰州剖面、定西剖面和环县剖面。

当沿着断面到东南部，S1的3个土壤逐渐发生融合，在秦安我们仍可以区分出3层土壤，但是到了天水，我们已经无法分辨出3个土壤的界线，3次成壤事件叠加在一起，因而形成了加积型的B层。庆阳、旬邑、宝鸡、蓝田的S1也发生了土壤融合现象。因此，保存在土壤剖面中的一些特性（比如，黏粒、碳酸钙）是后期改造的结果。对上述发生土壤融合的S1做高分辨率的气候重建显然是不科学的。

3.3 S1的土壤地层和年代地层

到目前为止，国内外学者对S1的土壤地层已经做了大量的释光测年工作。图3.10列举了部分测年结果，从中我们可以看到，S1的年代在50～150 ka之间，多数在70～150 ka之间（渭南、榆林蔡家沟、榆林石峁、会宁、临夏北塬、临夏塬堡、西宁土巷道）。所以，可以相信，S1确实是在末次间冰期发育形成的。但是，土壤发生过程未必与沉积过程是同步的，期待的年龄与实测的释光年龄可能存在一定的差距。例如，在黄土高原东部的渭南剖面，S1土壤地层底界（12.16 m）的测年结果为134.38±17.68 ka（刘嘉麒等，1994）或者134.5±17.7 ka（聂高众等，1996），如果不考虑误差，S1底部的年龄要老于轨道调谐获得的年龄（128 ka）。基于郭正堂等（1994）对该剖面土壤微形态的研究，聂高众指出，释光年龄偏老的原因是S1/L2的原始界线（或称岩石地层界线）在土壤地层底界之上0.36 m（即，11.86 m处）。也就是说S1土壤发育的母质部分是早先沉积的L2黄土。

我们的测年结果（见图3.11、3.12）与前人对S1的测年结果是比较一致的，同样证明S1形成于末次间冰期。野外观察结合实验室的粒度分析表明黄土高原西部的东南边缘的天水剖面在末次间冰期初期土壤也是向下发育的，虽然我们根据测年结果不能确认此处S1释光年龄是否偏老，但是，在黄土高原东部地区的环县剖面和蓝田剖面，若不计误差，S1底部的年龄都表现得比期望的128 ka要老。这应该与S1发育期间对下伏黄土的成壤改造有关。总而言之，只要地表相对稳定、气候条件适宜，S1古土壤总要向下发育，结果必然导致土壤底界的年龄较128 ka偏老。

众所周知，热释光或者光释光的测年误差较大，比如，前人的测年资料和我们的测年结果中S1底界的年龄误差值大多超过10 ka。而且一些不确定因素（Oches等，1998；李虎侯，2000）又会导致释光测年得到的年龄产生较大的偏差，例如，定西剖面和庆阳剖面顶部的年龄（约60 ka）比其理论值（约73 ka）小了许多。因此，这些释光年龄不能满足建立精确的年代地层序列的要求，只能作为S1的年代参考框架。

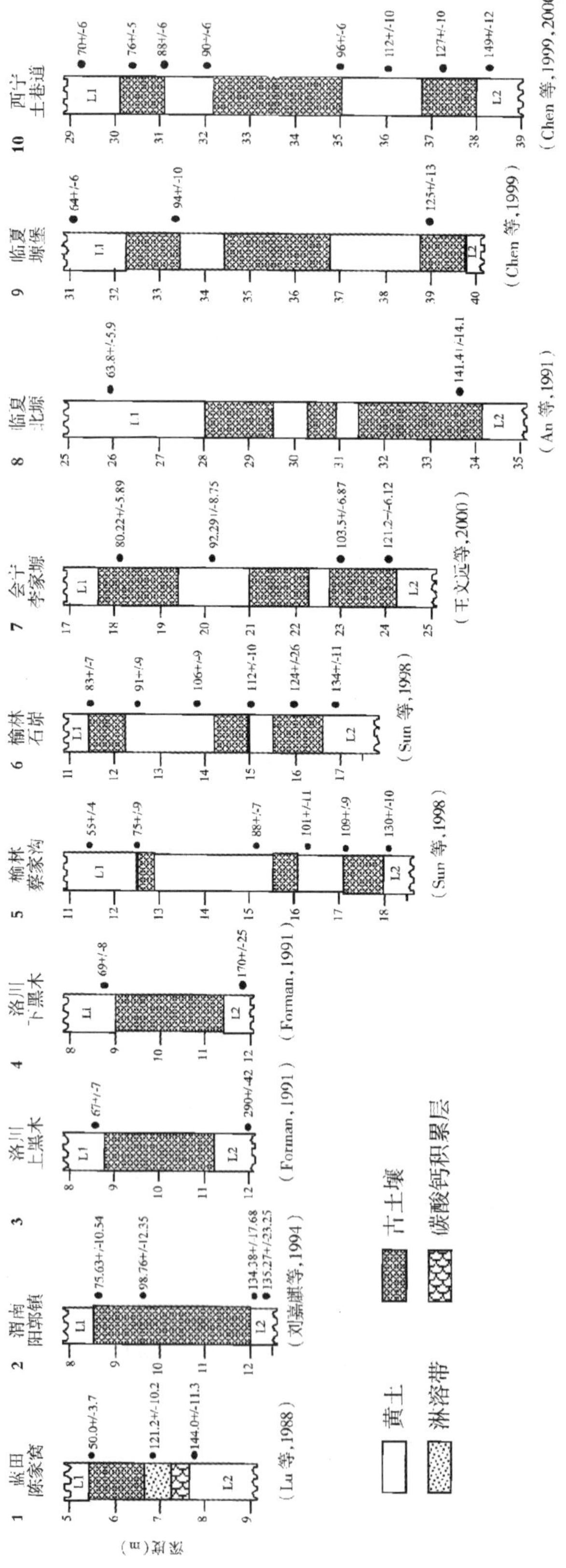

图 3.10 黄土高原S1的部分热释光测年结果(年龄单位:ka)

(注:参考文献均列于本章末尾)

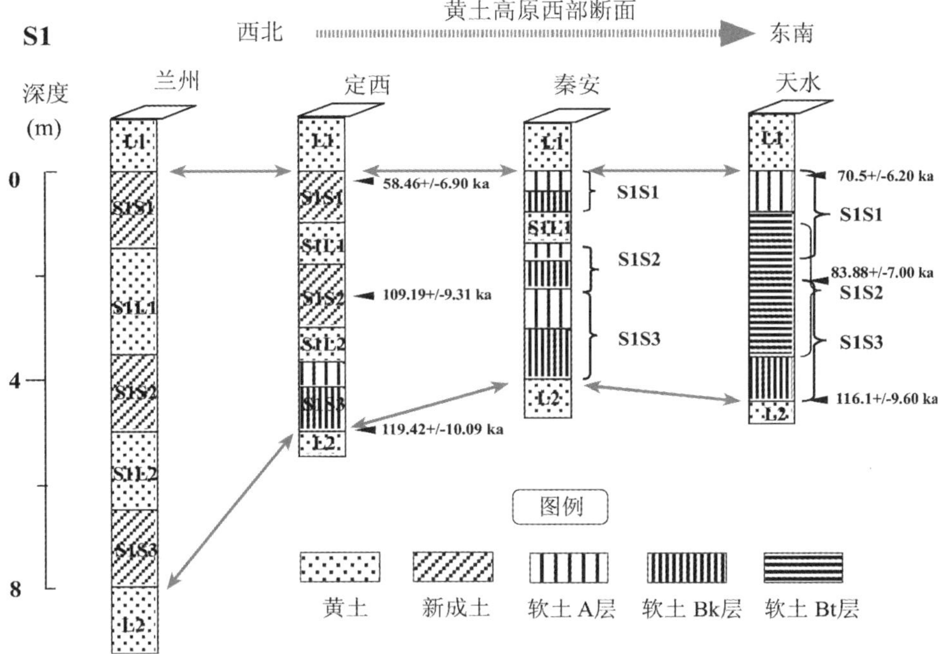

图3.11 黄土高原西部地区S1的土壤地层与光释光年代

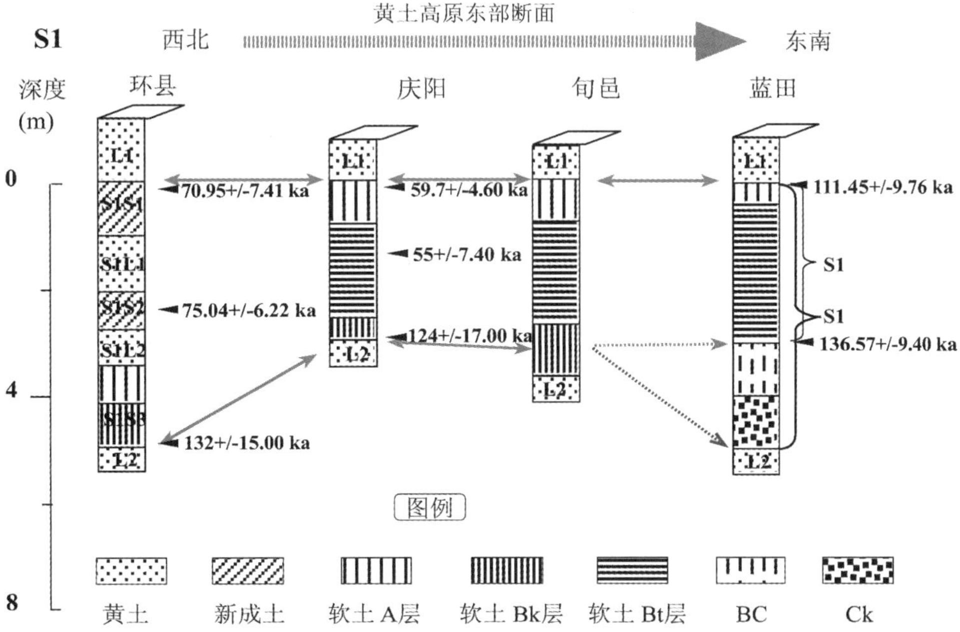

图3.12 黄土高原东部地区S1的土壤地层与光释光年代

参考文献

陈发虎，张维信. 甘青地区的黄土地层学与第四纪冰川问题. 北京：科学出版社，1993.

方小敏，戴雪荣，李吉均，等. 亚洲季风演化的突发性与不稳定性——以末次间冰期土壤发生为例. 中国科学（D辑），1996，26 (2) : 154-160.

郭正堂，刘东生，安芷生. 渭南黄土沉积中15万年来的古土壤及其形成的古环境. 第四纪研究，1994，3：256-269.

黄昌勇. 土壤学. 中国农业出版社，2000.

李虎侯. 光释光断代. 核电子学与探测技术，2000，20 (3): 217-228.

刘东生. 中国的黄土堆积. 北京：科学出版社，1965.

刘东生. 黄土与环境. 北京：科学出版社，1985.

刘嘉麒，陈铁梅，聂高众，等. 渭南黄土剖面的年龄测定及十五万年来高分辨时间序列的建立. 第四纪研究，1994，3: 193-202.

聂高众，刘嘉麒，郭正堂. 渭南黄土剖面十五万年以来的主要地层界线和气候事件——年代学方面的证据. 第四纪研究，1996，3: 221-231.

王文远，刘嘉麒，潘懋，等. 末次间冰期以来黄土-古土壤的热释光测年——渭南、会宁剖面的对比研究. 海洋地质与第四纪地质，2000，20(3): 67-71.

张宗祜，张之一，王芸生. 中国黄土. 北京：地质出版社，1989.

An Z S, Kukla G, Porter S C, et al. Magnetic susceptibility evidence of monsoon variation on the Loess Plateau of central China during the last 130, 000 years. Quaternary Research, 1991, 36: 29-36.

Birkeland. Soils and Geomorphology. 3rd ed. Oxford: Oxford University Press, 1999.

Buol S W, Hole F D, McCracken R J. Soil Genesis and Classification. Ames, IA: The Iowa State University Press, 1989.

Catt J A. Soils and Quaternary Geology: A handbook for Field Scientists. Oxford: Clarendon Press, 1986.

Chen F H, Boemandel J, Feng Z D, et al. East Asian Monsoon Variations during Oxygen Isotope Stage 5: Evidence from the Northwestern Margin of the Chinese Loess Plateau. Quaternary Science Reviews, 1999, 18: 1127-1135.

Chen F H, Feng Z D, Zhang J W. Loess particle size data indicative of stable winter monsoon during the last interglacial in the western part of the Chinese Loess Plateau. Catena, 2000, 39: 233-244.

Ding Z L, Rutter N W, Liu T S. Pedostratigraphy of Chinese loess deposits and climatic cycles in the last 2.5 Ma. Catena，1993, 20: 73-91.

Feng Z D, Wang H B, Olson C G. Pedogenic factors affecting magnetic susceptibility of the last interglacial paleosol S1 in the Chinese Loess Plateau. Earth Surface Processes and Landforms, 2004a, 29: 1389–1402.

Feng Z D, Wang H B, Olson C G, et al. Chronological discord between the last interglacial paleosol (S1) and its parent material in the Chinese Loess Plateau. Quaternary International, 2004b, 117: 17–26.

Forman S L. Late Pleistocene chronology of loess deposition near Luochuan, China. Quaternary Research, 1991, 36: 19–28.

Foth H D. Fundamentals of Soil Science. 6th ed. New York: John Wiley, 1978.

Lu Y C, Zhang J Z, Xie J. Thermoluninescence dating of loess and paleosol from the Lantian section, Shaanxi Province, China. Quaternary Research, 1988, 7: 245–250.

Morrison R B. How Can the Treatment of Pedostratigraphic Units in the North American Stratigraphic Code Be Improved? Presented at Paleopedology Symposium, PP NL 10 Part D, 1993.

Nettleton W D, Olson C G, Wysocki D A. Paleosol classification: problems and solutions. Catena, 2000, 41: 61–92.

Oches E A, Banerjee S K, Soheid P A, et al. High-resolution proxies of climate variability in the Alaska loess record // Busacca A J. International Symposium on Dust Aerosols, Loess Soil and Global Change. Washington State University' s CAHE MISC0190: Pullman, WA, 1998: 167–170.

O' Green A T, Busacca A J. Faunal burrows as indicators of paleovegetation in eastern Washington, USA. Paleogeography, Paleoclimatology, Paleoecology, 2001, 169: 23–37.

Soil Survey Staff. Keys to Soil Taxonomy. 9th ed. Natural Resources Conservation Service, United States Department of Agriculture: Washington, DC, 2003.

Stoops G, Eswaran H. Soil Micromorphology. New York: Hutchinson Ross, 1986.

Sun J M, Ding Z L. Deposits and soils of the past 130, 000 years at the desert–loess transition in the Northern China. Quaternary Research, 1998, 50:148–156.

4 中国黄土高原末次间冰期古土壤的粒度分布

4.1 粒度作为冬季风指标的潜在问题

将粒度分布作为冬季风的指标之初是基于如下假设的：黄土高原的物源区是固定的，较强的冬季风带来较粗的颗粒（An等，1991；丁仲礼等，1991；Ding等，1992；刘东生，1985；Liu，1987）。后来，丁仲礼将这一假设做了修改：季风-沙漠系统共同控制着粒度的分布，即冬季风的强度和沙漠的收缩扩张（距离沙漠的远近）同时决定着沉积区粒度的波动，只不过源区的远近对粒度分布的影响要小一些（Ding等，1999；丁仲礼等，1999a，1999b）。可是，我们认为，这个假设还不够完美，理由有两点：其一，由于经历较强的风化作用，作为潜在的粉尘源区之一的塔里木盆地与河西走廊的洪积扇和湖床在末次间冰期向黄土高原输送的粉尘本身可能就比较细（Assallay等，1998；Wright，2001）。其二，另外一个潜在的物源区——蒙古高原在末次间冰期由于较强的风化作用产生了较多的粉砂和黏粒（Feng和Chen，1999）。换言之，中国黄土高原黄土-古土壤序列的粒度分布还取决于源区物质的粗细。因此，将粒度作为冬季风的替代性指标的有效性值得怀疑。

不过，全样粒度或石英粒径目前仍是被用作重建末次冰期旋回冬季风强度的主要指标（An等，1991；Porter和An，1995；Xiao等，1995；An和Porter，1997；Chen等，1997；Ding等，1992）。可是，以前这些工作所暗含的前提并没有经过验证。比如，石英颗粒抗蚀能力很强，沉积的成壤改造作用对其影响不大（Xiao等，1995；An和Porter，1997）。事实上，末次间冰期气候温暖湿润，植被条件较好，有机酸在石英颗粒表面的溶蚀作用加强。例如，六盘山以东的灵台剖面S1土壤中石英颗粒表面可见浅坑和次生硅质沉淀，指示石英经过了溶蚀作用（孙有斌等，2000）。Howard等（1995）对美国弗吉尼亚州不同年龄的土壤中的石英颗粒表面的微结构进行了研究，他们认为石英的强烈溶蚀可以在热带气候条件下发生，也可以在温带气候条件并辅以足够长的时间的情况下发生。土壤的黏粒由两部分组成：硅酸盐矿物和氧化物。土壤中的游离氧化铁一部分继承自母质，但多数是在风化过程中释放再沉淀的结果（熊毅和许冀泉，1964），因此游离氧化铁的含量可以反映风化成壤的强度（马毅杰等，1998）。游离氧化铁与氧化铁全量之比（Fed/Fet）可以剔除土壤中碳酸钙的影响，能更准确地反映风化强度，有大量的工作表明间冰期土壤中Fed/Fet值较高（Guo等，1996a，1996b，1998，1999；郝青振等，2001；魏建晶等，2003；杨石岭等，2000），也就是说风化作用较强，这意味着大颗粒就地分解成了较细的颗粒。Rb/Sr的变化反映了黄土物质在风化成壤过程中的淋失程度，洛川黑木沟S1的Rb/Sr较高，意味着有较多的就地风化释放的不稳定元素（如Ca、Sr、P、Mg、Na等）被淋溶出了古土壤（陈骏等，1996）。如果黄土沉积后经受了明显的风化，那么将粒度作为冬季风强度代用指标的论据就受到了挑战。

有大量的研究阐述过成壤过程中粉砂、黏粒的迁移现象，以下是一些关于这方面的文献：Al-Barrak和Lewis（1978），Birkeland （1999），Buol等（1973），Buol和Hole（1959，1961），Catt （1986，1990），Feng（1997），Foth （1978），Gile和Grossman（1968），Hallberg等（1978），Johnson和Watson-Stegner（1987），Mack等（1993），Moore （1978），Nettleton等（1969，2000），Olson和Nettleton （1998），Ruhe （1984），Ruhe等 （1955），Valentine和Dalrymple （1976），Walker和Chittleborough （1986），Yaalon（1971）。在加拿大西北部（Moore，1978）和美国的德克萨斯州（Gile，1979）带有成熟的Bt层的厚约1 m的土壤在4～7 kys内就可以形成（注：kys=千年）。在黄土质古土壤当中Bt层的黏粒含量通常高达A层或C层的数倍（Ruhe和Olson，1979，1980），毫无疑问，末次间冰期黄土高原东部的S1完全有条件发育Bt层，那么黏粒（甚或粉砂）的迁移也必定可以发生。可见，沉积后物质的就地转化和迁移过程势必对土壤中的粒度分布造成影响，粒度分布作为冬季风指标的可靠性自然会受到影响。

4.2 粒度分布的地理分异

上述分析说明，沉积前源区的风化作用、沉积后的就地风化（残积黏化）和细颗粒在剖面中的迁移（例如淀积黏化）都使得粒度分布作为冬季风指标的可靠性受到挑战，以下我们对黄土高原的各剖面进行详细说明。

4.2.1 西部断面

兰州剖面： 黄土高原的西北边缘的兰州九州台S1的厚度约为8 m。从图4.1中的粗颗粒（>63 μm）含量和细颗粒（<10 μm）含量的变化可以看到，不管是3个土壤单元（S1S1、S1S2、S1S3）还是其间夹的2个黄土单元（S1L1、S1L2），整个S1土壤复合体与上覆的L1和下伏的L2存在非常明显的差别：S1的>63 μm含量整体偏低、<10 mm含量整体偏高。另外，从图4.1中也可以看到>63 μm含量和<10 μm含量的变化呈现括号形“（）”的趋势。S1L1和S1L2的磁化率降至冰期的水平，而粒度并没有大幅度的变化，这可能意味着源区的粒度在末次间冰期的时候比末次冰期和倒数第二次冰期要细。也就是说，如果磁化率在沉积前受到的增强改造并不显著，而且末次间冰期气候波动是相对平稳的话，则源区前期（对应于S1S3和S1S2）的风化作用为后期粉尘沉积制造了细颗粒。紧随磁化率的峰值之后，碳酸钙与黏粒在S1S3和S1S2的底部都出现了一个峰值，这表明，即使在较为干旱的黄土高原西北部，黏粒也发生了迁移，只不过迁移的深度有限。

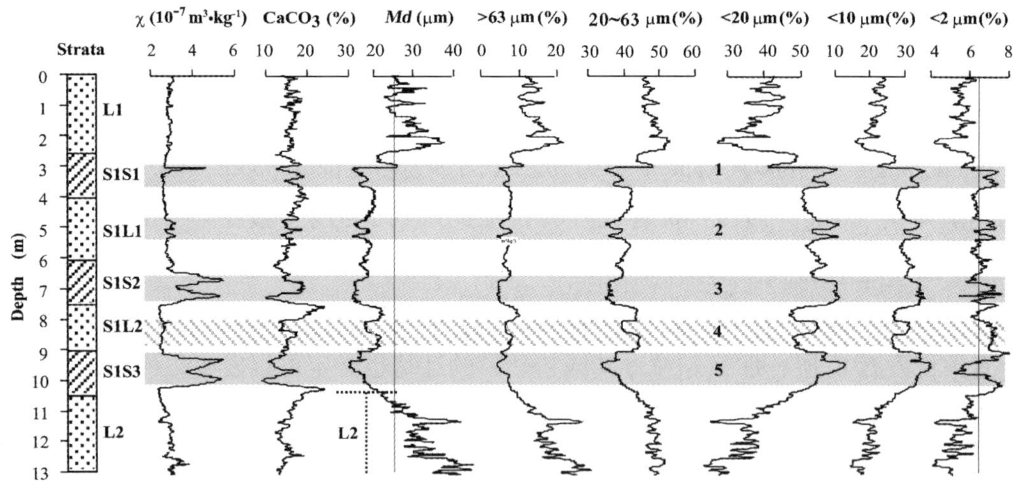

图4.1 兰州剖面磁化率、$CaCO_3$含量、粒度分布曲线

定西剖面： 从兰州向东南方向来到定西，这里的S1厚约5 m，这是大致对应于MIS 5a和MIS 5c的两个新成土（A—C结构），比兰州剖面发育得稍好。从图4.2可以看到，像兰州剖面一样，>63 μm含量和<10 μm含量可以很好地将S1同下伏L2和上覆L1区分开。我们依然可以看到S1中>63 μm含量波动曲线和<10 μm含量波动曲线的括号“（）”趋势。S1中的黄土单元S1L1和S1L2的粒度虽然变粗但变化幅度不大，而磁化率则降低至冰期的水平，再次表明S1的母质的粒度在末次间冰期的时

候远比冰期的时候要细。S1S1潜在的磁化率峰值没有出现在定西剖面，很可能与剖面中碳酸钙的稀释作用有关。值得注意的是S1S1中黏粒峰值与碳酸钙的峰值几乎是同步的，指示了相对干旱的条件下淋溶作用非常弱。S1S2底部和S1S3底部的碳酸盐峰值和黏粒含量的峰值较磁化率峰值滞后，指示了碳酸盐和黏粒都发生了淋溶迁移。由于滞后的深度较兰州剖面明显，所以定西的淋溶作用比兰州稍强。还有两个特征值得一提：其一，S1L2的全部和S1L1的下部较高的黏粒含量仍有可能指示源区前期较强的风化作用为后期的物质堆积准备了较细的颗粒；其二，中值粒径、粗颗粒含量和细颗粒含量变化显示，S1S3的底部已经逐渐变粗，因此S1S3底部的粒度分布可能反映的是倒数第二次冰期晚期的风尘状况。

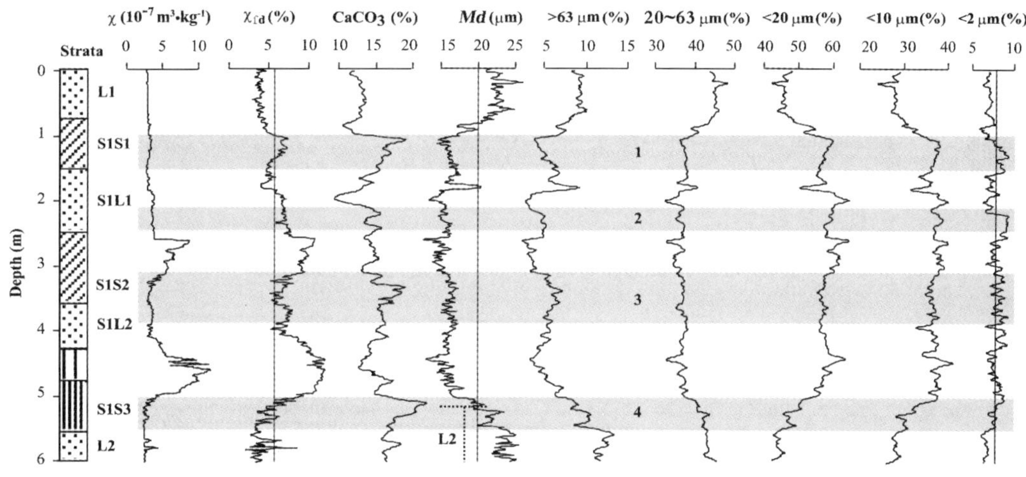

图 4.2　定西剖面磁化率、$CaCO_3$含量、粒度分布曲线

秦安剖面：进一步向东南方向来到秦安剖面，这里的S1土壤复合体厚度约为4 m。3个土壤层（S1S1、S1S2、S1S3）都能从剖面中分辨出来，可是，潜在的S1L2黄土单元为S1S2侵吞而不复存在，仅有S1L1保存下来。如图4.3所示，>63 μm含量、<10 μm含量和中值粒径可以清楚地划分S1与L1、L2岩性界线，>63 μm含量和<10 μm含量的括号“（）”趋势仍然存在。该剖面一个非常显著的特征就是S1S2和S1S3碳酸钙或者黏粒的淋溶带和淀积带非常分明，这是A—Bk型土壤剖面的典型特征（Birkeland，1999）。这意味着沉积后的风化或者风化后的迁移的确在S1中发生过。此外，S1S3的底部粒度（见图4.3的中值粒径*Md*）逐渐变粗。值得注意的是，虽然S1S3的土壤发育程度最高，可是粒度反而比另外两个土壤的粒度更粗，这反映出S1S3的发育至少部分地以L2的顶部作为母质。也就是说，风尘的堆积速率比成壤的速率要慢。如同孙东怀等（1995）发现黄土高原东部地区的古土壤最下一层（S1S3）磁化率并非如“期待”中的最大那样，秦安剖面S1S3的磁化率也就没有表

现出“潜在”的最高峰。我们认为，原因可能是S1S3的母质是前期较粗的物质，磁化率虽经成壤作用有所增强，但始终不如在细物质上经类似的成壤改造（S1S2）而具有更高的磁化率。既然如此，S1S3底部的粒度分布反映的应当是倒数第二次冰期末期的风尘状况。

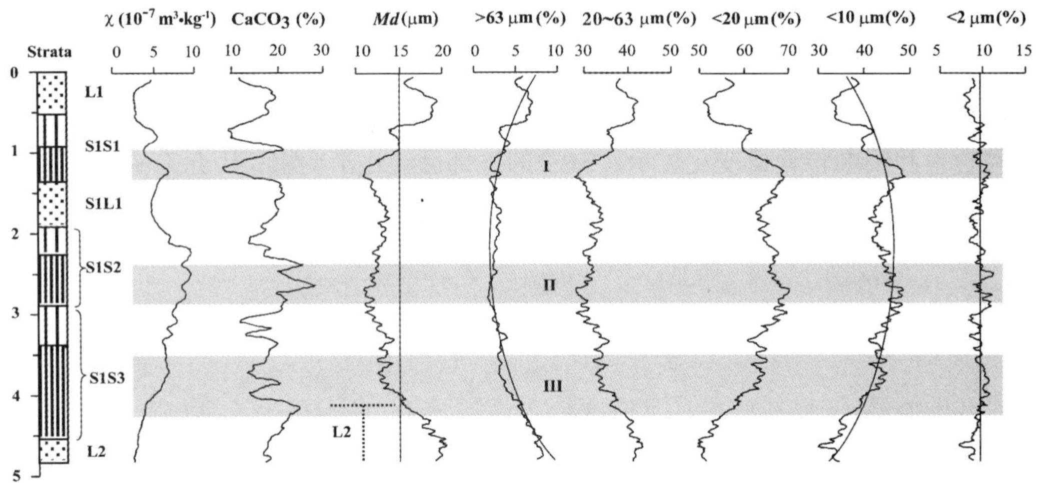

图 4.3　秦安剖面磁化率、$CaCO_3$含量、粒度分布曲线

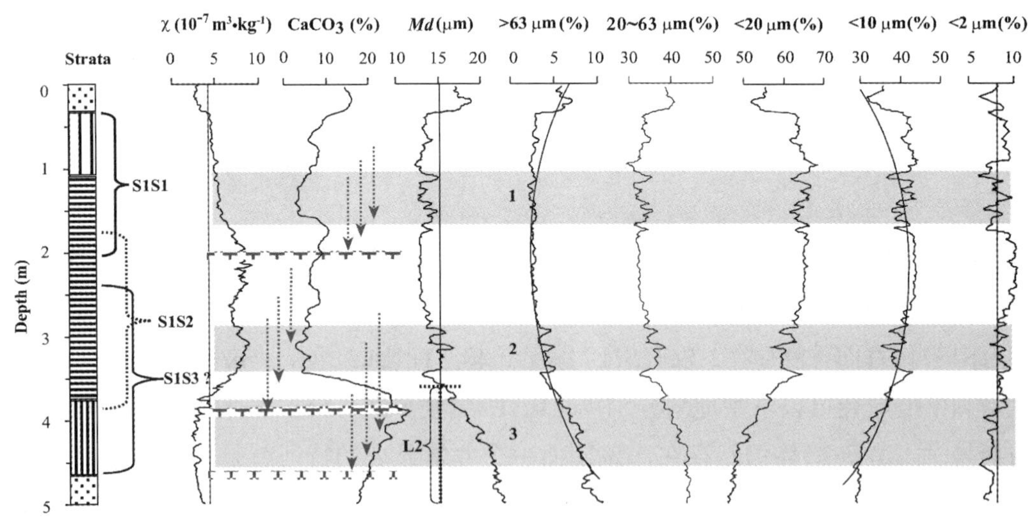

图 4.4　天水剖面磁化率、$CaCO_3$含量、粒度分布曲线

天水剖面：位于黄土高原西部的东南边缘，降水和气温都有所增高。天水剖面的S1完全发育成了一个“单一”的复合型土壤，即，S1S2侵吞了“潜在”的S1L2，并楔入S1S3的上部，而S1S1吞化了S1L1后侵入了S1S2的上部。如图4.4，我们仍然可以用>63 μm含量和<10 μm含量的波动情况来界定S1、L1和L2的岩性地

层。与前面的3个剖面相比，天水剖面叠加在括号趋势上的粒度波动非常平稳，没有明显的起落，同时，磁化率也没有出现“期待”中的三峰二谷。这些都意味着S1发生了融合。表现出粒度变粗趋势的阴影带“1”可能是S1S1与S1S2彼此融合后遗留的残迹，而阴影带“2”则可能是S1S2与S1S3彼此融合后遗留的残迹。碳酸钙含量较高的Bk很可能来自“潜在”的S1S2和S1S3的碳酸钙被淋溶下来而形成的碳酸盐淀积带（Feng等，2004a，2004b）。较低的碳酸盐含量、较高的磁化率和黏粒含量出现在S1的中部，表明此处曾经历过较为明显的就地风化作用（包括残积黏化）。大量出现在Bt层中虫孔表面的黏粒胶膜，反映出黏粒在剖面中的迁移。S1底部变粗的趋势再次表明，L2顶部的物质成了S1发育的母质。

4.2.2 东部断面

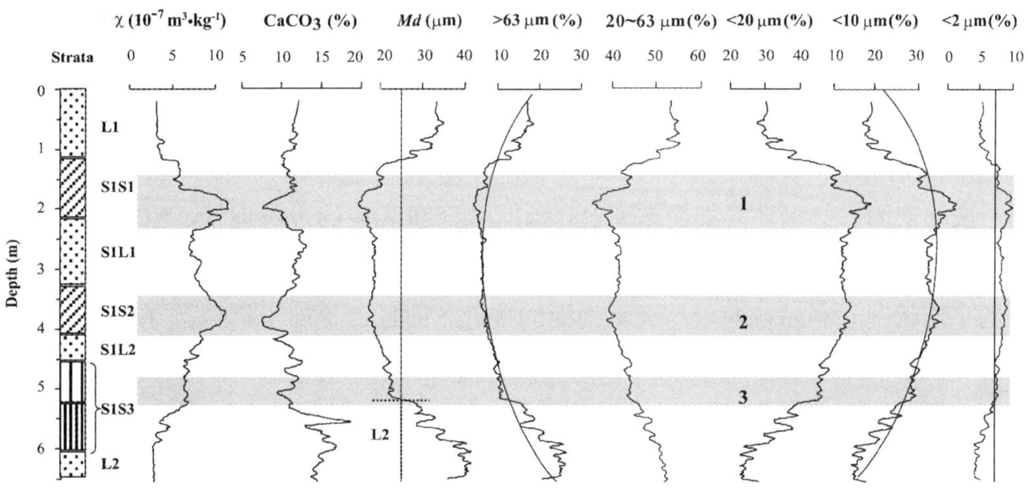

图 4.5 环县剖面磁化率、$CaCO_3$含量、粒度分布曲线

环县剖面：环县剖面位于黄土高原东部的北端，从野外的地层看，与黄土高原西部的定西剖面相似，实验室的数据却表明它更像秦安剖面。这也验证了“成土要素”学说的正确性，即如果成壤时间一样，成壤的环境相似，则土壤的发育程度也应该是接近的。如黄土高原西部地区的兰州剖面、定西剖面和秦安剖面一样，环县剖面的粒度分布也表现出3个层次的波动：首先，依据>63 μm含量和<10 μm含量的波动情况可以界定S1、L1和L2的岩性地层。其次，S1的粒度分布依然表现为括号形“（）”的趋势。最后，依据叠加在括号趋势上的粒度变化可以分辨出S1的5个层次单元：S1S1—S1L1—S1S2—S1L2—S1S3。3个碳酸钙含量的低谷对应于黏粒和<10 μm含量的高峰，说明在黄土高原北部末次间冰期古土壤S1也经历了明显的

就地风化作用甚至可能也发生了黏粒的迁移。众所周知，MIS 5e的气候应该是最好的，可是环县S1S3的粒度并没有如我们期望的那样是最细的，而且磁化率也仅仅展现一个较平的峰，说明S1S3发育的母质大部分是倒数第二次冰期晚期沉积的物质。

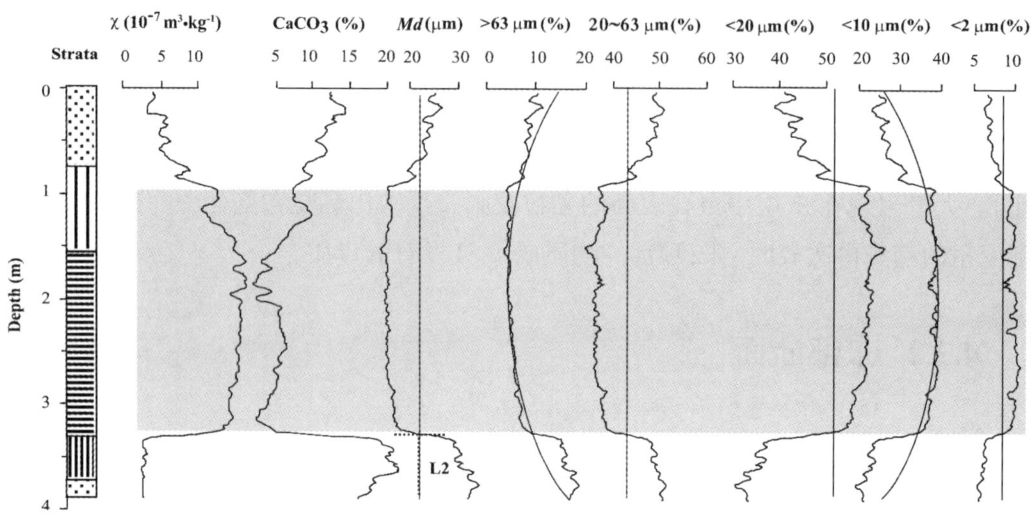

图 4.6　庆阳剖面磁化率、$CaCO_3$含量、粒度分布曲线

庆阳剖面：位于环县剖面东南100 km，属于董志塬的边缘地带。粗颗粒含量和细颗粒含量仍旧可以作为S1、L1和L2的岩性标准。这里的中值粒径（反映粒度分布的平均状况）和黏粒含量与天水剖面的接近，而且，叠加于括号“（）”趋势之上的粒度变化也是比较平稳的，说明潜在的S1S1、S1S2、S1S3在这里也发生了融合。对比天水和庆阳两地的$CaCO_3$含量变化，庆阳剖面S1中部的$CaCO_3$被淋失的程度更甚，说明庆阳剖面S1的土壤化作用更强。S1的Bk层的粒度分布完全是冰期的水平，可以断定S1发育的初期，地表相对稳定，因而土壤是向下发育的，即S1伸入到了较早堆积的L2。野外观测到S1沿坡路有起伏（见图3.8的照片），可能反映了一定的沟蚀过程。如果侵蚀事件倾向于发生在气候温暖湿润的时期（张信宝等，1996；邓成龙和袁宝印，2001；周杰等，1998），那么S1S3对应的MIS 5e期间发生较为强烈侵蚀的可能性最大。换言之，末次间冰期早期的侵蚀奠定了槽形地形的基础。这与我们所有的其他剖面不同，包括下文要讨论的旬邑剖面和蓝田剖面，庆阳剖面L2向S1的过渡是非常“突然”的：从3.22 m到3.12 m，中值粒径迅速从30.17 μm减小到18.15 μm，>63 μm粗颗粒含量从16.38%猛然降低到8.20%，<10 μm的细颗粒含量从23.17%陡然升高至35.08%，黏粒含量也由6.33%迅速增加到9.22%。这种粒度分布的突然变化令我们怀疑，采样点在末次间冰期的早期也发生过坡面侵蚀。

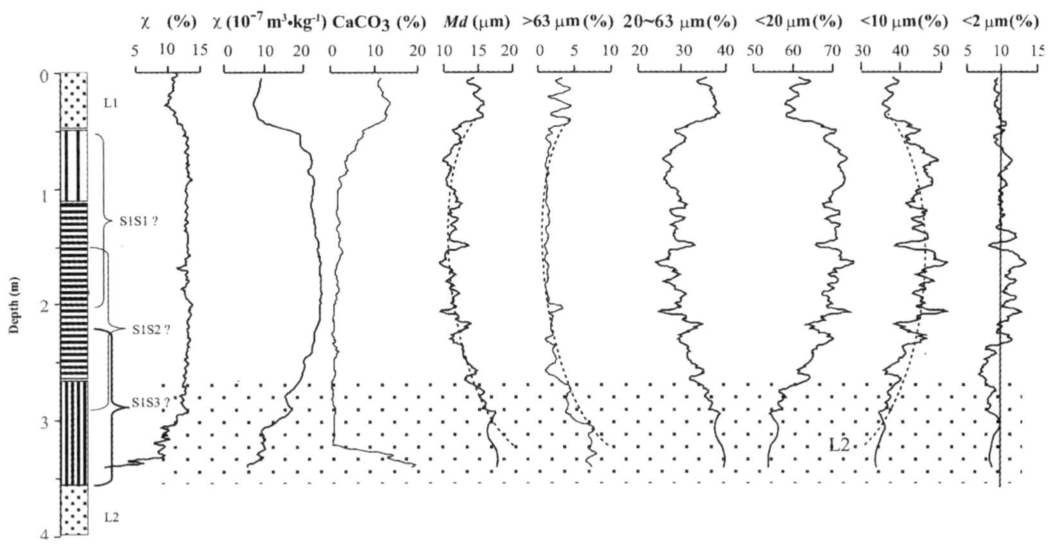

图 4.7　旬邑剖面磁化率、$CaCO_3$含量、粒度分布曲线

旬邑剖面：该剖面在庆阳剖面东南90 km处，著名的西峰剖面和洛川剖面就介于庆阳剖面和旬邑剖面之间。根据中值粒径、>63 μm含量和<10 μm含量，我们可以分辨出S1、L1和L2。由于距离源区更远，旬邑剖面的中值粒径比庆阳剖面的更小。更好的降水和热量条件使这里$CaCO_3$的淋溶比庆阳剖面和黄土高原东部的天水剖面更加彻底。叠加于括号“（）”趋势上的>63 μm颗粒含量缺乏显著的变化，而且磁化率也没有将潜在的S1S1、S1S2、S1S3区分开，说明较低的风尘堆积速率和较高的成壤改造速率使得这里S1的各个层次也融合在一起。<10 μm含量存在比较显著的波动，黏粒含量也有显著的变化，不过频繁波动的黏粒曲线的峰值区出现在S1的中部。这些特征意味着S1不仅发生了强烈的就地风化作用（使大颗粒变成小颗粒），而且发生了显著的黏粒迁移过程。而颗粒的转化和迁移增加了粒度分布的不确定性，这可能是造成粒度分布频繁波动的原因。在旬邑剖面，我们仍然可以看到S1底部粒度变粗的过程，再次有力地证明，形成于末次间冰期的S1在其发育的早期是以倒数第二次冰期期间沉积的黄土L2的上部作为母质的。

蓝田剖面：位于黄土高原东部断面的最南端。蓝田剖面是庆阳剖面和旬邑剖面的“压缩版本”。根据中值粒径、>63 μm含量和<10 μm含量，我们可以分辨出S1、L1和L2。不过野外观测表明，L1的底部也经历了成壤改造。直观的形态学特征（颜色、土壤结构）显示蓝田剖面L1土壤的发育程度比兰州剖面中发育最好的古土壤S1S3的发育程度还要高，加之远离源区，蓝田剖面L1的粒度较细，与S1的粒度分布比较接近。棱块状结构体表面的黏粒团和粉砂团表明不仅黏粒而且粉砂也在剖面当中随降雨迁移。S1中部黏粒的峰值对应于磁化率的峰值，表明强烈的残积黏化作用。叠加于括

号“（）”趋势线上的>63 μm含量波动非常平稳，富含黏粒的Bt层厚达2.5 m，这些意味着潜在的S1S2将S1S3的A层转化为B层并可能影响着S1S3的B层，而S1S1将S1S2的A层亦改造成B层，甚至影响着S1S2乃至S1S3的B层，最终形成了一个加积型的Bt层。强烈的就地风化以及较细颗粒（黏粒和细粉砂）在剖面当中的迁移，都造成S1粒度分布的一些不确定性，叠加于括号“（）”趋势线上的粒度波动当然没有任何有效的气候意义。此外，S1下部粒度变粗的趋势再次表明：风尘的加积速率很低造就了相对稳定的地表状况，这又促使土壤向下发育，S1至少向L2深入了1 m，如果加上BC层和Ck层，则S1侵入早先沉积的L2达3 m之多。因此，在黄土高原东南部试图利用类似的S1古土壤建立所谓的高分辨率的气候变化历史是不现实的。

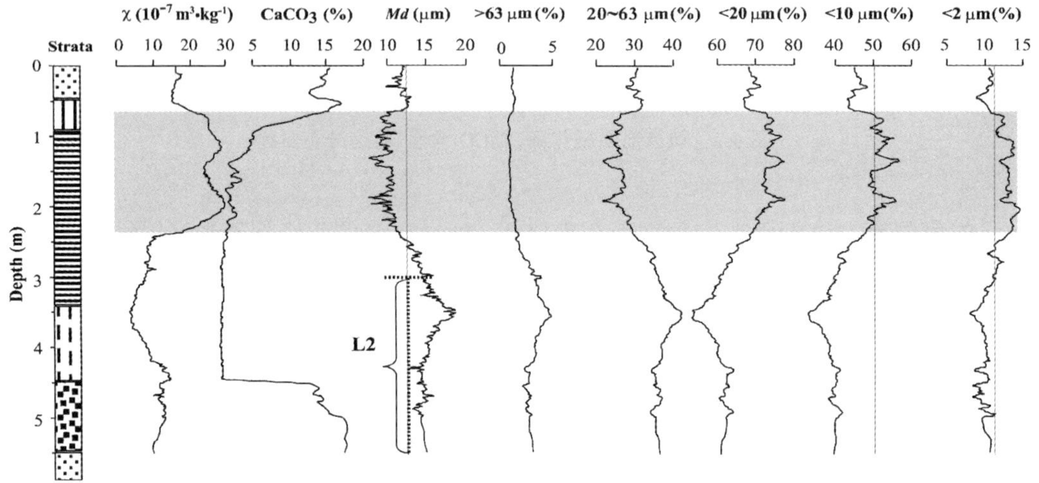

图 4.8　蓝田剖面磁化率、$CaCO_3$含量、粒度分布曲线

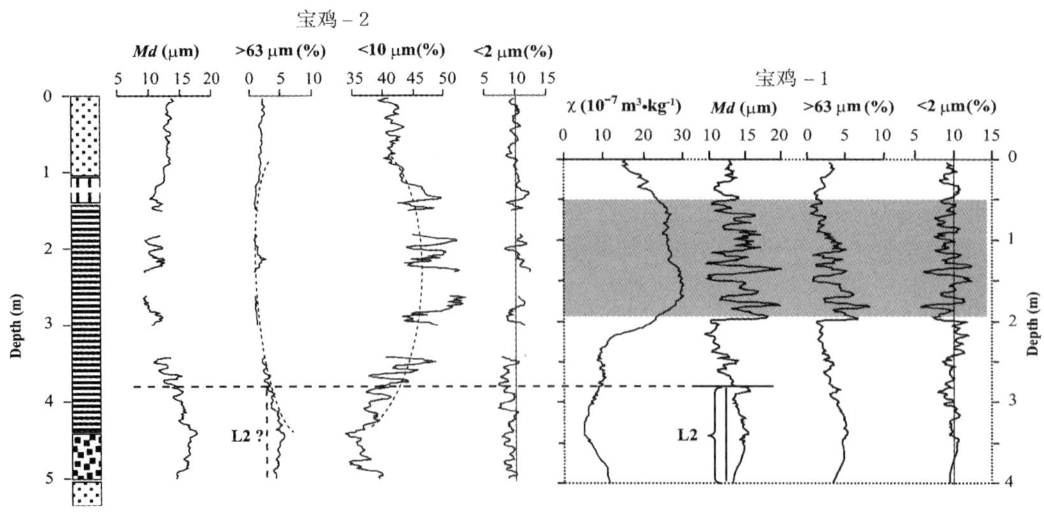

图 4.9　宝鸡剖面粒度分布、磁化率曲线

宝鸡剖面： 宝鸡剖面处于黄土高原东部的蓝田剖面和黄土高原西部的天水剖面之间。需要说明一下，宝鸡剖面我们采了两次样，第一次采的样做了粒度和磁化率分析，第二次采的样仅做了粒度分析，但第二次采的样有部分丢失。分析结果如图4.9。第一次的粒度分析结果在Bt层表现得非常混乱，而且黏粒含量整体偏低，这可能是实验过程中前处理不当造成的。与前次粒度分布相比，第二次的粒度分析结果更值得采信。磁化率结果几乎是蓝田剖面的“翻版”。单从第二次“幸存”的样品粒度分析数据看，叠加在括号趋势线上的>63 μm含量变化很小，而首次样品的磁化率在Bt层的上部呈现平坦的高值，说明宝鸡剖面的S1S3、S1S2、S1S1也融合到了一起。中值粒径在Bt层的底部逐渐变粗的趋势再次表明S1的部分母质是早先沉积的L2黄土的上部。野外观测到土壤结构体表面有许多黏粒胶膜或黏粒团，说明黏粒曾经在剖面中发生过迁移。

4.3 小　结

从黄土高原的西北端到东南端，粉尘的堆积速率呈递减趋势，而成壤作用逐渐加强，因此，造成了末次间冰期古土壤S1的地理分异。沿黄土高原西部S1的断面，在西北边缘，对应于MIS 5中3个暖的亚阶段（5a、5c、5e）的3层古土壤（S1S1、S1S2、S1S3）以及对应于MIS 5中2个冷的亚阶段（5b、5d）的2层黄土都完整地保存下来了（如兰州剖面和定西剖面）。向东南来到秦安剖面，S1L2受到后期的成壤改造而被S1S2吞并了。而且秦安剖面的S1S1、S1S2、S1S3的发育程度都比兰州剖面或定西剖面的高。继续向东南便是天水剖面，不仅S1L2而且S1L1皆为后期的土壤发育（S1S2，S1S1）所吞噬，故3个土壤（S1S1、S1S2、S1S3）部分地融合到一起。沿黄土高原的东部断面，环县剖面S1的土壤地层与定西剖面相似，3层古土壤嵌2层黄土的结构也完整地保存了下来，而发育程度最高的S1S3伸入了下伏的L2黄土。庆阳剖面和旬邑剖面是天水剖面的“压缩版”，即S1L1、S1L2由于受到后期的成壤改造而分别成为S1S1、S1S2的组成部分；3个土壤（S1S1、S1S2、S1S3）完全地融合在一起，形成1个类软土状的加积型土壤复合体：1个厚的A层加1个因加积而“过厚”的B层。在东南端，宝鸡剖面和蓝田剖面的S1亦为经多次成壤（S1S1、S1S2、S1S3）作用形成的土壤复合体，并且呈现为1个单一的土壤剖面，Bt层发育得很好。

就粒度分布而言，其波动情形在我们所考察的剖面中表现出3个层次：（1）第一级的波动体现在S1与上覆的L1和下伏的L2的粒度分布存在显著的差别，意味着源区提供的S1的母质在末次间冰期就相对细或（和）与源区的距离在末次间冰期比末次冰期和倒数第二次冰期都要大得多。(2）第二级的波动表现为>63 μm含量和<10 μm含量的括号形“（）”趋势（粗组分由两端向中间减小和细组分由两端向中间增大)。这种趋势可能反映了源区物质供应对气候的滞后响应，具体地说，在末次间冰期的早期为气候最宜期（最暖湿的5e)，之后尽管气候趋于恶化（见Guo等，1996b，1999)，但末次间冰期早期或气候最宜期（最暖湿的5e）在源区准备的细粒母质成为末次间冰期的中期黄土最细物质的来源。换句话说，粒度由末次间冰期早期到中期变细的趋势表明，末次间冰期的气候最宜期使源区为后期（主要是S1S2）的粉尘沉积准备了最细的物质。末次间冰期中期之后粒度逐渐变粗反映了5e之后的气候整体恶化趋势。(3）第三级的波动为叠加在括号形“（）”趋势之上的<10 μm组分含量的变化，且其波动与频率磁化率有良好的对应关系。这些可能反映了成壤作用生成的细颗粒（<10 μm）和超细的顺磁性颗粒（由频率磁化率表征）仅仅是S1土壤中所有细粒的很少的一部分。值得注意的是，土壤的融合和吞并过程使得第三级的波动在天水剖面、蓝田剖面、旬邑剖面、庆阳剖面并不清晰。此外，<10 μm含量第三级的波动峰值、野外观察到的土壤结构体表面的黏粒胶膜和碳酸钙的淋溶都表明物质在古土壤剖面中的迁移。

总之，由>63 μm组分含量显示S1S3下部粒度粗化的趋势，表明绝大多数剖面（兰州剖面除外）的先前沉积L2黄土的顶部都遭受了成壤改造。以间冰期前沉积的黄土的粒度来重建末次间冰期的冬季风强度显然是不合适的。还需要强调的是，通过类似的土壤复合体来重建高分辨率的气候是不现实的，因为除了冬季风以外，有众多的因素控制着粒度分布。这些因素包括沉积前物质在源区经历的风化作用、沉积后的风化作用、细颗粒的迁移以及土壤向下发育。

参考文献

陈骏，仇纲，鹿化煜，等. 最近130 ka黄土高原夏季风变迁的Rb和Sr地球化学证据. 科学通报，1996，41 (21): 1963-1966.

邓成龙，袁宝印. 末次间冰期以来黄河中游黄土高原沟谷侵蚀—堆积过程初探. 地理学报，2001，56 (1): 92-98.

丁仲礼，任剑璋，杨石岭，等. 最后两个冰期旋回季风-沙漠系统不稳定性的高分辨率黄土记录. 第四纪研究，1999a，1: 49-58.

丁仲礼，孙继敏，刘东生. 联系沙漠-黄土演变过程中耦合关系的沉积学指标. 中国科学（D辑)，1999a，29(1): 82-87.

丁仲礼，余志伟，刘东生. 中国黄土研究新进展：（三）时间标尺. 第四纪研究，1991，4: 336–348.

郝青振，郭正堂. 1.2 Ma以来黄土-古土壤序列风化成壤强度的定量化研究与东亚夏季风演化. 中国科学（D辑），2001，31 (6): 520–528.

刘东生.黄土与环境. 北京：科学出版社，1985.

马毅杰，陈家坊. 我国红壤中氧化铁形态及其特性和功能. 土壤，1998，1: 1–6.

孙东怀，周杰，蒋复初，等. 末次间冰期黄土高原夏季风气候的初步研究. 科学通报，1995，40 (20): 1873–1875.

孙有斌，安芷生. 风尘堆积物中石英颗粒表面微结构特征及其沉积学指示. 沉积学报，2000，18 (4): 506–509.

魏建晶，郭正堂. 900 ka以来黄土-古土壤序列记录的风尘铁含量变化及其古气候意义. 科学通报，2003，48 (11) : 1214–1218.

熊毅，许冀泉. 中国土壤中粘粒矿物的分布规律. 土壤学报，1964，3：266–271.

杨石岭，丁仲礼. 7.0 Ma 以来中国北方风尘沉积的游离铁/全铁值变化及其古季风指示意义，科学通报，2000，45 (22): 2453–2456.

张信宝，周杰. 晚更新世以来黄渤海海侵与黄土高原地貌区域分异. 中国沙漠，1996，16 (4): 411–416.

周杰，张信宝，陈惠中，等. 130 ka BP前后黄土高原东部地区的气候侵蚀事件. 中国沙漠，1998，18 (2): 105–109.

Al-Barrak S, Lewis D T. Soils of a grassland-forest ectone in eastern Nebraska. Soil Science Society of American Journal, 1978, 42: 334–338.

An Z S, Kukla G, Porter S C, et al. Late Quaternary dust flux on the Chinese Loess Plateau. Catena, 1991, 18, 125–132.

An Z S, Porter S C. Millennial-scale climatic oscillations during the last interglaciation in central China. Geology, 1997, 25 (7): 603–606.

Assallay A M, Rogers C D F, Smalley I J, et al. Silt, 2–62 m, 9–4. Earth Science Reviews, 1998, 45: 61–88.

Birkeland. Soils and Geomorphology. 3rd ed. Oxford: Oxford University Press, 1999.

Buol S W, Hole F D. Some of characteristics of clay skins on peds in soil B horizons of a gray-brown Podzol soil. Soil Science Society of American Journal, 1959, 23: 239–241.

Buol S W, Hole F D. Clay skin genesis in Wisconsin soils. Soil Science Society of American Journal, 1961, 25: 377–379.

Buol S W, Hole F D, McCracken R J. Soil Genesis and Classification. Ames, Iowa: The Iowa State University Press , 1973.

Catt J A. Soils and Quaternary Geology: a handbook for field scientists. Oxford: Clarendon

Press, 1986.

Catt J A. Paleopedology Manual. Quaternary International, 1990, 6: 1–95.

Chen F H, Boemandel J, Wang J M, et al. High - resolution multiproxy climatic records from Chinese loess: evidence for rapid climatic changes over the last 75 kyr. Paleogeography, Paleoclimatology, Paleoecology, 1997, 130: 323–335.

Ding Z L, Rutter N W, Han J M, et al. A coupled environmental system formed at about 2.5 Ma over eastern Asia. Paleogeography, Paleoclimatology, Paleoecology, 1992, 94, 223–224.

Ding Z L, Sun J M, Rutter N W, et al. Changes in sand content of loess deposits along a North - South transect of the Chinese Loess Plateau and the implications for desert variations. Quaternary Research, 1999, 52: 56–62.

Feng Z D. Geochemical characteristics of a loess - soil sequence in central Kansas, USA. Soil Science Society of American Journal, 1997, 61, 534–541.

Feng Z D, Chen F H. Problems of magnetic susceptibility signature as the summer monsoon proxy in Chinese loess sequences. Chinese Science Bulletin, 1999, 44 (suppl. 1): 97–104.

Feng Z D, Wang H B, Olson C G, et al. Pedogenic factors affecting magnetic susceptibility of the last interglacial paleosol S1 in the Chinese Loess Plateau. Earth Surface Processes and Landforms, 2004a, 29: 1389–1402.

Feng Z D, Wang H B, Olson C G, et al. Chronological discord between the last interglacial paleosol (S1) and its parent material in the Chinese Loess Plateau. Quaternary International, 2004b, 117: 17–26.

Foth H D. Fundamentals of Soil Science. 6th ed. New York: John Wiley and Sons Inc, 1978.

Gile L H. Holocene soils in eolian sediments of Bailey County, Texas. Soil Science Society of American Journal, 1979, 49: 994–1005.

Gile L H, Grossman R B. Morphology of argillic horizon in desert soils of southern New Mexico. Soil Sciences, 1968, 106: 6–15.

Guo Z T, Fedoroff N, Liu T S. The Micromorphology of the loess - paleosol last 130 ka in China and paleoclimatic events. Sciences in China (Series B), 1996a, 39(5): 468–477.

Guo Z T, Liu T S, Fedoroff N, et al. Climate extremes in loess of China coupled with the strength of deep - water formation in the North Atlantic. Global and Planetary Change, 1998, 18: 113–128.

Guo Z T, Liu T S, Guiot J, et al. High frequency pulses of East Asian monsoon climate in the last two glaciations: link with the North Atlantic. Climate Dynamics, 1996b, 12: 701–709.

Guo Z T, Peng S Z, Wei L Y. Weathering signals of millennial - scale oscillations of the East Asian summer monsoon over the last 220, 000 years. Chinese Science Bulletin, 1999, 44 (suppl. 1), 20–25.

Hallberg G R, Wollenhaupt N C, Miller G A. A century of soil development in spoil derived from loess in Iowa. Soil Science Society of American Journal, 1978, 42: 339–343.

Howard J L, Amos D F, Daniels W L. Micromorphology and dissolution of quartz sand in some exceptionally ancient soils. Sedimentary Geology, 1995, 105: 51–62.

Johnson D L, Watson-Stegner D. Evolution model of pedogenesis. Soil Science, 1987, 143: 349–366.

Liu T S. New Aspects of Loess Research. Beijing: Ocean Press, 1987.

Mack G H, James W C, Monger H C. Classification of paleosols. Geological Society of America Bulletin, 1993, 105: 129–136.

Moore T R. Soil formation in northeastern Canada. Annals of the Association of American Geographers, 1978, 68: 518–537.

Nettleton W D, Flach K W, Brasher B R. Argillic horizons without clay skins. Soil Science Society of American Journal, 1969, 33: 121–125.

Nettleton W D, Olson C G, Wysocki D A. Paleosol classification: problems and solutions. Catena, 2000, 41: 61–92.

Olson C G, Nettleton W D. Paleosols and the effects of alteration. Quaternary International, 1998, 51–52: 185–194.

Porter S C, An Z S. Correlation between climate events in the North-Atlantic and China during the last glaciation. Nature, 1995, 375: 305–308.

Ruhe R V. Soil-climate system across the prairies in Midwestern USA. Geoderma, 1984, 34: 201–219.

Ruhe R V, Olson C G. Estimate of clay content: additions of proportions of soil clay to constant standard. Clay Mineralogy, 1979, 27: 322–326.

Ruhe R V, Olson, C G. Soil welding. Soil Sciences, 1980, 130: 132–139.

Ruhe R V, Prill R C, Piecken F F. Profile characteristics of some loess-derived soils and soil aeration. Soil Science Society of American Journal, 1955, 19: 345–348.

Valentine K W G, Dalrymple J B. Quaternary buried paleosols: a critical review. Quaternary Research, 1976, 6: 209–222.

Walker P H, Chittleborough D J. Development of particle size distribution in some Alfisols in southeastern Australia. Soil Science Society of American Journal, 1986, 50: 394–400.

Wright J T. "Desert" loess versus "glacial" loess: quartz silt formation, source areas and sediment pathways in the formation of loess deposits. Geomorphology, 2001, 36: 231–256.

Xiao J L, Porter S C, An Z S, et al. Grain Size of Quartz as an Indicator of Winter Monsoon Strength on the Loess Plateau of Central China during the Last 130, 000 Yr. Quaternary Research, 1995, 43: 22–29.

Yaalon D H. Paleopedology. Jerusalem: Israel University Press, 1971.

5 影响末次间冰期土壤磁化率的成壤过程和成壤因素

5.1 黄土-古土壤磁化率研究进展

对中国黄土-古土壤序列的磁化率测量工作在20世纪70年代已有零星开展（李华梅等，1974；安芷生等，1977）。自Heller和Liu（1986）认识到中国的黄土-古土壤序列的磁化率可以同深海氧同位素进行对比之后，加之环境磁学渐趋成熟（Thompson和Oldfield，1986），中国黄土-古土壤的磁学研究才进入快速发展阶段，目前有关黄土磁化率的文献数以千计。

Heller和Liu（1982）率先建立了中国黄土高原地区的磁性地层，George Kukla等人（Kukla，1987；Kukla和An，1989）则利用磁性倒转事件和磁化率建立了第一个非常详细的中国黄土磁性地层。中国黄土磁化率与深海和极地冰芯氧同位素的可比性（Heller和Liu，1986；Kukla等，1988；李吉均等，1990）表明磁化率是一个良好的气候代用指标，安芷生等最先将磁化率视为夏季风强度的指标（安芷生等，1990）。此后，有许多工作将磁化率作为夏季风强度变化的半定量指标（An等，1991，1993；苏志珠等，1994；孙继敏等，1997；Chen等，1997；Fang等，1999；周杰等，1995）。也有学者基于对降水和磁化率的统计分析建立的转换方程来定量地计算古降水（Heller等，1993；吕厚远等，2003；孙东怀等，1995；Liu等，1995；Maher和Thompson，1995；Maher等，1994，2002，2003a）。可是，磁化率与气候之间联系的机制尚无法完全确定，换言之，磁化率的成因还存在着争论。目前，争论的焦点集中于“沉积成因”和“成壤成因”。

5.1.1 磁性矿物与磁性颗粒的大小

不管是“成壤成因”还是“沉积成因”，抑或是二者共同作用的结果，磁化率最终取决于作为磁化率载体的磁性矿物的种类、浓度以及磁性矿物的颗粒大小。依据磁性行为，磁性矿物可以分为亚铁磁性矿物、反铁磁性矿物、顺磁性矿物、抗磁性矿物。亚铁磁性矿物包括磁铁矿（Fe_3O_4）、磁赤铁矿（γ-Fe_2O_3）、钛磁铁矿（Fe_3O_4- Fe_2TiO_4）、钛赤铁矿（Fe_2O_3- $FeTiO_3$）、磁黄铁矿（Fe_7S_8）、胶黄铁矿（Fe_3S_4）。反铁磁性矿物包括赤铁矿（α-Fe_2O_3）和针铁矿（α-FeOOH）。顺磁性矿物包括部分硅酸盐矿物和一些含铁矿物，如纤铁矿（γ-FeOOH）、钛铁矿（$FeTiO_3$）、菱铁矿（$FeCO_3$）、黄铁矿（FeS）。抗磁性物质包括水、有机质、石英、碳酸钙等，它们通常具有弱的负磁化率。土壤中常见的磁性矿物如表5.1所示，对磁学研究具有重要意义的磁性矿物主要是亚铁磁性矿物（Thompson和Oldfield，1986；刘秀铭等，1991，1992）。中国黄土-古土壤序列中的亚铁磁性矿物主要是磁铁矿和磁赤铁矿。

表5.1　土壤中常见的磁性矿物及其特征

磁性矿物	化学式	颜色	磁性行为	形态	磁化率 /$10^{-8}m^3 \cdot kg^{-1}$	矫顽力 /mT
磁铁矿	Fe_3O_4	—	亚铁磁性	晶形铁	39000～110000	20
磁赤铁矿	γ-Fe_2O_3	2.5YR-5YR	亚铁磁性	晶形铁	28600～44000	30～40
赤铁矿	α-Fe_2O_3	7.5YR-5YR	反铁磁性	晶形铁	27～169	760
针铁矿	α-FeOOH	7.5YR-2.5Y	反铁磁性	晶形铁	35～126	—
纤铁矿	γ-FeOOH	5YR-7.5YR 色度值≥6	顺磁性	晶形铁	50～75	—
水铁矿	$Fe_5O_7OH \cdot 4H_2O$	5YR-7.5YR 色度值≤6	顺磁性	隐晶质铁	113～130	—

亚铁磁性矿物可分为多畴（Multidomain，MD，粒径>1 μm）、假单畴（Psuedo single domain，PSD，粒径为0.04～1 μm）、稳定单畴（Stable single domain，SSD，粒径为0.02～0.04 μm）以及超顺磁性颗粒（Superparamagnetic grain，SP，粒径<0.02 μm）（Thompson和Oldfield，1986；卢升高等，2003）。通过对合成和天然磁铁矿的磁性特征的测量，Maher（1988）给出了磁性参数随磁性颗粒粒度变化的规律。磁化率随晶粒的变化呈双峰形（见图5.1），SP有极低的饱和等温剩磁（SIRM）和很高的磁化率，MD颗粒呈弱而不稳定的剩磁，磁化率在50 μm附近出现次高峰，SSD具有强

而稳定的剩磁，且磁化率较高。

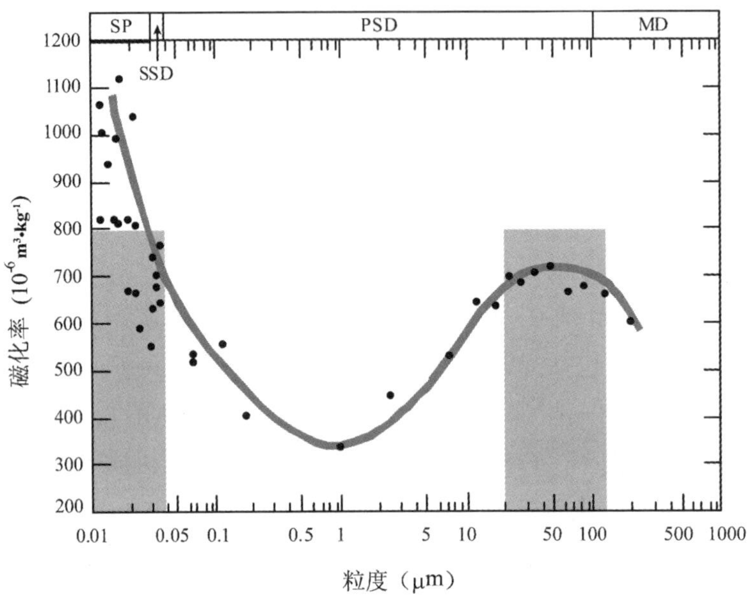

图5.1 不同粒径磁铁矿的磁化率

在不同的土壤发生条件下，铁可以发生价态（Fe^{2+}、Fe^{3+}）的转换（Diao和Wen，1997；徐仁扣，1994；中国科学院地球化学研究所，1981）和不同形态的转化：离子态↔非晶质↔隐晶质↔晶质（陈家坊，1981；于天仁和陈志诚，1990；雷梅等，2001）。为DCB所溶解的无定形铁、隐晶质铁、晶形铁统称为游离氧化铁，但磁铁矿不属于游离氧化铁的范畴。土壤中Fe^{2+}的含量表征了土壤的氧化-还原状态，磁化率对Fe^{2+}的含量变化的响应呈现一个类正态分布，即，极端的还原条件或极端的氧化条件都会使磁化率降低（顾兆炎等，2000）。刁桂仪（1982）对黄土中几种赋存形态的铁进行了总结，他认为黄土中的铁可以分为铝硅酸盐矿物铁、晶形铁、无定形铁、有机铁（络合铁）、代换态铁、碳酸盐结合铁、氧化锰结合铁等。黄土-古土壤中铁的形态转化过程包括：土体中原生铝硅酸盐矿物（如绿泥石）晶格被破坏后释放出来的铁，与水结合形成无定形非晶体的氧化铁（活性氧化铁）。它们以凝胶形式包被在黏粒表面，这类铁不稳定，极易发生迁移转化，并进一步脱水结晶生成晶质态的氧化铁（老化过程），如针铁矿和赤铁矿。晶质态铁又可转化为离子态铁（活化过程）。因此，土壤发育得越好，土体中原生矿物风化释放的游离氧化铁越多，而活性铁相对较少，换言之，游离度（游离氧化铁与全铁的比值）和活化度可以指示土壤的风化程度（郭正堂等，1999a，1999b）。

5.1.2 沉积成因

Kukla的“磁通量稀释模式”主张“磁通量”保持恒定，粗颗粒粉尘输入速率调节着磁化率的最终结果，黄土中的磁化率之所以比古土壤中的小，是因为在给定的一个时段内，弱磁性的粗颗粒物质输入较多，磁信号被稀释了（Kukla，1987；Kukla和An，1989）。这一假说中携带“磁通量”的细颗粒载体并没有得到实验的证实，而且，根据Feng（1996）的计算，兰州、北塬、洛川黑木沟、西峰、白马坡、清水河等6地的末次冰期黄土（L1）的年均磁化率为末次间冰期古土壤（S1）的年均体积磁化率的2倍以上，因此，Kukla的“磁通量稀释模式”有明显的缺陷。

研究表明，阿拉斯加黄土、西伯利亚黄土以及中国沙地或沙漠附近的部分风尘沉积物中的磁化率与土壤发育程度呈负相关（Begét等，1990；Chlachula，1997；Sun和Liu，2000），同中国黄土高原的磁化率与黄土-古土壤的匹配模式相比有很大的差别。由于阿拉斯加黄土记录的磁化率变化与深海钻的磁化率记录非常相似（间冰期磁化率较低），并且后者是反映风力搬运的，所以，Begét等（1990）将风力搬运沿用到对阿拉斯加黄土磁化率波动的解释。随后的实验使Begét等（1990）认为磁化率反映的是风力搬运的密度分选。他们认为，距离源区近或者风力强盛导致较高的磁化率，距离源区远则磁铁矿少，磁化率相应较低（Begét等，1990；Begét，1996）。因此，在一个给定的地点，冰期—间冰期风力强弱的交替变化将导致磁化率信号的波动。Chlachula等（1997，1998）也用此假说来解释西伯利亚黄土的磁化率。可是不论是阿拉斯加黄土还是西伯利亚黄土，研究人员都没有对其中的磁性矿物进行过检测，因此也遭到了Liu等（1999b）的反驳。Liu等（1999b）认为，在高纬度地区（如阿拉斯加和西伯利亚），间冰期时沼泽条件下的还原作用可能减弱了黄土的磁化率信号；而冰期时在完全冻结的干燥地面上沉积的黄土则保留了其母质原有的较高磁化率信号。

Sun和Liu（2000）对位于沙地中的内蒙古赤峰剖面和黑龙江泰来剖面进行了研究，结果表明赤峰剖面的部分条带和泰来剖面的全部磁化率的来源主要是颗粒较大（63～350 μm）的碎屑颗粒，磁性颗粒的大小主要集中在30 μm以上。根据风力搬运与颗粒大小的关系，他们推断近源的物质对磁化率的增强有重要贡献。

此外，现代粉尘的磁化率较高，意味着磁化率在沉积前就受到了同时代气候的影响（Meng等，1997；孙东怀，2001），因此，磁性矿物可能大部分或部分已经在源区就形成了（Liu等，1999a）。郭正堂等（1999a，1999b）认为，铁的总量和游离铁的含量基本反映了原始风尘的情况。因此，由沉积作用导致的古上壤中氧化铁含量增加必然是其磁化率增高的原因之一。

5.1.3 成壤成因

由于黄土和古土壤中的磁性矿物的种类和形态并不相同，代表超顺磁颗粒含量的参数（频率磁化率χ_{fd}和$\chi_{ARM/SIRM}$）均显示古土壤中超顺磁颗粒比黄土中的多。因此，Zhou等（1990）、Maher和Thompson（1991）提出了成壤过程导致磁化率增加的主张。成壤过程或因素对磁化率贡献或正或负，其实质是成壤环境中氧化铁的转化导致磁性特征的改变（见图5.2）。成壤过程或因素可以归结为以下几个方面。

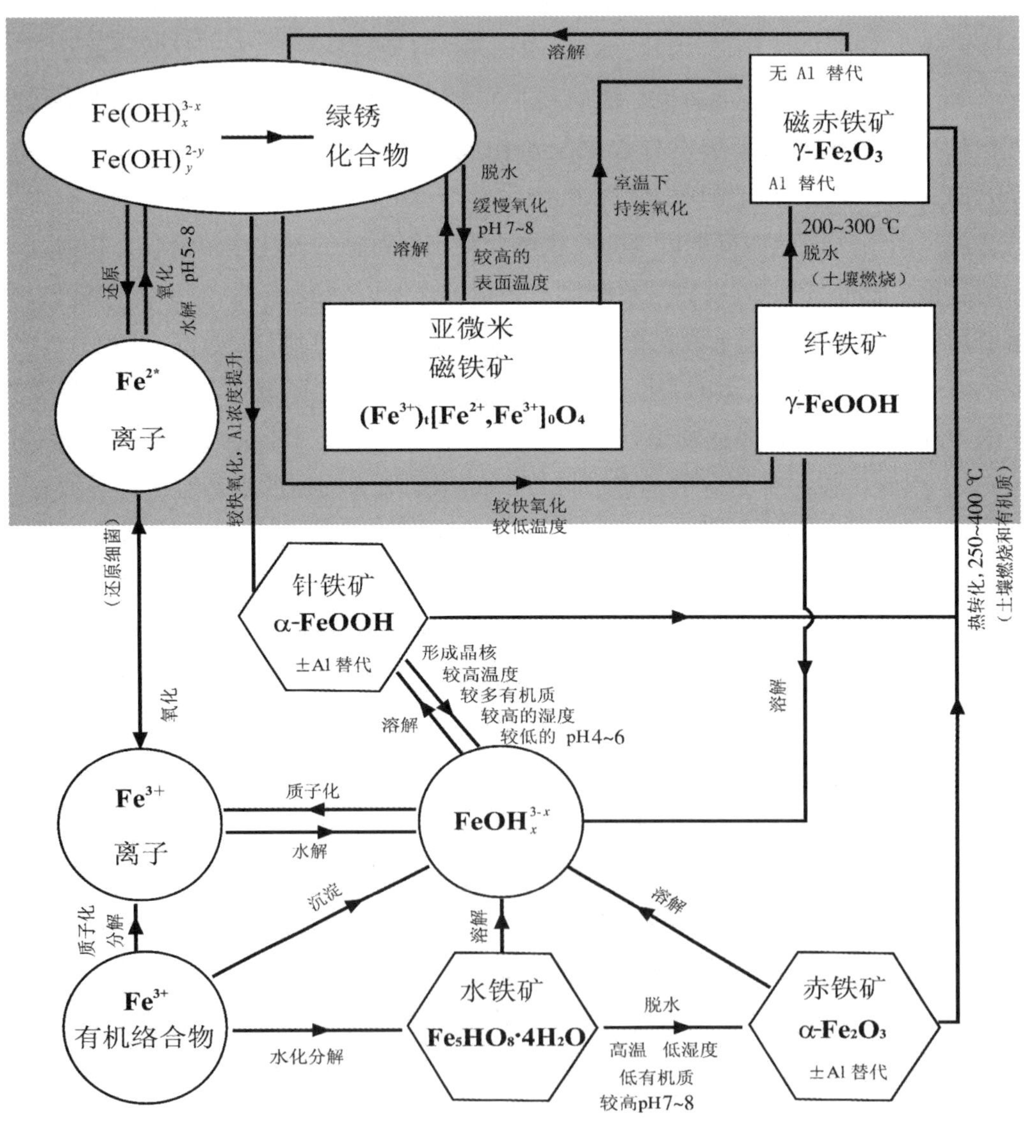

图 5.2 成壤环境中氧化铁的转化过程（铁还原细菌可能参与了许多溶解和还原步骤）

（自Schwertmann和Taylor，1987，转引自Maher等，2003b）

5.1.3.1 有机体因素对磁化率增强的作用

有机质同磁化率具有良好的相关关系（胡雪峰，2004；彭先芝和贾蓉芬，2001；贾蓉芬等，1992；孙继敏等，1995a，1995b），这种良好的相关关系，可能反映了成壤过程中生物主导的因素（需要无机化学过程的参与）对磁性矿物的生成和转变起了关键作用。

5.1.3.1.1 微生物合成

首先，由于有机质的适度存在，土壤中的微生物活动加强，微生物利用土壤中的铁合成了超细磁性矿物，这是一个生物矿化过程。Lowenstam（1981）将生物矿化分为两种模式：（1）生物诱导矿化作用（BIM），例如，Lovely等（1987）从土壤中提取出铁还原细菌，它能使通过还原作用和自身的分泌过程产生的Fe^{2+}和外部环境中产生的Fe^{3+}相互作用生成超细粒的磁性矿物。（2）生物控制矿化作用（BCM）。趋磁细菌属于BCM型生物，潘永信等（2004）对趋磁细菌的研究做了非常有益的评述。Blakemore（1975）研究发现，趋磁细菌（Magentotactic bacteria，简称MB）的细胞内包含有一条或多条磁小体（Magnetosome，简称MS），而MS的铁的形态主要是磁铁矿。Frankel等人（1983）提出了磁小体形成的一个概念模型：环境中的Fe^{3+}被趋磁细菌主动吸收后，细胞膜将其还原成Fe^{2+}。进入磁小体膜后Fe^{2+}重新被氧化形成低密度含水Fe^{3+}氧化物，之后又经脱水作用形成高密度的Fe^{3+}氧化物（水铁矿），最后，1/3的Fe^{3+}被还原并进一步脱水生成磁铁矿。中国黄土高原黄土-古土壤序列也存在趋磁细菌，贾蓉芬的小组对此开展了不少研究工作（贾蓉芬等，1996，2001，2003；李荣森等，1996；Fan等，1996；彭先芝等，2000，2002；彭先芝和贾蓉芬，2001）。彭先芝等（2000）的实验表明，趋磁细菌适度存在可以导致磁化率的增加，但是，当细菌过量或者外界的铁补给不充分的时候，磁化率会降低。他们给出的理由是，在其生命活动的能量交换过程中超磁细菌可将体内储存的Fe^{2+}全部变为Fe^{3+}并排出体外，致使MS在体内消失（彭先芝等，2000；贾蓉芬等，2003）。

5.1.3.1.2 植物体分解

植物体本身含有磁性矿物，其残体的分解导致了土壤中磁性矿物的增加，从而提高了磁化率。Meng等（1997）研究发现，中国北方现代粉尘的磁化率比黄土的要高，其中含有较多的细粒磁性矿物，这些细粒磁性矿物主要是植物残体分解产生的。Meng等据此将黄土高原土壤中磁化率的增高归因于当时气候条件下磁化率较高的粉尘的输入。孙东怀等（2001）对黄土高原现代天然降尘的磁化率研究结果也支持Meng等的观测，孙东怀等还认为除了源区的磁信号外，后期的改造也应对磁化率有贡献。也就是说，即使植物残体分解对磁化率的贡献是显著的，也不能排除就地的植物分解过程对磁化率的增强作用。现代C3、C4植物的燃烧试验表明土壤的磁化率在植被燃烧后升高，且C4植物比C3植物对磁化率的贡献更显著（吕厚远和刘东生，2001）。

5.1.3.1.3 有机溶解或还原与无机化学改造相结合

植物分解产生的有机质可以作为还原剂，引起铁的活化，活化铁最后又被氧化、沉淀为磁赤铁矿（Rivers等，1999）。这一过程中有机化学反应和无机化学反应彼此呼应，有机质的存在是溶解和还原的前提。另外，有机质的存在，在一定程度上可以阻滞氧化铁的老化（雷梅等，2001；胡雪峰，2004）。需要指出的是，目前还缺乏足够的证据表明，在有机质的存在条件下无定形铁老化过程中倾向于形成磁赤铁矿（胡雪峰，2004）。

5.1.3.2 氧化-还原过程对磁化率的影响

黄土-古土壤中的磁赤铁矿，一般被认为是次生的，它是磁铁矿在化学风化过程中产生的（季峻峰等，1999；陈天虎等，2003），可能涉及低温氧化的作用（Maher和Thompson，1994；Verosub等，1993；刘青松等，2003）。但氧化-还原作用不是必然地增强磁化率，它也可能导致磁化率的降低。

吕厚远等（2003）研究发现，磁化率与年均温和年降水量的正相关关系仅存在于一定的温度和降水量范围内，当年均温超过15 ℃，年降水量超过1100 mm时，土壤的磁化率则随温度或（和）降水的增加而减小。其中的原因是铁的氧化和老化过程较为强盛，土壤中形成了较多的赤铁矿。

前人研究表明阿拉斯加黄土-古土壤磁化率的差异是风力分选的结果（Begét等，1990；Begét，1996）。Liu等（1999b）对阿拉斯加黄土-古土壤的磁性矿物进行了深入的研究后发现黄土中的磁性颗粒大小、浓度和种类与古土壤中的都有所不同。因此Liu等提出，沉积后的潜育化作用使古土壤中的亚铁磁性矿物受到了破坏从而引起磁化率的降低，并提出了中国黄土高原黄土与阿拉斯加黄土磁化率的成壤改造的差异模式图（如图5.3）。Feng等（1998）的研究表明临夏盆地的北塬剖面S1底部的磁化率低值也是渍水还原造成的。

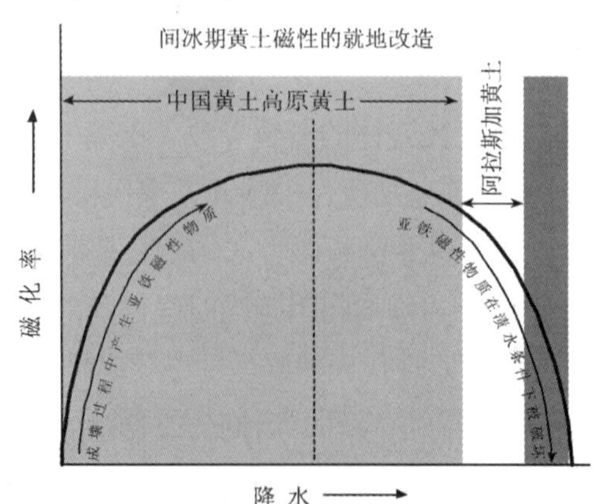

图5.3 降水与亚铁磁性矿物生成关系图（自Liu等，1999b）

5.1.3.3 碳酸盐对磁化率的影响

Heller和Liu（1986）认为黄土中的碳酸盐积累对磁化率信号存在着稀释作用，而碳酸盐的淋失可以增强磁化率。其他一些学者也报道了类似的现象（如：Feng和Johnson，1995； Feng，1997）。但也有学者表明，碳酸盐的淋失和积累对磁化率的贡献可能是非常有限的（韩家楙等，1991；刘秀铭等，1993）。由于剖面中的碳酸盐含量与所在层位的成壤强度的对应关系有时是不明确的，受到碳酸盐的稀释和增强作用的磁化率不可以被轻率地认为指示成壤强度（Feng和Chen，1999）。

综上所述，影响磁化率信号强弱的因素很多，源区的物质和成壤过程共同控制着磁化率信号的最终结果。要精确地重建古气候（如古降水），我们必须厘清沉积前原生的磁性矿物和沉积后次生的磁性矿物的贡献，同时还必须解析沉积–成壤的过程。

5.2 成壤过程对黄土高原末次间冰期古土壤S1的磁化率的影响

粒度分布一方面受控于源区的物质，另一方面受制于成壤过程。碳酸盐的含量在剖面中的分布也是成壤过程的结果。在本节，我们期望通过分析磁化率与粒度分布和碳酸盐含量的统计关系来阐述成壤过程对磁化率的贡献。我们将8个剖面（兰州、定西、秦安、天水、蓝田、旬邑、庆阳、环县）的多个粒级的含量和碳酸钙含量与磁化率的关系做了线性相关分析。在进行线性相关分析前，所有的数据先进行3点滑动平均。分析结果显示，在各个粒级中，>63 μm、2～10 μm、<2 μm与磁化率具有较高的相关系数。

表5.2 各剖面磁化率和频率磁化率与粒度和$CaCO_3$含量的相关系数

剖面	变量	>63 μm	2～10 μm	<2 μm	$CaCO_3$	χ_{fd}
兰州（n=648）	χ	−0.219	0.421	0.056	−0.505	0.864
	χ_{fd}	−0.446	0.632	0.267	−0.335	—
定西（n=298）	χ	−0.501	0.565	0.133	−0.114	0.887
	χ_{fd}	−0.705	0.780	0.376	0.012	—
秦安（n=238）	χ	−0.824	0.825	0.491	−0.094	0.873
	χ_{fd}	−0.866	0.849	0.615	0.126	—

续表 5.2

剖面	变量	>63 μm	2～10 μm	<2 μm	$CaCO_3$	χ_{fd}
天水（n=248）	χ	−0.732	0.727	0.627	−0.748	0.948
	χ_{fd}	−0.764	0.769	0.640	−0.665	—
蓝田（n=253）	χ	−0.886	0.918	0.793	0.119	0.834
	χ_{fd}	−0.914	0.838	0.787	0.172	—
旬邑（n=188）	χ	−0.804	0.882	0.596	−0.715	0.851
	χ_{fd}	−0.825	0.804	0.452	−0.682	—
庆阳（n=198）	χ	−0.838	0.973	0.955	−0.933	0.963
	χ_{fd}	−0.899	0.967	0.948	−0.943	—
环县（n=303）	χ	−0.853	0.935	0.946	−0.733	0.924
	χ_{fd}	−0.877	0.940	0.957	−0.641	—

5.2.1 兰州剖面

从图5.4和表5.2可以看到几个特征：首先，磁化率和粒度各自的整体趋势差别较大，S1的磁化率曲线总体趋势是一波三折，表现为“三峰二谷”，S1中的两个黄土单元（S1L1和S1L2）的磁化率值与冰期黄土（L1和L2）的磁化率没有显著差别；而粒度，例如如*Md*和>63 μm含量在S1当中则是整体偏低，包括S1L1和S1L2的粒度都远较冰期的黄土L1和L2的粒度细，尽管它们比3个土壤单元的粒度要稍

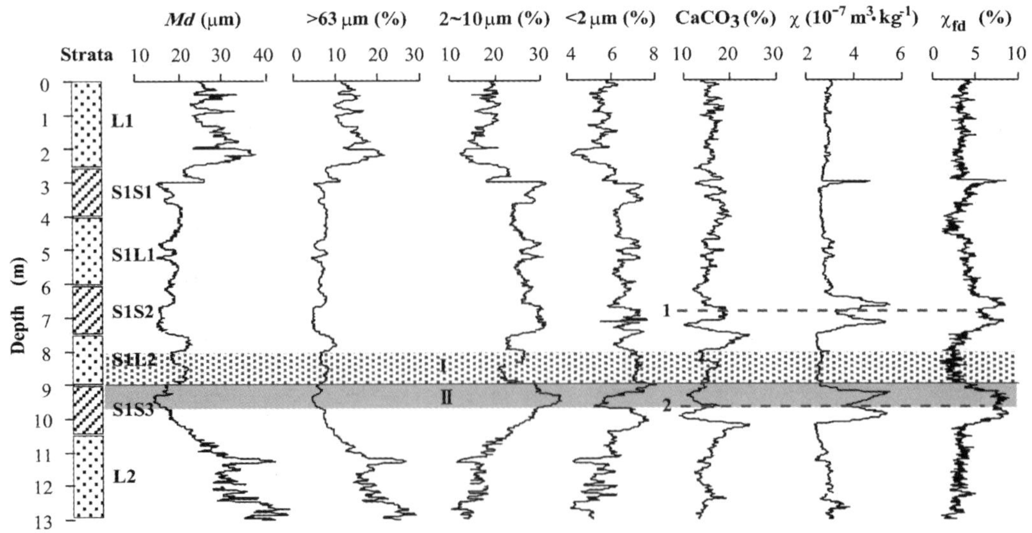

图5.4 兰州剖面中值粒径（*Md*）、>63 μm含量、2～10 μm含量、<2 μm含量、$CaCO_3$含量、磁化率、频率磁化率变化曲线

粗。第二，黏粒的含量与磁化率的相关系数极低（r=0.056），而且在某些层位两者存在负相关的关系：在8～9 m深度，黏粒的含量较高，而对应的磁化率是低值（见图5.4的灰色条带Ⅰ）；在9～10 m深度，黏粒含量表现为一个低谷，而磁化率却呈现出一个高峰（见图5.4的灰色条带Ⅱ）。第三，在所有的粒级中，2～10 μm含量与磁化率和频率磁化率的相关系数最大。第四，磁化率的第一级的波动是由>63 μm含量和2～10 μm含量的变化来控制的。而它的次一级变化则可以由$CaCO_3$含量的变化来解释。总的说来，磁化率的高值对应于碳酸钙的低值（r=−0.505），特别清晰的是，S1S2和S1S3各为一个磁化率的高峰，而这两个峰中的小谷均对应于$CaCO_3$的高值（见图5.4的虚线1、2）。

5.2.2 定西剖面

与兰州剖面相似，磁化率与粒度的整体趋势仍然有明显差别，尽管S1中的两个黄土单元（S1L1和S1L2）的粒度明显比冰期黄土细，但它们的磁化率却仍然很低。只不过，S1L1和S1L2的磁化率看起来要比L1和L2稍高一点。磁化率对>63 μm和2～10 μm的含量的相关系数分别为−0.501和0.565，较兰州剖面的相关性有所提高。而磁化率与黏粒（<2 μm）含量的相关性仍然很差，系数仅为0.133。单就磁化率和$CaCO_3$含量的相关系数（r=−0.114）看，二者几乎没有关系。有趣的是，在定西剖

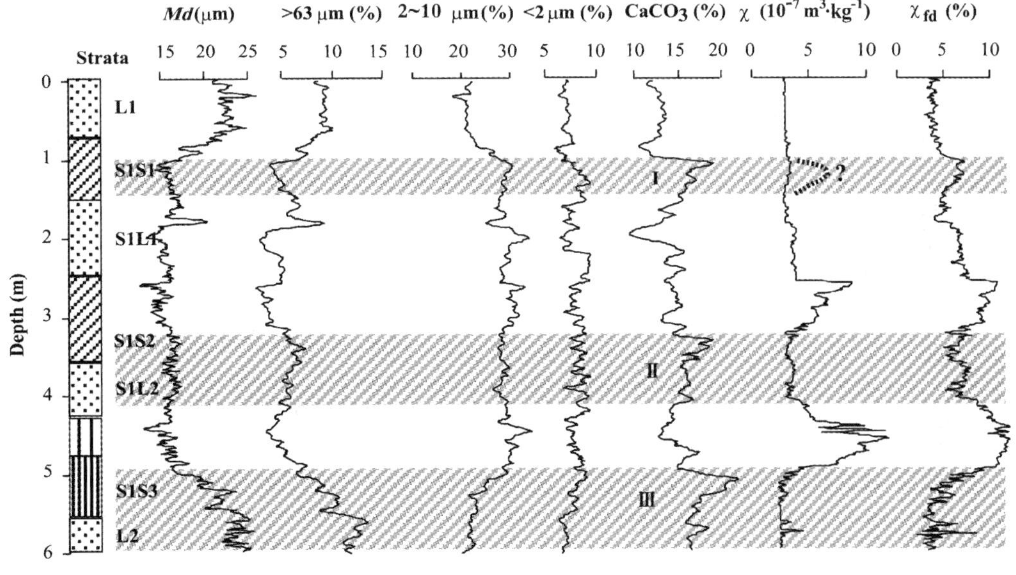

图5.5 定西剖面中值粒径（Md）、>63 μm含量、2～10 μm含量、<2 μm含量、$CaCO_3$含量、磁化率、频率磁化率变化曲线

面，S1S1潜在的磁化率峰值消失了，而频率磁化率的峰值仍然存在。根据磁化率与>63 μm含量和2～10 μm含量之间的线性回归方程得到磁化率的模拟曲线（见图5.5），S1S1的磁化率峰值应该是存在的。那么，造成此峰消失的原因是什么？通过进一步计算，我们注意到频率磁化率与$CaCO_3$含量的相关系数在2.5～6 m深度为负值（r=-0.585），而在0～2.5 m深度两者的相关系数为正值（r=0.415），这说明频率磁化率不依赖于碳酸盐含量的变化。观察到图中Ⅱ、Ⅲ带$CaCO_3$含量的高值对应的是磁化率和频率磁化率的低值，而Ⅰ带$CaCO_3$含量仍然很高，联系到碳酸盐对磁化率的稀释作用，我们认为，Ⅰ带磁化率的潜在峰值被高含量的$CaCO_3$抑制了，即$CaCO_3$的淀积稀释了磁性矿物的浓度。

5.2.3 秦安剖面

不管是磁化率还是频率磁化率，对>63 μm含量或2～10 μm含量的相关性都有所增加。80%以上的磁化率波动是由>63 μm含量或2～10 μm含量控制的。与前面的两个剖面不同，秦安剖面黏粒含量与磁化率的相关性大大增加（$r\chi$=0.491，$r\chi_{fd}$=0.615）。类似定西剖面，秦安剖面$CaCO_3$含量与磁化率整体上相关性极弱（r=-0.094），不过，从图5.6的Ⅰ、Ⅱ、Ⅲ、Ⅳ带可以看出，$CaCO_3$含量的变化与磁化率的次一级的波动有较好的反向对应关系。值得关注的是，野外观察表明S1S3的土壤发育程度是最高的，可是磁化率对此没有体现，显然，粒度在S1S3逐渐变粗的趋势抑制了潜在的磁化率最高峰。S1S2和S1S3之间的S1L2的缺失使得S1S3不太容易用磁化率加以分辨。

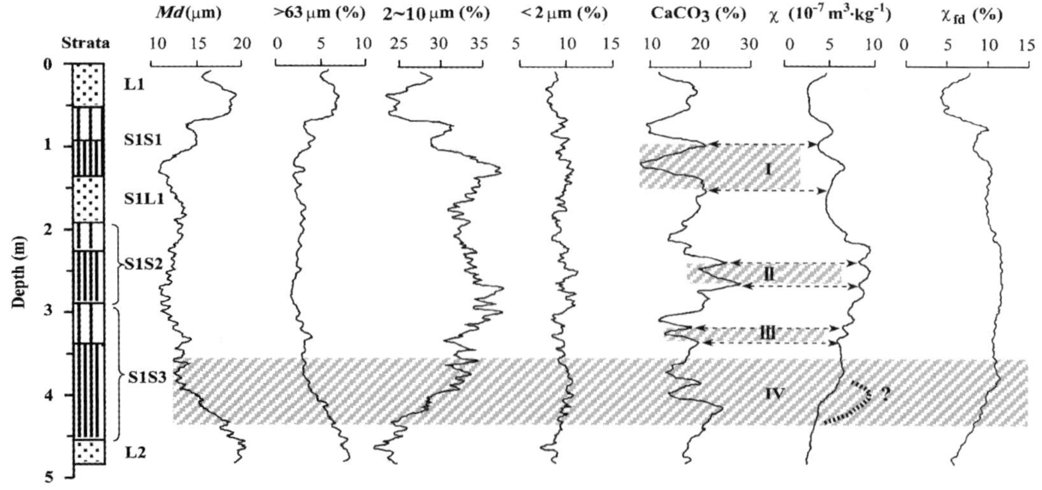

图5.6　秦安剖面中值粒径（Md）、>63 μm含量、2～10 μm含量、<2 μm含量、$CaCO_3$含量、磁化率、频率磁化率变化曲线

5.2.4 天水剖面

天水剖面的S1是一个土壤复合体，S1L1和S1L2在剖面中缺失，土壤形态特征以及$CaCO_3$含量在剖面上的表现都说明S1S1、S1S2和S1S3部分地发生融合。如图5.7中的箭头（对应2、3）所示，S1S2和S1S3两个土壤都发育成Bk层，占据整个S1的大部分。图5.7中富含碳酸盐的层次1可能指示了S1S1的底界，或至少是S1S1内$CaCO_3$淋溶的后期阶段，并且S1S1在发育过程中很可能吞并了S1S2的最上部（如层次1之上的箭头所指）。由于成壤速率与沉积速率的落差增大，土壤的融合过程不仅将两个黄土单元S1L1和S1L2改造成土壤，而且将S1S2和S1S3的A层转化为B层。因此，磁化率无法区分出3次成壤事件。磁化率同>63 μm含量、2～10 μm含量、黏粒含量、$CaCO_3$含量的相关性都较好，相关系数分别是：-0.732、0.727、0.627、-0.748。

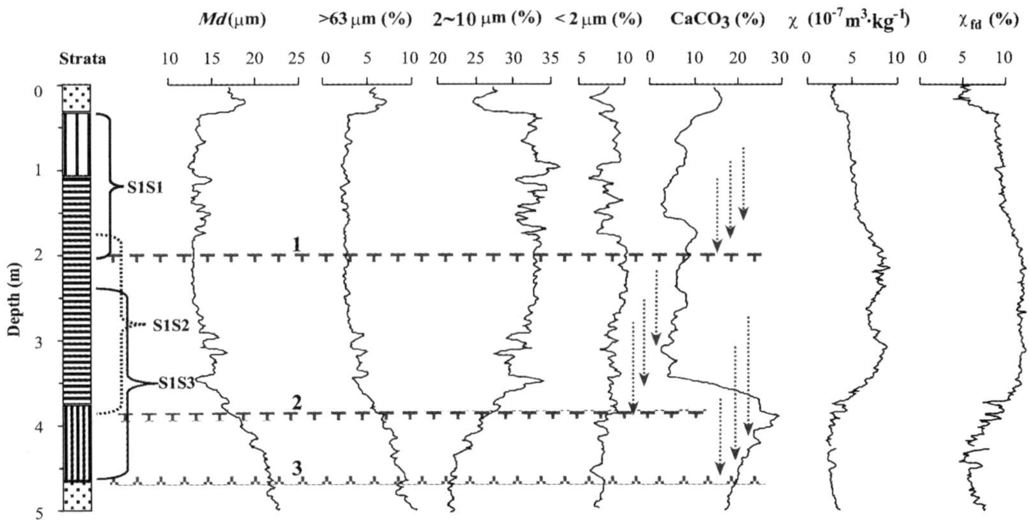

图5.7　天水剖面中值粒径（*Md*）、>63 μm含量、2～10 μm含量、<2 μm含量、$CaCO_3$含量、磁化率、频率磁化率变化曲线

5.2.5 蓝田剖面

黄土高原西北部的3次成壤序列在蓝田表现为一个单一的土壤剖面。此剖面有两个非常显著的特点：第一，S1的大部分是在较粗的母质上发育的，表明S1主要是在较老的L2上部发育的。第二，$CaCO_3$的含量在Bt和BC层都很低，在Ck层很高，意味着Ck层可能是3次成壤事件（S1S1、S1S2、S1S3）的淀积层。2～10 μm的含

量与磁化率具有很高的相关系数（$r=0.918$），>63 μm的含量与其磁化率的相关性（$r=-0.886$）次之，黏粒含量与其相关性（$r=0.793$）居后，而$CaCO_3$的含量变化对磁化率几乎没有贡献（$r=0.119$）。显然，2.5～4.5 m粒度的变粗是造成磁化率变低的原因。

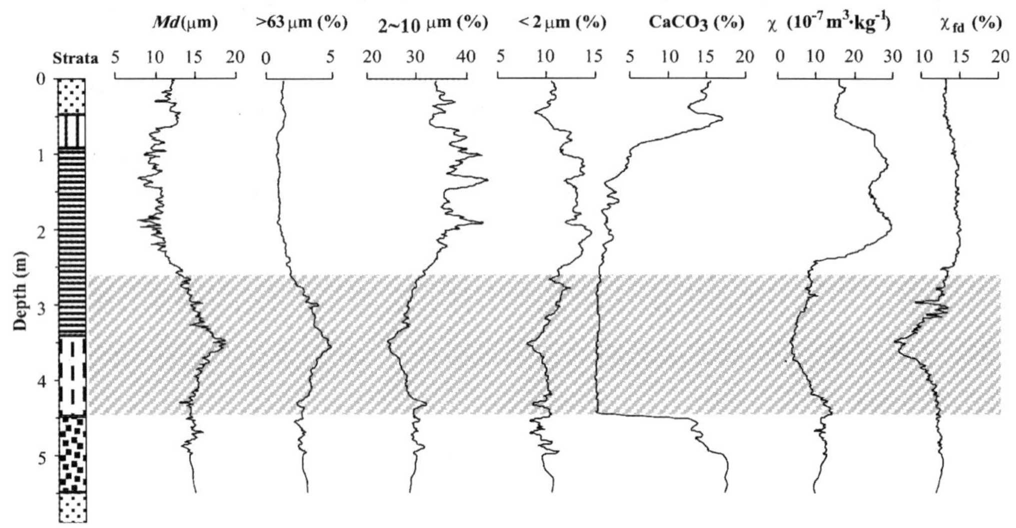

图5.8　蓝田剖面中值粒径(Md)、63 μm含量、10～2 μm含量、<2 μm含量、$CaCO_3$含量、磁化率、频率磁化率变化曲线

5.2.6　旬邑剖面

旬邑剖面位于黄土高原东部子午岭的西南角，它也是由一个单一的土壤剖面构成的：A层、Bt层和Bk层（见图5.9），相当于蓝田剖面的扩展版。磁化率与>63 μm含量、2～10 μm含量、<2 μm含量、$CaCO_3$的含量都有较好的相关性，其中与2～10 μm的相关系数最高（$r=0.882$），与<2 μm含量的相关系数最低（$r=0.596$）。磁化率和粒度都不能向我们提供有关3次成壤事件界线的信息。

5.2.7　庆阳剖面

庆阳剖面位于黄土高原东部的中间，它与著名的洛川剖面和西峰剖面处于相同的生物气候带。这是蓝田剖面的又一个扩展版。磁化率与>63 μm含量、2～10 μm含量、<2 μm含量、$CaCO_3$的含量有很好的相关性，相关系数分别为-0.838，0.973，0.955，-0.933。不管是磁化率还是粒度都不能区分出S1S1、S1S2、S1S3（见图5.10）。

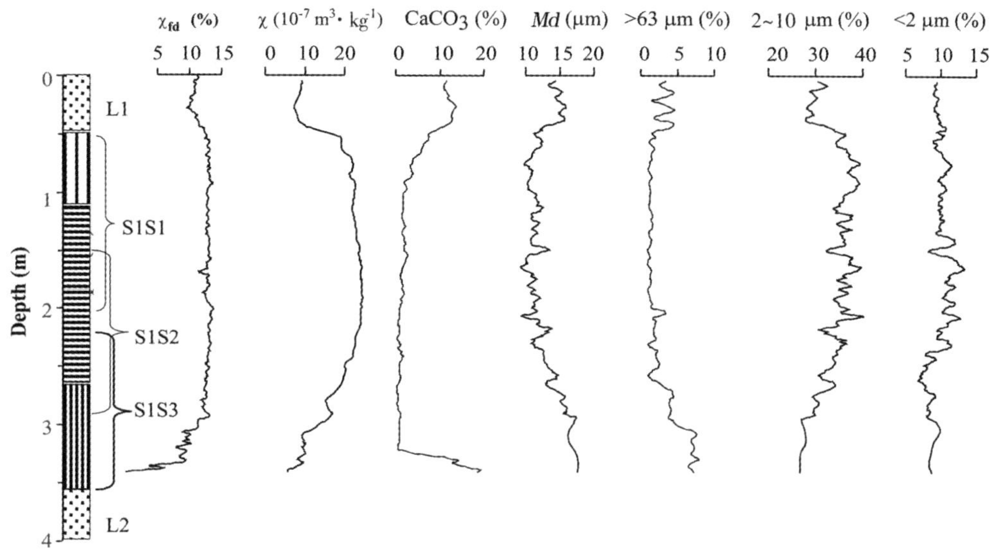

图5.9 旬邑剖面中值粒径(*Md*)、>63 μm含量、2～10 μm含量、<2 μm含量、$CaCO_3$含量、磁化率、频率磁化率变化曲线

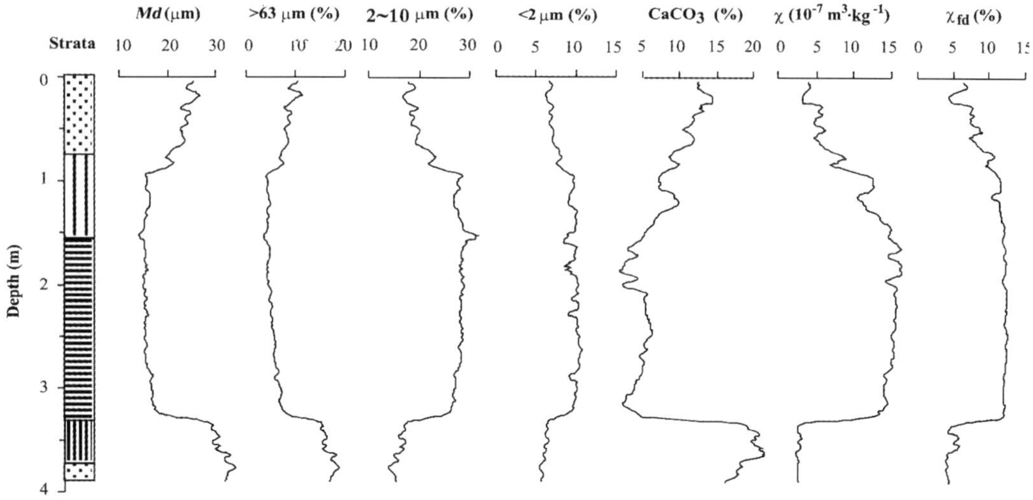

图5.10 庆阳剖面中值粒径(*Md*)、>63 μm含量、2～10 μm含量、<2 μm含量、$CaCO_3$含量、磁化率、频率磁化率变化曲线

5.2.8 环县剖面

在黄土高原东部的西北端，不仅S1S1、S1S2、S1S3而且这三层土壤所夹的S1L1和S1L2都得到了保存。看起来，>63 μm含量控制着磁化率曲线总体趋势（$r=-0.853$），而碳酸钙含量明显调节着磁化率的次一级波动（$r=-0.733$）（见图

5.11中条带Ⅰ和Ⅱ)。如我们在秦安剖面所见，磁化率信号没能很好地体现出S1S3的发育程度是最高的。粒度变粗（见图5.11中条带Ⅲ）应该是造成S1S3的磁化率降低的原因。

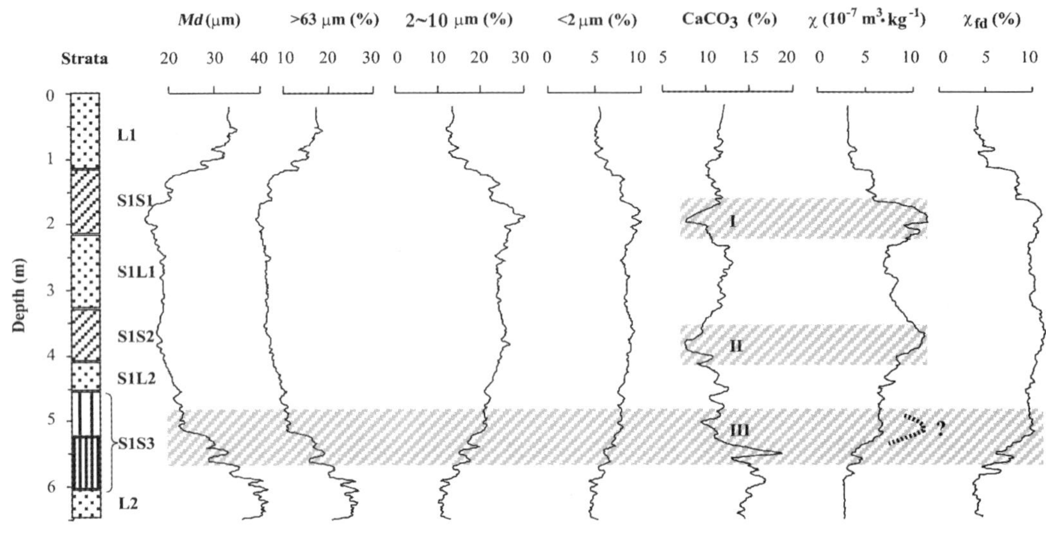

图5.11　环县剖面中值粒径（*Md*）、>63 μm含量、2～10 μm含量、<2 μm含量、$CaCO_3$含量、磁化率、频率磁化率变化曲线

我们的分析结果表明，2～10 μm的颗粒组分是磁化率的主要贡献者，这和Han和Jiang（1999）所做的不同颗粒组分对磁化率的贡献的试验结果是一致的。如果超细（<0.03 μm）的超顺磁性颗粒是控制频率磁化率的要素，而2～10 μm对高频磁化率和低频磁化率的贡献的重要性显然也不能被否认，这就与磁性矿物颗粒粒径对磁化率的贡献的经典模式图（见图5.1）有出入。也许，经风化作用附着于粉砂颗粒上的纳米级的风化壳（Cui等，1994；Liu等，1995；Maher和Thompson，2000）可以解释这种分歧。也就是说，那些超细的超顺磁性颗粒通常存在于这些风化壳中，因而2～10 μm含量不仅调节着磁化率而且左右着频率磁化率的变化。另外的可能性是超细颗粒强烈地附着在大颗粒的表面。一些研究表明氧化铁有强烈的胶结作用，对于2～20 μm含量和水稳定团聚体（>250 μm）贡献显著（Duiker等，2003；Barberis等，1991）。如果用DCB（Dithionite Citrate Bicarbonate，连二亚硫酸钠）去除土壤样品中的游离铁，那么<2 μm和<20 μm的颗粒都会明显增加（胡国成等，2002；Barberis等，1991）。而我们的粒度实验的前处理都不采用DCB处理。为了检验这种可能性，我们对若干典型样品在显微镜下做了观察，结果表明，超细颗粒的黏附主要发生在黏粒组分，而不是在2～10 μm组分。

看起来，2～10 μm是磁化率最重要的正向调控者，>63 μm是磁化率的负向控制者。黏粒含量在黄土高原东部对磁化率的贡献比较显著，在黄土高原西部地区的贡献不大。我们的解释是在风化作用相对较弱的剖面粉砂级的风化壳控制着磁化率信号；而在风化作用较强的剖面，风化产生的黏粒级的磁性颗粒决定着磁化率信号。野外观察、X射线衍射分析都显示了Bt和Bk层黏粒胶膜的存在，这意味着黏粒在S1剖面中有迁移；实验室粒度分析的黏粒结果也表明黏粒在剖面中有迁移。毫无疑问，部分磁性颗粒随着黏粒向下迁移，因此，我们得到的磁化率反映的仅仅是迁移后磁性矿物分布的情况。另外，在大多数剖面中，S1S3的发育伸入到了L2的上部，因而土壤发育强度最高的S1S3根本不能通过磁化率值反映出来。$CaCO_3$遭受的淋溶作用的强弱造成了其含量与磁化率的相关性具有不确定性，而$CaCO_3$含量与磁化率具有负相关关系主要是以下两个原因造成的：（1）风化较强并且磁化率较高的层中$CaCO_3$通常被淋失；（2）被淋溶的$CaCO_3$一般淀积在淋失层之下。但是，如果淋溶作用不是很强烈，$CaCO_3$也会在磁化率增强的风化层内积累，例如定西剖面的上部（0～2.5 m）。在这种情况下，$CaCO_3$的含量就抑制了磁化率的峰值。总而言之，使用磁化率重建末次间冰期的高分辨率气候是一件有风险的事。

参考文献

安芷生，Kukla G，Porter S C，等. 最近13万年黄土高原季风的变迁的磁化率证据. 科学通报，1990(7): 529–532.

安芷生，王俊达，李华梅. 洛川黄土剖面的古地磁研究. 地球化学，1977 (4): 239–249.

陈家坊. 土壤胶体中的氧化物. 土壤通报，1981，2: 44–49.

陈天虎，季峻峰，陈骏. 黄土中强磁性矿物透射电子显微镜观察和成因分析. 科学通报，2003，48 (17):1183–1189.

刁桂仪. 黄土中游离氧化铁的古气候意义. 地质地球化学，1982，9: 58–59.

郭正堂，彭淑贞，魏兰英，等. 二十二万年以来东亚夏季风的千年尺度变化及其在不同时期的差异. 第四纪研究，1999a，4: 299–305.

郭正堂，魏兰英，吕厚远，等. 晚第四纪风尘物质的成分变化及其环境意义. 第四纪研究，1999b，1: 41–48.

顾兆炎，韩家楙，刘东生. 中国第四纪黄土地球化学研究进展. 第四纪研究，2000，20 (1): 41–55.

韩家楙，Hus J J，刘东生，等. 马兰黄土和离石黄土的磁学性质. 第四纪研究，1991，4: 310–325.

胡国成，章明奎. 氧化铁对土粒胶结作用的矿物学证据. 土壤通报，2002，33 (1): 25–27.

胡雪峰. “黄土-古土壤”序列中氧化铁和有机质对磁化率的影响. 土壤学报，2004，41 (1): 7-11.

季峻峰，陈骏，刘连文，等. 洛川黄土中绿泥石的化学风化与磁化率增强. 自然科学进展，1999，9 (7):619-623.

贾蓉芬，李荣森，范国昌，等. 陕西段家坡黄土剖面中趋磁细菌特征与环境意义. 中国科学（D辑），1996，26 (5): 411-416.

贾蓉芬，刘东生，林本海. 陕西蓝田段家坡黄土剖面有机质磁性的初步研究. 地球化学，1992，3: 234-242.

贾蓉芬，彭先芝，高梅影，等. 中国黄土剖面趋磁细菌的组成特征与生态意义. 岩石矿物学杂志，2001，20 (4): 428-432.

贾蓉芬，彭先芝，高梅影，等. 趋磁细菌——生物地球化学作用的范例. 第四纪研究，2003，23 (5): 537-545.

雷梅，常庆瑞，冯立孝，等. 太白山土壤特性及氧化铁发生学特征. 地理研究，2001，20 (1): 83-90.

李华梅，安芷生，王俊达. 午城黄土剖面古地磁研究的初步结果. 地球化学，1974(2): 93-104.

李吉均，朱俊杰，康建成，等. 末次冰期旋回兰州黄土剖面与南极东方站冰岩芯的对比. 中国科学（B辑），1990，10: 1086-1094.

李荣森，范国昌，贾蓉芬，等. 黄土剖面中趋磁细菌及其磁小体的初步研究. 地球化学，1996，25 (3): 251-254.

刘青松，Banerjee S K，Jackson M J，等. 低温氧化作用对中国黄土记录剩磁的影响. 科学通报，2003，48 (2): 193-198.

刘秀铭，Heller F，许同春，等. 低温岩石磁学与黄土磁颗粒特征. 科学通报，1991，36 (2): 125-128

刘秀铭，刘东生，Heller F，等. 中国黄土磁化率与第四纪古气候研究. 地质科学，1992，增刊: 279-285.

刘秀铭，刘东生，Shaw J. 中国黄土磁性矿物特征及其古气候意义. 第四纪研究，1993，3: 281-287.

卢升高. 中国土壤磁性与环境. 北京：高等教育出版社，2003.

吕厚远，韩家楙，吴乃琴，等. 中国现代土壤磁化率分析及其古气候意义. 中国科学（B辑），2003，24:1290-1297.

吕厚远，刘东生. C3和C4植物及燃烧对土壤磁化率的影响. 中国科学（D辑），2001，31 (1): 43-53.

潘永信，邓成龙，刘青松，等. 趋磁细菌磁小体的生物矿化作用和磁学性质研究进展. 科学通报，2004，49 (24): 2505-2510.

彭先芝，贾蓉芬. 西峰与段家坡黄土剖面中有机质的特征及古环境信息. 地理科学，2001，21 (1): 36-40.

彭先芝，贾蓉芬，李荣森，等. 黄土-古土壤序列中趋磁细菌分布和磁小体形成的古环境研究. 科学通报，2000，45（增刊）: 2710-2715.

彭先芝，贾蓉芬，李荣森，等. 趋磁细菌及磁小体对黄土-古土壤序列磁化率贡献的模拟实验研究. 第四纪研究，2002，22 (2): 188-194.

苏志珠，董光荣. 130 ka 来陕北黄土高原北部的气候变迁. 中国沙漠，1994，14 (1): 45-51.

孙东怀，苏瑞侠，陈发虎，等. 黄土高原现代天然降尘的组成、通量和磁化率. 地理学报，2001，56 (2): 171-180.

孙东怀，周杰，蒋复初，等. 末次间冰期黄土高原夏季风气候的初步研究. 科学通报，1995，40 (20): 1873-1875.

孙继敏，丁仲礼. 浅议中国黄土磁化率的物理意义. 地球物理学进展，1995b，10 (4): 88-93.

孙继敏，丁仲礼. 近13万年来黄土高原干湿气候的时空变迁. 第四纪研究，1997，2: 168-175.

孙继敏，丁仲礼，刘东生，等. 末次间冰期以来沙漠-黄土边界带的环境演变. 第四纪研究，1995a，5: 117-122.

徐仁扣. 土壤中氧化铁的有机还原溶解动力学. 热带亚热带土壤科学，1994，3 (2): 71-76.

于天仁，陈志诚. 土壤发生过程中的化学过程. 北京：科学出版社，1990.

中国科学院地球化学研究所. 铁的地球化学. 北京：科学出版社，1981.

周杰，周卫健，陈惠忠，等. 新仙女木时期东亚夏季风降水不稳定的证据. 科学通报，1995，44 (2): 205-208.

An Z S, Kukla G, Porter S C, et al. Magnetic susceptibility evidence of monsoon variation on the Loess Plateau of central China during the last 130,000 years. Quaternary Research, 1991, 36: 29-36.

An Z S, Porter S C, Zhou W J, et al. Episode of strengthened summer monsoon climate of Younger Dryas age on the loess plateau of central China. Quaternary Research, 1993, 39: 45-54.

Barberis E, Ajmonemarsan J, Boero V, et al. Aggregation of soil particles by iron oxides in various size fractions of soil B horizons. Journal of Soil Science, 1991, 42: 535-542.

Begét J. Tephrochronolgy and paleoclimatology of the last interglacial cycle recorded in Alaska loess deposits. Quaternary International, 1996, 34-36: 121-126.

Begét J, Stone D, Hawkins D. Paleoclimate forcing of magnetic susceptibility variations in

Alaskan loess. Geology, 1990, 18: 40–43.

Blakemore R R. Magnetotactic bacteria. Science, 1975, 190: 377–379.

Chen F H, Bloemendal J, Wang J M, et al. High - resolution multiproxy climate records from Chinese loess: evidence for rapid climatic changes over the last 75 kyr. Palaeogeography, Palaeoclimatology, Palaeoecology, 1997, 130: 323–335.

Chlachula J, Evans M E, Rutter N W. A magnetic investigation of a late Quaternary loess/palaeosol record in Siberia. Geophysical Journal International, 1998, 132: 128–132.

Chlachula J, Rutter N W, Evans M E. A late Quaternary loess - paleosol record at Kurtak, southern Siberia. Canadian Journal of Earth Science, 1997, 34: 679–686.

Cui Y L, Verosub K L, Roberts A P. The effect of low–temperature oxidation on large multi - domain magnetite. Geophysical Research Letters, 1994, 21: 757–760.

Diao G Y, Wen Q Z. The paleoclimatic variation records of carbonate and iron oxides in the Weinan loess section. Chinese Journal of Geochemistry, 1997, 16 (1): 62–68.

Duiker S W, Rhoton F E, Torrent J, et al. Iron (Hydr)oxide crystalinity effects on soil aggregation. Soil Science Society of America Journal, 2003, 67: 606–611.

Fan G C, Li R S, Li X G, et al. Distribution of magnetotactic bacteria in China and characterization of magnetosomes. Chinese Science Bulletin, 1996, 41 (11): 944–948.

Fang X M, Ono Y, Fukusawa H, et al. Asian summer monsoon instability during the past 60, 000 years: magnetic susceptibility and pedogenic evidence from the western Chinese Loess Plateau. Earth and Planetary Science Letters, 1999, 168: 219–232.

Feng Z D. Climatic implications of magnetic susceptibility and ^{10}Be flux in Chinese loess. Catena, 1996, 27: 143–147.

Feng Z D. Geochemical characteristics of a loess - soil sequence in central Kansas, USA. Soil Science Society of American Journal, 1997, 61: 534–541.

Feng Z D, Johnson W C. Factors affecting the magnetic susceptibility of a loess - soil sequence, Barton County, Kansas, USA. Catena, 1995, 24: 25–37.

Feng Z D, Chen F H. Problems of magnetic susceptibility signature as the proxy of the summer monsoon intensity in Chinese Loess Plateau. International Symposium on Paleosols and Climate Change, Chinese Science Bulletin, 1999, 44 (suppl. 1): 97–104.

Feng Z D, Chen F H, Tang L Y, et al. East Asian monsoon variations and Gobi dynamics in marine isotope stages 4 and 3. Catena, 1998, 33: 29–46.

Frankel R B, Papaefthymiou G C, Blakemore R P, et al. Fe_3O_4 precipitation in magnetotactic bacteria. Biochim Biophys Acta, 1983, 763: 147–159.

Han J M, Jiang W Y. Particle size contribution to bulk magnetic susceptibility record of Chinese loess/paleosol sequence. Geophysical Journal International, 1999, 122: 97–107.

Heller F, Liu T. Magnetostratigraphic dating of loess deposits in China. Nature, 1982, 300: 431–433.

Heller F, Liu T S. Paleoclimatic and sedimentary history from magnetic susceptibility of loess in China. Geophysical Research Letters, 1986, 13 (11): 1169–1172.

Heller F, Shen C D, Beer J, et al. Quantitative estimates and paleoclimatic implications of pedogenic ferromagnetic mineral formation in Chinese loess. Earth Planetary Science Letters, 1993, 114: 385–390.

Kukla G. Loess stratigraphy in central China. Reviews, 1987, 6: 191–219.

Kukla G, An Z S. Loess stratigraphy in central China. Palaeogeography, Palaeoclimatology, Palaeoecology, 1989, 72: 203–225.

Kukla G, Heller F, Liu X M, et al. Pleistocene climates in China dated by magnetic susceptibility. Geology, 1988, 16: 811–814.

Liu X M, Hesse P, Rolph T. Origin of maghaemite in Chinese loess deposits: aeolian or pedogenic? Physics of the Earth and Planetary Interiors, 1999a, 112: 191–201.

Liu X M, Hesse P, Rolph T, et al. Properties of magnetic mineralogy of Alaskan loess: evidence for Pedogenesis. Quaternary International, 1999b, 62: 93–102.

Liu X M, Rolph T, Bloemendal J, et al. Quantitative estimates of paleoprecipitation at Xifeng, in the Loess Plateau of China. Palaeogeography, Palaeoclimatology, Palaeoecology, 1995, 113: 243–248.

Lovely R R, Stolz J F, Nord G L. Anaerobic productivity of magnetite by a dissimilatory iron-reducing microorganism. Nature, 1987, 330: 252–254.

Lowenstam H A. Minerals formed by organisms. Science, 1981, 211: 1126–1131.

Maher B A. Magnetic properties of some synthetic submicron magnetites. Geophysical Journal, 1988, 94: 83–96.

Maher B A, Alekseev A, Alekseeva T. Magnetic mineralogy of soils across the Russian steppe: climatic dependence of pedogenic magnetite formation. Palaeogeography, Palaeoclimatology, Palaeoecology, 2003a, 201: 321–341.

Maher B A, Alekseev A, Alekseeva T. Variation of soil magnetism across the Russian steppe: Its significance for use of soil magnetism as a paleorainfall proxy. Quaternary Science Review, 2002, 21: 1571–1576.

Maher B A, Hu M Y, Roberts H M, et al. Holocence loess accumulation and soil development at the western edge of the Chinese loess plateau: implications for magnetic proxies of palaeorainfall. Quaternary Science Reviews, 2003b, 22: 445–451.

Maher B A, Thompson R. mineral magnetic record of the Chinese loess and paleosols. Geology, 1991, 19: 3–8.

Maher B A, Thompson R. Paleorainfall reconstructions from pedogenic magnetic susceptibility variations in the Chinese loess and paleosols. Quaternary Research, 1995, 44: 383–391.

Maher B A, Thompson R. Paleomonsoons I: the magnetic record of palaeoclimate in the terrestrial loess and paleosol sequence // Maher B A, Thompson R. Quaternary Climates, Environments and Magnetism. New York: Cambridge University Press, 2000: 83–125.

Maher B A, Thompson R, Zhou L P. Spatial and temporal reconstructions of changes in the Asian paleomonsoon: A new mineral magnetic approach. Earth Planetary Science Letters, 1994, 125: 461–471.

Maher B A, Thompson R. Pedogenesis and paleoclimate: interpretation of the magnetic susceptibility record of Chinese loess - paleosol sequences: comment. Geology, 1994, 22: 857–858.

Meng X M, Debershire E, Kemp R A. Origin of the magnetic susceptibility signal in Chinese loess. Quaternary Science Reviews, 1997, 16: 833–839.

Rivers J M, Nyquist J E, Roh Y, et al. Investigation into the origin of magnetic soils on the Oak Ridge Reservation, Tennessee. Soil Science Society of America Journal, 1999, 68: 1772–1779.

Sun J M, Liu T S. Multiple origins and interpretations of the magnetic susceptibility signal in Chinese wind-blown sediments. Earth and Planetary Science Letters, 2000, 180: 287–296.

Thompson R, Oldfield F. Environmental Magnetism. London: Allen & Unwin, 1986.

Verosub K L, Fine P, Singer M J. Pedogenesis and paleoclimate: interpretation of the magnetic susceptibility record of Chinese loess-paleosol sequence. Geology, 1993, 21: 1011–1014.

Zhou L P, Oldfield F, Wintle A C, et al. Partly pedogenic origin of magnetic variations in Chinese loess. Nature, 1990, 346: 737–739.

6 定西剖面、天水剖面、蓝田剖面S1地理分异的进一步研究

土壤的形态特征、微形态特征、矿物风化程度以及一些物理化学指标都可以确定土壤的风化程度。就化学风化而言，氧化铁及其游离度、硅铝比（SiO_2/Al_2O_3）、淋溶指数［（Na_2O+K_2O+CaO）/Al_2O_3］、Rb/Sr都是良好的土壤风化指标（Chen等，1999；Guo等，1996；郭正堂等，1999a；刁桂仪，1982）。

我们选择的剖面是定西剖面、天水剖面和蓝田剖面，理由是这三个剖面气候—植被梯度显著，便于探讨风化作用的地理分异。

6.1 定西剖面、天水剖面、蓝田剖面的土壤微形态特征

6.1.1 定西剖面

对剖面自下而上进行了土壤微形态观察，L2为块状结构（Massive），颗粒较粗（见图6.1.a）。S1S3的底部与L2的土壤微形态相似，不过可观察到碳酸钙斑点和浸染状的黏粒分布（红褐色），可能与上层的淋溶有关（见图6.1.b），反映当时土壤生物扰动微弱，植被覆盖度低。S1S3的中上部呈强烈的团聚细颗粒并有黏粒胶膜出现（见图6.1.c），是发育较好的S1S3的B层的典型特征。S1S3的上部，黏粒嵌于基质（Groundmass）中，次生的碳酸钙附着在孔道壁上（见图6.1.d），可能的过程是孔道周围的基质脱钙后碳酸钙重新淀积。S1L2为带碳酸钙斑点的块状结构（见图6.1.e），反映了相对干冷、地表裸露的环境条件。S1S2土壤亦缺乏结构，可见黏粒分布于基质中（见图6.1.f），指示了一定的残积黏化作用。S1L1表现为海绵状微结构，与图6.1.b比较接近，指示了微弱的土壤发育。S1S1表现为中等破碎棱块状微结构（见图6.1.g），

表 6.1 定西剖面铁与磁化率、频率磁化率和$CaCO_3$的相关系数（$n=121$）

变量	Fet	Fetr	Fed	Fedr	Fed/Fet
χ	0.549	0.493	0.716	0.696	0.616
χ_{fd}	0.642	0.685	0.806	0.819	0.690
$CaCO_3$	−0.384	0.170*	−0.183*	0.020	−0.034*
>63 μm	−0.838	−0.870	−0.622	−0.621	−0.372
2～10 μm	0.779	0.863	0.678	0.698	0.472
<2 μm	0.145*	0.373	0.232	0.315	0.231*

*未通过0.01置信水平上的验证。

6.2.1.2 天水剖面

Fet和Fed的总体趋势表现为“括号形”，由Fet和Fetr曲线无法判别出对应于S1S1、S1S2和S1S3的3次成壤过程的界线。条带Ⅱ的游离度（Fed/Fet）表现为一个次高峰，野外观察到对应深度的土壤当中出现较多的黏粒胶膜，我们猜测铁的游离度的次高峰正是这些黏粒淀积的结果，即少量的黏粒淀积亦足以显著提升铁的游离度。图6.5中2段（虚线之间）的游离度、Fed和Fet值的降低可能与粉尘加积速率增高对风化过程的阻滞有关，如我们在上一章所指出的，1段（虚线之间）极可能是S1S2与S1S3融合的残余特征。整个条带Ⅰ可能囊括S1S2、S1L2的全部和S1S3顶部。有意思的是，图6.5中的1段（两虚线之间）的游离度和游离氧化铁的含量出现了一个峰值，然而磁化率和频率磁化率对此无任何响应，而且对应的较细颗粒（<2 μm，2～10 μm）的含量整体趋势也是降低的。这种现象指示风化作用产生了较多的游离铁，而且可能是源区的风化作用占主导作用；或者可能是风化过程中产生的磁性矿物包含了较多的针铁矿抑或磁性矿物的颗粒较大。从表6.2可以看到，$CaCO_3$与Fet、Fed的相关性很高，尽管如此，$CaCO_3$对Fet和Fed的影响却有不同的意义，校正前后相关系数的差异表明Fet受$CaCO_3$的影响显著，可是$CaCO_3$对Fed几乎没有任何影响。之所以Fed与$CaCO_3$有显著的相关关系，是因为游离氧化铁的生成首先取决于风尘沉积中铁的总量。Fet和Fed与各个粒级含量的相关系数证明铁是亲细颗粒的物质，并且倾向于在2～10 μm的粒级富集。

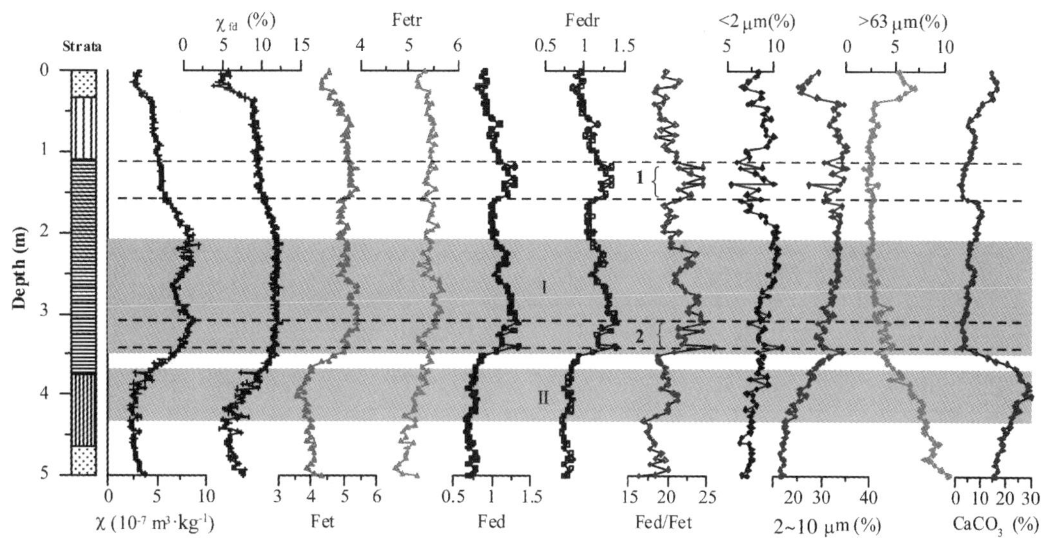

图 6.5　天水剖面磁化率(χ)、频率磁化率(χ_{fd})、全铁含量(Fet)、Fetr、游离铁含量(Fed)、Fedr、游离度(Fed/Fet)、粒度、$CaCO_3$的变化曲线

Fetr为去掉$CaCO_3$后计算的氧化铁总量，Fetr=Fet/(1−$CaCO_3$%)

Fedr为去掉$CaCO_3$后计算的游离氧化铁含量，Fedr=Fed/(1−$CaCO_3$%)

表 6.2　天水剖面铁与磁化率、频率磁化率和$CaCO_3$的相关系数 (n=101)

变量	Fet	Fetr	Fed	Fedr	Fed/Fet
χ	0.781	0.664	0.786	0.787	0.625
χ_{fd}	0.731	0.725	0.741	0.743	0.601
$CaCO_3$	−0.965	−0.625	−0.889	−0.889	−0.604
>63 μm	−0.845	−0.842	−0.766	−0.768	−0.536
2～10 μm	0.821	0.828	0.723	0.725	0.484
<2 μm	0.410	0.427	0.377	0.379	0.277

6.2.1.3　蓝田剖面

蓝田剖面Bt层游离氧化铁含量呈现出一个缺少频繁波动的高峰，A层和BC层的含量相对较少，这是“单一型”土壤剖面具备的典型特征（Birkeland，1999），这显然同黏粒（Fed与<2 μm的相关系数为0.690）在Bt层中部的淀积有关（见图6.6），反映了地表在很长的时间内处于稳定状态。从图6.6可以看到，粒度自2.5 m以下至4.5 m处逐渐变粗，Fed和Fed/Fet虽然有所降低，但大体维持在某个水平之上，较天水剖面和定西剖面的值都高。这意味着由于地表状况非常稳定，土壤持续向下发育促使游离铁就地生成，同时黏粒的迁移也是游离铁含量增高的原因。Fet和Fed与各个粒级的相关系数表明在风化作用强烈的黄土高原东南边缘铁更倾向于

在黏粒级颗粒中富集，这与天水剖面和定西剖面的铁在2～10 μm富集有所不同。$CaCO_3$与Fet、Fetr和Fed、Fedr的相关系数再次表明Fet受$CaCO_3$的制约非常明显，Fed则不受$CaCO_3$的影响。

表6.3　蓝田剖面铁与磁化率、频率磁化率和$CaCO_3$的相关系数（n=106）

变量	Fet	Fetr	Fed	Fedr	Fed/Fet
χ	0.282	0.651	0.393	0.393	0.396
χ_{fd}	0.242	0.742	0.341	0.342	0.333
$CaCO_3$	−0.944	−0.360	−0.877	−0.877	−0.854
>63 μm	−0.158	−0.660	−0.246	−0.247	−0.241
2～10 μm	0.250	0.631	0.329	0. 329	0. 325
<2 μm	0.575	0.693	0.690	0.690	0.693

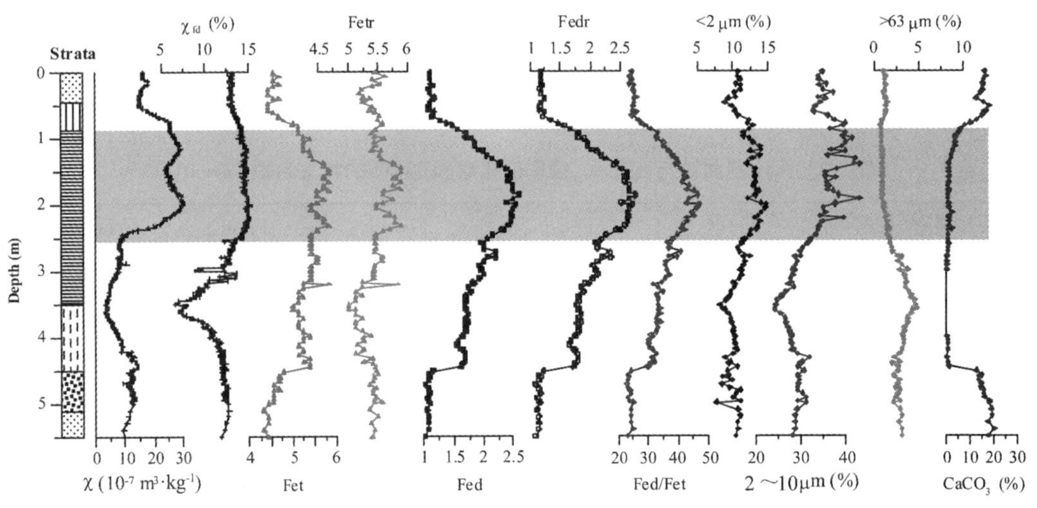

图6.6　蓝田剖面磁化率（χ）、频率磁化率（χ_{fd}）、全铁含量（Fet）、Fetr、游离铁含量（Fed）、Fedr、游离度（Fed/Fet）、粒度、$CaCO_3$的变化曲线

Fetr为去掉$CaCO_3$后计算的氧化铁总量，Fetr=Fet/（1-$CaCO_3$%）

Fedr为去掉$CaCO_3$后计算的游离氧化铁含量，Fedr=Fed/（1-$CaCO_3$%）

从黄土高原西部的定西剖面、天水剖面到黄土高原东部的蓝田剖面，Fed、Fed/Fet的值总体是逐渐增大的，意味着风化作用逐渐增强。尤其是蓝田剖面铁的游离度峰值超过了40%，可能处于脱硅富铁化阶段（常庆瑞等，1999）。从上述3个剖面磁化率或频率磁化率与Fet和Fed的相关系数来看，Fed对磁化率的贡献比Fet对磁化率的贡献要稍大些，表明成壤风化作用确实可以增强磁化率。总的说来，铁倾向于在细颗粒部分富集，随着风化作用的加强，黏粒含量与Fed或Fet的相关系数呈增高的趋势，反映了风化过程形成的次生氧化铁向黏粒富集的趋势。由相关系数判断，$CaCO_3$对Fet的影响是非常显著的，Fetr曲线与Fet曲线的较大差异可以证明其影响。$CaCO_3$和Fed的相关系数与$CaCO_3$和Fedr的相关系数差距很小，表明淋溶过程对游离氧化铁几乎没有影响，Fed或Fed/Fet是更可靠的风化指标。但是需要指出的是，黏粒在剖面中的迁移必然导致游离氧化铁的迁移，尽管数量可能非常有限。

6.2.2 其他地球化学指标所反映的古土壤S1化学风化的地理分异

土壤发生的实质是各种元素的重新组合及其迁移（陈家坊，1981），而表生作用过程中化学元素的迁移富集是元素对环境条件变化响应的表现。地球化学的观点认为土壤的风化产物可以分为残留部分和移动部分，因此，可以计算土壤或黏粒中各有关元素的比值以判断物质的残留或迁移。例如，灰壤B层的硅铁铝率比A_2层为低，意味着铁和铝从A_2层迁移出而在B层淀积。又如，矿物中的K_2O、Na_2O和CaO易于淋失，而Al_2O_3则较稳定，因此（K_2O+Na_2O+CaO）/Al_2O_3物质的量比被建议作为风化程度的一个指标，该比率越大则风化程度越低。块状岩石中的K_2O和Na_2O的含量相近，其K/Na约在0.8～0.9之间，而海水中的K/Na则在0.035～0.038之间，表明在风化过程中淋溶速率是Na大于K，因此，土壤或土壤黏粒中K_2O / Na_2O物质的量比也可用作迁移值的计算（Jackson，1979）。K_2O / Na_2O还同硅酸盐矿物中K的释放有关，其比值也可指示土壤中斜长石的风化程度。

Chen等（1999）对洛川黄土-古土壤化学风化过程的研究发现，以Al的变化率为参照，黄土中绝大多数元素都保持稳定，活动性元素仅有Ca、Sr、P、Mg和Na；化学风化处于脱Ca、Na的初级阶段。Gu等（1997）应用^{10}Be作为示踪剂对黄土中古土壤的风化淋滤程度进行估算，结果是Ca、Na、Mg和U的淋滤程度较高，Si和K淋滤的程度较低。刁桂仪和文启忠（1999）对渭南黄土剖面中主要化学组分在风化成土过程中的迁移富集的研究表明，$CaCO_3$、FeO、MgO、Na_2O、K_2O、SiO_2以迁移为主，而Al_2O_3、Fe_2O_3、TiO_2等以淀积为主。康建成和穆德芬（1998）对北塬剖面的地球化学分析研究表明古土壤层中元素的迁移能力按下列顺序排列：Ca^{2+}>Mg^{2+}>Fe^{3+}>K^{+}>Na^{+} >Si^{4+}>Fe^{2+}>Al^{3+}（原文如此，但笔者认为Fe^{3+}、Fe^{2+}的顺序应该互换）。这些研究均表明，中国黄土-古土壤的化学风化为去除易溶碱性元素的过程。微量元素中，Rb、Sr、U和Ce在古土壤中易于淋失，Th、Sc、Co、Zr、Hf、Ti和Nb等在母岩风化、搬运、沉积和后期成壤过程中几乎等量地转移到沉积物中而不发生迁移或流失（Galllet等，1996）。

进而，元素地球化学分析为提取黄土-古土壤序列中蕴藏的古气候和古环境提供了新的思路。Liu等（1995）基于Ti在风化过程中难移动性及抗风化的石英矿物在粉尘组粒级富集的特征，提出SiO_2/TiO_2比值可以作为冬季风强度的的替代指标。由于Si和Al在土壤中相对稳定，SiO_2/Al_2O_3比值与<50 μm粒级含量有良好的线性关系，Peng和Guo（2001）认为硅铝率（SiO_2/Al_2O_3）可以作为另外一个可供选择的冬季风的代用指标。Zr和Rb在黄土—古土壤中的地球化学行为都相对稳定，受成壤作用的影响小。Rb倾向于在黏粒级的细颗粒富集，而Zr多存在于锆石中，而锆石抗物理风化能力强，基本能保持原来的形态，与石英、长石等在粗颗粒富集，因此Zr/Rb比值的变化反映了粗、细颗粒含量的相对含量，故Zr/Rb比值也可以作为冬季风的指标（Liu等，2002）。由于影响磁化率的因素较多，成壤过程又未必是增强磁化率的，因此，寻找新的夏季风代用指标非常必要。Guo等（1996）将土壤学中常用的铁的游离度和淋溶指数引入了黄土研究，并将它们作为夏季风的代用指标。关于铁的游离度，我们已经在上节有所表述，这里不再重复。Guo等将淋溶指数（K_2O+Na_2O+CaO）/Al_2O_3修改为（$Na_2O+CaO+Al_2O_3$）/Al_2O_3并称之为化学风化指数（CIW）。研究表明，Rb主要赋存于较稳定的含K矿物（如云母、钾长石和伊利石）中，而Sr主要赋存在易风化的含Ca的矿物（如角闪石、斜长石、辉石、碳酸盐）中，因此，含Ca矿物的风化和Sr迁出，必然造成风化剖面中Rb/Sr比值的升高。Rb/Sr比值主要取决于Sr的淋失程度，Sr的淋失程度又受制于降水的多少，在黄土高原降水量的大小又受控于夏季风的盛衰，因此，陈骏等（1997）将Rb/Sr比值作为夏季风的替代性指标。

本小节将通过淋溶指数（K_2O+Na_2O+CaO）/Al_2O_3、硅铝率SiO_2/Al_2O_3、硅铁铝率$SiO_2/(Fe_2O_3+Al_2O_3)$、硅钛比SiO_2/TiO_2、钾钠比K/Na、铷锶比Rb/Sr、锆铷比Zr/Rb等指标来考察定西、天水、蓝田3个剖面的化学风化的地理分异。

6.2.2.1 定西剖面

从图6.7可以看到，淋溶指数（Leaching Index）与$CaCO_3$含量的变化具有高度的一致性。总体看来，淋溶指数在每个土壤（S1S1、S1S2、S1S3）的上部较小，在土壤的下部较大，意味着淋溶作用不太强，因此，$CaCO_3$的淀积深度非常浅。K_2O/Na_2O比值呈现出向较早的年代递增的趋势。有意思的是，图中的Ⅰ灰色条带的淋溶指数在整个剖面中处于非常突出的低谷，硅铝铁率$SiO_2/(Al_2O_3+Fe_2O_3)$和硅钛比值SiO_2/TiO_2也处于极端的谷值，而且游离铁的含量和游离度都很高，似乎指示了强烈的风化淋溶过程。但是在Ⅰ带的下部$CaCO_3$并没有出现对应的显著的淀积，并且K_2O/Na_2O表明K也没有相对Na在Ⅰ带富集。我们怀疑这种强烈的风化淋溶迹象可能主要继承自源区，也就是说，源区的风化作用使得细物质增多、$CaCO_3$含量降低、Al和Fe相对富集，并且使Fe的游离度增大。S1（0.7～5.5 m，平均值为15.09%）的$CaCO_3$含量比上覆黄土段和下伏黄土段的（平均值为14.38%）要高。部分原因可能是由于末次间冰期降水的增加导致生物量的增加，从而引起植物根系和微生物的呼吸作用加强以及引起微生物对植物残体的分解作用增强，最终使土壤中CO_2浓度增高、有机酸增多，水的活性增大，促使硅酸盐矿物中Ca的释放（于天仁和陈志诚，1990）。概而言之，在风化较弱的西部地区，化学元素或成分在剖面中的变化需要考虑其对母质的继承性。

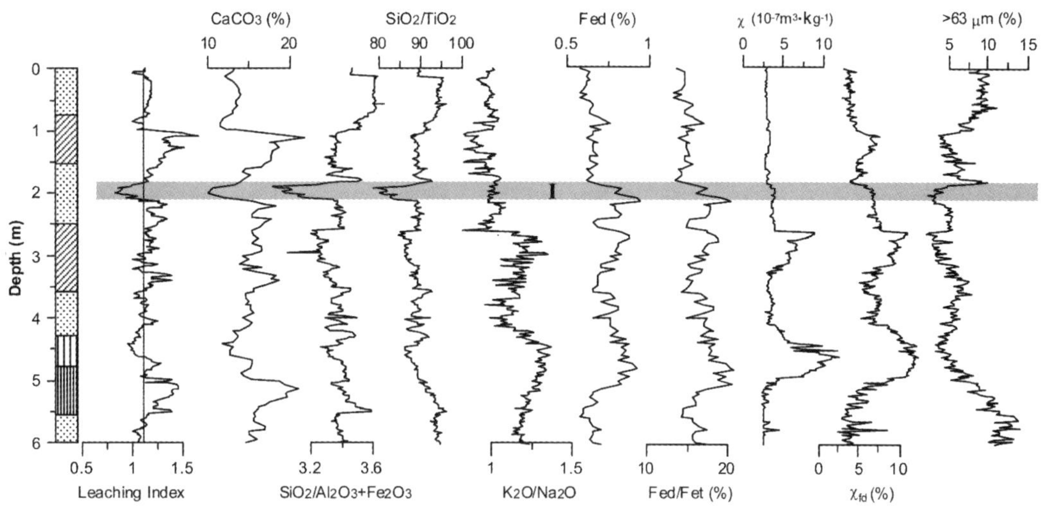

图6.7　定西剖面淋溶指数(Leaching Index)、$CaCO_3$含量、硅铝铁率$SiO_2/(Al_2O_3+Fe_2O_3)$、SiO_2/TiO_2比值、K_2O/Na_2O比值、游离铁含量、游离度、磁化率、频率磁化率、>63 μm变化曲线

$$\text{Leaching Index}=(K_2O+Na_2O+CaO)/Al_2O_3$$

6.2.2.2　天水剖面

天水剖面的淋溶指数（见图6.8）显示土壤A层和Bt层的易溶元素等（如Ca、Na、K）淋失严重，Bk接受了上层淋溶物质。从细节上说淋溶指数、硅铝铁率、硅钛比、K_2O/Na_2O比值、Rb/Sr比值、游离铁的含量以及铁的游离度指示了Ⅰ、Ⅱ、Ⅲ条带发生了较强的风化作用。但是，Ⅰ带存在着看似矛盾的地方：第一，Ⅰ带的SiO_2/TiO_2比值处于整条曲线的最低谷，与前面提到的几个指标相比有异常的表现；第二，磁化率在此带不是很高。我们猜测，Ⅰ带的风化特征既继承了母质的特性，又受到沉积后成壤改造。值得一提的是Zr/Rb比值在剖面中的表现，在总体趋势上，Zr/Rb比值的变化与K_2O/Na_2O比值、Rb/Sr比值、游离铁的含量以及铁的游离度等相反，而与淋溶指数、硅铝铁率和硅钛比的变化同向。但在次一级的变化上，却存在相反的表现，例如Ⅰ带和Ⅱ带。或者说，在S1当中Zr/Rb比的谷值区相对于Fed/Fet等的峰值区有一定的滞后性。这个滞后性首先是由Rb的地球化学行为的活跃性和Zr的稳定性造成的，也可能是由于黏粒对Rb较强的吸附性使然，换言之，Rb对少量的黏粒迁移的反应非常敏感。若果真如此，则将Zr/Rb比作为冬季风的代

用指标是不恰当的。

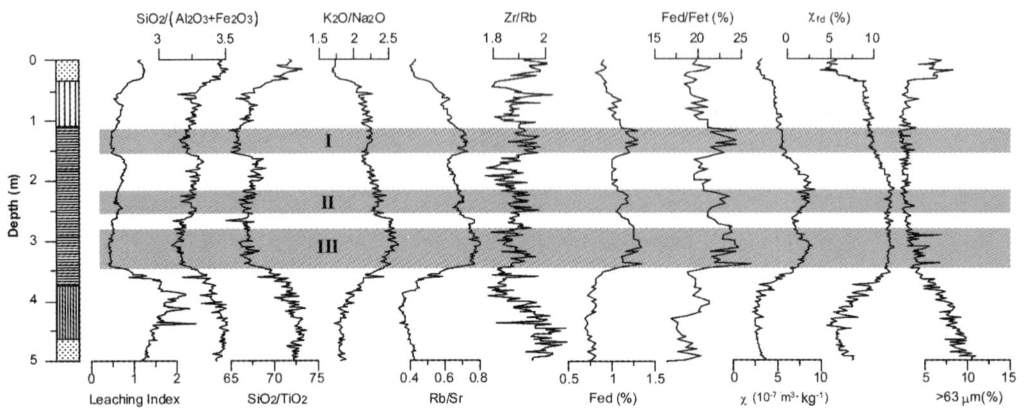

图6.8　天水剖面淋溶指数(Leaching Index)、$CaCO_3$含量、硅铝铁率$SiO_2/(Al_2O_3+Fe_2O_3)$、SiO_2/TiO_2比值、K_2O/Na_2O比值、Rb/Sr比值、Zr/Rb比值、游离铁含量、游离度、磁化率、频率磁化率、>63 μm变化曲线

Leaching Index＝$(K_2O+Na_2O+CaO)/Al_2O_3$

6.2.2.3　蓝田剖面

蓝田剖面的Bt和BC层（0.8～4.5 m）的淋溶作用表现得非常强烈和彻底（图6.9），淋溶指数曲线近乎一条直线。如图6.9，SiO_2/TiO_2比值在Ⅰ、Ⅱ灰色条带是两个谷值，而硅铝铁率（$SiO_2/Al_2O_3+Fe_2O_3$）的谷值区“1”段（虚线之间）落后于Ⅰ带、“2”段（虚线之间）落后于Ⅱ带，反映了黄土高原的东南端在末次间冰期的土壤S1由于丰沛的降水和充足的热量（高温）发生了一定的脱硅富铁铝作用。K_2O/Na_2O比值的两个峰值亦对应于1、2段，对SiO_2/TiO_2比值的谷值也是落后的，这反映了S1

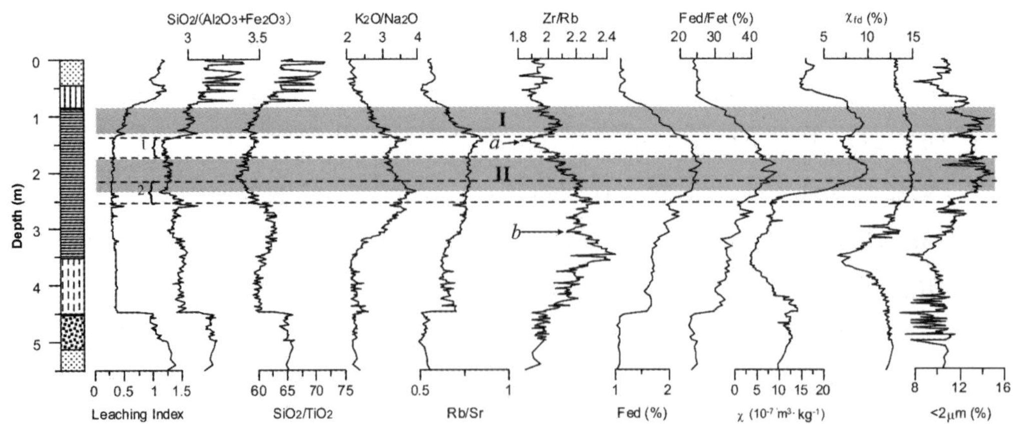

图6.9　蓝田剖面淋溶指数(Leaching Index)、$CaCO_3$含量、硅铝铁率$SiO_2/(Al_2O_3+Fe_2O_3)$、SiO_2/TiO_2比值、K_2O/Na_2O比值、Rb/Sr比值、Zr/Rb比值、游离铁含量、游离度、磁化率、频率磁化率、<2 μm变化曲线

Leaching Index＝（K_2O+Na_2O+CaO）/ Al_2O_3

发育过程经历了去K阶段（Nesbitt等，1980）。Zr/Rb比值的两个峰值*a*、*b*可能还反映了黏粒的迁移淀积过程，不过，由于Bt层和BC层通体淋溶作用强盛，Rb的淋失严重，*a*、*b*都没有明显低于黄土层的Zr/Rb比值。

综上所述，由于黄土高原气候梯度和植被带梯度的存在，土壤发育的地理分异非常显著。在黄土高原西部的定西剖面，风化作用处于初级的脱碱（去Ca、Na）阶段。由于风化作用较弱，化学成分在剖面的变化存在着对沉积前母质的继承的特点。在黄土高原西部的东南端（天水剖面），风化淋溶作用明显加强，Zr/Rb比值显示黏粒的迁移显著，但风化作用仍处于初级的去Ca、Na阶段。在黄土高原东部的东南边缘（蓝田剖面），土壤风化淋溶作用非常强烈，K_2O/Na_2O比值的变化反映出土壤发育经历了中级的去K阶段，而硅铝铁率甚至反映出了土壤发育进入了脱硅阶段。

参考文献

常庆瑞，冯立孝，闫湘. 陕西汉中土壤氧化铁及其发生学意义研究. 土壤通报，1999，30 (1): 14–16.

陈家坊. 土壤胶体中的氧化物. 土壤通报，1981，2: 44–49.

陈骏，季俊峰，仇纲. 陕西洛川黄土化学风化程度的地球化学研究.中国科学（D辑），1997，27（6）：531–536.

刁桂仪. 黄土中游离氧化铁的古气候意义. 地质地球化学，1982，9: 58–59.

刁桂仪，文启忠. 黄土成土过程中主要元素迁移序列. 地质地球化学，1999，27（1）：21–26.

郭正堂，刘东生，吴乃琴，等. 最后两个冰期黄土中记录的Heinrich型气候节拍. 第四纪研究，1996，1: 21–29.

郭正堂，彭淑贞，魏兰英，等. 二十二万年以来东亚夏季风的千年尺度变化及其在不同时期的差异. 第四纪研究，1999a，4: 299–305.

郭正堂，魏兰英，吕厚远，等. 晚第四纪风尘物质的成分变化及其环境意义. 第四纪研究，1999b，1: 41–48.

郝青振，郭正堂. 1.2 Ma以来黄土–古土壤序列风化成壤强度的定量化研究与东亚夏季风演化. 中国科学（D辑），2001，31 (6): 520–528.

康建成，穆德芬. 甘肃临夏黄土剖面地球化学特征. 兰州大学学报：自然科学版，1998，34（2）：119–125.

于天仁，陈志诚.土壤发生中的化学过程. 北京：科学出版社，1990.

魏建晶，郭正堂. 900 ka以来黄土–古土壤序列记录的风尘铁含量变化及其古气候意义.

科学通报，2003，48 (11): 1214-1218.

魏明建，孙建中，封达庄，等. 黄土中铁与25万年来的古气候. 西安地质学院学报，1988，3: 93-99.

杨石岭，丁仲礼. 7.0 Ma以来中国北方风尘沉积的游离铁/全铁值变化及其古季风指示意义. 科学通报，2000，45 (22): 2453-2456.

张宗祜，魏明建. 黄土中全氧化铁与气候指标的定量关系. 科学通报，1995，40 (13): 1219-1221.

Birkeland P W. Soils and Geomorphology. 3rd ed. New York: Oxford University Press, 1999.

Chen J, An Z S, Head J. Variation of Rb/Sr ratios in the loess - paleosol sequences of central China during the last 130,000 years and their implications for monsoon paleoclimatology. Quaternary Research, 1999, 51： 215-219.

Gallet S, Jahn B, Torii M. Geochemical characterization of the Luochuan loess - paleosol sequence, China, and paleoclimatic implications. Chemical Geology, 1996, 133: 67-88.

Gu Z Y, Lal D, Liu T S, et al. Weathering histories of Chinese loess deposits based on U - Th series nuclides and cosmogenic ^{10}Be. Geochimica et Cosmochimica Acta, 1997, 61: 5221-5231.

Guo Z T, Liu T S, Fedoroff N, et al. Climate extremes in loess of China coupled with the strength of deep - water formation in the North Atlantic. Global and Planetary Change, 1998, 18: 113-128.

Guo Z T, Liu T S, Guiot J, et al. High frequency pulses of east Asian monsoon climate in the last two glaciations: link with the North Atlantic. Climate Dynamics, 1996, 12: 701-709.

Jackson N L. Soil chemical analyses — Advanced course. 3rd ed. Madison: University of Wisconsin, 1979.

Ji J F, Chen J, Balsam W, et al. High resolution hematite/goethite records from Chinese loess sequences for the last glacial - interglacial cycle: rapid climatic response of the East Asian monsoon to the tropic Pacific. Geophysical Research Letters, 2004, 31: 203-207.

Liu L, Chen J, Chen Y, et al. Variation of Zr/Rb ratios on the Loess Plateau of Central China during the last 130000 years and its implications for winter monsoon. Chinese Science Bulletin, 2002, 47(15): 1298-1302.

Liu X M, Rolph T, Bloemendal J, et al. Quantitative estimates of paleoprecipitation at Xifeng, in the Loess Plateau of China. Palaeogeography, Palaeoclimatology, Palaeoecology, 1995, 113: 243-248.

Nesbitt H W, Markovics G, Price R C. Chemical processes affecting alkalis and alkaline earths during continental weathering. Geochim Cosmochim Acta, 1980, 44 (1): 1659-1666.

Peng S Z, Guo Z T. Geochemical indicator of original eolian grain size and the implications on winter monsoon evolution. Sciences in China (Series D), 2001, 44 (Suppl): 261-266.

附录

黄土高原西部地区黄土粒度的环境指示意义*

汪海斌，陈发虎，张家武

摘要：通常把>30 μm颗粒含量作为冬季风的替代指标。对黄土高原西部地区的兰州九州台剖面、西宁土巷道剖面粒度主成分和聚类分析表明：>40 μm颗粒的含量是黄土高原西部地区更为敏感的古冬季风替代指标，<2 μm颗粒含量的变化所指示的古气候意义可能与黄土高原中部地区不同。

Abstract: Chinese loess paleosol sequence has provided some the most detailed terrestrial records of climate changes in Quaternary. Grain size and magnetic susceptibility have proved to be good proxies of East Asian Winter Monsoon and Summer Monsoon variations respectively. Studies on loess sections through Loess Plateau in Central China suggested that >30 μm size fraction is a sensitive proxy of winter monsoon strength for central part of loess plateau. However, one thing that should be reemphasized is that grain size distribution becomes finer leeward, from northwest through southeast, gradually on Chinese Loess Plateau. Therefore >30 μm size fraction should be argued when it was issued as an indicator of winter monsoon strength of west Chinese Loess Plateau. While western part of Chinese Loess Plateau has great potentials to provide much higher - resolution climatic records than Central Chinese Loess Plateau does. So it is necessary to find out a sensitive proxy of winter monsoon strength for West Chinese Loess Plateau. This paper focuses on discussing grain size distribution characteristics of two typical loess sections, Tuxiangdao Section in Xining and Jiuzhoutai Section in Lanzhou, on West Chinese Loess Plateau so as to obtain related climatic information and appropriate proxy of winter monsoon strength.

Using SPSS for Window 8.0, we conduct Principal Component Analysis on amounts of size distribution data of these two Loess sections. Output accomplished with SPSS shows that the cumulative loading of the initial three components of Jiuzhoutai section and Tuxiangdao section accounts for 95.37%, 96.07% respectively, which suggests that these three extracted principal components are fully credible. Results also indicate that the first component and the

* 本文发表于：中国沙漠，2002，22(1)：21-26.

third component is linked to winter monsoon variation in Jiuzhoutai section; while the first component and the second component is related to winter monsoon variation in Tuxlangdao section. To determine candidate for winter monsoon strength proxy, we employ classifying analysis that is a useful way to tell threshold value. The threshold level is 40.2～43.9 μm in Jiuzhoutai section and 38.9～42.6 μm in Tuxiangdao section. Therefore, we conclude that coarser size fraction > 40 μm is a proper indicator of winter monsoon strength for west Chinese Loess Plateau.

关键词：风尘；冬季风；古气候；主成分分析

Key words: eolian dust; winter monsoon; paleoclimate; Principal Component Analysis

中国分类号：P532　　**文献标识码**：A

中国黄土高原黄土-古土壤堆积序列是记录第四纪气候变化的最佳陆源载体之一[1]，其粒度、磁化率分别是记录了东亚冬季风、夏季风演化历史的良好替代性指标。中国黄土高原的古气候记录与全球其他地区的气候记录对比，表明中国黄土高原的古气候记录具有全球意义。指示东亚冬季风变迁的常用替代指标有中值粒径、平均粒径、>30 μm粗颗粒含量、>40 μm粗颗粒含量[2-8]，另外，肖举乐等曾用提纯的石英颗粒的含量作为反映冬季风的代用指标[9]。中值粒径大致反映了粒度组成的平均状况（与平均粒径较为接近，但比平均粒径小），由于受到后期成壤作用的影响，尤其是在黄土高原中东部地区所受影响更甚，所以真实细致的古气候信息可能得不到可靠的反映。相对而言，用粗颗粒含量指标来反映东亚冬季风变化更为敏感。鹿化煜等对黄土高原中部的洛川地区的粒度的古气候意义做过细致的研究工作，指出>40 μm粗颗粒含量是冬季风敏感的代用指标[3-5]。不过需要强调的是，黄土高原内部的粒度组成具有向下风向（从西北到东南）逐渐变细的特征。基于这一事实，鹿化煜等[10]在六盘山以东地区，由北向南取3个剖面研究了粒度的空间分布特征，认为冬季风指标的选取需考虑黄土堆积区与源地的远近。因此，将>30 μm粗颗粒含量同样作为黄土高原西部地区敏感的冬季风指标值得进一步的讨论。同时，鉴于黄土高原西部地区在提供高分辨率（如L_1中2 cm≈100 a，S_1中2 cm≈200 a）的气候记录方面比黄土高原中部地区更有潜力[5-8, 11-13]，因此，有必要对黄土高原西部地区的粒度分布特征进行研究，以提取相关的古气候信息，获得敏感的东亚冬季风代用指标。

1 材料与方法

1.1 样品采集与实验室处理

样品采自黄土高原西部两个典型的黄土剖面（图1）：（1）兰州九州台剖面，黄土堆积深厚，是良好的天然剖面[11]。所采样品为S_1、S_2古土壤层，并在各古土壤层顶部往上、底部往下各采2 m左右。以2 cm厚度连续采样，每段古土壤层各得650个样品，总计1300个样品。（2）西宁土巷道剖面，按2～4 cm间隔采样，共采样品347个[8]。

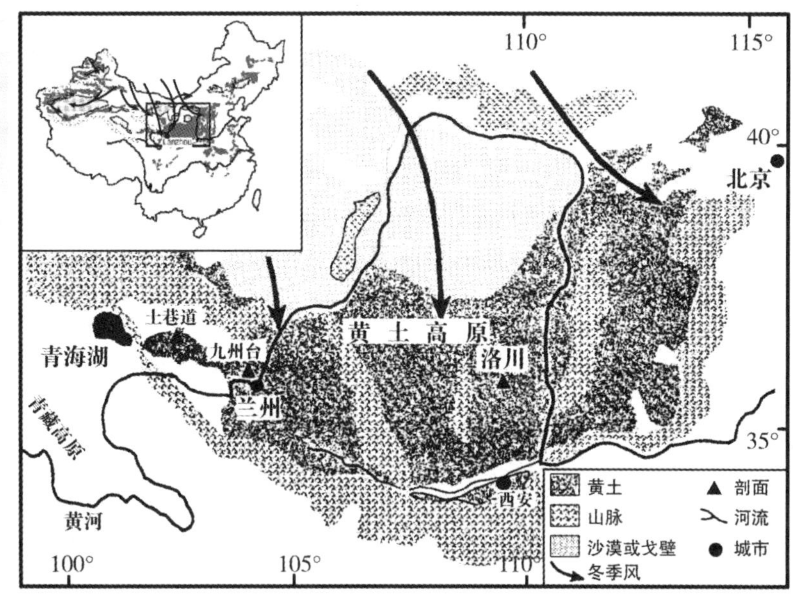

图1 九州台剖面与土巷道剖面位置示意图

Fig. 1 Location of Jiuzhoutai section and Tuxiangdao section

粒度样品的实验室处理过程同文献［7］，所不同的是，对所有样品进行洗酸处理，即将样品溶液用蒸馏水洗至中性，除去离子。超声振荡时间为7 min。实验证明，7 min可以将样品充分分散，延长时间可以击碎较大颗粒，反而影响粒度的测量。九州台粒度样品测量在兰州大学资源环境学院环境分析实验室用英国Malvern公司制造的Mastersizer 2000型粒度仪完成。Mastersizer 2000型粒度仪测量精度高，实验误差小。土巷道粒度样品在英国Liverpool大学用美国生产的Coulter粒度仪完成。

1.2 数据处理

提取冬季风的代用指标，主成分分析（原理与基本过程见文献［13］）是有效的手段之一[5, 15]。主成分分析之前先要对粒度进行粒径分级。研究表明，风力搬运（输送）与粒径大小呈指数关系，而不是呈线性关系[16]，因此，本文的粒级划分均是按照对数尺度由粒度仪配套软件给出的。由于九州台剖面粒度与土巷道剖面粒度在分级上存在差别，这就首先需要检验分级对主成分分析结果的影响：第一，需要检验粒径范围对分析结果的影响；第二，需要检验分级数目对分析结果的影响。限于手头无土巷道剖面的原始粒度测量数据，这里仅分析九州台剖面的粒度。将九州台粒度按两种粒径范围进行分析：0.25～128 μm（>128 μm单列为一级），0.37～219.86 μm。然后将0.25～128 μm粒径范围按照3种分级方法分级：21级，35级，70级。有效分级（粒级对应百分含量为零不参与主成分分析）分别为21、34、67级。0.37～219.86 μm粒径范围划分为60级。主成分分析的各因子贡献率表明，粒级划分方法对分析结果影响不大（表1）。

表1　因子累积贡献率表

Tab. 1　Cumulative loading on the three principal components

粒径范围(μm)及粒级		贡献率占总方差/%			累积贡献率/%		
		1	2	3	1	2	3
九州台剖面	0.37～219.86(60)	69.86	13.00	8.44	69.86	82.85	91.29
	0.25～128.0(21)	73.28	13.49	8.56	73.28	86.77	95.33
	0.25～128.0(34)	72.86	13.94	8.33	72.86	86.79	95.13
	0.25～128.0(67)	73.16	13.74	8.46	73.16	86.91	95.37
土巷道剖面	0.1～139.2(81)	84.54	8.76	2.76	84.54	93.31	96.07

分级愈细，愈能反映粒度分布的细节，从而反映各主成分贡献率随粒级分布的细节。因此，我们将用九州台剖面67级粒度分级数据分析结果与土巷道剖面81级（粒径范围：0.1～139.2 μm，>139.2 μm单列一级）粒度分级数据分析结果进行讨论。所有粒度数据的主成分分析是由社会科学统计软件包SPSS（Statistical Package for Social Science）for Windows 8.0完成的，旋转方法：方差极大旋转（Varimax），旋转的目的是因子载荷向两极偏，即正值向1偏，负值向-1偏；正规化方法：Kaiser正规化。

2　结果分析

根据软件计算的结果，九州台剖面、土巷道剖面前三个主成分的累积贡献率分别为95.37%和96.07%，表明提取的主成分是完全可信的。九州台剖面的第一主成分的贡献率占73.16%，土巷道剖面的第一主成分占84.54%，二者存在较明显的差别，同时九州台剖面与黄土高原中部地区的分析结果（87%）也存在较大的差别[5]。造成这一差别的原因可能是：(1) 参与主成分分析的数据量存在差异；(2) 不同采样点本身的粒度组成存在差异。通过极大方差旋转因子载荷在粒级的分布图（图2），可以发现，第一主成分突出贡献于粉砂部分（2～63 μm）和极细砂（63～125 μm）部分。在物理机制上可能指示着主要由锋面活动引起的尘暴的粉尘输入以及中等或弱性的大气条件下的粉尘输入。有意思的是，九州台剖面的第三主成分与土巷道的第二主成分的载荷在粒级分布上表现形式相近，而它们对粗粉砂以上（>32 μm）的粒级存在较大的贡献，指示的物理意义比较特殊，可能映射了尘暴的某些信息。单从图2看，相对而言，土巷道剖面黄土堆积过程中所受尘暴贡献要较九州台剖面的显著，实际的粒度组成上，土巷道剖面比九州台剖面的要粗。九州台剖面的第二主成分、土巷道剖面的第三主成分对黏粒部分（<2 μm）的贡献率是显著的。黏粒部分是非常值得讨论的，在成因上这部分容易与成壤作用联系在一起，在黄土高原中部地区，这一推断是合乎逻辑的[3, 17]。不过，师育新等[18]研究了距九

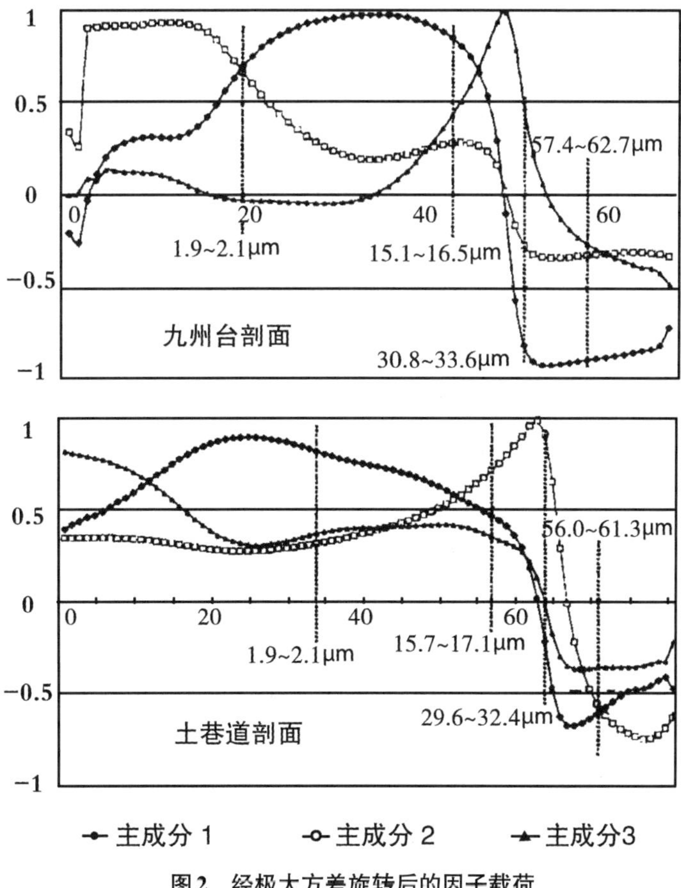

图2　经极大方差旋转后的因子载荷

Fig. 2　Loading on components via varimax rotation

州台10 km之遥的皋兰山剖面的黏土矿物，指出兰州地区的黏土矿物主要是碎屑成因的，并不是由后期成壤作用形成的，与现代尘暴粉尘的黏土矿物组合特征基本相同。我们收集到的8个粉尘样的黏粒部分的含量（平均为7.52%）略高于S1中黏粒的含量（九州台剖面平均为6.60%）。不排除成壤作用的存在，我们认为，黄土高原西部地区的黏粒部分主要是由非成壤因素控制的。首先，就九州台剖面而言，<2 μm颗粒含量变化与粗颗粒的含量变化、频率磁化率（χ_{fd}）的波动存在不“协调性”：（1）末次间冰期（5e）内>40 μm含量与<2 μm含量表现出同步地减少，在倒数第二次间冰期亦有类似现象。尽管频率磁化率在5e内存在小幅度的波动，但是，可以发现，<2 μm含量之低谷却对应于它的峰值，因此，无法以成壤强度来解释<2 μm含量的波动。（2）氧同位素5e阶段，>40 μm含量和频率磁化率与<2 μm含量的可比性也不是很好。其次，在两个剖面，与>40 μm含量同频率磁化率的变化在5e存在的相差①相一致，黏粒含量的变化与频率磁化率亦存在相差。这个相差可能以黏粒的碎屑成因而非后期成壤作用来解释更加合理。研究表明，末次间冰期（5e），地中海地区的希腊Ioannina湖泊多气候指标记录显示该区域在124.7～118.1 ka BP表现为一个温度降低、降水增加的时段[19]。西风带南迁，可能是该地区降水增加的原因[20]。作为大气气溶胶的背景物质，<2 μm物质的含量与西风带位置存在较大的联系[1，21]。但是，在九州台剖面5e中<2 μm物质的含量的急剧减少与西风环流南迁导致北支急流的减弱是否存在很大关系，尚难以下结论，因为两地剖面在黏粒含量上的可比性较差。在土巷道剖面，第一主成分在黏粒段的贡献率也较显著（见图2），反映黏粒的沉积与粗颗粒的搬运有较大联系。这或许正是土巷道剖面<2 μm含量与>40 μm含量存在良好的负相关的原因，也反映了土巷道剖面的物质来源比较单一。

通过上述的分析，我们基本确定了各个主成分所指示的物理机制，九州台剖面的第一、第三主成分与广义的冬季风有特定的联系，而土巷道剖面的第一、第二主成分则与广义的冬季风存在特定的联系，九州台剖面的第二主成分、土巷道剖面的第三主成分指示的物理意义尚不确定。

在选择冬季风的代用指标上，聚类是一个方法[22]：将因子载荷作成三维聚点图，即在前三个主分量（主成分）场中，把在三维空间中坐标点距离相近者归为一类。我们发现，散点在三维空间中按一种规律排列：相邻的两点在粒级上是连续的。这为进一步聚类提供了方便。由冬季风所映射的各主成分，又将九州台剖面的载荷散点投射至一、三主分量场中，将土巷道剖面的载荷散点投射至一、二主分量场中，得到平面载荷散点图（图3）。载荷同时出现负值的起始点可能表征了冬季风搬运的一个临界状态，因此，可以把包括此点及其以后的点聚为一类。九州台剖

①Chen F H, Feng H B. The stable east Asia monsoon climate during the last interglacial (Eemian) documented in the paleosol S1 of the western part of Chinese Loess Plateau. Global and Planetary Changes, 2000(in press).

面的阈值粒级为40.2～43.9 μm；土巷道剖面的临界粒级为38.9～42.6 μm。这样，我们选择>40 μm粗颗粒的含量作为黄土高原西部地区的冬季风指标。这意味着，黄土高原中部与西部地区冬季风的指标存在差异，这种差异符合粉尘搬运沉积的实际情况。

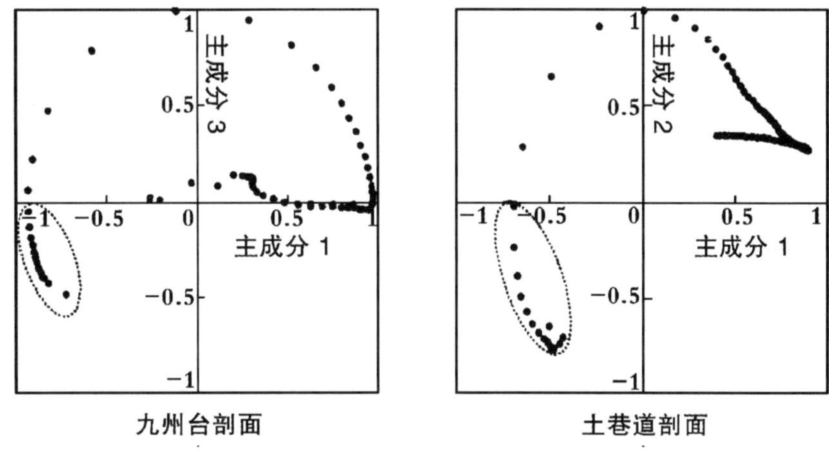

图3　载荷散点图(纵坐标为无量纲的载荷值,横坐标为粒级数)

Fig. 3　Scatter diagram of loading on components

3　讨论与结论

西伯利亚—蒙古高压将东亚冬季风与全球冰量联系在一起，因此，可以将>40 μm粗颗粒含量变化与反映全球冰量变化的深海氧同位素$\delta^{18}O$ [23] 变化进行比较（图4），对比表明，在黄土高原西部地区>40 μm粗颗粒含量是良好的冬季风替代指标。只不过由于分辨率的差异，粒度变化与深海氧同位素的波动在细节上存在差别。相对于>30 μm粗颗粒含量而言，>40 μm粗颗粒含量能够更加突出强调冬季风事件 [24]，同时，如前所述，40 μm表征着一个临界状态，因此，>40 μm粗颗粒含量变化是更为敏感的冬季风替代指标。在黄土高原西部地区，较为干旱的环境，使得黏粒（<2 μm）部分指示的环境意义比较特殊 [25]。不可排除黏粒黏附于粗颗粒搬运形式的存在，总的说来，黏粒含量的变化是相对独立的，尤其是在九州台剖面，其波动的频率远比>40 μm粗颗粒含量变化频率快。因此，<2 μm颗粒含量的变化所指示的古气候意义可能与黄土高原中部地区不同。

通过上面的分析，我们认为：

（1）>30 μm颗粒含量作为东亚冬季风的代用指标，在黄土高原地区不具有通用性，需要根据特定区域做相应的分析，对黄土高原西部地区的两个典型剖面的粒度因子分析表明，>40 μm颗粒含量作为冬季风的替代指标在本区域更为理想。

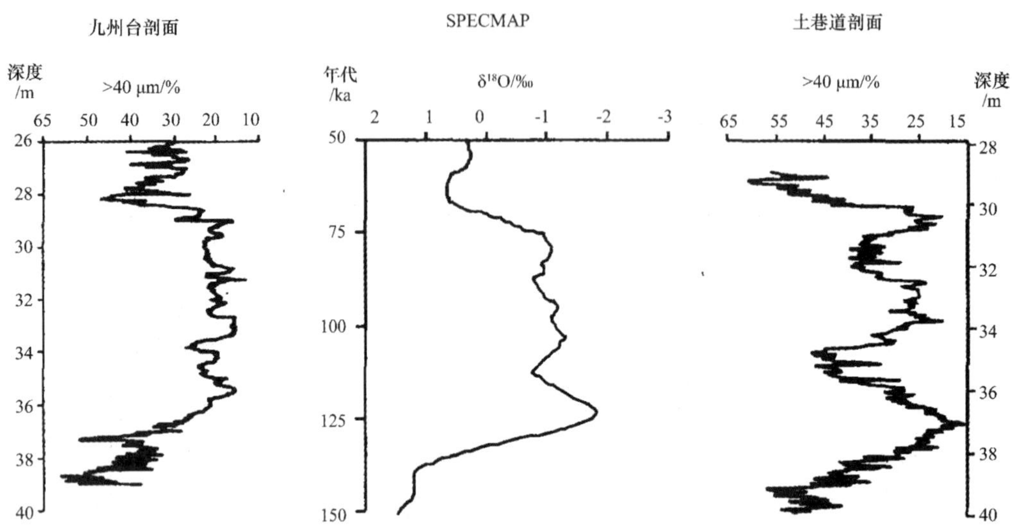

图4　>40 μm粗颗粒含量变化与SPECMAP深海氧同位素($\delta^{18}O$)对比

Fig. 4　Comparison between >40 μm size fraction variation, western part of Loess Plateau, and $\delta^{18}O$ variation, SPECMAP

(2) 在气候更干旱、粉尘沉积速率更高的黄土高原西部地区，<2 μm的黏粒物质含量的变化与后期成壤作用关系不大。黏粒的形成机制尚有待深入的研究，在黄土高原西部地区，黏粒含量的变化可能隐含着全球大气环流系统中某一因子的变化。

致谢：感谢曹继秀高工、吴海斌先生、吴庆龙先生、孟飞先生在野外采样给予的帮助，感谢徐齐治高工、鹿化煜副研究员、王华先生、楼永辉先生、李安先生和李世萍小姐在实验室工作中给予的指导或帮助。

参考文献（References）

[1] 刘东生. 黄土与环境[M]. 北京:科学出版社,1985:191-358.

[2]丁仲礼,任剑璋,杨石龄,等. 最后两个冰期旋回季风——沙漠系统不稳定性的高分辨率黄土记录[J]. 第四纪研究,1999 (1):150-157.

[3]鹿化煜,安芷生. 洛川黄土粒度组成的古气候意义[J]. 科学通报,1997,42(1):166-169.

[4]鹿化煜,Huissteden K V,周杰,等. 中国北方更新世极端冷期冬季风快速变化[J]. 中国沙漠,2000,20(2):192-196.

[5]鹿化煜. Huissteden K V,安芷生,等. 早、中更新世东亚冬季风强度的快速变化[J]. 海洋地质与第四纪地质,1999,19(2):75-83.

[6]Porter S C, An Z S. Correlation between climate events in the North Atlantic and China during the last glaciation[J]. Nature,1995,375:305-308.

[7]An Z S, Porter S C. Millennial-scale climatic oscillations during the last interglaciation in Central China[J]. Geology,1997,25:603-606.

[8]Chen F H, Bloemendal J, Feng Z D, et al. East Asian Monsoon variation during Oxygen Isotope Stage 5, evidence from the northwestern margin of the Chinese Loess Plateau[J]. Quaternary Science Review,1999(18):1127-1135.

[9]Xiao Jule, Porter S C, An Z S, et al. Grain size of Quartz as an indicator of Winter Monsoon strength on the Loess Plateau of central China during the last 130000 a [J]. Quaternary Research,1995,43:22-29.

[10]鹿化煜,安芷生. 黄土高原黄土粒度组成的古气候意义[J]. 中国科学(D辑),1998,28(3):278-283.

[11]陈发虎,张维信. 甘青地区的黄土地层学与第四纪冰川问题[M]. 北京:科学出版社,1993:9-24.

[12]Chen F H, Bloemendal J, Wang J M, et al. High-resolution multiproxy climate records from Chinese loess: evidence for rapid climatic changes between 70 ka and 10 ka[J]. Paleogeography, Paleoclimatology, Palaeontology,1997,130:323-335.

[13]庞奖励. 晚更新世以来黄土高原地区古季风的时空演化[J]. 中国沙漠,1999,19(1):72-76.

[14]张孟威,康德梦. 环境问题的数学解法及计算机应用[M]. 北京:中国环境科学出版社,1989:48-84.

[15]Huissteden K V, Nugteren G, Vandenberghe J, et al. Spectral analysis of grain size record of the Loess deposit in Central China[A]. Proc. 30th Int'l Geol. Congr. [C]. VSP, The Netherland,1997,Vol. 2 & 3:313-325.

[16]刘毅,张华,周明煜. 一次沙尘暴天气沙尘输送过程的数值模拟[J]. 南京气象学院学报,1997,20(4):511-517.

[17]王永焱,滕志宏. 中国黄土的微结构及其在时代上和区域上的变化——扫描电子显微镜下的研究[J]. 科学通报,1982,(2):102-105.

[18]师育新,戴雪荣,李节通,等. 末次间冰期兰州黄土记录中的黏土矿物及其环境意义探讨[J]. 海洋地质与第四纪地质,1997,17(1):87-94.

[19]Frogley M R, Tzedakis P C, Henton T H E. Climate variability in Northwest Greece during the Last interglacial[J]. Science,1999,285:1886-1888.

[20]于革,王苏民. 耿亚大陆湖泊记录和两万年来大气环流变化[J]. 第四纪研究,1998

(4):360-365.

[21]张小曳,张光宇,朱光华,等. 中国源区粉尘的元素示踪[J]. 中国科学(D辑). 1996,26(5):423-430.

[22]张佳华,孔昭宸,杜乃秋. 主成分分析对恢复过去植被和环境作用的再分析——以北京坟庄剖面为例[J]. 地理科学. 1997,17(4):316-321.

[23]Martinson D G, Pisias N G, Hays J D, et al. Age dating and the orbital theory of the ice ages: development of a high-resolution 0 to 300000 a chronostratigraphy[J]. Quaternary Research, 1987,27:1-29.

[24]戴雪荣,李吉均,俞立中,等. 末次间冰期甘肃沙尘暴演化历史的黄土记录分析[J]. 地理学报,1999,57:445-453.

[25]同满存,王光谦,董光荣,等. 巴丹吉林沙漠沙山发育与环境演变研究[J]. 中国沙漠,2001,21(4):361-366.

Chronological discord between the last interglacial paleosol (S1) and its parent material in the Chinese Loess Plateau*

Z.D. Feng, H.B. Wang, C. Olson, G.A. Pope,
F.H. Chen, J.W. Zhang, C.B. An

Abstract: An and Porter (Geology 25 (1997) 603) reported six high dust-influx events of millennial timescales recovered from the last interglacial paleosol S1 and correlated them to six cool events of millennial timescale in the North Atlantic. However, the complexity of soil-forming processes may have made the chronological correlation with the North Atlantic records inadequate. To examine the complexity of the S1 formation, the S1 paleosol was traced laterally and identified based on the preserved characteristics observed in the field and analyzed in the laboratory. Our data show that from the northwest to the southeast, the S1 paleosol gradually converges from three distinctive soil profiles into a single welded profile because the net rate of loess accumulation was attenuated to the southeast and pedogenic development intensified southeastward during the last interglacial. Three soil-forming events within the S1 paleosol (S1S1, S1S2 and S1S3) separated by two loess units (S1L1 and S1L2) in the northwestern part of the Loess Plateau are stratigraphically coeval with a single soil profile in the southeastern margin of the Loess Plateau. In the southeast, the S1 paleosol developed into underlying older loess L2 (e.g., at the Lantian section). The three paleosols (S1S1, S1S2 and S1S3) are partially welded in the central part of the Chinese Loess Plateau (e.g., at the Tianshui section), where the lower portion of S1 paleosol developed in the underlying older loess unit L2. In the northwestern margin of the Chinese Loess Plateau (e.g., at the Lanzhou section), the preservation of the repeating soil–loess sequence (S1S1, S1L1, S1S2, S1L2 and S1S3) continuously documented the climatic events of the last interglacial. Our data also show that the magnetic signatures and particle-size information are more or less acceptable climatic proxies only for the northwestern sections, where the degree of pedogenesis was lower and the rate of eolian influx was greater during the last interglacial. It appears that in all cases investigated, the median grain size and the coarse fraction (>63 μm) content define the upper and lower boundaries of the S1 paleosol reasonably well and can be used to estimate the

*本文发表于：Quaternary International, 2004, 117: 17–26.

timetransgressive nature of the S1 paleosol relative to its parent material. Soil welding, bioturbation and material translocation within the S1 soil profiles make it impossible to preserve the detailed and high-resolution information of climate changes in those S1 profiles in the southeastern part (including the popularly called central part) of the Chinese Loess Plateau.

1 Introduction

Climatic systems changed at different temporal scales and the instrument-observed data are insufficient for establishing the temporal patterns of the change. As a result, we rely on various proxies from sedimentary sequences for reconstructing the temporal patterns. The loess-soil sequence in the Chinese Loess Plateau has proven to be one of the best such sedimentary sequences because it has been deposited to a certain degree continuously through time and is located in the climatically sensitive East Asian Monsoon area. To comprehend the scope of the future changes, the last interglacial deserves special attentions because it provides the most reliable understanding of the natural processes during interglacial times (Rind and Overpeck, 1993). The last interglacial climate was reported to have fluctuated dramatically on millennial timescales around the North Atlantic (Dansgaard et al., 1993; McManus et al., 1994; GRIP Members, 1995). In the Chinese Loess Plateau, six high dust-influx events of millennial timescales were reportedly recorded in the last interglacial S1 paleosol and correlated to six cool events of millennial timescales in the North Atlantic (An and Porter, 1997). The complexity of soil-forming processes may have made the chronological correlation with the North Atlantic records inadequate. This paper examines the complexity of the soil-forming processes during the last interglacial and argues that the high-resolution climatic reconstructions from the S1 paleosol in the southeastern part (including the popularly known central part) of the Chinese Loess Plateau are highly questionable.

2 Modern environments and S1 chronological problems

Due to the interaction between the winter and summer monsoons, there is an apparent SE–NW gradient of modern climate in the Chinese Loess Plateau (Li et al, 1988). That is, both the mean annual temperature and precipitation increase gradually from the northwestern margin to the northwestern margin (Fig. 1a), whereas the aridity (the ratio of evaporation and precipitation) increases gradually towards the northwest. The vegetation closely follows the aridity trend (Fig. 1b). For the sake of convenience, we use the 500 mm isohyet to divide the Chinese Loess Plateau into northwestern and southeastern parts, and the popularly called central part where the Luochuan and Xifeng sections are situated falls in the southeastern part. The Liupan Mountain divides the Loess Plateau into eastern and western parts.

The paleoclimatic information from the Chinese loess - soil sequence has been intensively explored during the past two decades. Based on the lithostratigraphic frameworks of Chinese loess (Liu, 1965, 1966), Heller and Liu (1982, 1984) established the magnetostratigraphy. Kukla and others (Kukla et al., 1988; Kukla and An, 1989) then made a breakthrough in establishing a high-resolution chronology and convincingly linked the magnetic susceptibility record of the Chinese loess to other global climatic records.

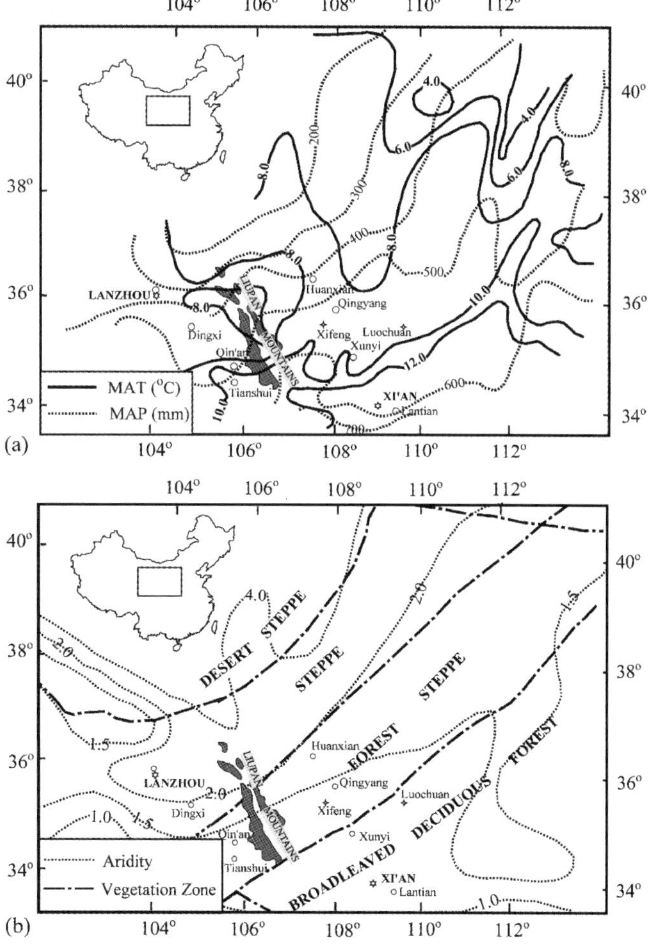

Fig. 1 (a) Mean annual temperature (MAT) and mean annual precipitation and (b) aridity (precipitation/evaporation) and vegetation distributions in the Chinese Loess Plateau

Maher' s group (Zhou et al., 1990; Maher and Thompson, 1992; Maher et al., 1994; Thompson and Maher, 1995) and Verosub's group (Fine et al., 1993, 1995; Verosub et al., 1993, 1994) substantiated the climatic significance of the magnetic susceptibility. Porter and An's group (An et al., 1991a, b; Ding et al., 1992; Porter and An, 1995; Zhou et al., 1996; An and Porter, 1997) further advanced the chronology and climatic interpretation with ever higher-resolution data of the magnetic susceptibility (as a proxy of the summer monsoon) and the grain size (as a proxy of the winter monsoon). With regard to the high-resolution reconstructions, the assumption was that the post-depositional alterations of the loess-soil sequence have been minimal. Yet, it is well known that pedogenesis can occur in nearly every environment and it has long been demonstrated to alter the physical and chemical properties of the parent materials (including bedrock) through soil-forming processes (Catt, 1986, 1990; Boul et al., 1989; Birkeland, 1990, 1999; Olson and Nettleton, 1998). Several authors (Bronger and Heinkele, 1989; Guo and Liu, 1993; Kemp, 1995; Kemp et al., 1995, 1997; Guo et al., 1996a, b) have recognized the characteristics of soil-forming processes of the last interglacial S1 paleosol in the Chinese Loess Plateau. However, the geographic differentiation and the chronological significance of the soil-horizon formation in altering the physical and chemical properties of the parent materials are not fully acknowledged. Specifically, the net rate of loess accumulation was attenuated and pedogenic development intensified southeastward during the last interglacial and the paleosol S1 must have responded to the southeastward trends. In addition, it has been shown that as loess thins systematically from the major sources, soils have progressively great development in the loess (e.g., Ruhe, 1973). These factors potentially discredit the use of some paleoclimatic proxies in reconstructing the high-resolution climatic changes. In an eolian environment where soil develops as the parent material is being deposited (accretionary), material translocations within modern and past soil profiles are well documented in the Midwestern USA (Ruhe et al., 1955; Al-Baraak and Lewis, 1978; Ruhe and Olson, 1980; Aandahl, 1982; Ruhe, 1984). Based on the SE-NW gradient of the modern environment in the Chinese Loess Plateau, the geographic differentiation of the soil-horizon formation must have occurred during the last interglacial (Li et al., 1988; Kemp et al., 1997; Chen et al., 1999) and thus the chronological significance of the geographic differentiation must be examined very closely in an effort to recover high-resolution climatic records.

3 Fieldwork strategies and laboratory methods

To investigate the geographic differentiation of the last interglacial paleosol S1 and its climatic significance, we chose two transects (see Fig. 1a and b): one across the western part of the Loess Plateau from Lanzhou to Tianshui extending to Lantian near Xi'an and another across the eastern part of the Loess Plateau from Lantian to Huanxian (Fig. 1). To examine the geographic differentiation of the S1 paleosol, the paleosol (S1 multiple paleosols or pedocomplex) was laterally traced by soil-horizon identification (Ruhe, 1973, 1983) and classified based on the preserved characteristics (Foth, 1978; Schaetzl and Sorenson, 1978; Catt, 1986; Boul et al., 1989; Birkeland, 1999; Nettleton et al., 2000). According to the definition of an isolated paleosol (Schaetzl and Sorenson, 1978), the thickness of the last glacial loess (L1) was sufficient to bury and isolate the last interglacial S1 paleosol from later pedogenic processes throughout the Chinese Loess Plateau. Thus, it is possible to examine the complexity of soil-forming processes during the last interglacial without the concern of post-burial alteration (Olson and Nettleton, 1998). The S1 soil profiles of the eight sections chosen on the two transects were first described in the field based on the characteristics of soil horizons (Foth, 1978; Catt, 1986, 1990; Boul et al., 1989; Birkeland, 1999) and then sampled at 2 cm intervals for grain size, magnetic and carbonate analyses. At all sections investigated, sampling began in the basal part of the L1 loess unit that overlies the S1 paleosol. The magnetic susceptibility (SI) was measured by the procedure of Thompson and Oldfield (1986) using a Bartington MS 2B susceptibility meter and the frequency-dependent susceptibility was calculated based on the high-frequency and low-frequency susceptibility measurements. The grain size of bulk samples was measured using a Malvern Co. Ltd. Mastersizer 2000 laser diffraction particle-size analyzer and the carbonate content was measured with the modified gas evolution method (Machette, 1986) using the Bascomb Calcimeter.

4 Soil profiles

An and Porter (1997) reported that the variations in the percentage of large quartz particles in the last interglacial paleosol (S1) from the type locality, Luochuan in the popularly known central part of Chinese Loess Plateau (in the southeastern part relative to the 500 mm isohyet divide), documented six high dust-influx events of the last interglacial.

They correlated these six high dust-influx events to the six cool events of millennial-scales in northern high latitudes reported by McManus et al. (1994). Due to uncertainties in the thermoluminescence (TL) dates of the S1 paleosol, the S1 paleosol is theoretically tuned to be bracketed by two ages: 73,000 and 128,000 yr BP (Kukla et al., 1988; Kukla and An, 1989), i.e., 55,000 years were available to form this 2.5 m thick S1 paleosol. Even if the S1 paleosol in the central part of the Loess Plateau was indeed formed during that time period under warm and humid interglacial conditions, it is likely that all or the lower part of the parent materials of the S1 paleosol was deposited prior to 128,000 yr BP. In other words, the 55,000 years of interglacial climate were more than sufficient to form a mature soil profile. It is well known that it took only 100 yr to form a mature A horizon in parent material in Iowa (Hallberg et al., 1978) and in Texas (Gile, 1979). It is also well documented that it took only 4000–7000 yr to form a thick soil with a mature Bt horizon on parent materials in northeastern Canada (Moore, 1978) and in Texas (Gile, 1979). As for the accretionary or cumulic loessial soils that developed as the parent material (loess) was being deposited (Johnson and Watson-Stegner, 1987; Phillips, 1993), the synchroneity between soil formation and the parent material deposition depends on the comparative rates of soil formation and eolian deposition (Valentine and Dalrymple, 1976; Ruhe and Olson, 1980; Boardman, 1985; Mack et al., 1993; Almond, 1998). Synchroneity of rates may be implied if the loessial soil consists of cumulic A horizons. That is, the eolian deposition was rapid enough to prevent the formation of soil B horizons, yet slow enough to permit the formation of soil A horizons (Feng et al., 1994a, b; Chen et al., 1997, 1999; Almond, 1998). In brief, the attenuation of the net accumulation of loess and the intensification of the pedogenesis southeastward in the Chinese Loess Plateau during the last interglacial should have differentiated the paleosol S1 from the northwest to the southeast and must have left traceable imprints.

4.1 Lanzhou and Dingxi sections

In the northwestern part of the Loess Plateau (e.g., at the Lanzhou section), an 8 m thick S1 pedocomplex consists of multiple A–C soil profiles (Derbyshire et al., 1995, 1997; Kemp et al., 1995, 1997; Chen et al., 1999), indicating that the rate of eolian deposition was episodically greater than the rate of soil formation (Fig. 2). Three incipient soils (A–C profiles) mark the marine isotope substages 5a (S1S1), 5c (S1S2) and 5e (S1S3). Two inter bedded loess units demarcate the substages 5b (S1L1) and 5d (S1L2) (Chen et al., 1999). These five units are well demonstrated by both the magnetic susceptibility and frequency-dependent susceptibility curves and to a lesser extent by the clay and carbonate contents (Fig. 2).

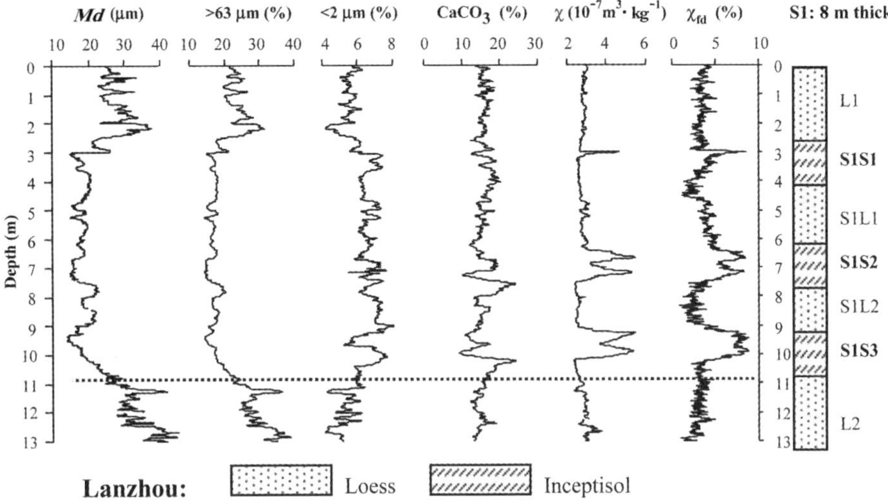

Fig. 2 Lanzhou section: field-observed pedostratigraphy and laboratory data. *Md*(μm), median size; >63 μm (%), percentage of coarse fraction (>63 μm); <2 μm (%), percentage of fine fraction (<2 μm); $CaCO_3$ (%), percentage of carbonate; χ, magnetic susceptibility (10 $m^3 \cdot kg^{-1}$); χ_{fd}, frequency-dependent susceptibility (%).

Southeastward near Dingxi where the S1 paleosol is 5 m thick, two incipient soils (A-C profiles) corresponding to the marine isotope substages 5a and 5c were better developed than those at the Lanzhou section. Corresponding to the substage 5e is a Mollisol-like soil with both an A horizon and a Bk horizon. The incipient soils at the Lanzhou and Dingxi sections are both characterized by slightly more compaction with observable granular structures and by a darker color with more rootlet channels than the overlying and underlying loess units. The Mollisol-like soil (S1S3) at the Dingxi section appears to be identical with modern Mollisols that characterize the surface soils in most parts of the Chinese Loess Plateau and has a dark (organic matter) and granular-structured A horizon and a slightly subangular blocky-structured Bk horizon. These three paleosols (S1S1, S1S2 and S1S3) at the Dingxi section are pronouncedly expressed by the contents of coarse fraction of the gain size (>63 μm) and carbonate and also by the frequency-dependent magnetic susceptibility curve, and to a lesser extent by the clay (<2 μm) content and the susceptibility curve (Fig. 3). It should be noted here that the susceptibility peak corresponding to the S1S1 was most likely suppressed by the high carbonate concentration. It is also notable that the Bk horizon was actually developed in the coarsening portion at the depth of 5.0–5.5 m, implying that the basal portion of the S1 paleosol complex developed into the underlying older and coarser loess L2 (Fig. 3).

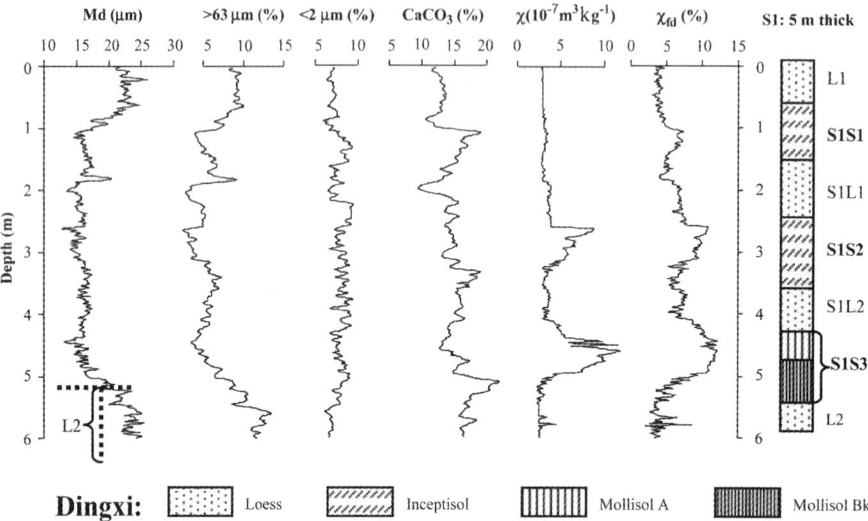

Fig. 3 Dingxi section: field-observed pedostratigraphy and laboratory data. ***Md*** **(μm), median size; >63μm (%), percentage of coarse fraction (>63 μm); <2 μm (%), percentage of fine fraction (<2 μm); $CaCO_3$ (%), percentage of carbonate; χ, magnetic susceptibility (10 $m^3 \cdot kg^{-1}$); χ_{fd}, frequency-dependent susceptibility (%).**

4.2 Qin'an and Tianshui sections

Farther to the southeast at Qin'an where the S1 paleosol complex is 4 m thick, three Mollisols-like soils corresponding to the three odd-numbered marine isotope substages (5a, 5c, and 5e) are present. The S1S1 and S1S2 paleosols, both having an A horizon and a Bk horizon, are separated by the S1L1 loess unit. The loess unit S1L2 between the S1S2 and S1S3 is not present here (Fig. 4). Carbonate content at this section is relatively high both in loess units and in the soil Bk horizons and lower in the soil A horizons. The S1S3 paleosol at the Qin'an section is of particular interest. Our field-observed characteristics including well-developed blocky structures and notable clay coatings on ped-faces suggest that the lower portion of the S1S3 is a Btk horizon, but the clay content and the magnetic susceptibility curves do not seem to indicate a Btk horizon. The coarsening trend of the grain size indicated by both the median grain size and the coarse (>63 μm) fraction content in the S1S3 paleosol is attributed to the lower clay content and magnetic signatures. This grain size coarsening trend also suggests that the S1S3 paleosol was developed in the underlying older loess unit L2 (Fig. 4).

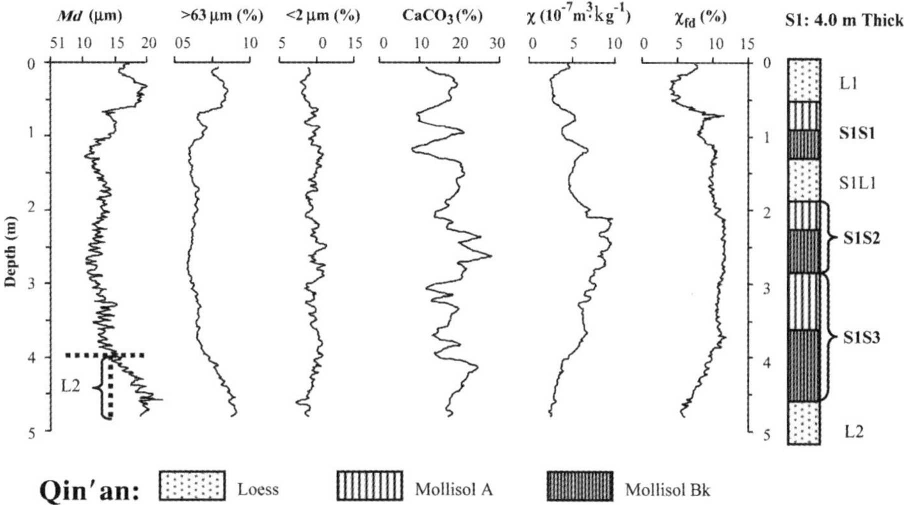

Fig. 4 Qin'an section: field-observed pedostratigraphy and laboratory data. *Md* (μm), median size; >63 μm (%), percentage of coarse fraction (>63 μm); <2 μm (%), percentage of fine fraction (<2 μm); $CaCO_3$ (%), percentage of carbonate; χ, magnetic susceptibility ($10^{-7}m^3 \cdot kg^{-1}$); χ_{fd}, frequency-dependent susceptibility (%).

The S1 at the Tianshui section is a paleosol complex without an interbedded loess unit, that is, both S1L1 and S1L2 are not present. This 4.5 m thick S1 paleosol has a thin (0.8 m thick) mollic A horizon at the top, a 2.5 m thick Bt horizon and 1.2 m thick Bk horizon (Fig. 5). Notable is that the entire S1 paleosol is bioturbated with abundant small burrows whose walls are coated with clay films. These burrows are most likely insect and wormcasts that occurred in the A horizon of the surface soil at the time (Foth, 1978; Stoops and Eswaran, 1986; Boul et al., 1989; O' Green and Busacca, 2001). Two features deserve special mentioning here: (1) rootlet channel - marked crumble - granular structures and worm and insect burrows, commonly A horizon characteristics, are preserved within the clay-coated prismatic columns of the B horizons (Bt and Bk), implying that A horizons were later altered to B horizons; and (2) the existence of carbonate (threads and filaments) throughout the B horizons (Bt and Bk) indicates that the B horizons were accretionary, that is, B horizons developed more or less continuously as carbonate-rich dust accumulated in the soil profile. Carbonate coats the illuvial clay on the burrow walls and ped-faces in the Bt horizon, and engulfs the entire matrix and fills burrows in the Bk horizon. A minor peak of carbonate concentration at the depth of 1.6–2.0 m may correspond to the S1L1 loess unit (5b) appeared at the Qin' an section, which is only about 50 km to the north. Our interpretation is that the multiple soils corresponding to the marine isotope substages 5a, 5c and 5e have become partially welded in this part of the Chinese Loess Plateau. That is, after the development of S1S3 (5e), S1S2 development "annexed" the upper portion of the S1S3 (A horizon and probably the upper portion of B horizon). The S1S1 development might have also "annexed" the uppermost part of the S1S2. The possible divisions of the three paleosols are indicated in Fig. 5. Welding of the S1 paleosols is well demonstrated by our laboratory data. For example, the magnetic signatures and grain-size data do not distinguish the S1 subdivisions and the well-developed Bk horizon might have been carbonate accumulation zones for both the S1S1 and S1S2 paleosols. Again, the coarsening trend towards the base of the S1 paleosol suggests that the S1 paleosol developed into the underlying older loess L2 (Fig. 5).

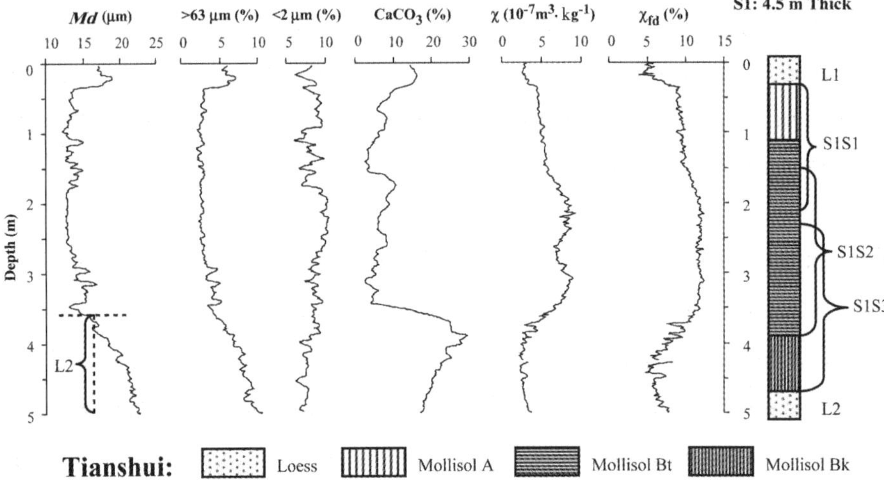

Fig. 5 Tianshui section: field-observed pedostratigraphy and laboratory data. *Md* (μm), median size; >63 μm (%), percentage of coarse fraction (>63 μm); <2 μm (%), percentage of fine fraction (<2 μm); $CaCO_3$ (%), percentage of carbonate; χ, magnetic susceptibility ($10^{-7}m^3 \cdot kg^{-1}$); χ_{fd}, frequency-dependent susceptibility (%).

4.3 Lantian section

Unlike at other sections reported here, the last glacial loess L1 (i.e., the Malan Loess) at the Lantian section is actually not loess. The loess units corresponding to the marine isotope stages 2 and 4 experienced much stronger pedogenesis than the soil units S1S1 and S1S2 at the Lanzhou and Dingxi sections and the "loess" unit corresponding to the marine isotope stage 3 is a well-developed accretionary mollic A horizons. The last interglacial paleosol S1 is basically a well-developed Bt horizon (Fig. 6). This Bt horizon is characterized by coarse prismatic peds, breaking to medium angular blocky peds. Small rounded clay or silt balls, probably formed by post - depositional bioturbations, are noticeable within these medium angular blocky peds. In comparison with other S1 paleosols or loss - paleosol complex, the S1 paleosol at the Lantian section is much better developed not only because the climate was warmer and wetter but also because the land surface was much more stable with less loess deposition during the last interglacial in this southeastern margin of the Chinese Loess Plateau.

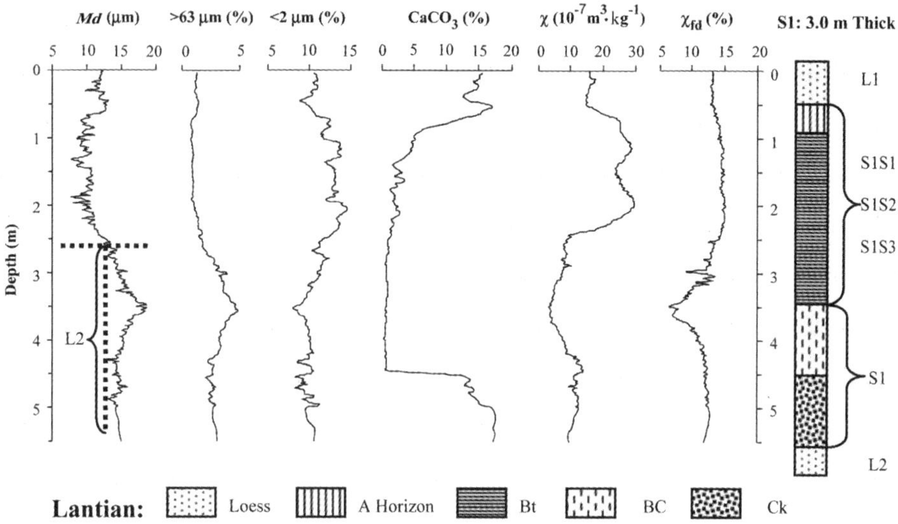

Fig. 6 Lantian section: field-observed pedostratigraphy and laboratory data. *Md* (μm), median size; >63 μm (%), percentage of coarse fraction (>63 μm); <2 μm (%), percentage of fine fraction (<2 μm); $CaCO_3$ (%), percentage of carbonate; χ, magnetic susceptibility ($10^{-7}m^3 \cdot kg^{-1}$); χ_{fd}, frequency-dependent susceptibility (%).

This reddish - brown and prismatically structured S1 paleosol was primarily resulted from a stable land surface during most of the 55,000 yr of the last interglacial. Yet, prominent carbonate filaments on clay coatings of ped - faces and pores indicate that the capillary force of evapotranspiration may have contributed to the carbonate filament coatings, implying that the climate was occasionally dry or seasonally dry during the last interglacial in the southeastern part of the Chinese Loess Plateau. Below the Bt horizon is a carbonate-leached BC horizon overlying 1 m thick carbonate-enriched Ck horizon. If the A and Bt horizons alone are included as the S1 paleosol, its thickness is only 3 m. But, if the BC and Ck horizons are also included, the S1 paleosol is as thick as 5 m. The coarsening trend in grain size at the depth of 2.5 m seems to indicate that at least the basal 1 m of the S1 paleosol may be developed in the underlying older loess L2 if the 3m thick S1 paleosol is assumed. If we assume that the total S1 paleosol thickness is 5 m, then the basal 3 m was developed in the underlying older loess L2. In either case, the grainsize - based (parent material) chronology of the S1 paleosol is highly questionable.

4.4 Xunyi and Qingyang sections

The Xunyi and Qingyang sections are located in the same bioclimatic settings as the well - known Luochuan and Xifeng sections (see Fig. 1b). The A horizons at both sections are characterized by friable structures, carbonate masses and filaments, and abundant medium and fine pores with root traces. The Bt horizons have angular - blocky structures with observable clay coatings on ped - faces. Carbonate coats the illuvial clay on ped - faces (threads and filaments) in the matrix of Bt horizons, and concentrates as masses or nodules in the Bk horizons at both sections. Not only are the field observations similar but also the laboratory analytical data (e.g., the magnetic signatures and grain size data) are similar at these two sections. The only differences between the two sections are: (1) both A horizon and Bk horizon at the Xunyi section (Fig. 7) are thinner than at the Qingyang section (Fig. 8); and (2) the coarsening trend of the grain size towards the base of the S1 paleosol is gradual at the Xunyi section and rather abrupt at the Qingyang section. At both sections, approximately 1 m of this 3.2 m thick S1 paleosol may be in the underlying older loess L2, again implying that the grainsize - based chronology of the S1 paleosol is highly questionable.

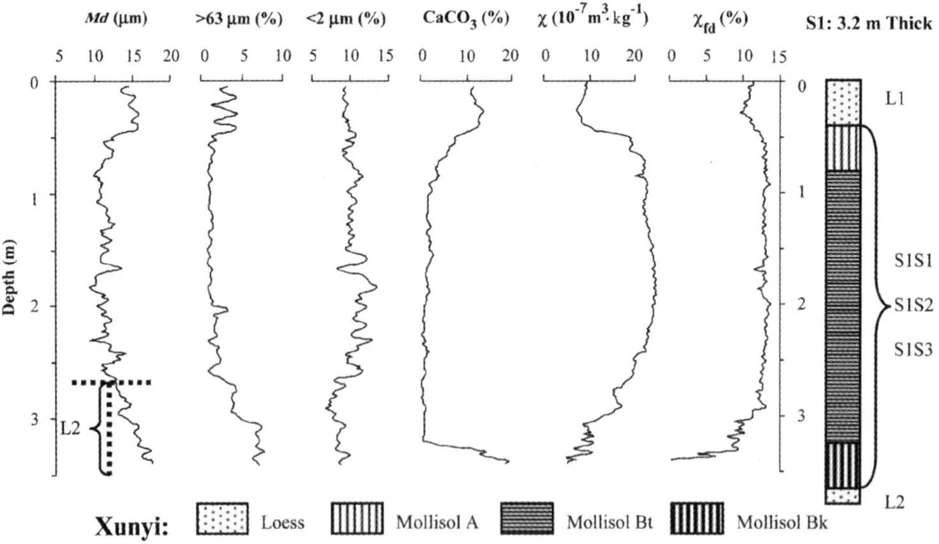

Fig. 7 Xunyi section: field - observed pedostratigraphy and laboratory data. *Md* (μm), median size; >63 μm(%), percentage of coarse fraction (>63 μm); <2 μm(%), percentage of fine fraction (<2 μm); $CaCO_3$ (%), percentage of carbonate; χ, magnetic susceptibility ($10^{-7}m^3 \cdot kg^{-1}$); χ_{fd}, frequency-dependent susceptibility (%).

Welding of the S1 paleosols is well demonstrated by our laboratory data: for example, the magnetic susceptibility and grainsize data do not distinguish the S1 subdivisions, and the well-developed Bk horizon may include carbonate accumulation zones for all three paleosols corresponding to the three marine isotope substages (5e, 5c, and 5a).

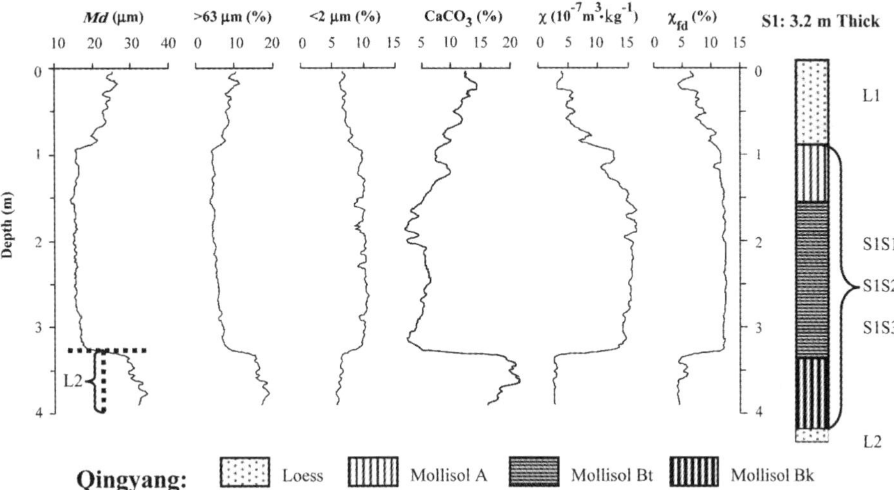

Fig. 8 Qingyang section: field - observed pedostratigraphy and laboratory data. *Md* (μm), median size; >63 μm(%), percentage of coarse fraction (>63 μm); <2 μm(%), percentage of fine fraction (<2 μm); $CaCO_3$ (%), percentage of carbonate; χ, magnetic susceptibility ($10^{-7}m^3 \cdot kg^{-1}$); χ_{fd}, frequency–dependent susceptibility (%).

4.5 Huanxian section

Farther to the northwest at the Huanxian section (Fig. 9), the field - observed pedostratigraphy is similar to that at the Dingxi section (see Fig. 3) and the laboratory analyses are similar to those at the Qin'an section (see Fig. 4). Specifically, all three paleosols (S1S1, S1S2 and S1S3) and the two intervening loess units (S1L1 and S1L2) are identifiable. The S1S3 paleosol is the best developed. Yet, the laboratory results, like those at the Qin'an section, do not support the field observations for the S1S3 paleosol. Again, the coarsening trend of the grain size indicated by both the median grain size and the content of >63 μm fraction in the S1S3 paleosol is attributed to the lower clay content and magnetic signatures. The S1S3 is 1.5 m thick and seems to have developed entirely within the underlying older loess L2, again suggesting that the grainsize-based chronology of the S1 paleosol is highly questionable.

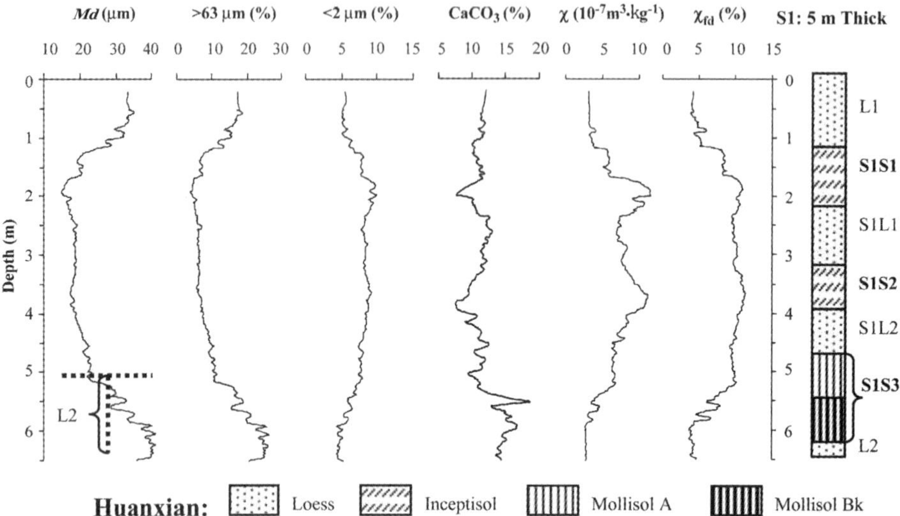

Fig. 9 Huanxian section: field - observed pedostratigraphy and laboratory data. *Md* (μm), median size; >63 μm(%), percentage of coarse fraction (>63 μm); <2 μm(%), percentage of fine fraction (<2 μm); χ, magnetic susceptibility ($10^{-7}m^3 \cdot kg^{-1}$); χ_{fd}, frequency - dependent susceptibility (%).

5 Conclusions

To summarize, the net accumulation of loess (deposition minus erosion) attenuated and the pedogenesis intensified southeastward in the Chinese Loess Plateau during the last interglacial. As a result, the last interglacial paleosol (S1) gradually differentiated from the northwest to the southeast. In the northwestern margin of the Loess Plateau, the three paleosols corresponding to the three odd - numbered marine isotope substages (5a, 5c and 5e) and the two intervening loess units (S1L1 and S1L2) are completely preserved (e.g., at the Dingxi and Lanzhou sections), implying that the loess - soil sequence of S1 paleosol continuously documented the climatic events of the last interglacial. It should be stressed here that the lower portion of the S1S3 at the Dingxi section developed in the underlying older and coarser loess L2 (see Figs. 3 and 10). The S1L2 was annexed by the later paleosol S1S2 development and the S1S3 intruded into the underlying loess L2 even more at the Qin'an section in the central part of the western Loess Plateau where the three paleosols (S1S1, S1S2 and S1S3) were better developed than those at the Lanzhou and Dingxi sections. The three paleosols (S1S1, S1S2 and S1S3) were partially welded at the Tianshui section where accretionary B horizons dominate the S1 paleosol profile and the lower portion of S1 paleosol developed in the underlying older and coarser loess L2 (see

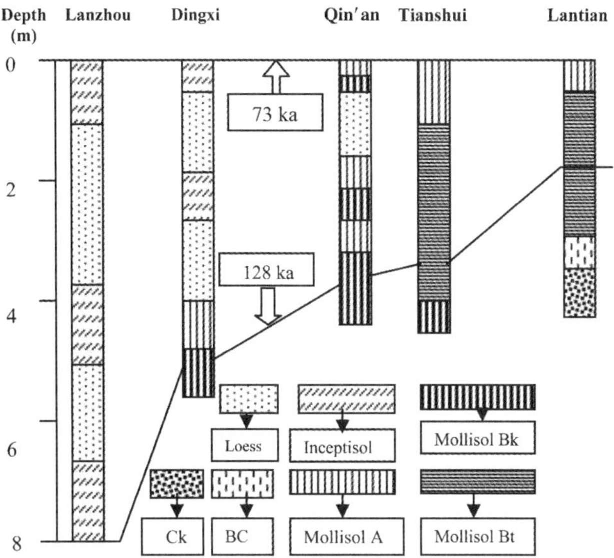

Fig. 10 Geographic differentiation of the S1 paleosol profiles from the northwestern margin to the southeastern margin of the Chinese Loess Plateau. The 73 ka line is the land surface around 73 ka when the S1 development stopped and the 128 ka line is the land surface around 128 ka when the S1 development started.

Figs. 5 and 10). The three soil-forming events occurred repeatedly just in one single soil profile in the southeastern margin of the Loess Plateau (i.e., completely welded at the Lantian section) and a major portion of the S1 paleosol developed in the underlying older loess L2 (see Figs. 6 and 10). At the Xunyi and Qingyang sections, the three soil-forming events occurred also repeatedly in one single soil profile (i.e., completely welded) but only a small portion of the S1 developed in the underlying older and coarser loess L2. The Huanxian section preserves all of the five pedostratigraphic units (S1S1, S1L1, S1S2, S1L2 and S1S3) but the S1S3 is not expressed by both the magnetic and grain-size signatures. The coarsening trend of the grain size is attributed to the suppression of the magnetic signatures and clay content. At this section, the S1S3 intruded into the underlying loess L2 deeper than at the Dingxi section. To sum up, only at such section as Lanzhou where the degree of pedogenesis was lower and the rate of eolian influx was greater during the last interglacial than other sections, are the magnetic signatures and grain size data more or less acceptable climatic proxies for the summer monsoon intensity (e.g., magnetic signatures) and for the winter monsoon intensity (e.g., grain size data). Carbonate concentration can not be used as a proxy to reconstruct the high-resolution records of the summer monsoon intensity even at this northwestern section simply due to the fact that carbonate can be easily leached down to a certain depth. It appears that in all cases investigated, the median grain size and the coarse fraction (>63 μm) content define the upper and lower boundaries of the S1 paleosol complex reasonably well and can be used to estimate the time - transgressive nature of the S1 paleosol relative to its parent material. The soil - forming and soil - welding processes make the grainsize - based (parent material) chronology of the S1 paleosol in the southeastern part (including the central part) of the Chinese Loess Plateau suspect. Furthermore, bioturbation and material translocation within the S1 paleosol profiles make it impossible to preserve the detailed and high - resolution information of climate changes at those southeastern S1 paleosol sections.

Acknowledgements

This research was financially supported by the US National Science Foundation grant (BCS-0078557) and a Chinese Education Ministry grant (No. 2000-65).

References

Aandahl, A.R., 1982. Soils of the Great Plains. The University of Nebraska Press, Lincoln, NE.

Al-Baraak, S., Lewis, D.T., 1978. Soils of a grassland - forest ecotone in eastern Nebraska. Soil Science Society of American Journal 42, 334-338.

Almond, P., 1998. Up - building soil formation in loess in a high rainfall environment, westland, New Zealand. In: Busacca, A.J. (Ed.), International Symposium on Dust Aerosols, Loess Soil and Global Change. Washington State University's CAHE MISC0190, Pullman, WA, pp. 207-211.

An, Z., Kukla, G., Porter, S.C., Xiao, J., 1991a. Late Quaternary dust flux on the Chinese Loess Plateau. Catena 18, 125-132.

An, Z.S., Porter, S.C., 1997. Millennial - scale climatic oscillations during the last interglaciation in central China. Geology 25, 603-606.

An, Z.S., Kukla, G.J., Porter, S.C., Xiao, J.L., 1991b. Magnetic susceptibility evidence of monsoon variation on the Loess Plateau of central China during the last 130,000 years. Quaternary Research 36, 29-36.

Birkeland, P.W., 1990. Soil - geomorphic research — a selective overview. Geomorphology 3, 207-224.

Birkeland, P.W., 1999. Soils and Geomorphology, 3rd Edition. Oxford University Press, New

York.

Boardman, J., 1985. Comparison of soils in Midwestern United States and Western Europe with the interglacial record. Quaternary Research 23, 62–75.

Bronger, A., Heinkele, T., 1989. Micromorphology and genesis of paleosols in the Luochuan loess section, China: pedostratigraphic and environmental implications. Geoderma 45, 123–143.

Buol, S.W., Hole, F.D., McCracken, R.J., 1989. Soil Genesis and Classification. The Iowa State University Press, Ames, IA.

Catt, J.A., 1986. Soils and Quaternary geology. Monographs on Soil and Resource Survey, Vol. 11. Clarendon Press, Oxford.

Catt, J.A., 1990. Paleopedology manual. Quaternary International 6, 1–95.

Chen, F.H., Bloemendal, J., Wang, J.M., Li, J.J., Oldfield, F., Ma, H.Z., 1997. High resolution multiproxy climate records from Chinese loess: evidence for rapid climatic changes over the last 75 kyr. Palaeogeography, Palaeoecology, Palaeoclimatology 130, 323–335.

Chen, F.H., Boemandel, J., Feng, Z.–D., Wang, J.M., Gou, Z.T., Park, E., Shi, Q., 1999. East Asian monsoon variations during oxygen isotope stage 5: evidence from the northwestern margin of the Chinese Loess Plateau. Quaternary Science Reviews 18, 1127–1135.

Dansgaard, W., Johnson, S.J., Clausen, H.B., Dahl–Jensen, D., Gundestrup, N.S., Hammer, C. U., Hvidberg, C.S., Steffensen, J.P., Sveinbjomsdottir, A.E., Jouzel, J., Bond, G., 1993. Evidence for general instability of past climate from a 250 - kya ice - core record. Nature 364, 218–220.

Derbyshire, E., Keen, D.H., Kemp, R.A., Rolph, T.A., Shaw, J., Meng, X.M., 1995. Loess - paleosol sequences as recorders of palaeoclimatic variations during the last glacial interglacial cycle: some problems of correlation in north - central china. Quaternary Proceedings 4, 7–18.

Derbyshire, E., Kemp, K.A., Meng, X.M., 1997. Climate change, loess and paleosols: proxy and resolution in north china. Journal of the Geological Society (London) 154, 793–805.

Ding, Z.L., Rutter, N., Han, J., Liu, T.S., 1992. A coupled environmental system formed at about 2.5Ma in East Asia. Paleogeography, Paleoclimatology, Paleoecology 94, 223–242.

Feng, Z.–D., Johnson, W.C., Diffendal, R.F., 1994a. Environment of eolian deposition in south - central Nebraska during the Last Glacial Maximum. Physical Geography 15, 250– 258. ARTICLE IN PRESS

Feng, Z.–D., Johnson, W.C., Sprowl, D.R., Lu, Y.–C., Ward, P.A., 1994b. Climatic signals from loess - soil sequences in the central Great Plains, USA. Palaeogeography, Palaeoecology,

Palaeoclimatology 110, 345–358.

Fine, P., Singer, M.J., Verosub, K.L., TenPas, J., 1993. New evidence for the origin of ferrimagnetic minerals in loess from China. Soil Science Society of American Journal 57, 1537–1542.

Fine, P., Verosub, K.L., Singer, M.L., 1995. Pedogenic and lithogenic contribution to the magnetic susceptibility record of the Chinese loess/ paleosol sequence. Geophysical Journal International 122, 97–107.

Foth, H.D., 1978. Fundamentals of Soil Science, 6th Edition. Wiley, New York, NY.

Gile, L.H., 1979. Holocene soils in eolian sediments of Bailey County, Texas. Soil Science Society of American Journal 49, 994–1005.

GRIP Members, 1995. Climate instability during the last interglacial period recorded in the GRIP ice core. Nature, 364, 203–207.

Guo, Z., Liu, T., Guiot, J., Wu, N., Lu, H., Han, J., Liu, J., Gu, Z., 1996a. High frequency pulses of east asian monsoon climate in the last two glaciations: link with the north atlantic. Climate Dynamics 12, 701–709.

Guo, Z.T., Liu, T.S., 1993. Paleosols as evidence of difference of climates between Holocene and the last interglacial. Quaternary Sciences 1993 (1), 41–55 (in Chinese).

Guo, Z.T., Fedoroff, N., Liu, T.S., 1996b. Micromorphology of the loess - paleosol sequence of the last 130 ka in China and paleoclimatic events. Science in China (Series D) 39, 469–477 (in Chinese).

Hallberg, G.R., Wollenhaupt, N.C., Miller, G.A., 1978. A century of soil development in spoil derived from loess in Iowa. Soil Science of American Journal 42, 339–343.

Heller, F., Liu, T.S., 1982. Magnetostratigraphical dating of loess deposits in China. Nature 300, 431–432.

Heller, F., Liu, T.S., 1984. Magnetism of Chinese loess deposits. Geophysical Research Journal 77, 125–141.

Johnson, D.L., Watson - Stegner, D., 1987. Evolution model of pedogenesis. Soil Science 143 (5), 349–364.

Kemp, R.A., 1995. Distribution and genesis of calcitic pedofeatures within a rapidly aggrading loess-paleosol sequence in China. Geoderma 65, 303–316.

Kemp, R.A., Derbyshire, E., Meng, X.M., Chen, F.H., Pan, B.T., 1995. Pedosendimentary reconstruction of a thick loess - paleosol sequence near Lanzhou in north - central China. Quaternary Research 43, 30–45.

Kemp, R.A., Derbyshire, E., Meng, X.M., 1997. Micromorphological variations of the S1 paleosol across northwest China. Catena 31, 77–90.

Kukla, G., An, Z.S., 1989. Loess stratigraphy in central China. Paleogeography, Paleoclimatology, Paleoecology 72, 203–225.

Kukla, G., Heller, F., Liu, X.M., Xu, T.C., Liu, T.S., An, Z.S., 1988. Pleistocene climates in China dated by magnetic susceptibility. Geology 16, 811–814.

Li, J.J., Feng, Z.D., Tang, L.Y., 1988. Late Quaternary monsoon patterns on the Loess Plateau of China. Earth Surface Processes and Landforms 13, 125–135.

Liu, T.S., 1965. Loess Deposits in China. Science Press, Beijing (in Chinese).

Liu, T.S., 1966. Composition and Texture of Chinese Loess. Science Press, Beijing (in Chinese).

Machette, M., 1986. Calciumand magnesium carbonates. In: Singer, M.J., Janitzky, P. (Eds.), Field and Laboratory Procedures used in a Soil Chronosequence Study. US Geological Survey Bulletin, 1648. US Government Printing Office, Washington, DC, pp. 30–33.

Mack, G.H., James, W.C., Monger, H.C., 1993. Classification of paleosols. Geological Society of America Bulletin 105, 129–136.

Maher, B.A., Thompson, R., 1992. Paleoclimatic significance of the mineral magnetic records of the Chinese loess and paleosols. Quaternary Research 37, 155–170.

Maher, B.A., Thompson, R., Zhou, L.P., 1994. Spatial and temporal reconstruction of changes in the Asian paleomonsoon: a new mineral magnetic approach. Earth and Planetary Science Letters 125, 461–471.

McManus, J.F., Bond, G.C., Broecker, W.S., Johnsen, S., Labeyrie, L., Higgins, S., 1994. High-resolution climatic records from the North Atlantic during the last interglaciation. Nature 371, 326–327.

Moore, T.R., 1978. Soil formation in northeastern Canada. Annals of the Association of American Geographers 68, 518–537.

Nettleton, W.D., Olson, C.G., Wysocki, D.A., 2000. Paleosol classification: problems and solutions. Catena 41, 61–92.

O' Green, A.T., Busacca, A.J., 2001. Faunal burrows as indicators of paleo - vegetation in eastern Washington, USA. Paleogeography, Paleoclimatology, Paleoecology 169, 23–37.

Olson, C.G., Nettleton, W.D., 1998. Paleosols and the effects of alteration. Quaternary International 51/52, 185–194.

Phillips, J.D., 1993. Progressive and regressive pedogenesis and complex soil evolution. Quaternary Research 40, 169–176.

Porter, S.C., An, Z.S., 1995. Correlation between climate events in the North Atlantic and China during the last glaciation. Nature 375, 305–308.

Rind, D., Overpeck, J., 1993. Hypothesized causes of decade - tocentury - scale climate variability: climate results. Quaternary Science Reviews 12, 357–374.

Ruhe, R.V., 1973. Background of model for loess - derived soils in the upper Mississippi River Basin. Soil Science 115 (3), 250–253.

Ruhe, R.V., 1983. Depositional environment of late Wisconsin loess in the mid - continental United States. In: Porter, S.C. (Ed.), Later Quaternary Environments of the United States. University of Minnesota Press, Minneapolis, MN, pp. 130–137.

Ruhe, R.V., 1984. Soil - climate system across the prairies in Midwestern USA. Geoderma 34, 201–219.

Ruhe, R.V., Olson, C.G., 1980. Soil welding. Soil Science 130, 132–139.

Ruhe, R.V., Prill, R.C., Piecken, F.F., 1955. Profile characteristics of some loess - derived soils and soil aeration. Soil Science of American Journal 19, 345–348.

Schaetzl, R.J., Sorenson, C.J., 1978. The concept of buried versus isolated paleosols: examples from northeastern Kansas. Soil Science 143 (6), 426–435.

Stoops, G., Eswaran, H. (Eds.), 1986. Soil Micromorphology. Hutchinson Ross, New York.

Thompson, R., Maher, B.A., 1995. Age models, sediment fluxes and paleoclimatic reconstruction for the Chinese loess and paleosol sequences. Geophysical Journal International 123, 611–622.

Thompson, R., Oldfield, F., 1986. Environmental Magnetism. Allen & Unwin, London.

Valentine, K.W.G., Dalrymple, J.B., 1976. Quaternary buried paleosols: a critical review. Quaternary Research 6, 209–222.

Verosub, K.L., Fine, P., Singer, M.J., TenPass, J., 1993. Pedogenesis and paleoclimate: interpretation of the magnetic susceptibility record of Chinese loess - paleosol sequences. Geology 21,1011–1014.

Verosub, K.L., Fine, P., Singer, M.J., TenPass, J., 1994. Reply to the comments on pedogenesis and paleoclimate: interpretation of the magnetic susceptibility record of Chinese loess - paleosol sequences. Geology 22, 859–860.

Zhou, L.P., Oldfield, F., Wintle, A.G., Robinson, S.G., Wang, J.T., 1990. Partly pedogenic origin of magnetic variations in Chinese loess. Nature 346, 1–3.

Zhou, W.J., Donahue, D.J., Porter, S.C., Jule, T.A., Li, Xi.Q., Stuiver, M., An, Z.S., Eiji, M., Dong, G.R., 1996. Variability of monsoon climate in East Asia at the end of the Last Glaciation. Quaternary Research 46, 219–229.

（注:参考文献为原杂志格式。）

Pedogenic factors affecting magnetic susceptibility of the last interglacial paleosol S1 in the Chinese Loess Plateau*

Z.-D. FENG, H. B. WANG, C. G. OLSON

Abstract: The magnetic susceptibility has been used as a quantitative or semi - quantitative proxy for reconstructing the summer monsoon intensity in the Chinese Loess Plateau based on extensive studies on climatic or/and environmental mechanisms producing the magnetic susceptibility signatures. However, the precise nature of the link between past climates and the susceptibility signatures has remained uncertain primarily due to lack of our understanding in the finalizing and preserving processes of the signatures. This paper attempts to examine the reliability or acceptability of this summer monsoon proxy from non - magnetic perspectives of soil - forming processes. We chose nine sections along two transects: one across the western part of the Chinese Loess Plateau and another across the eastern part. Several conclusions can be drawn from our analytical data. First, clay translocation within the S1 paleosol profiles, as indicated by field - observed clay coatings on ped - faces in Bt and Bk horizons and demonstrated by laboratory - analysed clay contents, must have moved some of the magnetic minerals downward so that the susceptibility reflects only the post - translocation distribution of the magnetic - susceptibility producing minerals. Second, the best - developed paleosol S1S3 at most of the sections studied is not expressed by the magnetic susceptibility because this paleosol developed in underlying coarse loess (L2) and coarse textures tend to lower the susceptibility. Third, carbonate concentration is normally negatively correlated with the magnetic susceptibility or simply suppresses the magnetic susceptibility peak when the susceptibility enhancement exceeds the carbonate dilution effect. To conclude, extreme caution must be observed when using magnetic susceptibility signatures to retrieve high - resolution records of the last interglacial palaeoclimate in the Chinese Loess Plateau.

Key words: last interglacial; paleosols; magnetic susceptibility; palaeoclimate

*本文发表于：Earth Surface Processes and Landforms, 2004, 29: 1389-1402.

Introduction

Various magnetic parameters have been employed to demonstrate the degree of pedogenesis within loess, and they have commonly been used as palaeoclimatic proxies in the Chinese Loess Plateau. The magnetic susceptibility signature in Chinese loess, which was the first to show a close correlation with the oceanic ^{18}O signature (Kukla et al., 1988), remains the most convincing climatic proxy (Derbyshire et al., 1997; Heller and Evans, 1995; Maher, 1998; Zhang and Chen, 1995). The susceptibility has therefore been used extensively as a semi-quantitative proxy for reconstructing the summer monsoon intensity (Kukla et al., 1988; An et al., 1991a, b; Kukla et al., 1990; Sun et al., 1995; Chen et al., 1997; Fang et al., 1999) as well as a quantitative proxy for reconstructing mean annual precipitation (Sun et al., 1995; Heller et al., 1993; Maher and Thompson, 1995; Maher et al., 1994). However, the precise nature of the link between past climates and the susceptibility has remained uncertain.

Three distinctive proposals for the magnetic susceptibility signature

Three distinctive hypotheses have been proposed to explain the link between the magnetic susceptibility and climate. First, it was proposed that the magnetic influx has remained constant, with the intensity of dustfall modulating the variation in the susceptibility (Kukla et al., 1988, 1990; An et al., 1991a, b). The second hypothesis states that the degree of pedogenesis has controlled the variation in the susceptibility (Maher and Thompson, 1991, 1992, 1995; Zhou et al., 1990). The third proposal states that the susceptibility signature is a combined result of pedogenic enhancement and detrital inheritance (Fine et al., 1993, 1995; Verosub et al., 1993; Zheng et al., 1991).

Feng (1996) argued that the annual magnetic susceptibility would have to have been constant through time if the first proposal holds. He then calculated the annual susceptibility MS_{annual} as:

$$MS_{annual} = (VS \times H)/T$$

where VS = volumetric susceptibility, H = thickness, and T = time span. The calculated results showed that the annual susceptibility of the last interglacial paleosol S1 is less than half that of the last glacial loess L1 in the northwestern part of the Chinese Loess Plateau where post-depositional alteration has been minimal, and thus the constant magnetic influx proposal does not pass the test. To test the second proposal, Feng (1996) demonstrated that the annual susceptibilities of both the last interglacial paleosol S1 and the last glacial loess L1 do not exhibit a southeasterly increasing trend, although the second proposal predicts such a trend. The third proposal seems reasonable, but it does not include other pedogenic factors that do not necessarily enhance the magnetic susceptibility signature. The pedogenic factors primarily refer to three in situ processes that produce susceptibility - enhancing minerals. They are (1) low - temperature oxidation, (2) geochemical alteration, and (3) biogenic formation (Banerjee et al., 1993; Cui et al., 1994; Derbyshire et al., 1995, 1997, 1998; Evans and Heller, 1994, 2001; Evans and Rokosh, 2000; Eyre and Shaw, 1994; Heller and Evans, 1995; Heller et al., 1993; Liu, 2000; Liu and Liu, 1993; Liu et al., 1992, 1995, 1999; Maher, 1998, 1999; Maher and Thompson, 1991, 1992, 1995, 2000; Meng et al., 1997, 1999; Mullins, 1977; Sun and Liu, 2000; Zhou et al., 1990).

Two components of the magnetic susceptibility signature

Based on stratigraphic comparison of the magnetic susceptibility (Kukla et al., 1988) and ^{10}Be flux (Shen et al., 1992) at the Luochuan section (see Fig. 1 for locations), Beer et al. (1993) and Heller et al. (1993) concluded that 45- 75 percent of the magnetic susceptibility signature is pedogenic in paleosols and only about 20 per cent in loess units. The remainder is the dust component. Evans and Heller (1994) demonstrated that the isothermal remanence magnetization (IRM) spectra remain identical from the northwest to the southeast on the Chinese Loess Plateau, suggesting that a uniform magnetic component-A is widespread across the plateau. Subtracting component-A from the total isolates component- B which increases southeastward, reflecting the summer monsoon pattern. Component-A is inherited from parent materials and component-B is pedogenic. This two-component proposal is in good agreement with the work by Banerjee et al. (1993) and was reconfirmed by Evans and Heller (2001). Fine et al. (1995) and Verosub et al. (1993) used the citrate - bicarbonate - dithionite (CBD) method to distinguish the pedogenically derived susceptibility signature from the parent material inherited signature. However, Liu et al. (1995) have proved that the CBD method is inadequate in separating these two types of signatures.

Other factors affecting the magnetic susceptibility signature

Dilution by carbonate concentration (Heller and Liu, 1986), magnetic enhancement by leaching processes (Anderson and Hallet, 1996), and magnetic alterations by redox cycles (Feng et al., 1994a, b, c, 1998; Feng and Chen, 1999; Feng and Johnson, 1995; Li et al., 1996; Liu, 2000; Liu et al., 1999; Sun and Liu, 2000; Virina et al., 2000; William, 1992) and even particle - size redistribution (Feng, 1997; Feng and Johnson, 1995; Han and Jiang, 1999; Wang et al., 1996; Zheng et al., 1991) are soil - forming processes that contribute to the finalization of the susceptibility signature. Each of the mentioned factors may be location - dependent and/or time - dependent. For example, Feng et al. (1998) showed that a reducing index and a leaching index are the two factors primarily modulating the variations in the magnetic susceptibility at the Beiyuan section in the Linxia Basin of western China, whereas the reducing index and particle size are the two factors primarily modulating the variations in the susceptibility of the northern Mongolian Plateau (Feng, 2001). In the Great Plains of the United States, variations in the susceptibility of the last glacial/interglacial loess - soil sequence are primarily controlled by three factors (Feng, 1997): particle size, carbonate concentration and an oxidizing index. In both the Great Plains of the United States and the Linxia Basin of western China, the variations in the susceptibility of the paleosol formed during the marine oxygen isotope stage 5 are primarily controlled by the carbonate concentration and oxidizing index, whereas the variations in the magnetic susceptibility of the unit formed during the marine isotope stage 3 in both places are basically controlled by the reducing index (Feng et al., 1998; Feng, 1997). It is worth mentioning here that soil - forming processes under persistent or occasional water - saturated conditions normally lower the magnetic susceptibility signature (Evans and Heller, 2001; Feng, 2001; Feng et al., 1994a, b, c, 1998; Feng and Chen, 1999; Liu et al., 1999; Sun and Liu, 2000; Virina et al., 2000). In conclusion, the susceptibility lows and highs might be the result of a combination of pedogenic factors, and the relations of these factors to the summer monsoon intensity are by no means easy to determine.

Fieldwork Strategies and Laboratory Methods

Because of the interaction between the winter and summer monsoons, there is an apparent SE–NW modern climatic gradient on the Chinese Loess Plateau (Li et al., 1988). That is, the mean annual precipitation (MAP) decreases gradually from the southeastern to the northwestern margins with the mean annual temperature (MAT) increasing southward (Fig. 1a), whereas the aridity (the ratio of evaporation and precipitation) increases gradually toward the northwest. The vegetation closely follows the aridity trend (Fig. 1b). The Liupan Mountains divide the Loess Plateau into eastern and western parts.

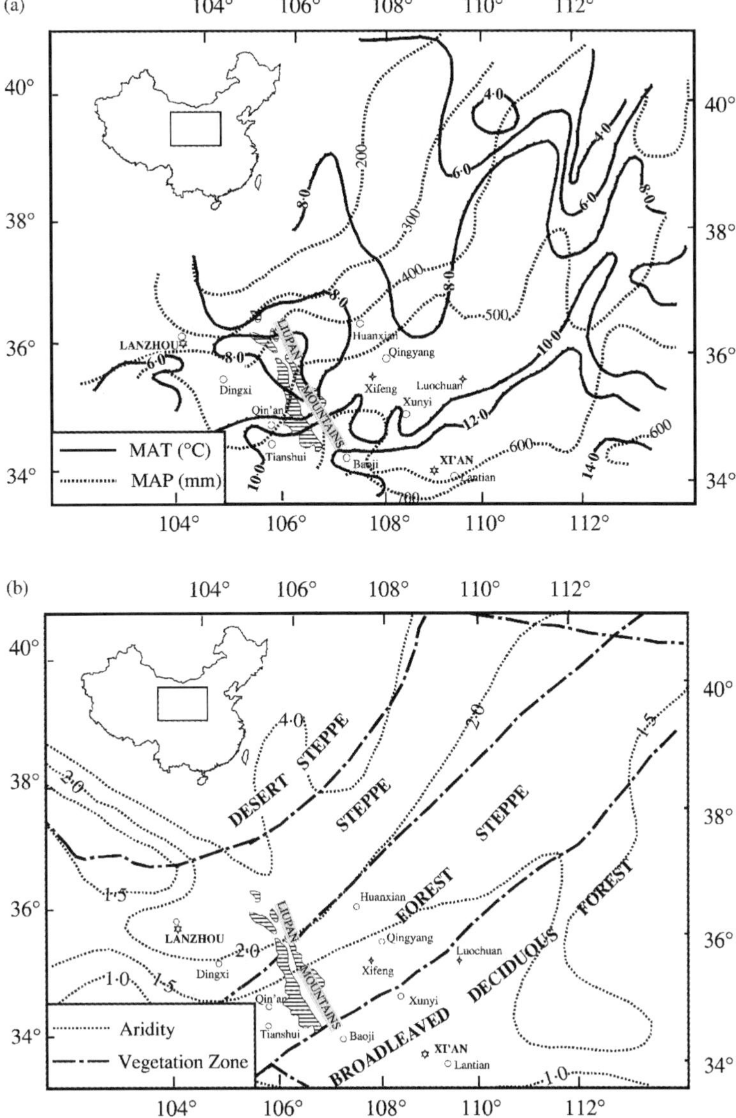

Fig. 1 (a) Mean annual temperature (MAT) and mean annual precipitation (MAP) in the Chinese Loess Plateau; (b) Aridity and natural vegetation distributions in the Chinese Loess Plateau

In order to investigate the geographic differentiation of the last interglacial paleosol S1 and its climatic significance, we chose two transects (see Fig. 1a and b): one across the eastern part of the Loess Plateau from Huanxian to Lantian near Xi'an, and another across the western part from Lanzhou to Tianshui extending to Lantian. The S1 paleosol profiles of the nine sections chosen on the two transects were first described in the field based on the characteristics of the soil horizons (Birkeland, 1999; Buol et al., 1989; Catt, 1986, 1990;

Foth, 1978) and then sampled at 2 cm intervals for laboratory analyses. At all sections investigated, sampling began in the basal part of the L1 loess unit that overlies the S1 paleosol and ended in the uppermost part of the L2 loess that underlies the S1 paleosol. The magnetic susceptibility (SI) was measured by the procedure of Thompson and Oldfield (1986) using a Bartington MS 2B susceptibility meter, and the frequency-dependent susceptibility was calculated based on the high- and low-frequency susceptibility measurements. The particle size of bulk samples was measured using a Malvern Co. Ltd Mastersizer 2000 laser diffraction particle size analyser (Chen et al., 1997) and pretreatments of the samples for particle size analysis include adding (1) H_2O_2 to remove organic and soluble salts, (2) diluted 6 mol/L HCl to remove carbonate, and (3) Na-hexametaphosphate to disperse the aggregates (Janitzky, 1987). The carbonate content was measured with the modified gas evolution method (Machette, 1986) using the Bascomb Calcimeter.

Geographic Variations of the Susceptibility Signature

The net accumulation of loess should have attenuated and the pedogenesis should have intensified southeastward during the last interglacial. Consequently, the last interglacial paleosol (S1) profiles and their relations to their parent materials should have systematically varied from the northwest to the southeast.

Geographic differentiation of the pedostratigraphy

In the northwestern part of the Loess Plateau (e.g. at the Lanzhou section in Fig. 1), an 8 m thick S1 pedocomplex consists of multiple A-C soil profiles (Chen et al., 1999; Derbyshire et al., 1995, 1997; Kemp et al., 1995, 1997). Three incipient soils (A-C profiles) mark the marine isotope substages 5a (S1S1), 5c (S1S2) and 5e (S1S3). Two interbedded loess units demarcate the substages 5b (S1L1) and 5d (S1L2) (Fig. 2). Southeastward near Dingxi where the S1 paleosol is 5 m thick, two incipient soils (A-C profiles) corresponding to the marine isotope substages 5a and 5c are better developed than those at the Lanzhou section. Corresponding to the substage 5e (i.e. S1S3) is a Mollisol-like soil with both A horizon and Bk horizon developed. Farther to the southeast near Qin'an where the S1 paleosol complex is 4 m thick, there are three Mollisol-like soils, each having an A horizon and a Bk horizon, corresponding to the three odd-numbered marine isotope substages (5a, 5c and 5e). The S1L1 loess unit separates the S1S1 and

S1S2 paleosols and the loess unit S1L2 between the S1S2 and S1S3 is not present here (see Fig. 2). The S1 at the Tianshui section, about 50 km south of the Qin'an section, is a pedocomplex without those two interbedded loess units, that is, neither S1L1 nor S1L2 is present. This 4.5 m thick S1 paleosol has a 0.8 m thick mollic A horizon, a 2.5 m thick Bt horizon and 1.2 m thick Bk horizon.

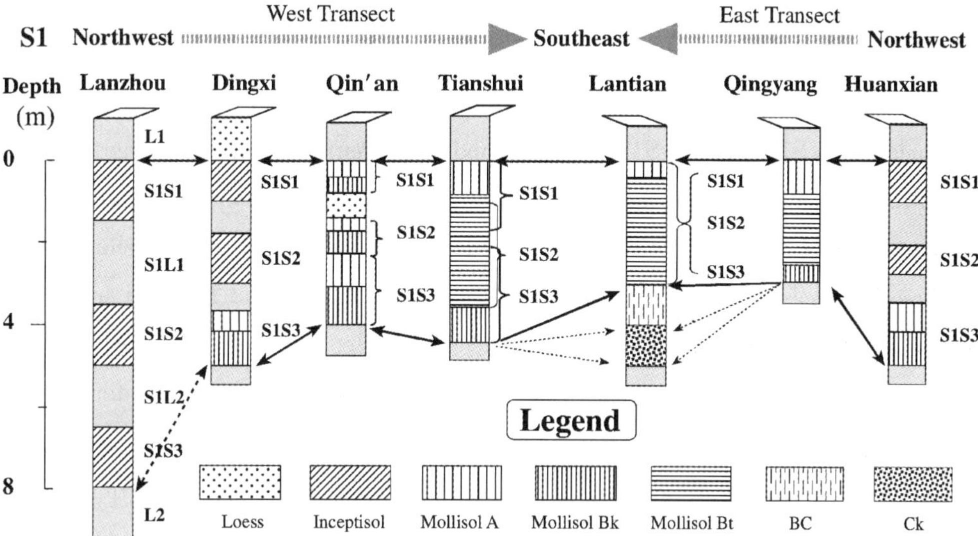

Fig. 2 The geographic differentiation of the S1 paleosol profiles from the northwestern margin to the southeastern margin in the Chinese Loess Plateau: all of the five pedostratigraphic units (S1S1, S1L1, S1S2, S1L2, S1S3) are preserved at the Lanzhou and Dingxi sections; the S1L2 was annexed by the S1S2 development at the Qin' an section and both the S1L2 and S1L1 were annexed at the Tianshui sections; the S1 at the Lantian section is a completely welded paleosol profile.

Unlike other sections reported here, the last glacial loess L1 (i.e. the Malan Loess) at the two sections selected in the Guanzhong Basin (Baoji and Lantian sections) is not loess. The loess units corresponding to the marine isotope stages (MIS) 2 and 4 experienced much stronger pedogenesis than the soil units S1S1 and S1S2 at the Lanzhou and Dingxi sections and the "loess" unit corresponding to the MIS 3 has well-developed accretionary mollic A horizons (i.e. cumulic soils). The last interglacial paleosol S1 is basically a well-developed Bt horizon. The Xunyi and Qingyang sections, located in the same bioclimatic settings as the well-known Luochuan and Xifeng sections in the eastern part of the Chinese Loess Plateau (Fig. 1b), are characterized by a single soil profile with an A horizon, a Bt horizon and a Bk horizon. Carbonate coats the illuvial clay on ped-faces (threads and filaments) in the matrix of Bt horizons, and concentrates as masses or nodules in the Bk horizons at both sections. Farther to the northwest at the Huanxian section, the field - observed pedostratigraphy is similar to that at the Dingxi section and the laboratory - analysed data are similar to those at the Qin' an section. Specifically, all three paleosols (S1S1, S1S2 and S1S3) and the two intervening loess units (S1L1 and S1L2) are identifiable and the S1S3 paleosol is the best developed (Fig. 2).

To sum up, the last interglacial paleosol (S1) profiles become gradually differentiated from the northwest to the southeast. Near the northwestern margin of the Loess Plateau, the three paleosols (S1S1, S1S2, S1S3) corresponding to marine isotope substages 5a, 5c and 5e and the two intervening loess units (S1L1 and S1L2) corresponding to marine isotope substages 5b and 5d are completely preserved (e.g. at the Dingxi and Lanzhou sections). The three paleosols (S1S1, S1S2, S1S3) are partially welded at the Tianshui section where accretionary B horizons dominate the S1 paleosol profile, and the lower portion of the S1 paleosol developed in the underlying older loess L2. During the same time interval (marine isotope stage 5), a single soil profile formed on the southeastern margin of the Loess Plateau (i.e. completely welded at the Lantian section) and a major portion of the S1 paleosol developed into the underlying older loess L2. Consequently, the magnetic susceptibility should have responded to the geographic variations as already noted by some researchers (Derbyshire et al., 1995; Evans and Rokosh, 2000; Feng et al., 2004; Rokosh et al., 2002; Zhu et al., 2001).

Geographic variations of the magnetic susceptibility signature

Before examining the geochemical contributions (e.g. oxidizing, reducing and leaching indices) to the magnetic susceptibility signature, we had established that particle size distributions and carbonate concentrations account for the majority of the variations in the magnetic susceptibility signature. Yet, particle size distributions and carbonate concentrations in the S1 paleosol profiles are the final results of pedogenic processes occurring during the entire soil-forming period. We first conducted a correlation analysis of the magnetic susceptibility signatures with seven particle size fractions and carbonate concentration for the nine chosen sections. We found that the following particle size fractions, as well as the carbonate concentrations, have the highest correlation coefficients with the magnetic signatures: >63 μm, 2–10 μm and <2 μm.

Lanzhou section. The following observations can be made from Tab. I and Fig. 3. First, the low-field magnetic susceptibility (χ) does not negatively follow the overall trends of the percentage of >63 μm (r =−0.219, n=650) and its dictated median size (Md). That is, the loess units within the S1 (S1L1 and S1L2) do not have higher magnetic susceptibility values than the L1 and L2, although the S1L1 and S1L2 are considerably finer. Second, the correlation between clay (<2 μm) content and the magnetic susceptibility (χ) is very low (r= 0.056) and the correlation becomes negative in two zones: first at the depth of 8−9 m (marked as I in Fig. 3) where higher clay contents correspond to lower magnetic susceptibility values, and second at the depth of 9−10 m (marked as Ⅱ in Fig. 3) where lower clay contents correspond to higher magnetic susceptibility values. Third, among all searched particle size fractions, the 2−20 μm fraction has the highest correlation coefficient with the magnetic susceptibility (r=0.421) and with the frequency-dependent susceptibility (r=0.632). Fourth, the variations in the >63 μm and 2−10 μm fraction account for the first-trend variations in the magnetic susceptibility. The second-trend variations superimposed on the first-trend ones are readily explained by the variations in the carbonate concentration. In general, the magnetic susceptibility highs are responsive to the carbonate lows (r=−0.505) and the magnetic susceptibility lows within the magnetic susceptibility peaks expressing the S1S2 and S1S3 (marked as 1 and 2 in Fig. 3) are responsive to the carbonate highs in particular.

Dingxi section. At the Dingxi section, the overall trend of the magnetic susceptibility from the L1 to the L2 through the S1 does not follow the particle size trends (both Md and > 63 μm fraction). That is, the loess units within the S1 (S1L1 and S1L2) do not have higher magnetic susceptibility than the L1 and L2 although the S1L1 and S1L2 are considerably finer. The correlation coefficients of the susceptibility with >63 μm fraction (r =−0.501, n = 300) and with 2−10 μm fraction (r = 0.565) are improved in comparison with those at the Lanzhou section. Again, the correlation with the clay (<2 μm) content remains very low (r = 0.133). It is also noticeable that the overall correlation coefficient between the magnetic susceptibility (χ) and carbonate concentration (percentage) is close to zero (r = 0.012) and the first magnetic susceptibility peak corresponding to the S1S1 is absent here, although the frequency-dependent susceptibility (χ_{fd}) does express the S1S1 well. According to the general correlation between the magnetic susceptibility (χ) and the frequency-dependent susceptibility (χ_{fd}) at the nine chosen sections (Tab. I), the magnetic susceptibility peak expressing S1S1 should be present at this section. To examine possible reasons why it is absent, we made two predictions of the magnetic susceptibility (χ), the first based on the correlation between the χ and χ_{fd} for the entire measured section (r = 0.887), and the second on the linear relationship of the χ with thc >63 μm fraction and 2−10 μm fraction for the entire measured section. Both predictions indicate the

Tab. I The correlation coefficients of the magnetic susceptibility (χ) and frequency-dependent magnetic susceptibility (χ_{fd}) with the percentages of particle size fractions and carbonate content at seven selected sections in the Chinese Loess Plateau

Section	Variables	>63 μm	2–10 μm	<2 μm	$CaCO_3$	χ_{fd}
Lanzhou (n=650)	χ	−0.219	0.421	0.056	−0.505	0.864
	χ_{fd}	−0.446	0.632	0.267	−0.335	—
Dingxi (n=300)	χ	−0.501	0.565	0.133	−0.114	0.887
	χ_{fd}	−0.705	0.780	0.376	0.012	—
Qin'an (n=250)	χ	−0.824	0.825	0.491	−0.094	0.987
	χ_{fd}	−0.866	0.849	0.615	0.126	—
Tianshui (n=250)	χ	−0.732	0.727	0.627	−0.749	0.948
	χ_{fd}	−0.764	0.769	0.640	−0.665	—
Lantian (n=300)	χ	−0.886	0.918	0.793	0.119	0.834
	χ_{fd}	−0.914	0.838	0.787	0.172	—
Qingyang (n=200)	χ	−0.838	0.973	0.955	−0.933	0.963
	χ_{fd}	−0.899	0.967	0.948	−0.943	—
Huanxian (n=350)	χ	−0.853	0.935	0.946	−0.733	0.924
	χ_{fd}	−0.877	0.940	0.957	−0.641	—

existence of the χ peak corresponding to the S1S1. We noticed that the correlation coefficient between the carbonate concentration and the frequency - dependent susceptibility (χ_{fd}) is negative in the lower (2.5 to 6 m) portion (r =−0.585) and positive in the upper (0 to 2.5 m) portion (r = 0.415). We also noticed that the two major carbonate concentration highs in the lower portion (marked as Ⅲ and Ⅱ in Fig. 4) correspond to two lows in both the susceptibility and the frequency - dependent susceptibility. However, the carbonate high at the upper portion (marked as Ⅰ in Fig. 4) is responsive to the frequency-dependent susceptibility high expressing the S1S1. We know that the frequency-dependent susceptibility is independent of the carbonate concentration and the susceptibility signature can be readily diluted by carbonate concentration. Therefore, the carbonate peak (marked as Ⅰ in Fig. 4) is responsible for the absence of the susceptibility peak expressing the S1S1.

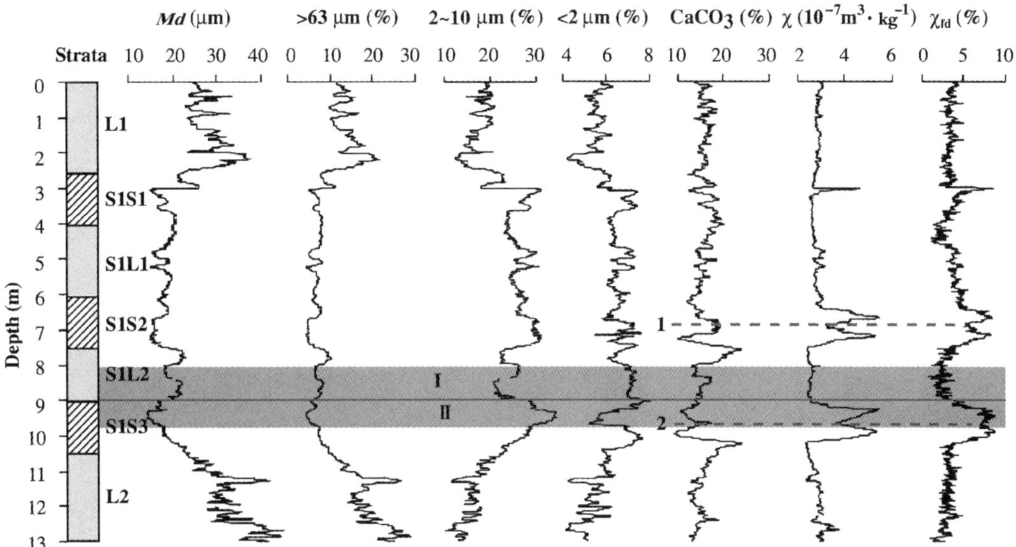

Fig. 3 Lanzhou section: field-observed pedostratigraphy and laboratory data. *Md*(μm), median size (μm); >63 μm (%), percentage of >63 μm fraction; 2–10 μm (%), percentage of 2–10 μm fraction; <2 μm (%), percentage of <2 μm fraction; $CaCO_3$ (%), percentage of carbonate; χ, magnetic susceptibility ($10^{-7}m^3 \cdot kg^{-1}$) and χ_{fd}, frequency-dependent susceptibility (%).

Qin' an section. At the Qin' an section, the correlation coefficients of both the susceptibility (χ) and frequency-dependent susceptibility (χ_{fd}) with the >63 μm fraction (negative) and 2–10 μm fraction (positive) are very high (see Tab. I) and account for over 80 per cent of the variations in the magnetic susceptibility signatures. Unlike at the Lanzhou and Dingxi sections, the clay (<2 μm) content is positively correlated with χ(r = 0.491, n = 250) and χ_{fd} (r = 0.615) at the Qin' an section. Again, the carbonate concentration does not appear to correlate with the overall trend of the susceptibility (r = – 0.094), but the carbonate variations correspond very well with the secondary variations in the magnetic susceptibility as marked in Fig. 5 (e.g., zones Ⅰ, Ⅱ, Ⅲ, and Ⅳ). It is most noticeable that neither χ nor χ_{fd} expresses the existence of the S1S3 unit although it is a much better developed paleosol than the S1S2 and S1S1 according to the field observations (see Feng et al., 2004). It is apparent that the coarsening trend of the particle size in S1S3 has suppressed the susceptibility peak. The absence of the S1L2 between the S1S3 and S1S2 had the effect of making S1S3 even less distinguishable in the susceptibility curves.

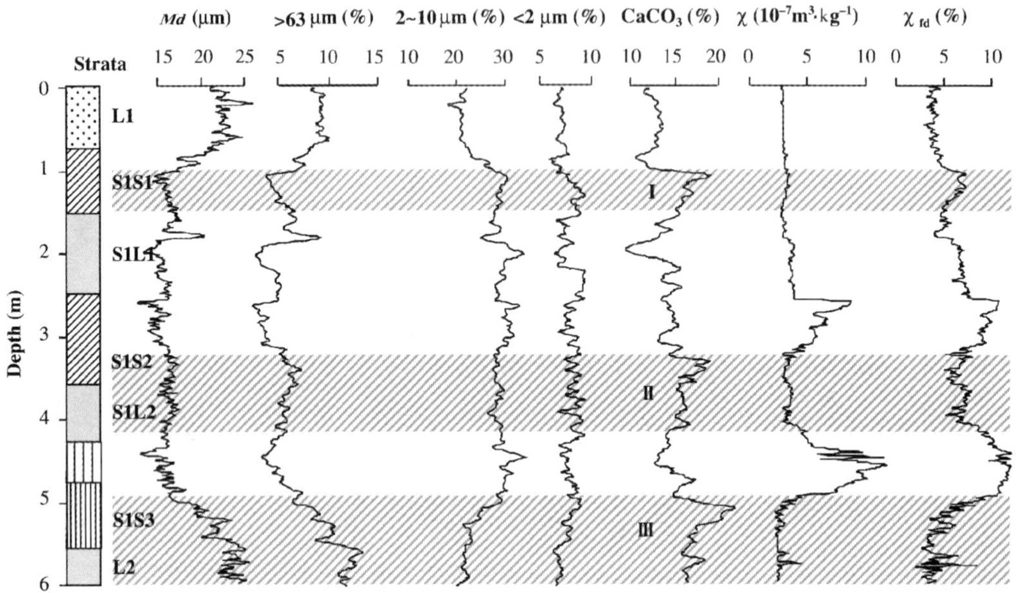

Fig. 4 Dingxi section: field-observed pedostratigraphy and laboratory data.

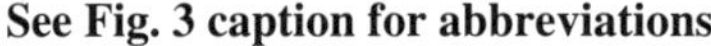
See Fig. 3 caption for abbreviations

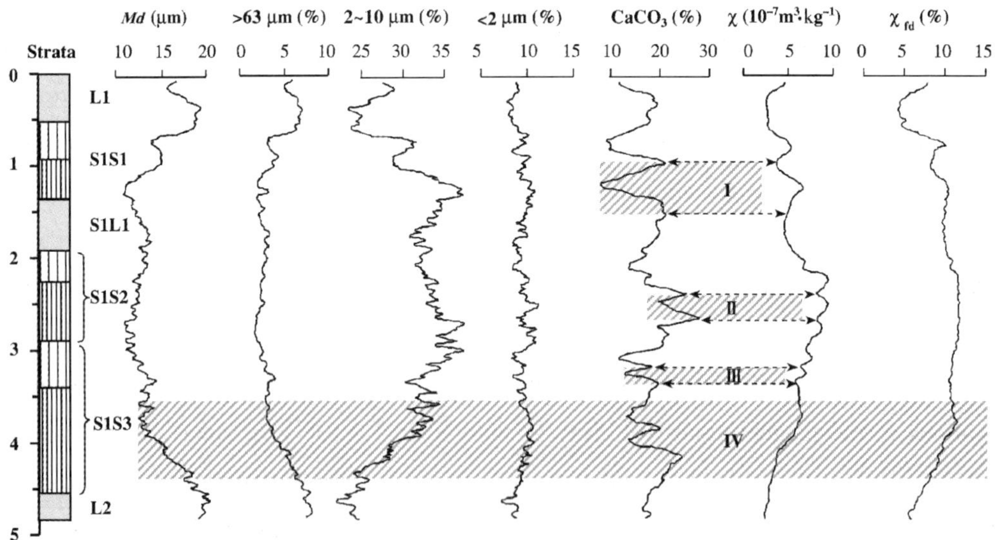

Fig. 5 Qin'an section: field-observed pedostratigraphy and laboratory data.

See Fig. 3 caption for abbreviations

Tianshui section. The S1 is a pedocomplex at the Tianshui section, both S1L2 and S1L1 being absent (Fig. 6). Carbonate concentration, as well as soil morphologic features (see Feng et al., 2004), suggest that the three paleosols (S1S1, S1S2 and S1S3) are partially welded. That is, both the S1S3 and S1S2 paleosol development formed the Bk horizon as indicated by arrows (associated with 3 and 2) in Fig. 6 and shared a major portion of the soil profile. The carbonate-enriched layer 1 in Fig. 6 may mark the bottom of the S1S1 or a later stage of the S1S1 carbonate leaching, and the S1S1 development might have annexed the uppermost portion of the S1S2 as the arrows indicate (associated with 1) in Fig. 6. The soil annexation and welding not only altered S1L1 and S1L2 into soils but also altered the soil A horizons of the S1S3 and S1S2 into later B horizons, forming thick accretionary B horizons. As a result, the magnetic susceptibility signature does not distinguish the three soil-forming events (S1S1, S1S2, S1S3). The magnetic susceptibility (χ) is well correlated with the >63 μm fraction (r =−0.732, n = 250), with the 2−10 μm fraction (r = 0.727) and with the carbonate concentration (r =−0.748). The clay content is also well correlated with the susceptibility (r = 0.627).

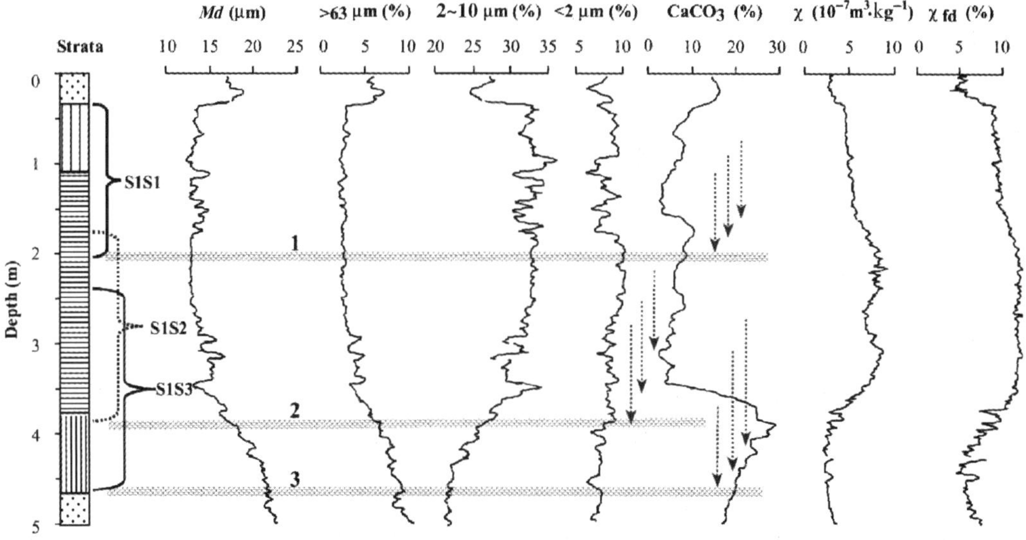

Fig. 6 Tianshui section: field-observed pedostratigraphy and laboratory data. See Fig. 3 caption for abbreviations

Lantian section. In the Guangzhong Basin of the eastern part of the Chinese Loess Plateau, we investigated two similar sections: Baoji and Lantian. We focus here on the Lantian Section. The three soil-forming sequences observed in the more northwesterly sites (discussed above) occur as one single soil profile at the Lantian section. Two features are quite noticeable at this section. First, a major portion of the S1 paleosol developed in a coarse parent material, suggesting that the paleosol mainly developed in underlying older loess L2. Second, the carbonate concentration is quite low in the Bt and BC horizons and very high in the Ck horizon, implying that the Ck horizon might have served as the carbonate accumulation zone for all of the three soil - forming events (S1S1, S1S2, S1S3). The 2–10 μm fraction has the highest correlation coefficient with the magnetic susceptibility (r = 0.918, n = 300), followed by the >63 μm fraction (r =–0.886) and the < 2 μm fraction (r = 0.793). The carbonate concentration plays almost no role in shaping the susceptibility curve (r = 0.119) except in the Ck horizon. The particle - size coarsening from 2.5 to 4.5 m deep (shaded zone in Fig. 7) is certainly responsible for lowering the susceptibility.

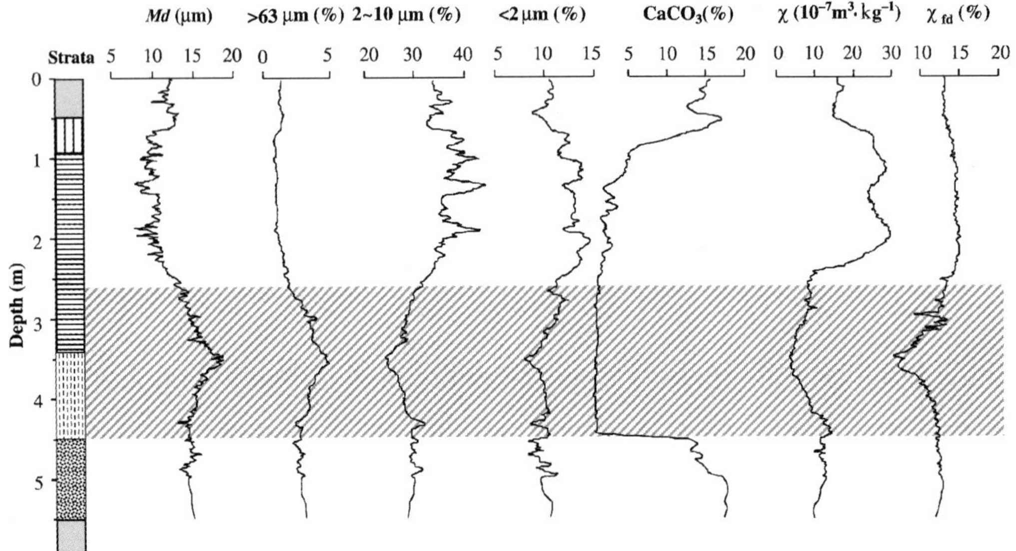

Fig. 7 Lantian section: field-observed pedostratigraphy and laboratory data. See Fig. 3 caption for abbreviations

Qingyang section. In the centre of the eastern part of the Chinese Loess Plateau, two similar sections, Xunyi and Qingyang, are located in the same bioclimatic settings as the well - known Luochuan and Xifeng sections. Qingyang section is focused on here. It is characterized by a single thick soil profile with an A horizon, a Bt horizon and a Bk horizon (Fig. 8). Not only are the correlation coefficients of the magnetic susceptibility (χ) with the >63 μm fraction (r =–0.838, n = 200) and with the 2–10 μm fraction (r = 0.967) very high, but the coefficients with the clay content (r = 0.955) and with the carbonate concentration (r =–0.933) are also extremely high. It seems that none of the parameters, magnetic or non - magnetic, can distinguish the three soil - forming events (S1S1, S1S2, S1S3) within the S1 paleosol.

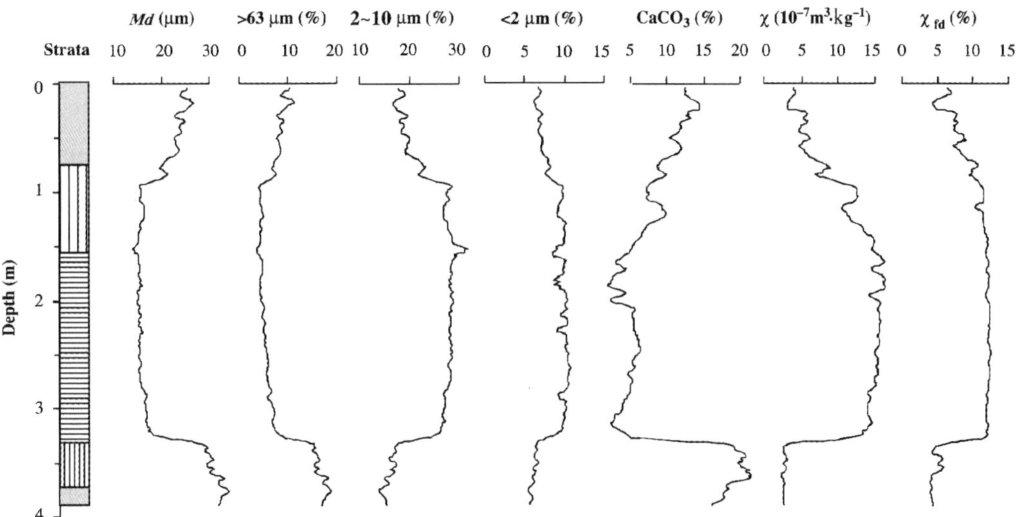

Fig. 8 Qingyang section: field-observed pedostratigraphy and laboratory data. See Fig. 3 caption for abbreviations

Huanxian section. Farther to the northwest along the eastern transect, not only are the three constituent S1 paleosols (S1S1, S1S2, S1S3) well preserved, but so are the intervening loess units (S1L1 and S1L2) (Fig. 9). It seems that the >63 μm fraction shapes the overall trend of the magnetic susceptibility (r =− 0.853, n = 350) and the carbonate concentration definitely modulates the secondary variations superimposed on the

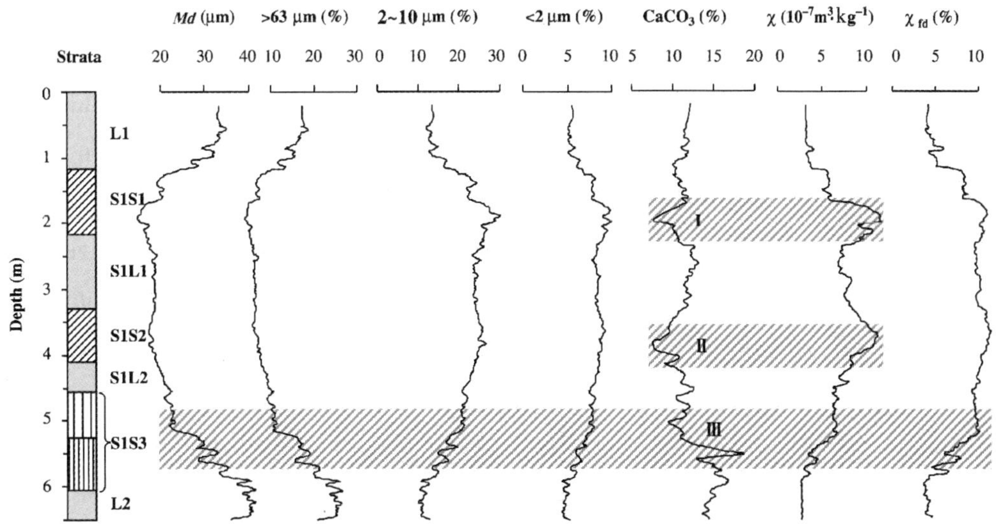

Fig. 9 Huanxian section: field-observed pedostratigraphy and laboratory data. See Fig. 3 caption for abbreviations

overall trend (r =− 0.733) as marked in Fig. 9 (Ⅰ and Ⅱ). Again, the magnetic susceptibility does not express the existence of S1S3 although it is the best - developed paleosol in this section. The magnetic susceptibility peak expressing S1S3 can be recovered by excluding the negative effect of the >63 μm fraction. In other words, the particle - size coarsening in zone Ⅲ (Figure 9) should be held responsible for suppressing the magnetic susceptibility peak expressing the S1S3.

Discussions and Conclusions

Our analyses confirm that the 2−10 μm fraction is a major contributor to the magnetic susceptibility signature, as reported by Han and Jiang (1999). If the so - called ultrafine superparamagnetic minerals are the ones that modulate the frequency - dependent susceptibility and the importance of the 2−10 μm fraction in contributing to both high - and low - frequency susceptibility is undeniable, well - weathered rinds of silt particles (several nanometers thick), as observed by Cui et al. (1994), Liu et al. (1995) and Maher and Thompson (2000), may be the answer to reconcile the discrepancy. That is, the ultrafine superparamagnetic minerals are primarily included in those weathered rinds of silt particles in the cases where the 2−10 μm fraction seems to be modulating both the magnetic susceptibility and frequency - dependent susceptibility signatures. Another possibility is that the ultrafine particles (<0.03 μm) adhere to larger particles (e.g. 2−10 μm) so strongly that standard procedures failed to separate the particles (E. Derbyshire, 2003, personal communication). To examine the possible adherence of ultrafine particles to larger ones, we observed several representative samples under the microscope and the results show that the adherence of ultrafine particles to the larger ones mainly occurs in the clay fraction, not in the 2−10 μm fraction.

It appears that the 2−10 μm fraction is the most important modulator (positive) which is in turn modulated primarily by the >63 μm fraction (negative). The clay content is a major player in shaping the magnetic susceptibility curves in the eastern part of the Chinese Loess Plateau and becomes an important player only in the southernmost section (e.g. at Tianshui) in the western part. Our explanation is that weathered magnetic rinds of silt - sized particles dominate the susceptibility signature in the sections where the weathering was relatively weaker during the last interglacial, whereas the weathering - produced magnetic clay - sized particles dominate the signature in the sections where the weathering was relatively strong. Clay translocation within the S1 paleosol profiles, as indicated by field and X-ray diffraction observations of clay coatings on ped-faces in Bt and Bk horizons (Feng et al., 2003) and demonstrated by laboratory-analysed clay-content curves, must have moved some of the magnetic minerals downward so that the susceptibility only reflects the post-translocation distribution of the magnetic susceptibility-producing minerals. Also documented by this study, the best-developed paleosol S1S3 at most of the sections studied is not expressed by the magnetic susceptibility at all because the S1S3 developed into underlying coarse loess (L2) and coarser texture lowers the susceptibility. Carbonate concentration is normally negatively correlated with the magnetic susceptibility for two reasons: (1) wellweathered and susceptibility-enhanced layers are normally carbonate-depleted (leached); and (2) the leached carbonate is normally accumulated in the layer immediately below the depleted layer. But carbonate can also accumulate in the susceptibility-enhanced weathered layer if carbonate leaching is not strong enough, such as in the upper portion (0- 2.5 m) of the Dingxi section. In this case, the carbonate concentration simply suppresses the magnetic susceptibility peak. To conclude, extreme caution must be taken when one uses the susceptibility signature to retrieve a high-resolution proxy record of the last interglacial palaeoclimate in the Chinese Loess Plateau.

Acknowledgement

This research is financially supported in part by a US National Science Foundation grant (BCS-0078557) and a Chinese Education Ministry grant (No. 2000-65).

References

An Z, Kukla GJ, Porter SC, Xiao JL. 1991a. Late Quaternary dust flux on the Chinese Loess Plateau. *Catena* 18: 125-132.

An ZS, Kukla GJ, Porter SC, Xiao JL. 1991b. Magnetic susceptibility evidence of monsoon variation on the Loess Plateau of central China during the last 130,000 years. *Quaternary Research* 36: 29-36.

Anderson RS, Hallet B. 1996. Simulating magnetic susceptibility profiles in loess as an aid in quantifying rates of dust deposition and pedogenic development. *Quaternary Research* 45: 1-16.

Banerjee SK, Hunt CP, Liu XM. 1993. Separation of local signal from regional paleomonsoon record of Chinese Loess Plateau: a rock magnetic approach. *Geophysical Research Letters* 20: 843–846.

Beer J, Shen CD, Heller F, Liu TS, Kubik PW. 1993. ^{10}Be and magnetic susceptibility in Chinese loess. *Geophysical Research Letters* 20: 57–60.

Birkeland PW. 1999. *Soils and Geomorphology* (3rd edition). Oxford University Press: New York.

Buol SW, Hole FD, McCracken RJ. 1989. *Soil Genesis and Classification*. The Iowa State University Press: Ames, Iowa.

Catt JA. 1986. *Soils and Quaternary Geology*. Monographs on Soil and Resource Survey, No. 11. Clarendon Press: Oxford.

Catt JA. 1990. Paleopedology Manual. *Quaternary International* 6: 1–95.

Chen FH, Bloemendal J, Wang JM, Li JJ, Oldfield F. 1997. High resolution multi-proxy climate records from Chinese loess: evidence for rapid climatic changes over the last 75 kyr. *Palaeogeography Palaeoclimatology Palaeoecology* 130: 323–335.

Chen FH, Boemandel J, Feng ZD, Wang JM, Gou ZG, Park E, Shi Q. 1999. East Asian monsoon variations during the Last Interglacial: evidence from the northwestern margin of the Chinese Loess Plateau. *Quaternary Science Reviews* 18: 1127–1135.

Cui YL, Verosub KL, Roberts AP. 1994. The effect of low-temperature oxidation on large multi-domain magnetite. *Geophysical Research Letters* 21: 757–760.

Derbyshire E, Keen DH, Kemp RA, Rolph TA, Shaw J, Meng XM. 1995. Loess - paleosol sequences as recorders of palaeoclimatic variations during the last glacial interglacial cycle: some problems of correlation in north-central China. *Quaternary Proceedings* 4: 7–18.

Derbyshire E, Kemp KA, Meng XM. 1997. Climate change, loess and paleosols: proxy and resolution in North China. *Journal of the Geological Society (London)* 154: 793–805.

Derbyshire E, Meng XM, Kemp KA. 1998. Provenance, transport and characteristics of modern aeolian dust in western Gansu Province, China, and interpretation of the Quaternary loess record. *Journal of Arid Environments* 39: 497–516.

Evans ME, Heller F. 1994. Magnetic enhancement and paleoclimate: study of a loess/paleosol couplet across the Loess Plateau of China. *Geophysical Journal International* 117: 257–264.

Evans ME, Heller F. 2001. Magnetism of loess/paleosol sequences: recent developments. *Earth Science Reviews* 54: 129–144.

Evans ME, Rokosh CD. 2000. The last interglacial in the Chinese Loess Plateau: a petromagnetic investigation of samples from a northsouth transect. *Quaternary International* 68–71: 77–82.

Eyre JK, Shaw J. 1994. Magnetic enhancement of Chinese loess — the role of Fe_2O_3? *Geophysical Journal International* 117: 265–171.

Fang XM, Ono Y, Fukusawa H, Pan BT, Li JJ, Guan DH, Oi K, Tsukamoto S, Torri M, Mishima T. 1999. Asian summer monsoon instability during the past 60,000 years: magnetic susceptibility and pedogenic evidence from the western Chinese Loess Plateau. *Earth and Planetary Science Letters* 168: 219–232.

Feng H, Pope GA, Feng Z-D, Cedfelli CE, Lanziotti A, Jones KW. 2003. Mineralogical and structural study of the S1 loess/paleosol composition of the Chinese Loess Plateau using XRD and XANES based on Synchronton technologies. *INQUA Conference*, 23–31 June 2003, Reno, USA, abstract.

Feng Z-D. 1996. Climatic implications of magnetic susceptibility and ^{10}Be flux in Chinese loess. *Catena* 27: 143–147.

Feng Z-D. 1997. Geochemical characteristics of a loess-soil sequence in central Kansas, USA. *Soil Science Society of American Journal* 61: 534–541.

Feng Z-D. 2001. Gobi dynamics in the northern Mongolian Plateau during the past 20,000 years: preliminary result. *Quaternary International* 76/77: 77–83.

Feng Z-D, Chen F-H. 1999. Problems of magnetic susceptibility signature as the proxy of the summer monsoon intensity in Chinese Loess Plateau. In *International Symposium on Paleosols and Climate Change, Chinese Science Bulletin* 44 (suppl. 1): 97–104.

Feng, Z-D, Johnson WC. 1995. Factors affecting the magnetic susceptibility of a loess-soil sequence, Barton County, Kansas, USA. *Catena* 24: 25–37.

Feng Z-D, Johnson WC, Diffendal RF. 1994a. Environment of eolian deposition in south-central Nebraska during the Last Glacial Maximum. *Physical Geography* 15(3): 250–258.

Feng Z-D, Johnson WC, Sprowl DR, Lu YC. 1994b. Loess accumulation and soil formation in central Kansas, USA, during the past 400,000 years. *Earth Surface Processes and Landforms* 19: 55–67.

Feng Z-D, Johnson WC, Sprowl DR, Lu YC, Ward PA. 1994c. Climatic signals from loess-soil sequences in the central Great Plains, USA. *Palaeogeography, Palaeoclimatology, Palaeoecology* 110: 345–358.

Feng Z-D, Chen FH, Tang LY, Kang JC. 1998. East Asian monsoon variations and Gobi dynamics in marine isotope stages 4 and 3. *Catena* 33: 29–46.

Feng Z-D, Wang HB, Olson CG, Pope GA, Chen FH, Zhang JW, An CB. 2004. Chronological discord between the last interglacial paleosol (S1) and its parent material in the Chinese Loess Plateau. *Quaternary International* 117: 17–26.

Fine P, Singer MJ, Verosub KL, TenPas J. 1993. New evidence for the origin of ferrimagnetic minerals in loess from China. *Soil Science Society of American Journal* 57: 1537–1542.

Fine P, Verosub KL, Singer ML. 1995. Pedogenic and lithogenic contribution to the magnetic susceptibility record of the Chinese loess/paleosol sequence. *Geophysical Journal International* 122: 97–107.

Foth HD. 1978. *Fundamentals of Soil Science* (6th edition). John Wiley and Sons: New York.

Han J- M, Jiang W- Y. 1999. Particle size contribution to bulk magnetic susceptibility in Chinese loess and paleosol. *Quaternary International* 62: 103–110.

Heller F, Evans ME. 1995. Loess magnetism. *Reviews of Geophysics*. 33: 211–240.

Heller F, Liu TS. 1986. Paleoclimatic and sedimentary history from magnetic susceptibility of loess in China. *Geophysical Research Letters* 13: 613–618.

Heller F, Shen CD, Beer J, Liu XM, Liu TS, Bronger A, Suter M, Bonani G. 1993. Quantitative estimates of pedogenic ferromagnetic mineral formation in Chinese loess and paleoclimatic implications. *Earth and Planetary Science Letters* 114: 385–390.

Janitzky, P. 1987. Particle size analysis. In *Field and Laboratory Procedures used in Soil Chronosequence Study*, Singer M, Janitzky P (eds). US Geological Survey Bulletin 1648. Government Printing Office: Washington, DC: 11–16.

Kemp RA, Derbyshire E, Meng X- M, Chen F- H, Pan B- T. 1995. Pedosedimentary reconstruction of a thick loess - paloesol sequence near Lanzhou in North - Central China. *Quaternary Research* 43: 30–45.

Kemp RA, Derbyshire E, Meng X–M. 1997. Micromorphological variations of the S1 paleosol across northwest China. *Catena* 31: 77–90.

Kukla G, Heller F, Liu XM, Xu TC, Liu TS, An ZS. 1988. Pleistocene climates in China dated by magnetic susceptibility. *Geology* 16: 811–814.

Kukla G, An ZS, Melice JL, Gavin J, Xiao J–L. 1990. Magnetic susceptibility record of Chinese loess. *Transactions of the Royal Society of Edinburgh* (*Earth Sciences*) 81: 263–288.

Li JJ, Feng Z–D, Tang LY. 1988. Late Quaternary monsoon patterns on the Loess Plateau of China. *Earth Surface Processes and Landforms* 13: 125–135.

Li Z, Zhou SK, Zeng DW. 1996. Relation between magnetic susceptibility and $Fe^{2+}/(Fe^{2+}+Fe^{3+})$ and relative contents of iron in Zhouyuan loess. *Marine Geology and Quaternary Geology* 16 (4): 105–112 (in Chinese).

Liu J. 2000. Reductive diagenesis of magnetic minerals: a review. *Marine Geology and Quaternary Geology* 20(4): 103–107 (in Chinese).

Liu XM, Liu TS. 1993. Magnetic mineral characteristics of Chinese loess and its paleoclimatic significance. *Quaternary Sciences* 3: 281–287 (in Chinese).

Liu XM, Shaw J, Liu TS, Heller F, Yuan BY. 1992. Magnetic mineralogy of Chinese Loess and its significance. *Geophysical Journal International* 108: 301–308.

Liu XM, Rolph T, Bloemendal J, 1995. The Citrate-Biicarbonate-Dithionite (CBD) removable magnetic component of Chinese loess. *Quaternary Proceedings* 4: 53–58.

Liu X–M, Hess P, Rolph T, Beget JE. 1999. Properties of magnetic mineralogy of Alaskan loess: evidence for pedogenesis. *Quaternary International* 62: 93–102.

Machette M. 1986. Calcium and magnesium carbonates. In *Field and Laboratory Procedures used in a Soil Chronosequence Study*, Singer MJ, Janitzky P (eds). US Geological Survey Bulletin 1648. US Government Printing Office: Washington, DC: 30–33.

Maher BA. 1998. Magnetic properties of modern soils and Quaternary loessic paleosols: paleoclimatic implications. *Palaeogeography Palaeoclimatology Palaeoecology* **137**: 25–54.

Maher BA. 1999. Comments on: origin of the magnetic susceptibility singanal in Chinese loess. *Quaternary Science Reviews* 18: 865–869.

Maher BA, Thompson R. 1991. Mineral magnetic records of the Chinese loess and paleosols. *Geology* 19: 3–6.

Maher BA, Thompson R. 1992. Paleoclimatic significance of the mineral magnetic records of the Chinese loess and paleosols. *Quaternary Research* 37: 155–170.

Maher BA, Thompson R. 1995. Paleorainfall reconstructions from pedogenic magnetic susceptibility variation in the Chinese loess and paleosols. *Quaternary Research* 44: 383–391.

Maher BA, Thompson R. 2000. Paleomonsoons I: the magnetic record of paleoclimate in the terrestrial loess and paleosol sequence. In *Quaternary Climates, Environments and Magnetism*, Maher BA, Thompson R (eds). Cambridge University Press: New York: 83–125.

Maher BA, Thompson R, Zhou LP. 1994. Spatial and temporal reconstruction of changes in the Asian paleomonsoon: a new mineral magnetic approach. *Earth and Planetary Science Letters* 125: 461–471.

Meng XM, Derbyshire E, Kemp RA. 1997. Origin of the magnetic susceptibility singanal in Chinese loess. *Quaternary Science Reviews* 16: 833–839.

Meng XM, Derbyshire E, Kemp RA. 1999. Reply to comments on: origin of the magnetic susceptibility singanal in Chinese loess. *Quaternary Science Reviews* 18: 871–875.

Mullins CE. 1977. Magnetic susceptibility of the soil and its significance in soil science–A review. *Journal of Soil Sciences* 28: 223–246.

Rokosh CD, Rutter NW, Ding Z, Sun J. 2002. Regional lithofacies and pedofacies variations along a north-south climatic gradient during the Last Glacial period in the central Loess Plateau, China. *Quaternary Science Reviews* 21: 811–817.

Shen CD, Beer J, Liu TS, Oeschger H, Bonani G, Suter M, Wolfli W. 1992. ^{10}Be in Chinese loess. *Earth and Planetary Science Letters* 109: 169–177.

Sun DH, Zhou J, Jiang WC, Porter SC. 1995. Last interglacial summer monsoon reconstruction in the Chinese Loess Plateau. *Chinese Science Bulletin* 40(20): 1873–1875 (in Chinese).

Sun, JM, Liu TS. 2000. Multiple origins and interpretations of the magnetic susceptibility signal in Chinese wind-blown sediments. *Earth and Planetary Science Letters* 180: 287–296.

Thompson R, Oldfield F. 1986. *Environmental Magnetism*. Allen and Oldwin: London.

Verosub LK, Fine P, Singer MJ, TenPass J. 1993. Pedogenesis and paleoclimate: interpretation of the magnetic susceptibility record of Chinese loess - paleosol sequences. *Geology* 21: 1011–1014.

Virina EI, Faustov SS, Heller E. 2000. Magnetism of loess - paleosol formation in relation to soil - forming and sedimentary processes. *Physics and Chemistry of the Earth* 25(5): 475–478.

Wang J, Liu ZC, Jiang WY, Dong LX, Zhu MZ, Gao F. 1996. A relationship between the magnetic susceptibility and grain size and minerals, and their paleo - environmental implications. *Acta Geographica Sinica* 15(2): 155–163 (in Chinese).

William M. 1992. Evidence for the dissolution of magnetite in recent Scottish peat. *Quaternary Research* 37: 171–182.

Zhang ZG, Chen Y. 1995. New development in the loess in China. *Episodes* 18: 58–60.

Zheng HB, Oldfield F, Yu LZ, Shaw J, An ZS. 1991. The magnetic properties of particle - sized samples from the Luo Chuan loess section: evidence for pedogenesis. *Physics of the Earth and Planetary Interiors* 68: 250–258.

Zhou LP, Oldfield F, Wintle AG, Robinson SG, Wang JT. 1990. Partly pedogenic origin of magnetic variations in Chinese loess. *Nature* 346: 1–3.

Zhu R, Deng C, Jackson MJ. 2001. A magnetic investigation along a NW–SE transect of the Chinese Loess Plateau and its implications. *Physics and Chemistry of the Earth* 26(11–12): 867–872.

（注：参考文献为原杂志格式。）

Pedostratigraphy and carbonate accumulation in the last interglacial pedocomplex of the Chinese Loess Plateau*

Z.-D. Feng and H. B. Wang

ABSTRACT: This paper examines the geographic variations of carbonate concentrations in last interglacial pedocomplex (S1) profiles along a northwest (NW) - southeast (SE) transect across the Chinese Loess Plateau. Average S1 carbonate concentration is the same as that of overlying loess (L1) and underlying loess (L2) at the northwesternmost site (Lanzhou), but variations in carbonate concentration within S1 pedocomplex are greater than the within loess (L1 and L2) variations, indicating that the carbonate translocation within the S1 pedocomplex had occurred. Carbonate was leached to greater depths to form more pronounced peaks in the three paleosols (S1S1, S1S2, S1S3) within the S1 pedocomplex at the Dingxi section. Farther SE to the Qin'an section, the three paleosols (S1S1, S1S2, S1S3) have more distinguishable carbonate leaching and accumulation zones than at the Dingxi section. The S1 carbonate concentration at the Tianshui section suggests that the three paleosols were partially welded, as evidenced by S1S3 and S1S2 paleosols sharing a major portion of the paleosol profile. Soil-forming events occurred repeatedly in a single paleosol profile and the Ck horizon might have served as the carbonate accumulation zone for all three paleosols (S1S1, S1S2, S1S3) at the southeasternsite (Lantian). Land surface stabiliiy complicated carbonate concentration processes in loessial paleosols and extra caution should be observed when interpreting climate implication of carbonate concentration data.

Soil formation is a function of time and environmental factors including climate, vegetation, topography, and parent material (Buol et al., 1989). The time factor has two implications: soil-forming duration and landsurface stability (Foth, 1978). If the duration of soil formation is too short for soil to reach the equilibrium with the climate and its

*本文发表于:Soil Science Society of America Journal, 2005, 69: 1094–1101.

associated vegetation, the soil (e.g., Entisols and Inceptisols) will not be a reliable indicator of the climate. If the duration of soil formation is too long for the soil to preserve the imprints of equilibrium status, the soil (e.g., Ultisols) may not reflect the climate and its associated vegetation (Birkeland, 1999). Second, soil formation requires land surface stability. A stable land surface regarding soil formation implies the downward soil development, that is, soil develops in an already deposited parent material. If the soil develops when all or part of the parent material is being added (Almond, 1998), it is an accretionary soil that does not reach its equilibrium with the climate and its associated vegetation. For example, if soil - formation rate is approximately equal to the rate of dust influx in a grassland, a mature Mollisol with a well - developed B horizon will not form. Instead, a thick cumulic pedocomplex may be formed consisting of multiple A horizons with little or no B horizon development (Almond, 1998; Feng et al., 1994a, 1994b, 1994c; Feng and Johnson, 1995; Feng, 1996, 1997; Feng and Chen, 1999).

If the time factor is known and the topography and parent material are constants, soil formation is basically a function of climate and the associated vegetation (Johnson and Watson - Stegner, 1987). The effort to quantify the factor relationships has been persistently attempted since the beginning of soil science (Birkeland, 1999; Retallack, 1994). Among other soil characteristics, carbonate enrichment in arid and semiarid soils has been widely investigated (Arkley, 1963; Gile et al., 1965, 1966; Kemp, 1995; Machette, 1985) to quantify its relationships with the climate and the associated vegetation. The formation of pedogenic carbonate is a function of carbonate - bicarbonate equilibria. Under soil - forming conditions, CO_2 (either from the atmosphere or released by biological activities) in the soil air reacts with soil water to form HCO_3^-. The percolating water carries both the HCO_3^- and weathering - released or/and dust - deposited Ca^{2+} to form carbonate - rich horizon at a certain depth where the solution (i.e., percolating water) becomes saturated with respect to carbonate (Machette, 1985; Marion et al., 1985; Schlesinger, 1985; Van der Hoven and Quade, 2002). The depth of carbonate leaching is basically a function of mean annual precipitation (Arkley, 1963; Zhao, 2000).

Many previous studies noted carbonate concentrations in loessial soils (modern and past) of the midcontinental USA (e.g., Aandahl, 1982; Olson and Nettleton, 1998; Ruhe, 1973, 1983, 1984; Ruhe and Olson, 1980; Ruhe et al., 1955; Schaetzl and Sorenson, 1987). Recent studies (Feng et al., 1994a, 1994b, 1994c; Feng and Johnson, 1995; Feng, 1997) closely examined carbonate concentrations and associated properties of paleosols and their relations to the soil-forming environments in the Great Plains of the USA. As for the calcic loessial soils in the Chinese Loess Plateau, Zhao (1991, 1993, 1994, 2000) was the first who systematically studied carbonate-concentrating processes and their relations to the soil-forming environments. Guo and his colleagues (Guo and Liu, 1993; Guo et al., 1996a, 1996b) carefully examined carbonate-related paleosol micromorphology in the Chinese loess sequence and attempted climatic interpretations of the carbonate-related micromorphology. Kemp and his colleagues (Kemp, 1995, 2001; Kemp et al., 1995, 1997) have comprehensively studied the geographic patterns of the carbonate-related micromorphology of the last interglacial pedocomplex S1 in the Chinese Loess Plateau. Chen et al. (1997, 1999) and Fang et al. (1996, 1999) went even further to reconstruct the abrupt climatic events from the last glacial loess (L1) and also from the last interglacial pedocomplex (S1) using carbonate concentration as a summer monsoon proxy. Yang et al. (2001) used carbonate-influenced light-reflectance spectra as a proxy for reconstructing summer monsoon intensity to support the last interglacial summer monsoon instability proposed by An and Porter (1997).

Because of the interaction between the winter and summer monsoons, there is a modern SE–NW gradient of climate in the Chinese Loess Plateau (Li et al., 1988). The mean annual precipitation decreases gradually from SE to NW with the mean annual temperature increasing southward, whereas aridity (the ratio of evaporation to precipitation) increases gradually toward the NW. The native vegetation closely follows the aridity trend (Fig. 1). Assuming that the climatic gradients and the associated vegetation existed during the last interglacial as they today in the Chinese Loess Plateau, the net loess accumulation should have decreased and soil development should have intensified southeastward. Consequently, the last interglacial pedocomplex (S1) should change from NW to SE and the pedocomplex should reflect the changes as noted by some researchers (Evans and Rokosh, 2000; Kemp et al., 1997; Rokosh et al., 2002; Zhu et al., 2001).

Materials and Methods

We investigated systematic geographic variation of carbonate accumulation in the last interglacial pedocomplex (S1) and its climatic significance along a NW–SE transect across the Chinese Loess Plateau extending from Lanzhou (36°03′ N, 103°53′ E) to Lantian (34°06′ N, 108°39′E) near Xi'an (Fig. 1) in hope that carbonate-related soil-

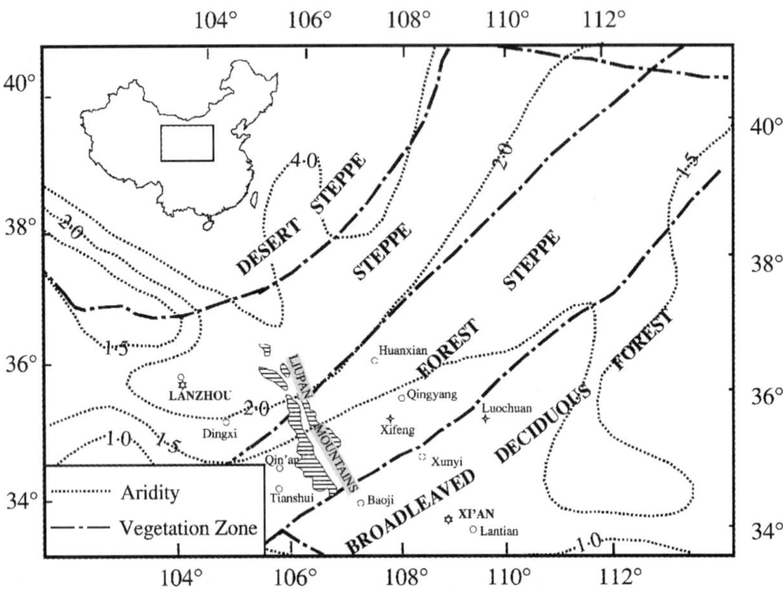

Fig. 1 Aridity (the ratio of evaporation to precipitation) and native vegetation distributions in the Chinese Loess Plateau

forming processes will be more fully considered when reconstructing high - resolution climatic records from loessial paleosols. The S1 pedocomplex of the five selected sections was described in the field based on characteristics of soil horizon (Birkeland, 1999; Buol et al., 1989; Catt, 1986, 1990; Foth, 1978) and then sampled at 2 cm intervals for laboratory analyses. At all sections investigated, sampling began in the basal L1 loess unit that overlies the S1 pedocomplex. Carbonate content was measured with a modified gas evolution method (Machette, 1986) using a Bascomb Calcimeter. Grain size of bulk samples was measured using a Malvern Co. Ltd. Mastersizer 2000 laser (Worceshire, UK) diffraction particle - size analyzer (Chen et al., 1997). Magnetic susceptibility (SI) was measured by the procedure of Thompson and Oldfield (1986) using a Bartington MS 2B susceptibility meter (Bartington, Oxford, UK).

In the northwestern part of the Loess Plateau (e.g., Lanzhou section at Jiuzhoutai: 36° 03′ N, 103° 53′ E, 1518 m above sea level [asl]), the 8 m thick S1 pedocomplex consists of three separate paleosols (Derbyshire et al., 1995, 1997; Kemp et al., 1995, 1997). Based on thermoluminescence (TL) dates and the comparability of S1 magnetic susceptibility signature with last interglacial marine isotopic signature (Chen et al., 1999, 2000; Feng et al., 2004a, 2004b; Kukla and An, 1989; Kukla et al., 1988, 1990), three Entisol - like paleosols with typical A−C profiles are interpreted as marking marine isotope substages 5a (S1S1), 5c (S1S2), and 5e (S1S3) and two interbedded loess units as demarcating substages 5b (S1L1) and 5d (S1L2) (Fig. 2). Southeastward near Dingxi (35°35′ N, 104°37′ E, 1898 m asl) the S1 pedocomplex is 5 m thick with two Entisol-like paleosols (A–C profiles) corresponding to the marine isotope substages 5a and 5c, which are better developed than those at the Lanzhou section. Marine isotope substage 5e is marked by a Mollisol-like paleosol with both an A horizon and a Bk horizon. Farther to the SE near Qin'an (34°52′ N, 105°40′ E, 1226 m asl) the S1 pedocomplex is 4 m thick with three Mollisol-like paleosols corresponding to the three odd-numbered marine isotope substages (5a, 5c, and 5e). The S1S1 and S1S2 paleosols are separated by the S1L1 loess unit. The loess unit S1L2 is not present between the S1S2 and S1S3 paleosols (see Fig. 2). The S1 at the Tianshui section (34°35′ N, 105°45′ E, 1142 m asl), about 50 km south of the Qin'an section, is a pedocomplex without the interbedded loess units. That is, both S1L1 and S1L2 are absent. This 4.5 m thick S1 pedocomplex has a 0.8 m thick A horizon at the top, a 2.5 m thick Bt horizon in the middle, and 1.2 m thick Bk horizon at the bottom. The S1 at Lantian section (34°06′ N, E108°39′, 800 m asl) near Xi'an is a pedocomplex containing a well-developed Bt horizon with a Ck horizon that is separated from the Bt by a

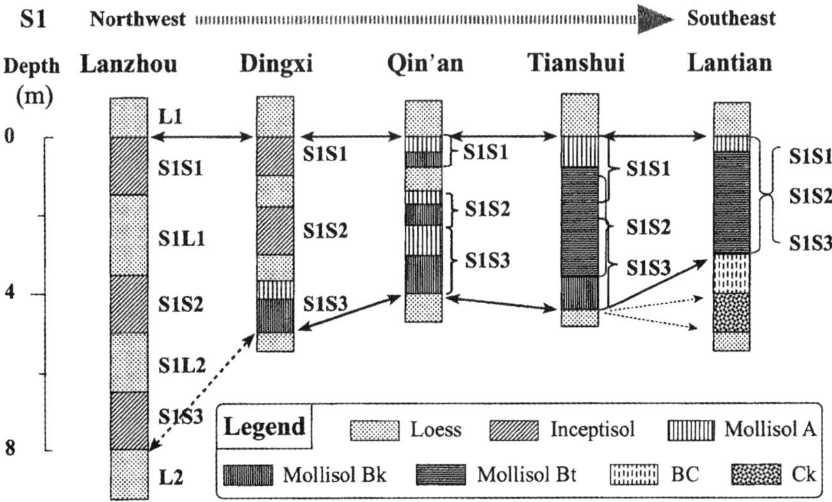

Fig. 2 The geographic variations of the S1 pedocomplex profiles from northwest to southeast across the Chinese Loess Plateau: all three paleosols (S1S1, S1S2, S1S3) and two interbedding loess units (S1L1 and S1L2) are preserved at the Lanzhou and Dingxi sections; the S1L2 loess unit was annexed by the S1S2 paleosol development at the Qin'an section and both the S1L2 and S1L1 loess units were annexed by later paleosol development at the Tianshui sections; the S1 pedocomplex at the Lantian section is a single composite paleosol profile.

0.8 m thick BC horizon (Feng et al., 2004a).

Results and Discussion

Lanzhou Section

Fig. 3 shows that carbonate concentration in the last interglacial pedocomplex S1 (15.8%) is not distinctively different from that of overlying L1 (16.0%) and underlying L2 (15.0%). Yet, the within - pedocomplex (S1) variations in carbonate concentration are greater than the within - loess (L1 and L2) variations, indicating that carbonate translocation (leaching and accumulation) within the pedocomlex profile had occurred during the last interglacial even at this northwestern section. Although variations in median grain size (the correlation coefficient between median gain size and magnetic susceptibility r =−0.65, sample number n = 600) and in the <10 μm fraction (the correlation coefficient between percentage of <10 μm fraction and magnetic susceptibility r = 0.74, n = 600)

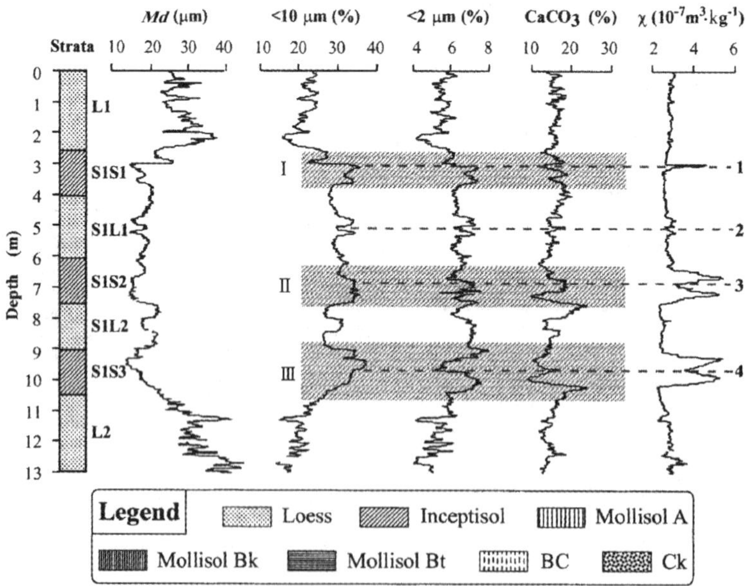

Fig. 3 Lanzhou Section: field - observed pedostratigraphy and laboratory data. *Md* (μm): median size; <10 μm (%): percentage of <10 μm fraction; <2 μm (%): percentage of <2 μm fraction; $CaCO_3$ (%): percentage of carbonate; and χ: magnetic susceptibility (10^{-7} $m^3 \cdot kg^{-1}$). Three shaded strips (Ⅰ, Ⅱ, Ⅲ) are paleosol zones (S1S1, S1S2, S1S3). Three dashed lines (1, 2, 3) indicate the relationship between carbonate concentration peaks and their lowered magnetic susceptibility within the three major magnetic susceptibility peaks corresponding to the three paleosols (S1S1, S1S2, S1S3).

account for the major portion of the variations in magnetic susceptibility (Feng et al., 2004b), carbonate concentration is also a major factor in shaping the magnetic susceptibility curve (the correlation coefficient between carbonate concentration and magnetic susceptibility $r = -0.51$, $n = 600$). Two other notable features deserve mentioning. First, carbonate concentration highs always occur in the layers immediately below the magnetic susceptibility highs and <10 μm fraction highs expressing the three paleosols (S1S1, S1S2, S1S3), suggesting that the carbonate was leached downward, although only to a limited depth and degree (marked as Ⅰ, Ⅱ, Ⅲ in Fig. 3). Second, carbonate concentration is sensibly responding to the minor susceptibility highs and lows within the major susceptibility (χ) peaks expressing the three paleosols (S1S1, S1S2, S1S3) within the S1 pedocomplex. For example, the susceptibility peak expressing S1S1 corresponds to a carbonate concentration low (marked as 1 in Fig. 3), and the two secondary susceptibility lows that are superimposed on two first-order susceptibility highs (S1S2, S1S3) correspond to two carbonate concentration highs (marked as 2, 3 in Fig. 3). It should also be noted that the clay content highs and carbonate concentration highs appear approximately at the same layers, again implying that carbonate leaching really happened but only to a limited depth.

Dingxi Section

The overall correlation coefficient between magnetic susceptibility (χ) and carbonate concentration (%) at the Dingxi section is close to zero ($r = 0.01$) and no magnetic susceptibility (χ) peak exists for the S1S1 paleosol although the frequency-dependent magnetic susceptibility (χ_{fd}) does express the S1S1 paleosol well (Fig. 4). To explain the lack of a magnetic susceptibility peak in the S1S1, we made two mathematical predictions of the magnetic susceptibility: one based on the correlation between the χ and χ_{fd} for the entire measured section ($r = 0.89$, $n = 300$), and the second based on the linear relationship of the χ with two major modulators, >63 μm fraction (negative) and 2 to 10 μm fraction (positive) for the entire measured section. Both predictions yield a susceptibility peak corresponding to the S1S1 paleosol. We noticed that the correlation coefficient between the carbonate concentration (%) and the frequency-dependent magnetic susceptibility (χ_{fd}) is negative in the lower portion (2.5–6 m) ($r = -0.59$, $n = 175$) and two major carbonate concentration highs in the lower portion (marked as Ⅲ and Ⅱ in Fig. 4) correspond well to two lows in the susceptibility. However, the correlation coefficient between the carbonate concentration (%) and the frequency-dependent susceptibility (χ_{fd}) turns into a positive value in the upper portion (0–2.5 m) ($r = 0.42$, $n = 125$) and the carbonate high in the upper portion (marked as I in Fig. 4) is responsive to the frequency - dependent susceptibility high expressing the S1S1 paleosol where the susceptibility peak is absent. Our predicted susceptibility peak and calculated contribution (negative) by the carbonate high (marked as I in Fig. 4) indicate that the susceptibility peak expressing the S1S1 was suppressed by the carbonate dilution effect.

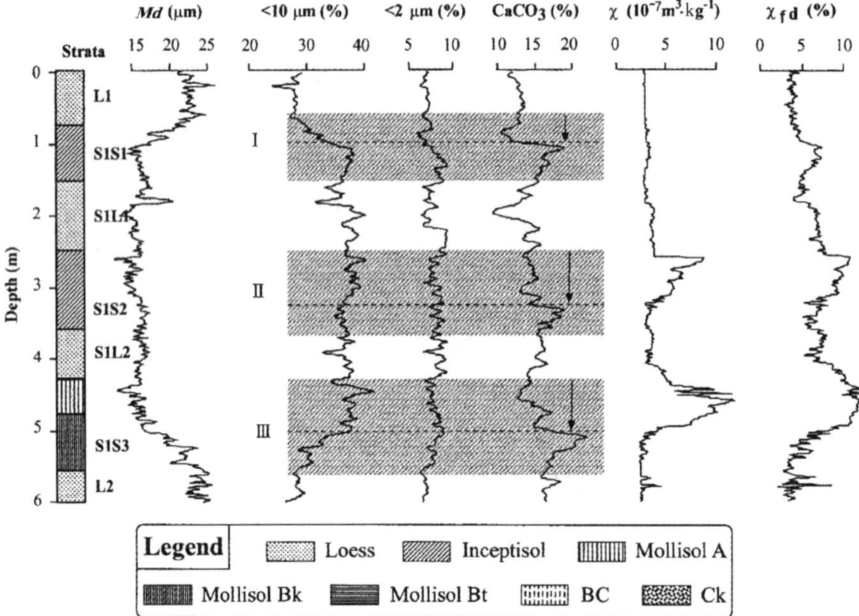

Fig. 4 Dingxi Section: field-observed pedostratigraphy and laboratory data. *Md* (μm): median size; <10 μm (%): percentage of <10 μm fraction; <2 μm (%): percentage of <2 μm fraction; $CaCO_3$ (%): percentage of carbonate; χ: magnetic susceptibility (10^{-7} $m^3 \cdot kg^{-1}$); and χ_{fd}: frequency -dependent susceptibility (%). Three shaded strips (Ⅰ, Ⅱ, Ⅲ) are paleosol zones (S1S1, S1S2, S1S3). Three arrows within the three shaded strips indicate carbonate leaching and accumulation in the three paleosols.

Qin'an Section

The clay (<2 μm) content is correlative with the susceptibility (r = 0.49, n = 250) at the Qin' an section. Like at the Dingxi section, the carbonate concentration seems not correlative with the first-order variations in the susceptibility (χ) that can be accounted for by the >63 μm fraction-dictated median grain size (negative) and 2 to 10 μm fraction-dictated <10 μm fraction (positive), but the carbonate variations correspond negatively with the second-order variations in the magnetic susceptibility (Fig. 5), especially in the upper portion (0–3.5 m deep). Although the best developed paleosol S1S3 is not proportionally expressed by the magnetic susceptibility mainly due to dilution of the coarse fractions, the carbonate concentration, as well as the clay content and <10 μm fraction to a lesser degree, expresses the S1S3 paleosol reasonably well. Both the S1S3 and paleosols have distinguishable carbonate leaching and accumulation zones as indicated by arrows in Fig. 5. The carbonate leaching and accumulation are somewhat complicated in the S1S1 paleosol. That is, a weakly weathered layer at the bottom of the L1 generated one carbonate concentration peak (marked as 1 in Fig. 5), and the S1S1 itself might have generated two peaks, one in the S1S1 Bk horizon (marked as 2 in Fig. 5) and the other below the Bk horizon (marked as 3 in Fig. 5).

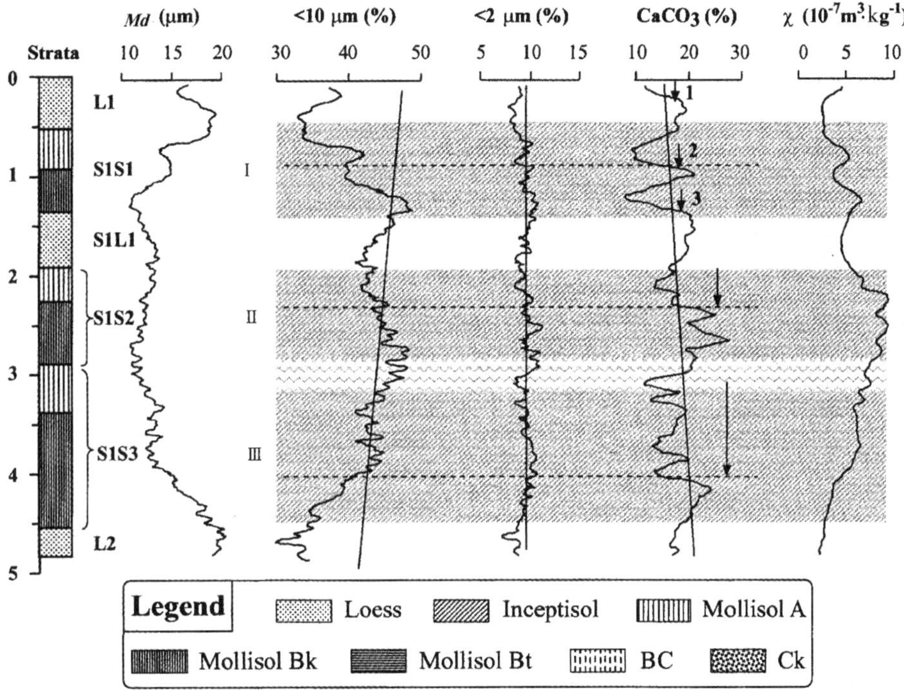

Fig. 5 Qin'an Section: field-observed pedostratigraphy and laboratory data. ***Md*** **(μm): median size; <10 μm (%): percentage of <10 μm fraction; <2 μm (%): percentage of <2 μm fraction; $CaCO_3$ (%): percentage of carbonate; and χ: magnetic susceptibility (10^{-7} $m^3 \cdot kg^{-1}$). Three shaded strips (Ⅰ, Ⅱ, Ⅲ) are paleosol zones (S1S1, S1S2, S1S3). The arrows indicate carbonate leaching and accumulation.**

Tianshui Section

Carbonate concentration, as well as soil morphologic features (e.g., clay coatings and granular structures throughout the 3.7 m thick B horizon), suggests that the S1 at Tianshui section is a partially welded pedocomplex with both S1L1 and S1L2 loess units being absent (Feng et al., 2004a). That is, both the S1S3 and S1S2 paleosol development formed the Bk horizon as arrows indicated (associated with 3 and 2) in Fig. 6 and shared a major portion of the paleosol profile. The carbonate - enriched layer at depth of 1.6 to 2.0 m may mark the bottom of the S1S1 paleosol or the leaching depth of later stage of the S1S1 development. The S1S1 paleosol development might have annexed the uppermost portion of the S1S2 paleosol as the arrows indicate (associated with 1) in Fig. 6. Soil annexation and welding not only altered S1L1 and S1L2 loess units into paleosols but also altered the A horizons of the S1S3 and S1S2 into later B horizons, forming thick accretionary B horizons. Carbonate coats the illuvial clay on the burrow walls and ped - faces in the Bt horizon, and engulfs the entire matrix and fills burrows in the Bk horizon that contains carbonate nodules.

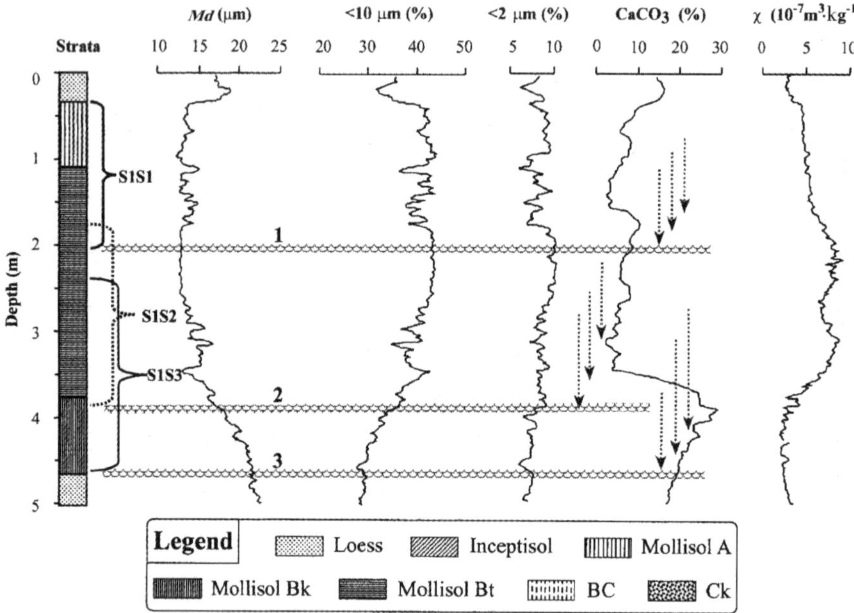

Fig. 6 Tianshui Section: field - observed pedostratigraphy and laboratory data. *Md* (μm): median size; <10 μm (%): percentage of <10 μm fraction; <2 μm (%): percentage of <2 μm fraction; $CaCO_3$ (%): percentage of carbonate; and χ: magnetic susceptibility (10^{-7} $m^3 \cdot kg^{-1}$). Three groups of arrows (associated with three dashed lines 1, 2, 3) indicate carbonate leaching and accumulation for all three paleosols (S1S1, S1S2, S1S3).

Lantian Section

The three soil-forming events (S1S1, S1S2, S1S3) occurred in a single paleosol profile at the Lantian section (Fig. 7). A noticeable feature at this section is that the carbonate concentration is low in the Bt and BC horizons (<5%) and high in the Ck horizon (about 20%), implying that the Ck horizon might have served as the carbonate accumulation zone for all three soil-forming events. The clay content is expectedly high in the Bt horizon. The coarsening grain size trend in the lower portion of the S1 pedocomplex profile (vertically shaded area in Fig. 7) implies that the S1 developed into the underlying older loess L2. Two features regarding the carbonate concentration deserve mentioning: (1) the carbonate in the Ck horizon exists primarily as nodules; and (2) ped - faces of the Btk horizon are nearly thoroughly coated with carbonate powder and small flutty threads although the total carbonate content is rather low in the Bt horizon at this southeasternmost site.

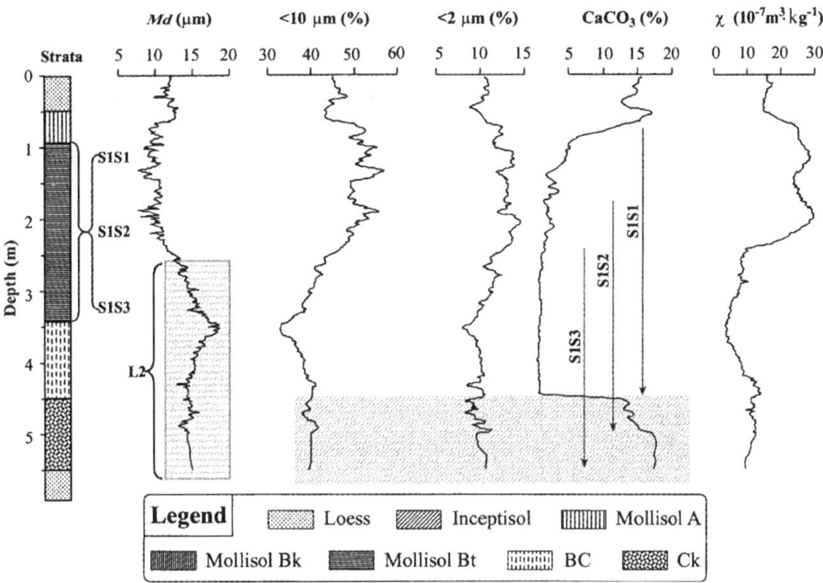

Fig. 7 Lantian Section: field - observed pedostratigraphy and laboratory data. *Md* (μm): median size; <10 μm (%): percentage of <10 μm fraction; <2 μm (%): percentage of <2 μm fraction; $CaCO_3$ (%): percentage of carbonate; and χ: magnetic susceptibility (10^{-7} $m^3 \cdot kg^{-1}$). The vertically shaded area indicates the chronological discord between parent material (older loess L2) and paleosol (later developed S1). the horizontally shaded area is carbonate accumulation zone for all three paleosols (S1S1, S1S2, S1S3).

The following observations can be made from the above mentioned carbonate data at the five sections investigated. At the northwestern section (Lanzhou), the average S1 carbonate concentration is nearly the same as that of overlying L1 and underlying L2 loess units. But, the within–S1 variations in carbonate concentration are greater than the within - loess (L1 and L2) variations, indicating that the carbonate translocation (leaching and accumulation) within the S1 pedocomplex had occurred, although to a limited depth and degree. Carbonate was leached to greater depths to form more pronounced carbonate peaks in the three paleosols (S1S1, S1S2, S1S3) at the Dingxi section than those at the Lanzhou section. The carbonate concentration high corresponding to the frequency - dependent magnetic susceptibility peak and predicted susceptibility peak expressing the S1S1 suggests that carbonate can accumulate in the susceptibility-enhanced weathered layer due to limited leaching.

Further SE at the Qin'an section, both the S1S3 and S1S2 paleosols have distinguishable carbonate leaching and accumulation zones. Nevertheless, carbonate leaching and accumulation in the S1S1 paleosol are more complicated. That is, the carbonate concentration peak in the S1S1 and two other peaks (one overlying the S1S1 and the other underlying the S1S1) may be indicative of carbonate accumulations not only during S1S1 formation but also before and after S1S1 formation. All five S1 subunits (S1S1, S1L1, S1S2, S1L2, S1S3) are preserved at both the Lanzhou and Dingxi sections, but S1L2 is absent at the Qin'an section. The carbonate concentration at the Tianshui section, as well as clay-coating characterized soil morphologic features (Feng et al., 2004a), suggests that the three paleosols (S1S1, S1S2, and S1S3) were partially welded with both S1L1 and S1L2 paleosols being absent. Soil annexation and welding not only altered the S1L1 and S1L2 loess units into paleosols but also altered the A horizons of the S1S3 and S1S2 paleosols into later B horizons, forming thick accretionary B horizons. At the Lantian section, three soil-forming events occurred in a single paleosol profile and nearly all carbonate was leached to a Ck horizon mainly consisting of carbonate nodules, suggesting that the Ck horizon might have served as the carbonate accumulation zone for all three soil-forming events.

Conclusions

Carbonate concentration in the S1 pedocomplex is not only a function of the last interglacial paleoclimate, but is strongly controlled by land-surface stability. For example, no composite paleosol or loess annexation occurs at the Lanzhou and Dingxi sections. The S1S2 paleosol development completely annexed the S1L2 loess unit at the Qin'an section. At the Tianshui section, not only were both the S1L1 and S1L2 loess units completely annexed, but also the uppermost part of the S1S2 paleosol was annexed by the S1S1 development. The S1S2 and S1S3 paleosols were nearly completely welded into one paleosol profile. The S1 pedocomplex at the Lantian section is a single composite paleosol profile, formed during three soil-forming events (S1S1, S1S2, S1S3). In other words, the single S1 paleosol at the Lantian section results not only from more intensive cyclic pedogenesis but also from much more stable land surface (i.e., limited eolian deposition) during the entire last interglacial (i.e., marine isotope Stage 5) spanning 55 000 yr (i.e., from 128 000–73 000 yr BP). It can be concluded that carbonate concentrations in loessial paleosols is not only a function of climate and its associated vegetation but also a function of land surface stability. Therefore, the climate interpretation of carbonate concentration is not straightforward considering the complexity of factors affecting land surface stability.

Acknowledgments

This research is financially supported by a US National Science Foundation grant (BCS–0078557) and a Chinese Education Ministry grant (No. 2000–65).

References

Aandahl, A.R. 1982. Soils of the Great Plains. The University of Nebraska Press, Lincoln.

Almond, P. 1998. Up-building soil formation in loess in a high rainfall environment, westland, New Zealand. p. 207–211. In A.J. Busacca (ed.) Int. Symp. on Dust Aerosols, Loess Soil and Global Change. CAHE MISC0190. Washington State University, Pullman, WA.

An, Z.S., and S.C. Porter. 1997. Millennial - scale climatic oscillations during the last interglaciation in central China. Geology 25:603–606.

Arkley, R.J. 1963. Calculation of carbonate and water movement in soil from climatic data. Soil Sci. 96:239–248.

Birkeland, P.W. 1999. Soils and geomorphology. 3rd ed. Oxford University Press, New York.

Buol, S.W., F.D. Hole, and R.J. McCracken. 1989. Soil genesis and classification. The Iowa State University Press, Ames.

Catt, J.A. 1986. Soils and quaternary geology. Monogr. Soil and Resource Surv. No. 11. Clarendon Press, Oxford.

Catt, J.A. 1990. Paleopedology manual. Quat. Int. 6:1–95.

Chen, F.H., J. Bloemendal, J.M. Wang, J.J. Li, F. Oldfield, and H.Z. Ma. 1997. High resolution multiproxy climate records from Chinese loess: Evidence for rapid climatic changes over the last 75 kyr. Palaeogeogr. Palaeoclimatol. Palaeoecol. 130:323–335.

Chen, F.H., J. Boemandel, Z.–D. Feng, J.M. Wang, S.T. Gou, E. Park, and Q. Shi. 1999. East Asian monsoon variations during oxygen isotope stage 5: Evidence from the Northwestern Margin of the Chinese Loess Plateau. Quat. Sci. Rev. 18: 1127–1135.

Chen, F.H., J.W. Zhang, and Z.–D. Feng. 2000. Loess particle size data indicative of stable winter monsoon during the last interglacial in the western part of Chinese Loess Plateau. Catena 39:233–244.

Derbyshire, E., D.H. Keen, R.A. Kemp, T.A. Rolph, J. Shaw, and X.M. Meng. 1995. Loess-paleosol sequences as recorders of palaeoclimatic variations during the last glacial interglacial cycle: Some problems of correlation in north-central China. Quat. Proc. 4:7–18.

Derbyshire, E., R.A. Kemp, and X.M. Meng. 1997. Climate change, loess and paloesols: Proxy and resolution in North China. J. Geol. Soc. (London) 154:793–805.

Evans, M.E., and C.D. Rokosh. 2000. The last interglacial in the Chinese Loess Plateau: A petromagnetic investigation of samples from a north-south transect. Quat. Int. 68–71:77–82.

Fang, X.M., X.R. Dai, J.J. Li, J.X. Cao, D.H. Guang, Y.P. Hao, J.L. Wang, and J.M. Wang. 1996. Abruptness and instability of Asian Monsoon — An example from soil genesis during the last interglacial. Sci. China B 26(2):154–160.

Fang, X.M., Y. Ono, H. Fukusawa, B.T. Pan, J.J. Li, D.H. Guan, K. Oi, S. Tsukamoto, M. Torri, and T. Mishima. 1999. Asian summer monsoon instability during the past 60,000 years: Magnetic susceptibility and pedogenic evidence from the western Chinese Loess Plateau. Earth Planet. Sci. Lett. 168:219–232.

Feng, Z.-D., H.B. Wang, C.G. Olson, G.A. Pope, F.H. Chen, J.W. Zhang, and C.B. An. 2004a. Chronological discord between the last interglacial paleosol (S1) and its parent material in the Chinese Loess Plateau. Quat. Int. 117:17–26.

Feng, Z.-D., H.B. Wang, and C.G. Olson. 2004b. Pedogenic factors affecting magnetic susceptibility of Last Interglacial paleosol S1 in the Chinese Loess Plateau. Earth Surf. Processes Landforms 29: 1384–1402.

Feng, Z.-D., and F.H. Chen. 1999. Problems of magnetic susceptibility signature as the summer monsoon proxy in Chinese loess sequences. p. 97–104. In Int. Symp. on Paleosols and Climate Change. Chinese Sci. Bull. 44 (suppl. 1). Science Press, Beijing.

Feng, Z.-D. 1997. Geochemical characteristics of a loess-soil sequence in central Kansas. Soil Sci. Soc. Am. J. 61:534–541.

Feng, Z.-D. 1996. Climatic implication of magnetic susceptibility and Be-10 in Chinese loess. Catena 25:211–216.

Feng, Z.-D., and W.C. Johnson. 1995. Factors affecting magnetic susceptibility of an eolian sequence in central Kansas. Catena 24:25–37.

Feng, Z.-D., W.C. Johnson, and R.F. Diffendal. 1994a. Environment of eolian deposition in south-central Nebraska during the Last Glacial Maximum. Phys. Geogr. 15:250–258.

Feng, Z.-D., W.C. Johnson, D.R. Sprowl, Y.-C. Lu, and P.A. Ward. 1994b. Climatic signals from loess - soil sequences in the central Great Plains, USA. Palaeogeogr. Palaeoclimatol. Palaeoecol. 110: 345–358.

Feng, Z.-D., W.C. Johnson, D.R. Sprowl, Y.-C. Lu, and P.A. Ward. 1994c. Loess accumulation and soil formation in central Kansas of the United States. Earth Surf. Processes Landforms 19:55–67.

Foth, H.D. 1978. Fundamentals of soil science. 6th ed. John Wiley & Sons Inc., New York.

Gile, L.H., F.F. Peterson, and R.B. Grossman. 1965. The K horizon: A master soil horizon of carbonate accumulation. Soil Sci. 99: 74–82.

Gile, L.H., F.F. Peterson, and R.B. Grossman. 1966. Morphological and genetic sequences of carbonate accumulation in desert soils. Soil Sci. 101:347–360.

Guo, Z.T., and T.S. Liu. 1993. Paleosols as evidence of difference of climates between Holocene and the last interglacial. (In Chinese.) Quat. Sci. 1:41–55.

Guo, Z., T. Liu, J. Guiot, N. Wu, H. Lu, J. Han, J. Liu, and Z. Gu. 1996a. High frequency pulses of East Asian monsoon climate in the last two glaciations: Link with the North Atlantic. Climate Dynamics 12:701–709.

Guo, Z.T., N. Fedoroff, and T.S. Liu. 1996b. Micromorphology of the loess-paleosol sequence of the last 130 ka in China and paleoclimatic events. (In Chinese.) Sci. China 39:469–477.

Johnson, D.L., and D. Watson - Stegner. 1987. Evolution model of pedogenesis. Soil Sci. 143: 349–364.

Kemp, R.A. 1995. Distribution and genesis of calcitic pedofeatures within a rapidly aggrading loess-paleosol sequence in China. Geoderma 65:303–316.

Kemp, R.A. 2001. Pedogenic modification of loess: Significance for paleoclimatic reconstruction. Earth Sci. Rev. 54:145–156.

Kemp, R.A. , E. Derbyshire, X.M. Meng, F.H. Chen, and B.T. Pan. 1995. Pedosendimentary reconstruction of a thick loess - paleosol sequence near Lanzhou in north - central China. Quat. Res. 43:30–45.

Kemp, R.A., E. Derbyshire, and X.M. Meng. 1997. Micromorphological variations of the S1 paleosol across northwest China. Catena 31:77–90.

Kukla, G., and Z.S. An. 1989. Loess stratigraphy in central China. Paleogeogr. Paleoecol. Paleoclimatol. 72:203–225.

Kukla, G., Z. S. An, J. L. Melice, J. Gavin, and J. L. Xiao. 1990. Magnetic susceptibility record of Chinese loess. Trans. R. Soc. Edinburgh 81:263–288.

Kukla, G., F. Heller, X.M. Liu, T.C. Xu, T.S. Liu, and Z.S. An. 1988. Pleistocene climates in China dated by magnetic susceptibility. Geology 16:811–814.

Li, J.J., Z.- D. Feng, and L.Y. Tang. 1988. Late Quaternary monsoon patterns on the Loess Plateau of China. Earth Surf. Processes Landforms 13:125–135.

Machette, M. 1985. Calcic soils of the southwestern United States. Geol. Soc. Am. Spec. Pap. 203:1–21.

Machette, M. 1986. Calcium and magnesium carbonates. p. 30– 33. In M.J. Singer and P. Janitzky (ed.) Field and laboratory procedures used in a soil chronosequence study. USGS Bull. 1648. U.S. Gov. Print. Office, Washington, DC.

Marion, G.M., W.H. Schlesinger, and P.J. Fonteryn. 1985. A regional model for soil carbonate deposition in southwestern deserts. Soil Sci. 139:468–481.

Olson, C.G., and W.D. Nettleton. 1998. Paleosols and the effects of alteration. Quat. Int. 51/52: 185–194.

Retallack, G.J. 1994. The environmental factor approach to the interpretation of paleosols. p. 31– 74. In R. Amundson et al. (ed.) Factors of soil formation: a fiftieth anniversary retrospective. SSSA Spec. Publ. 33. SSSA, Madison, WI.

Rokosh, C.D., N.W. Rutter, Z. Ding, and J. Sun. 2002. Regional lithofacies and pedofacies variations along a north - south climatic gradient during the Last Glacial period in the central Loess Plateau, China. Quat. Sci. Rev. 21:811–817.

Ruhe, R.V. 1973. Background of model for loess - derived soils in the upper Mississippi River Basin. Soil Sci. 115:250–253.

Ruhe, R.V. 1983. Depositional environment of late Wisconsin loess in the mid - continental United States. p. 130– 137. In S.C. Porter (ed.) Later quaternary environments of the United States, University of Minnesota Press.

Ruhe, R.V. 1984. Soil - climate system across the prairies in Midwestern U.S.A. Geoderma 34: 201–219.

Ruhe, R.V., and C.G. Olson. 1980. Soil welding. Soil Sci. 130:132–139. Ruhe, R.V., R.C. Prill, and F.F. Biecken. 1955. Profile characteristics of some loess - derived soils and soil aeration. Soil Sci. Soc. Am. J. 19:345–348.

Schaetzl, R.J., and C.J. Sorenson. 1987. The concept of "buried" versus "isolated" paleosols: Examples from northeastern Kansas. Soil Sci. 143: 426–435.

Schlesinger, W.H. 1985. The formation of caliché in soils of the Mojave Desert, California. Geochem. Cosmochem. Acta 49: 57–66.

Thompson, R., and F. Oldfield. 1986. Environmental Magnetism. Allen and Oldwin, London.

Van der Hoven, S.J., and J. Quade. 2002. Tracing spatial and temporal variations in the sources of calcium in pedogenic carbonates in a semiarid environment. Geoderma 108: 259–276.

Yang, S.L., X.M. Fang, J.J. Li, Z.S. An, and S.Y. Chen. 2001. Quantitative approach to soil color as a proxy for paleoclimate. (In Chinese.) Sci. China B 31(suppl.): 176–181.

Zhao, J.P. 1991. $CaCO_3$ leaching depth in the paleosols in the Guanzhong Basin. (In Chinese.) Chinese Sci. Bull. 18: 1397–1400.

Zhao, J.P. 1993. Carbonate and sedimentary environment of loess strata. (In Chinese.) Acta Sedimentologica Sinica 11: 137–142.

Zhao, J.P. 1994. Quaternary paleosols and the environments in the loess - covered areas of NW China. (In Chinese.) Shaanxi Science and Technology Press, Xi'an.

Zhao, J.P. 2000. A new geological theory about eluvial zone of carbonate and the accumulation depth. (In Chinese.) Acta Sedimentogica Sinica 18: 29–35

Zhu, R., C. Deng, and M.J. Jackson. 2001. A magnetic investigation along a NW–SE transect of the Chinese Loess Plateau and its implications. Phys. Chem. Earth 26: 867–872.

（注:参考文献为原杂志格式。）

Geographic variations in particle size distribution of the last interglacial pedocomplex S1 across the Chinese Loess Plateau: Their chronological and pedogenic implications*

Z.-D. Feng, H.B. Wang

Abstract: Due to northwestward attenuation of the summer monsoon and northwestward intensification of loess deposition during the last interglacial, the last interglacial pedocomplex S1 gradually differentiated from the northwest to the southeast. The three paleosols (S1S1, S1S2, S1S3) corresponding to the marine isotope substages 5a, 5c, and 5e and the two intercalated loess units (S1L1, S1L2) corresponding to the marine isotope substages 5b and 5d are completely preserved at northwestern sections. Towards southeast, both the S1L1 and S1L2 were annexed by the subsequent paleosol development (S1S1 and S1S2) and the three paleosols (S1S1, S1S2, and S1S3) were partially welded. At the southeasternmost site, the three soil-forming events (S1S1, S1S2, and S1S3) repeatedly occurred in a single paleosol profile. The three observed orders of particle-size variations are interpreted to have imprinted important chronological and pedogenic signatures. First-order variations, i.e., a remarkable difference between the interglacial pedocomplex S1 and the glacial loess units (L1 and L2), implies that the S1 parent material was considerably finer in the source areas or/and the proximity to the source areas was much farther during interglacial period than during the preceding (L2) and following (L1) glacial periods. Second-order variation, i.e., the parenthetical trends in >63 μm and <10 μm fraction curves, might have resulted from the delayed response of the source material supplies to the climate changes. The third-order variations in <10 μm fraction correspond well to the variations in frequency-dependent magnetic susceptibility, suggesting that pedogenically formed finer particles (i.e., <10 μm fraction) and the associated ultra-fine paramagnetic minerals as expressed by the frequency-dependent susceptibility occurred only as a minor component of the <10 μm fraction. The third-order variations seem to be obscured by soil welding and annexation at southeastern sections where the paleosols within the S1 were partially or completely welded. The laboratory data-

*本文发表于:Catena, 2006, 65: 315-328.

indicated <10 μm fraction peaks of the third - order and field - observed clay coatings on ped - faces, together with carbonate leaching and accumulation, in the paleosols within the S1 indicate occurrence of within - S1 material translocation. To sum up, it is unrealistic to reconstruct high - resolution climatic records from the S1 pedocomplex because a number of factors might have undermined the validity of the particle size as a winter monsoon proxy. These factors include weathering in the source areas, in situ post - depositional weathering and fine fraction translocation, and downward penetration of soil formation into underlying previously deposited materials on stable land surfaces.

Key words: Particle size distribution; Paleosol; Last interglacial; Chinese Loess Plateau

1 Introduction

The last interglacial climate was reported to have abruptly fluctuated six times (i.e., cool events) on millennium time scales around the North Atlantic (Dansgaard et al., 1993; GRIP Members, 1993; McManus et al., 1994). To search for regional responses to large - scale climatic changes of the millennium time scale during the last interglacial, An Zhisheng and his colleagues (An and Porter, 1997; Li et al., 1998) claimed that six high dust - influx events (or stronger winter monsoon events) of millennium time scales are recorded by the percentage of coarse quartz fraction in the last interglacial pedocomplex S1 at the well - known Luochuan Section in the eastern part of the Chinese Loess Plateau and that they are correlative with the six cool events documented around the North Atlantic. Nevertheless, the pedogenic processes during the last interglacial might have made the chronological correlation with the North Atlantic records problematic and the high - resolution paleoclimatic reconstruction questionable.

1.1 Potential chronological problems of S1 pedocomplex

Although chronological correlation has been made between the dust - influx events in Chinese Loess Plateau (An and Porter, 1997) and the cool events in the North Atlantic, the chronology of the S1 pedocomplex (only 2.5 m thick at the Luochuan Section) is far from certain. The thermoluminescence (TL) dates of S1 pedocomplex are not sufficiently accurate to bracket the ages of the S1 due to the large errors (e.g., 125 ± 15 ka) and the uncertainties associated with this method (Oches et al., 1998). Consequently, the S1 pedocomplex is theoretically tuned to be bracketed by two ages: 73,000 and 128,000 years

BP., i.e., 55,000years of time span (Kukla et al., 1988; Kukla and An, 1989). Even if the pedocomplex S1 in the eastern part of the Loess Plateau was indeed formed during that time period under warm and humid interglacial conditions, it is likely that all or part of the parent materials of the S1 pedocomplex were deposited prior to 128,000 years BP. In other words, 55,000-year interglacial climate might be sufficient to form a mature soil profile in previously deposited parent materials on stable land surfaces.

It is well known that soil formation is a function of time and environmental factors (Buol et al., 1973). The time factor has two connotations: soil-forming duration and land surface stability (Foth, 1978). A stable land surface regarding soil formation implies downward soil development, i.e., soil develops in a previously deposited parent material on a stable land surface. If the soil develops when all or part of the parent material is being added (Almond, 1998), it is an accretionary soil. For example, if soil-formation rate is approximately equal to the rate of dust influx in grasslands, a mature Mollisol with a well-developed B horizon will not form. Instead, a thick cumulic pedocomplex may be formed consisting of multiple A horizons with little or no B horizon development (Feng et al., 1994a, b, c; Feng and Johnson, 1995; Feng, 1996, 1997; Almond, 1998; Feng and Chen, 1999).

But, the S1 pedocomplex from Qin'an to Luochuan in the eastern part of the Loess Plateau is not characterized by cumulic A horizons. Instead, the S1 is ubiquitously a composite paleosol with a thickness of only about 2.5 m (Zhao, 1994; Zhang and Chen, 1995), implying that the rate of soil formation was much higher than the rate of eolian deposition. For example, an exposure of a composite paleosol S1 at Huanglin near Qin'an, directly south of the well-known Luochuan Section and within the same climatic zone (sub-humid) as Luochuan and Xifeng (Li et al., 1988), exhibits three overlapping B horizons (B1, B2, B3), implying that earlier paleosol A horizons and probably the upper parts of earlier B horizons were altered as subsequent B horizons developed (Zhang and Chen, 1995; Feng and Chen, 1999). If so, at least the lower part of the composite paleosol was most likely formed in previously deposited parent materials of a glacial origin (i.e., before 128 ka), suggesting a possibility that the penultimate glacial particle size was inappropriately used to reconstruct the last interglacial winter monsoon intensity.

1.2 Potential problems of particle size as a winter monsoon proxy

Previous research assumed that Chinese loess was derived from a finite source area and that larger particle resulted from stronger winter monsoon (Liu, 1985, 1987; An et al., 1991a; Ding et al., 1992). Later, that assumption was modified to include the proximity to the source area as another factor controlling the particle size distribution (Ding et al., 1999). This modified assumption should be further amended to include pre-windborne weathering in the source areas. For example, the particle size in one of possible source areas, e.g., the Tibetan Plateau - supplied fluvial fans and lake beds in the Tarim Basin and Gansu (i.e., Hexi) Corridor, could be considerably finer during interglacial times due to the fact that more silt and clay weathered in the Tibetan Plateau might have been brought to the fluvial fans and lake beds (Assallay et al., 1998; Wright, 2001). The particle size in another possible source area, the Mongolian Plateau, was definitely finer during interglacial times simply due to much stronger weathering as observed by Feng and Chen (1999). In other words, the particle size in the Chinese loess/paleosol sequences might also be dependent on the particle size of source materials, thus undermining the validity of the particle size as a winter monsoon proxy.

Several authors (An et al., 1991a; Ding et al., 1992; Porter and An, 1995; An and Porter, 1997; Chen et al., 1997a,b) used particle size (quartz or bulk) to reconstruct the intensity of the winter monsoon for the last interglacial/ glacial cycle. However, the assumptions on which the winter monsoon proxy relies are untested. The fault lies primarily in the presupposition that quartz particles (Porter and An, 1995; An and Porter, 1997; Sun et al., 2000) and even other coarse particles (Ding et al., 1992; Lu and An, 1997, 1998, Chen et al., 1997a,b) in loess remain immutable after deposition. In fact, even the quartz particles, supposedly being most resistant to weathering, can undergo significant chemical dissolution under certain conditions, particularly in the presence of salts (Goudie et al., 1979) and organic acids (Dixon et al., 1984; Pope, 1995). Smaller particles may be the result of weaker winter monsoon during warmer periods. However, there is little to prevent one from saying that smaller particles may also be the result of organic acid-accelerated weathering under forests or forest - steppes during warmer and moister interglacial periods in the Loess Plateau (Derbyshire et al., 1995, 1997). In fact, higher rates of loess weathering, indicated by higher ratios of free iron (weathering released) and total iron, during warmer and more mesic periods have already been convincingly demonstrated (Guo et al., 1993, 1994, 1996a,b, 1999; Hao and Guo, 2001), meaning that some of larger particles must have broken down in situ. More interestingly, much stronger leaching of unstable elements that were probably released by the in situ weathering and a much higher Sr/Rb leaching index in the paleosols relative to that in the loess units at the well-known Luochuan Section suggest that some of the weathered unstable elements were leached out of the paleosols (Chen et al., 1997b). This implies that the post-depositional weathering and leaching must have changed the original particle size distribution, also undermining the validity of the particle size as a winter monsoon proxy.

Furthermore, pedogenic translocation of fine particles (transported or/and in situ weathered) within a soil (modern or past) profile has been abundantly documented (e.g., Ruhe et al., 1955; Ruhe, 1984; Mack et al., 1993; Olson and Nettleton, 1998; Birkeland, 1999; Nettleton et al., 2000). It is well documented that it took only four to seven thousand years to form a thick soil with a mature Bt horizon in previously deposited parent materials on stable land surfaces (Moore, 1978; Gile, 1979). It is quite common that the clay content in Bt horizon (accumulated) of a loessial paleosol is two times higher than that in C horizon (parent material) and three times higher than that in A horizon (leached) (Ruhe and Olson, 1979, 1980). It is likely that clay and even fine silt translocation has occurred in the last interglacial pedocomplex S1 in the Chinese Loess Plateau, once again undermining the validity of the particle size as a winter monsoon proxy.

2 Sampling strategies and laboratory methods

Because of the interaction between the winter and summer monsoons, there is a modern SE–NW gradient of climate in the Chinese Loess Plateau (Li et al., 1988). That is, both the mean annual temperature and precipitation increase gradually from the northwest to the southeast, whereas the aridity (the ratio of evaporation to precipitation) increases toward the northwest. The native vegetation closely follows the aridity trend (Fig. 1). If the climatic gradients and the associated vegetation existed during the last interglacial as they do today, the net loess accumulation should have decreased and soil development should have intensified southeastward. Consequently, the last interglacial pedocomplex S1 should gradually change from the northwest to the southeast and the pedocomplex characteristics should reflect the changes as noted by some researchers (Kemp et al., 1995, 1997; Evans and Rokosh, 2000; Zhu et al., 2001; Rokosh et al., 2002). To investigate the geographic variations of the last interglacial pedocomplex S1 and its climatic significance, we chose two transects (Fig. 1): one across the western part of the Loess Plateau from Lanzhou to Tianshui and another across the eastern part from Huanxian to Lantian. The Liupan Mountain is the dividing line between the eastern and western parts. The pedocomplex was laterally traced by soil horizon identification (Ruhe, 1973, 1983) and classified based on the preserved characteristics in the field (Foth, 1978; Catt, 1986; Birkeland, 1999; Nettleton et al., 2000). Since the last glacial loess L1 is thick enough (5–30 m) to isolate the last interglacial S1 pedocomplex from the alteration of later pedogenic processes

(Schaetzl and Sorenson, 1987) throughout the Chinese Loess Plateau, it is thus possible to examine the last interglacial soil - forming processes without the concern of post - burial alteration (Olson and Nettleton, 1998).

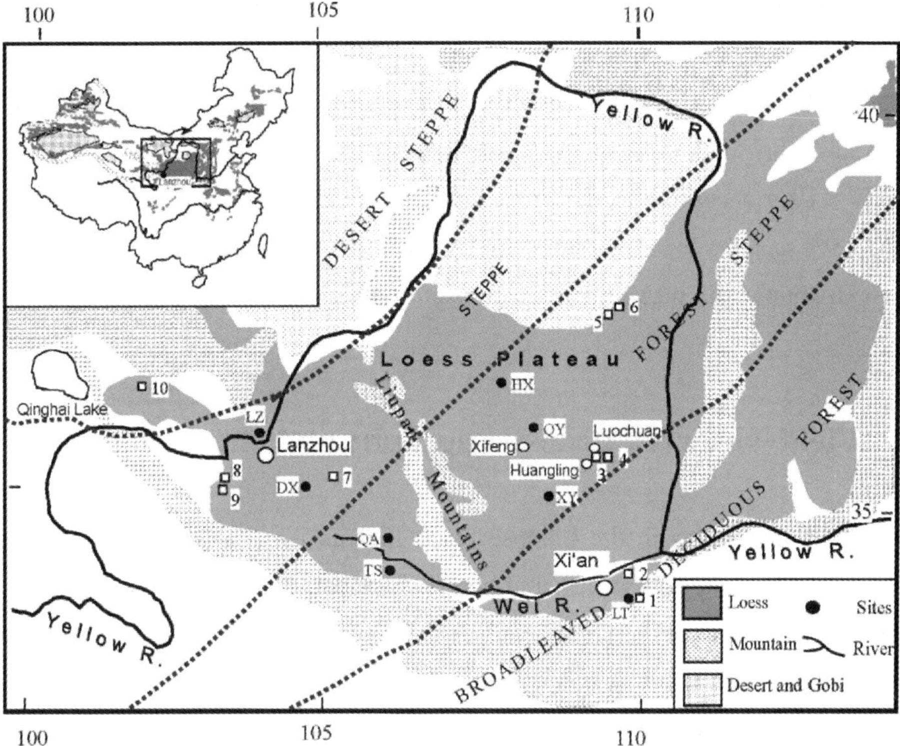

Fig. 1 Sketch map of the Chinese Loess Plateau showing the aridity - associated vegetation distribution and eight sections investigated. Western transect: Lanzhou (LZ), Dingxi (DX), Qin'an (QA) and Tianshui (TS). Eastern transect: Huanxian (HX), Qingyang (QY), Xunyi (XY) and Lantian (LT). Numbers 1–10 are the locations of the S1 sections that were previously TL dated by others (see Fig. 2 for chronostratigraphy and references of these 10 sections).

At all sections investigated, sampling began in the basal L1 loess unit that overlies the S1 pedocomplex and ended at the top part of the L2 that underlies the S1, and samples were taken at 2 cm intervals at each one of the eight sections for particle size, magnetic and carbonate analyses. The particle size of bulk samples was measured using a Malvern Co. Ltd. Mastersizer 2000 laser diffraction particle size analyzer (Chen et al., 1997a,b) and pretreatments of the samples for particle size analysis include adding (1) H_2O_2 to remove organic, (2) diluted 6 mol/L HCl to remove salts, and (3) sodium - hexametaphosphate to disperse the aggregates (Janitzky, 1987). The magnetic susceptibility was measured by the procedure of Thompson and Oldfield (1986) using a Bartington MS 2B susceptibility meter and the frequency - dependent susceptibility (χ_{fd}) was calculated based on the high - frequency (χ_h) and low-frequency (χ_l) susceptibility measurements (i.e., $\chi_{fd}=[(\chi_l-\chi_h)/\chi_l]\times 100\%$). The carbonate content was measured with the modified gas evolution method (Machette, 1986) using a Bascomb Calcimeter. To reaffirm our confidence in laterally tracing the pedocomplex S1 and explore the chronological discord between the S1 pedocomplex and its parent materials, we have also IRSL/OSL dated 14 samples. Five (5) samples were measured in Professor Stephen Stocks' Laboratory at University of Cambridge (UK) according to the procedures described by Murray and Wintle (2000), and nine (9) samples were measured in Professor Glenn Berger's Laboratory at Desert Research Institute (Reno, USA) according to the procedures described by Aitken (1998).

3 Field-observed pedostratigraphy and chronology

The S1 pedocomplex in the Chinese Loess Plateau is a ubiquitously distributed and laterally traceable pedostratigraphic unit across the landscape. Its age was first speculated to be of last interglacial based on the comparability of S1 magnetic susceptibility signature with last interglacial marine isotopic signature (Heller and Liu, 1982, 1984; Kukla et al., 1988), but attempts have been persistently made to determine the absolute age of the pedocomplex using thermoluminescence (TL) and other relevant methods (e.g., Lu et al., 1988; Forman, 1991; An et al., 1991b; Liu et al., 1994; Sun and Ding, 1998; Chen et al., 1999, 2000; Wang et al., 2000). Fig. 2, a summary of some published TL dates, shows that although the TL dates of S1 pedocomplex range widely from 50 ka to 150 ka, the S1 pedocomplex is approximately bracketed by 70 ka and 140 ka at seven of the ten listed sections (i.e., Weinan, Yulin-Caijiagou, Yulin–Simao, Huining, Linxia-Beiyuan, Linxia-Yuanbao, and Tuxiangdao sections), suggesting that the S1 was indeed formed during the last interglacial (i.e., marine isotope stage 5). But, as mentioned above, TL dates are not sufficiently accurate to bracket the ages of the S1 due to the large errors and the uncertainties associated with this method, and it is thus impossible to establish a detailed S1 chronology that can be used to bracket the subunits (e.g., equivalents to marine isotope substages 5a–5e) of the S1 pedocomplex.

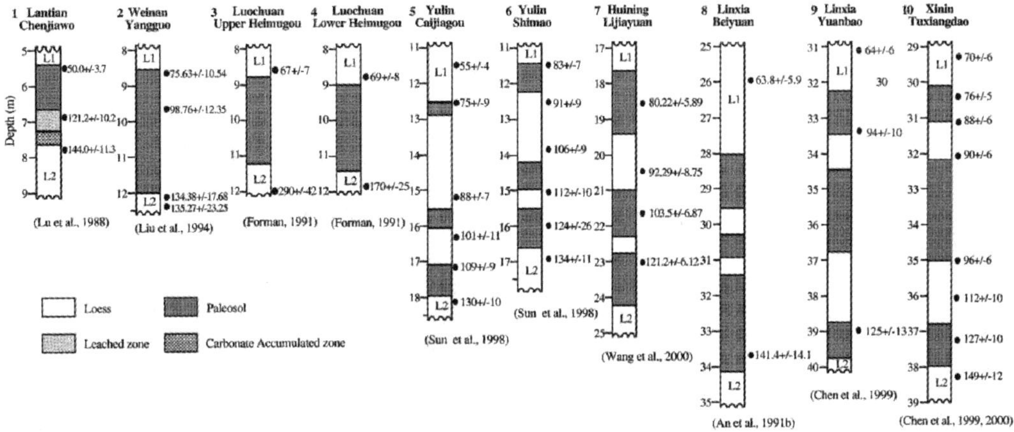

Fig. 2 Some published TL dates of the last interglacial pedocomplex S1 in the Chinese Plateau. The site locations are shown in Fig. 1 (numbered as 1– 10).

3.1 Western transect

3.1.1 Lanzhou Section

At this section (Fig. 3A) in the northwestern part of the Loess Plateau, the S1 pedocomplex (8 m thick) is characterized by interbedding of soil and loess units (Derbyshire et al., 1995, 1997; Kemp et al., 1995, 1997; Chen et al., 1997a,b, 1999, 2000). Three Entisol-like (A–C profiles) paleosols are interpreted as marking the marine isotope substages 5a (S1S1), 5c (S1S2) and 5e (S1S3) and two interbedded loess units as demarcating the substages 5b (S1L1) and 5d (S1L2). The Entisol-like paleosols are characterized by a little more compaction with observable granular structures and by a darker color with more rootlet canals than the loess units (S1L1 and S1L2).

3.1.2 Dingxi Section

Southeastward at Dingxi Section (S1=5 m thick), two Entisol-like (A–C profiles) paleosols corresponding to the marine isotope substages 5a and 5c were better developed than those at Lanzhou. Corresponding to the substage 5e is a Mollisol-like paleosol with an A horizon and a Bk horizon. The Mollisol-like paleosol has a granular-structured A horizon and a slightly subangular blocky-structured Bk horizon (Fig. 3A). Three IRSL/OSL dates were obtained from the top (58.46 ± 6.90 ka), middle (109.19 ± 9.31 ka) and bottom (119 ± 10.09 ka) of the S1.

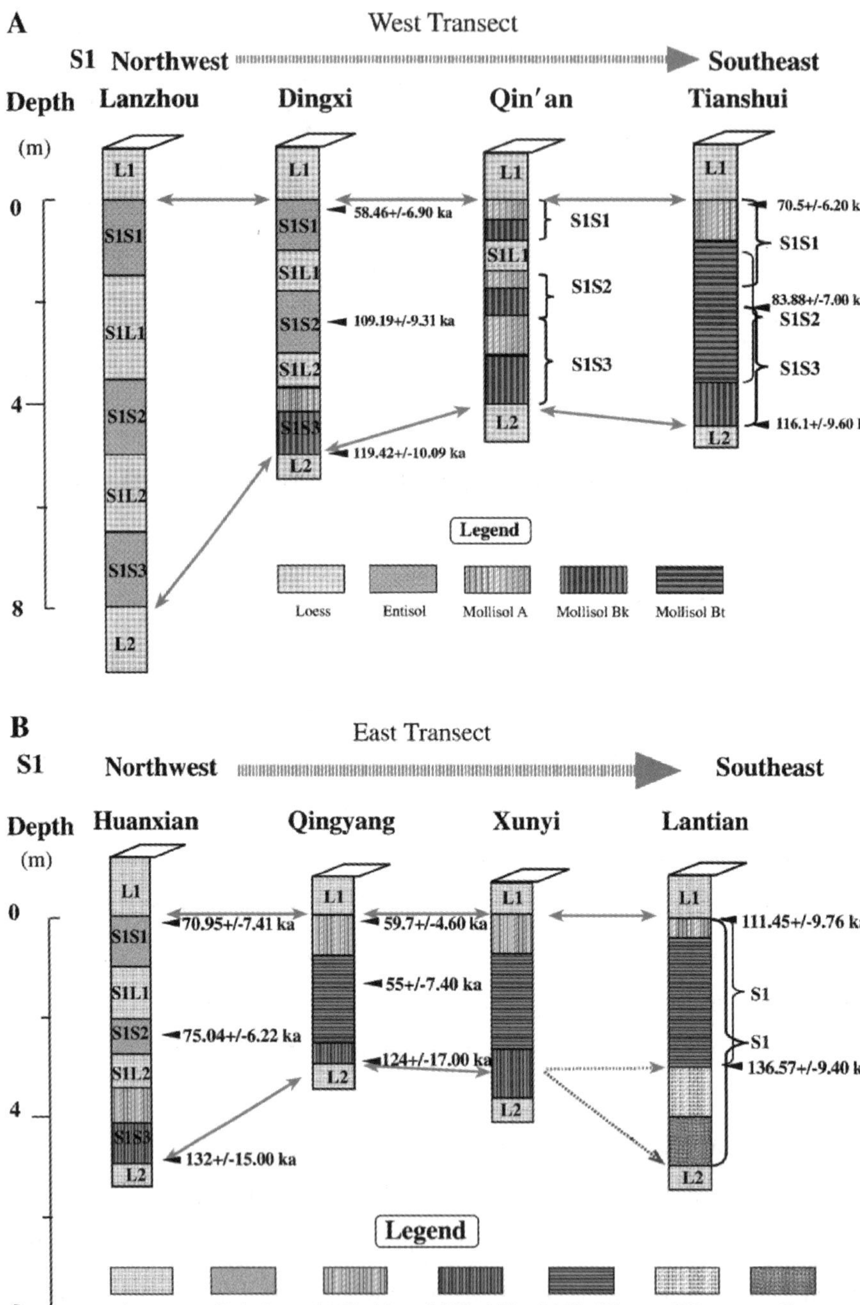

Fig. 3 （A）The geographic differentiation of the S1 pedocomplex profiles from the northwest to the southeast along the western transect. The top, middle and bottom of the S1 at Dingxi and Tianshui sections were TL dated.（B）The geographic differentiation of the S1 pedocomplex profiles from the northwest to the southeast along the eastern transect. Three TL dates were obtained from the top, middle and bottom of the S1 both at Huanxian and at Qingyang sections and two TL dates were obtained from the top and middle of the S1 at Lantian section.

3.1.3 Qin'an Section

Further southeastward at Qin' an Section where the S1 pedocomplex is 4 m thick, three Mollisol-like paleosols corresponding to the three odd marine isotope substages (5a, 5c, and 5e) were developed. The S1S1 and S1S2, both having an A horizon and a Bk horizon, are intercalated by the S1L1 loess unit. The loess unit S1L2 between the S1S2 and S1S3 is absent (Fig. 3A). The S1S3 at Qin'an Section is a Btk horizon with well-developed blocky structure and notable clay coatings on ped-faces. Carbonate translocation within the pedocomplex is stronger than at the Lanzhou and Dingxi Sections.

3.1.4 Tianshui Section

The S1 at this section is a pedocomplex with both S1L1 and S1L2 being absent. This 4.5-m-thick S1 consists of a 0.8-m-thick A horizon, a 2.5-m-thick Bt horizon and a 1.2-m-thick Bk horizon (Fig. 3A). Three features deserve special mentioning: (1) entire S1 pedocomplex is bioturbated with abundant small burrows whose walls are coated with clay films, (2) rootlet channel-marked granular-crumble structures and worm and insect burrows of A-horizon characteristics are preserved within the clay-coated prismatic columns of B horizon, implying that A horizons were later altered into a B horizon; and (3) the existence of carbonate throughout the B horizon indicates that this B horizon is accretionary, i.e., B horizon was aggraded when the S1 surface was raised by dust accumulation (see Feng et al., 2004a, b; Feng and Wang, 2005 for details). The top is IRSL/OSL dated at 70.50 ± 6.20 ka, the middle at 83.88 ± 7.08 ka and the bottom at 116.10 ± 9.60 ka.

3.2 Eastern transect

3.2.1 Huanxian Section

Field-observed pedostratigraphy at Huanxian Section, the northernmost site in the eastern part of the Loess Plateau, is quite similar to that at Dingxi Section in the western part (Fig. 3B). Specifically, two Entisol-like paleosols corresponding to the marine isotope substages 5a and 5c were developed. Corresponding to the substage 5e is a Mollisol-like paleosol with an A horizon and a Bk horizon. Three IRSL/OSL dates obtained are 70.95 ± 7.41ka (top), 75.04 ± 6.22ka (middle) and 132.00 ± 15.00ka (bottom).

3.2.2 Qingyang and Xunyi Sections

Qingyang and Xunyi Sections are located in the same bioclimatic settings as the well-known Luochuan and Xifeng Sections (see Fig. 1). The S1 is a mature Mollisol-like paleosol with a relatively thick A horizon and a well-structured and over-thickened Bt horizon. The A horizon is characterized by friable structures, carbonate masses and filaments, abundant medium and fine pores with root traces. The Bt horizon is angular-blocky structured with observable clay coatings on ped-faces. Although carbonate coatings on ped-faces in the Bt horizon are quite noticeable, it was nearly completely leached from Bt horizon (only about 5%) and accumulated in Bk horizon (about 20%) as masses or nodules. The S1 is only 2.5 m thick if only A and Bt horizons are taken as the S1 and it is as thick as 4.5 m if BC and Ck horizons are also taken as the S1 (Fig. 3B). Three IRSL/OSL dates obtained from the S1 at Qingyang Section are 59.70 ± 4.60 ka (top), 55.00 ± 7.40 ka (middle) and 124.00 ± 17.00 ka (bottom).

3.2.3 Lantian Section

The S1 at this section is a composite paleosol with a well-developed Bt horizon. The Bt horizon is characterized by large prismatic peds, which consist of medium-sized angular blocky peds. Small rounded clay or silt balls are quite noticeable within these medium-sized angular blocky peds. This reddish-brown and prismatic-structured S1 is most likely an Alfisol or Ultisol (Buol et al., 1973; Birkeland, 1999) that developed on a stable land surface over the 55,000 years of the last interglacial. Below the Bt horizon is a well-leached BC horizon overlying 1-m-thick Ck horizon. The top is IRSL/OSL dated at 111.45 ± 9.76 ka and the bottom of Bt horizon (3 m deep) at 136.57 ± 9.40ka.

It should be particularly noted that the TL/IRSL/OSL dates are generally supportive to the lateral tracing of the S1 pedocomplex, but their large error bars and uncertainties involved in these techniques prevented us from ascertaining the chronological discord between the S1 pedocomplex and its parent material.

4 Geographic variations of particle size distribution

4.1 Western transect

4.1.1 Lanzhou Section

Fig. 4 exhibits three orders of particle-size variations. The first order shows that not only are the paleosols (S1S1, S1S2, S1S3) but also the loess units (S1L1, S1L2) within the S1 pedocomplex remarkably distinguishable from the overlying L1 and underlying L2 by the percentages of >63 μm and <10 μm fractions. The second order refers to the gentle parenthetical or bowed trends in >63 μm and <10 μm fraction curves [i.e., dashed (–) as indicated in Fig. 4] within the S1 pedocomplex. The third-order variations in <10 μm fraction, as well as in >63 μm fraction, correspond to the variations in frequency-dependent magnetic susceptibility (e.g., the shaded areas 1, 2, 3 in Fig. 4). It should also be noted that the <10 μm fraction peaks in the middle portions and carbonate peaks in the lower portions of paleosols S1S2 and S1S3 indicate that both fine fraction (<10 μm) and carbonate were translocated within these two paleosols.

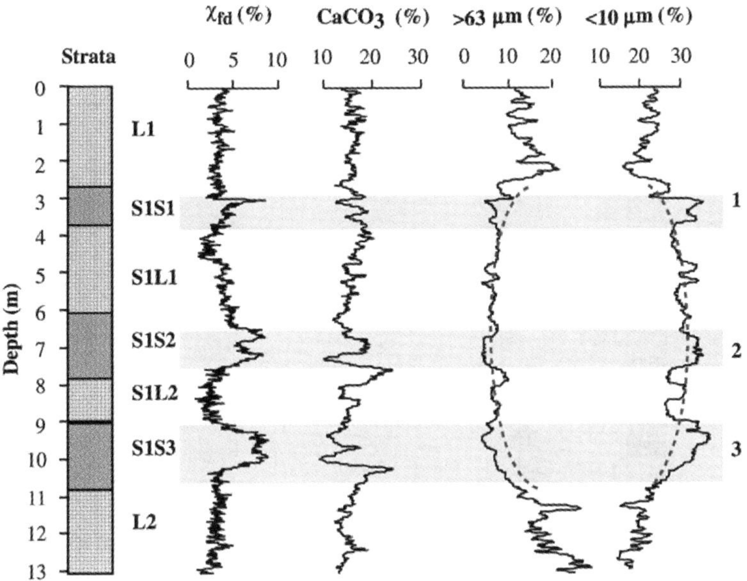

Fig. 4 Lanzhou Section: field-observed pedostratigraphy and laboratory data. Laboratory data include χ_{fd} (%), frequency-dependent magnetic susceptibility; $CaCO_3$ (%), percentage of carbonate; >63 μm (%), percentage of >63 μm fraction; <10 μm (%), percentage of <10 μm fraction.

4.1.2 Dingxi Section

The three-order variations observed at the Lanzhou Section are also present at Dingxi Section (Fig. 5). Again, the <10 μm fraction peaks in the middle portions and carbonate peaks in the lower portions of paleosols S1S2 and S1S3 also indicate that both fine fraction (<10 μm) and carbonate were translocated within these two paleosols. Another quite noticeable feature at this section is that the lower portion of the paleosol S1S3 developed in the coarsening portion (as expressed by the percentage of >63 μm fraction), suggesting that the S1S3 developed into the underlying older loess L2.

4.1.3 Qin'an Section

Again, three orders of particle-size variations are observable at Qin'an Section (Fig. 6). It is also notable that the <10 μm fraction peaks of the third order that are superimposed on the second-order parenthetical trend in the Bt horizons of the three paleosols (S1S1, S1S2 and S1S3) also indicate the occurrence of material translocation within these paleosols. Like at the Dingxi Section, the lower portion of the paleosol S1S3 also developed in the coarsening portion of the underlying older loess L2.

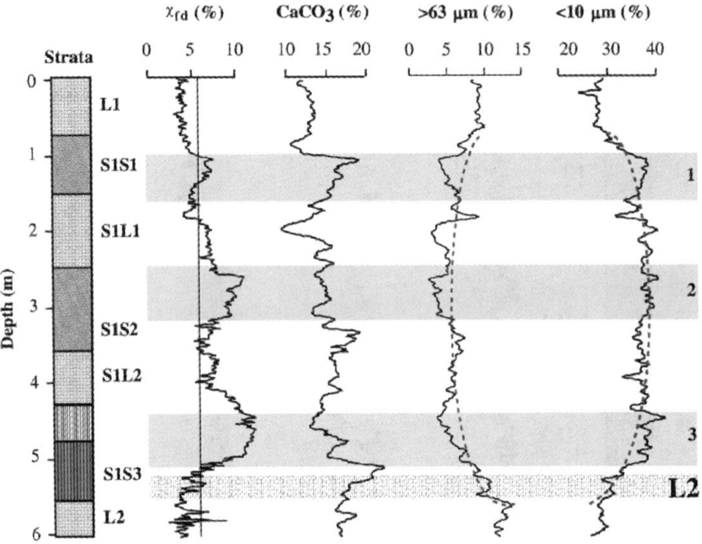

Fig. 5 Dingxi Section: field-observed pedostratigraphy and laboratory data. Laboratory data include χ_{fd} (%), frequency-dependent magnetic susceptibility; $CaCO_3$ (%), percentage of carbonate; >63 μm (%), percentage of >63 μm fraction; <10 μm (%), percentage of <10 μm fraction.

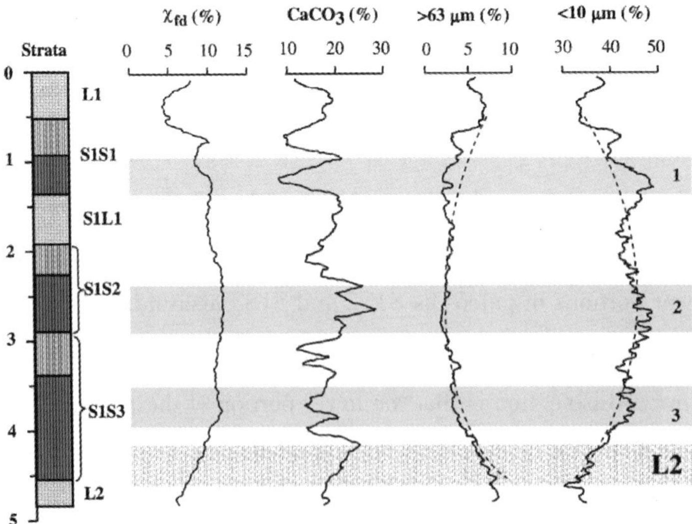

Fig. 6 Qin'an Section: field-observed pedostratigraphy and laboratory data. Laboratory data include χ_{fd} (%), frequency-dependent magnetic susceptibility; $CaCO_3$ (%), percentage of carbonate; >63 μm (%), percentage of >63 μm fraction; <10 μm (%), percentage of <10 μm fraction.

4.1.4 Tianshui Section

The S1 at the Tianshui Section is a pedocomplex without the interbedded loess units. Our interpretation is that the multiple paleosols corresponding to the marine isotope substages 5a, 5c and 5e have become partially welded. That is, after the development of S1S3 (5e), S1S2 (5c) development not only altered the underlying loess S1L2 (5d) into a part of the S1S2 but also "annexed" the upper portion of the S1S3 (5e). The S1S1 (5a) development has not only altered the underlying loess S1L1 (5b) into a part of the S1S1 but also "annexed" the uppermost part of the S1S2 (5c). The particle - size difference between glacial loess units (L1 and L2) and interglacial pedocomplex S1 (i.e., first - order variations) and the parenthetical trends of particle size distribution (i.e., second - order variations) are also observable. The third - order variations that were observed in previously mentioned three sections (Lanzhou, Dingxi, Qin'an) are not observable at Tianshui Section again due to paleosol welding (Feng et al., 2004a,b; Feng and Wang, 2005). Nevertheless, Three coarser zones expressed in <10 μm fraction (marked as −1,−2,−3 in Fig. 7) deserve attentions. The − 1 coarser zone might be the relic of S1S1 - annexed S1L1 and the − 2 coarser zone might be the relic of S2S2 - annexed S1L2. Again, the downward coarsening trend at the base of the S1 pedocomplex (marked as − 3) suggests that a part of S1 pedocomplex developed into the underlying older loess L2.

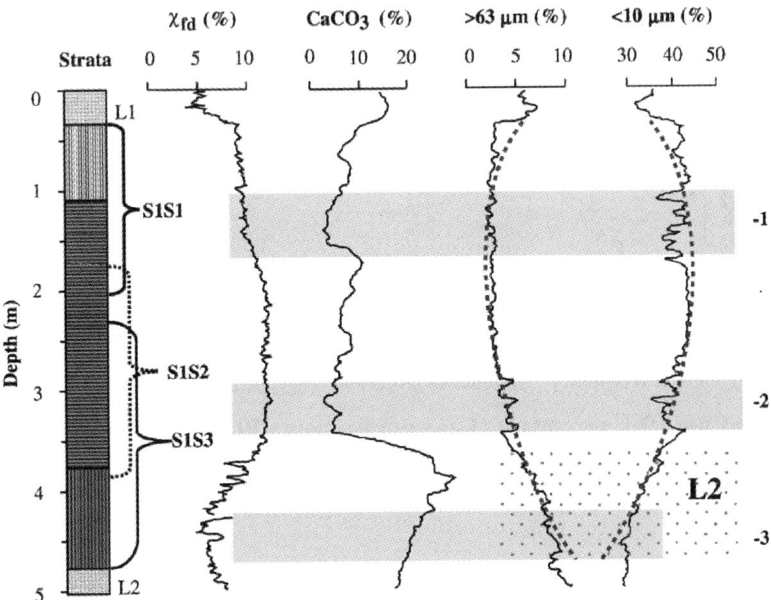

Fig. 7 Tianshui Section: field - observed pedostratigraphy and laboratory data. Laboratory data include χ_{fd}(%), frequency - dependent magnetic susceptibility; $CaCO_3$(%), percentage of carbonate; >63 μm (%), percentage of >63 μm fraction; <10 μm (%), percentage of <10 μm fraction.

4.2 Eastern transect

4.2.1 Huanxian Section

Three orders of particle - size variations observed along the western transect (Fig. 8) are also present at Huanxian Section. Three carbonate troughs associated with three minor < 10 μm peaks (shaded areas 1, 2, 3 in Fig. 8) indicate not only a stronger in situ weathering but probably also a traceable translocation of fine fraction within the S1. Another quite noticeable feature is that the S1S3 paleosol is expressed neither by the frequency - dependent magnetic susceptibility nor by the percentage of <10 μm fraction although it is the best - developed paleosol based on field observations (Feng et al., 2004a,b; Feng and Wang, 2005). Again, our interpretation is that the S1S3 development penetrated into the underlying older loess L2.

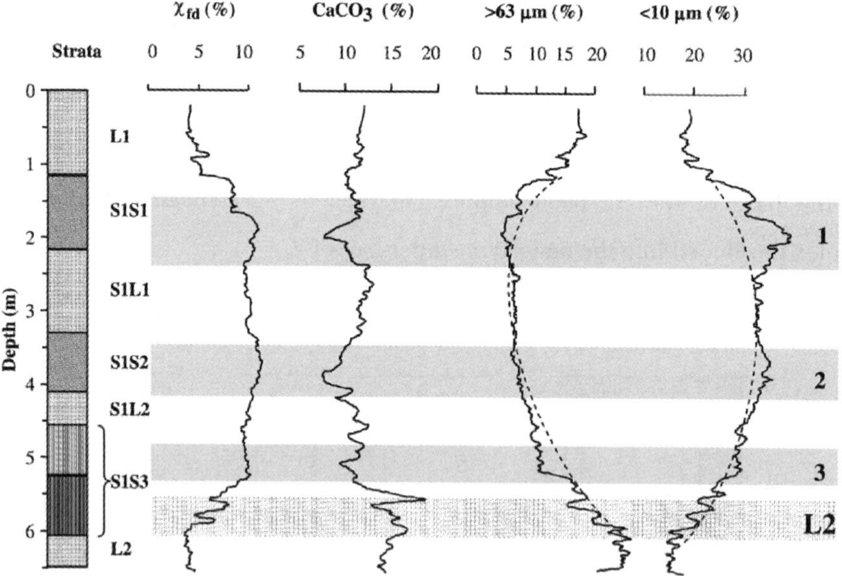

Fig. 8 Huanxian Section: field - observed pedostratigraphy and laboratory data. Laboratory data include χ_{fd} (%), frequency - dependent magnetic susceptibility; $CaCO_3$ (%), percentage of carbonate; >63 μm (%), percentage of >63 μm fraction; <10 μm (%), percentage of <10 μm fraction.

4.2.2 Qingyang and Xunyi Sections

The S1 at these two sections is a pedocomplex without the interbedded loess units (Figs. 9 and 10). Like at the Huanxian Section, the particle - size difference between glacial loess units (L1 and L2) and interglacial pedocomplex S1 (i.e., first - order variations) is observable and the parenthetical trends of particle size distribution (i.e., second - order variations) are also present. The third - order variations that were observed at the Huanxian Section seem to be obscured by soil welding. It should be added that the carbonate - enriched Bk horizon indicates leaching of not only carbonate but probably also other unstable elements as documented at the Luochuan Section by Chen et al. (1997b). Again, the downward coarsening trend at the base of the S1 suggests that a part of S1 pedocomplex developed into the underlying older loess L2.

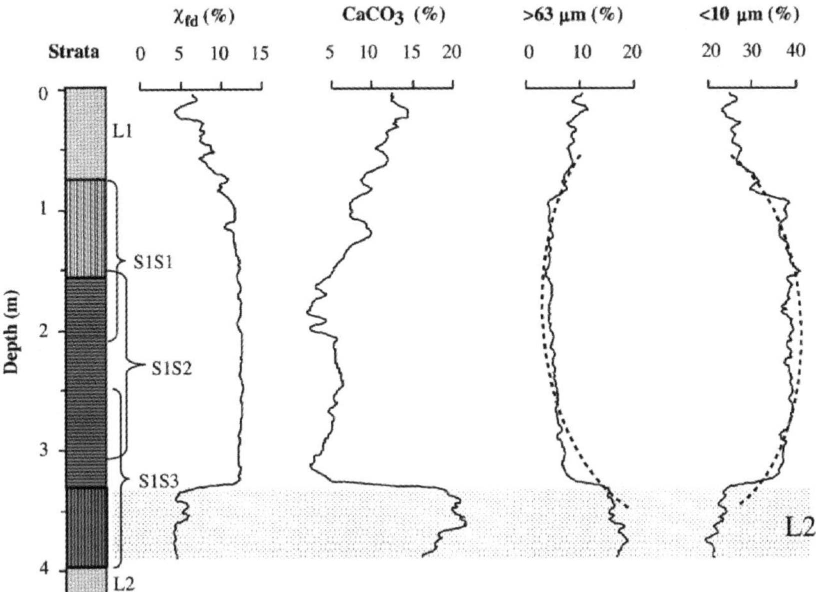

Fig. 9 Qingyang Section: field - observed pedostratigraphy and laboratory data. Laboratory data include χ_{fd} (%), frequency - dependent magnetic susceptibility; $CaCO_3$ (%), percentage of carbonate; >63 μm (%), percentage of >63 μm fraction; <10 μm (%), percentage of <10 μm fraction.

4.2.3 Lantian Section

The S1 paleosol at this section is basically a well - developed Bt horizon that is characterized by coarse prismatic peds, breaking to medium angular blocky peds. Small rounded clay or silt balls within these medium angular blocky peds, together with the clay - enriched thick Bt horizon, not only indicates a stronger in situ weathering but probably also within - S1 translocation of fine fractions. The well - leached BC horizon and the underlying carbonate - enriched Ck horizon in this reddish paleosol also indicate the occurrence of strong leaching of carbonate and probably other unstable elements. The coarsening trend in the particle size distribution from 3.0 to 5.5 m deep seems to indicate that at least the basal 2.5 m of the S1 composite paleosol might have developed in the underlying older loess L2 (Fig. 11).

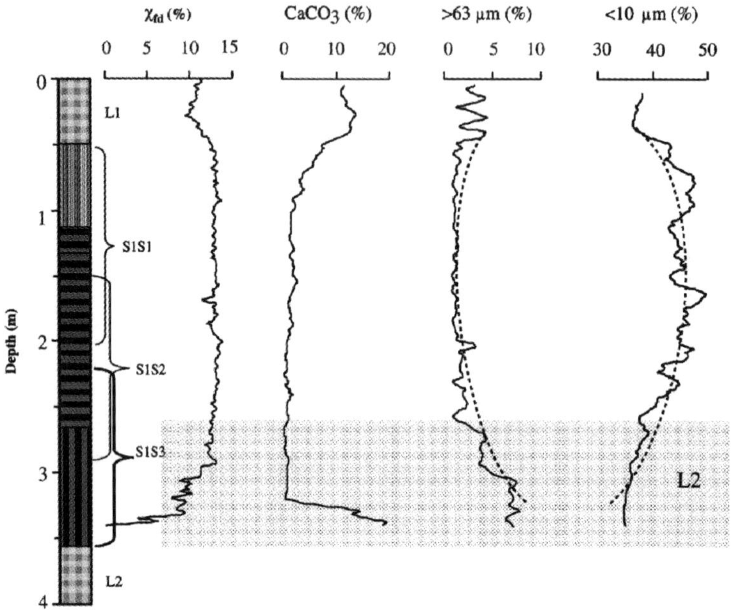

Fig. 10 Xunyi Section: field-observed pedostratigraphy and laboratory data. Laboratory data include χ_{fd} (%), frequency-dependent magnetic susceptibility; $CaCO_3$ (%), percentage of carbonate; >63 μm (%), percentage of >63 μm fraction; <10 μm (%), percentage of <10 μm fraction.

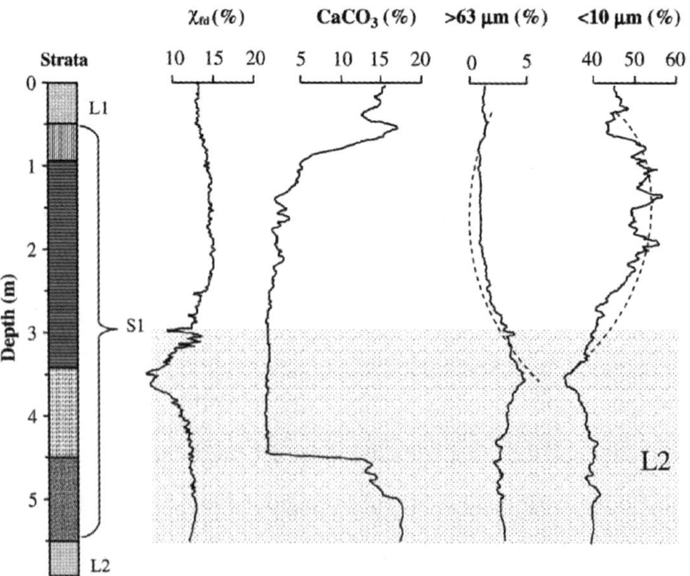

Fig. 11 Lantian Section: field-observed pedostratigraphy and laboratory data. Laboratory data include χ_{fd} (%), frequency-dependent magnetic susceptibility; $CaCO_3$ (%), percentage of carbonate; >63 μm (%), percentage of >63 μm fraction; <10 μm (%), percentage of <10 μm fraction.

5 Discussion

In the northwestern margin of the Chinese Loess Plateau along the western transect, the three paleosols (S1S1, S1S2, S1S3) corresponding to marine isotope substages (5a, 5c and 5e) and the two intercalated loess units (S1L1 and S1L2) corresponding to marine isotope substages 5b and 5d are completely preserved (e.g., at Dingxi and Lanzhou Sections). Southeastward at the Qin' an Section where the three paleosols (S1S1, S1S2, S1S3) were better developed than those at the Lanzhou and Dingxi Sections, the S1L2 was annexed by the later paleosol S1S2 development (Fig. 12). Further southeast at the Tianshui Section, both the S1L2 and S1L1 were annexed by the subsequent paleosol development (S1S2 and S1S1) and the three paleosols were partially welded. Along the eastern transect, the Huanxian Section exhibits similar pedostratigraphic and analytical data - indicated characteristics to those at the Dingxi Section. The Qingyang and Xunyi Sections are compressed versions of the Tianshui section. That is, both the S1L2 and S1L1 were completely annexed by the subsequent paleosol development (S1S2 and S1S1) and the three paleosols were completely welded into an accretionary Mollisol - like pedocomplex with an over - thickened B horizon (or cumulic B horizons). The S1 at the Lantian Section,

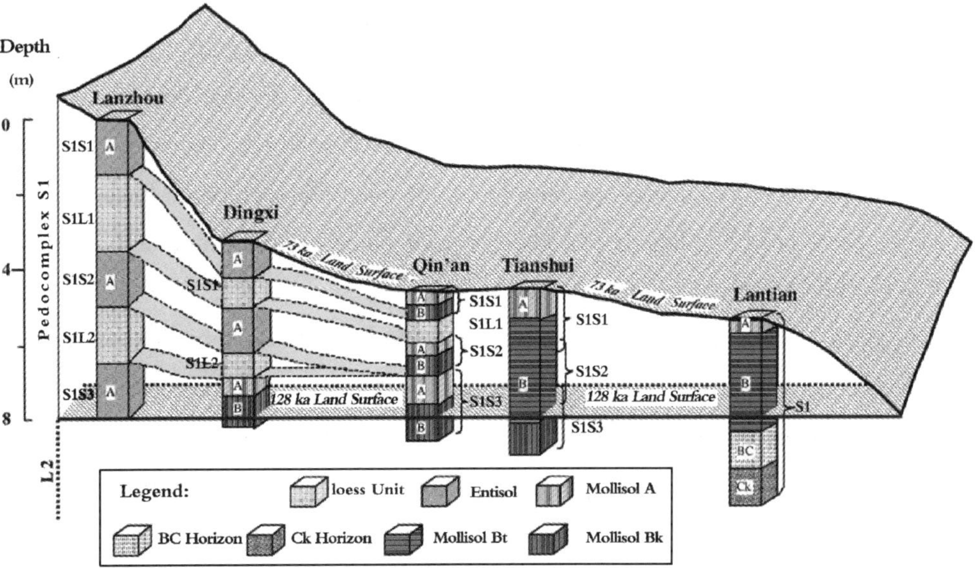

Fig. 12 A sketch model showing the geographic variations of the last interglacial pedocomplex S1 profiles and the relationship between the S1 profiles and their parent materials from the northwestern margin (Lanzhou) to the southeastern margin (Lantian) of the Chinese Loess Plateau (see Discussion for details).

the southeasternmost section, is a composite paleosol with a well - developed Bt horizon, indicating that this S1 profile is the result of multiple soil-forming events.

As for the particle size distribution, the focus of this paper, there are three orders of particle - size variations. First order variations, i.e., a remarkable difference between the interglacial S1 and the glacial loess units (L1 and L2), implies that the S1 parent material was considerably finer in the source areas or/and the proximity to the source areas was farther during interglacial period than during the preceding (L2) and following (L1) glacial periods.

Second order variations, i.e., the parenthetical trends in >63 μm and <10 μm fraction curves, appear to be similar to those widely documented bow - shaped particle size distribution in well - developed soil profiles. In those well - developed soil profiles, gradual intensification of pedogenes at the beginning of a climate amelioration and gradual weakening of pedogenesis at the end of a climatic amelioration are held responsible for the bow-shaped distribution (Ruhe et al., 1955; Zhao, 1994; Birkeland, 1999). But, the overall parenthetical trends of particle size distribution in the entire S1 pedocomplex of the Chinese Loess Plateau need a different explanation because the multiple cumulic paleosols within the S1 pedocomplex that were formed under multiple climatic ameliorations do not exhibit multiple bowed-shapes in the particle size distribution curves. Our interpretation is that although the climate started to deteriorate after the climatic optimum (i.e., the wettest and warmest marine isotope substage 5e) as demonstrated by Guo et al. (1996b, 1999), the parent material gradually reached the finest in the middle of the last interglacial (i.e., the middle portion of the S1 pedocomplex). The fining trend from the beginning to the middle suggests that the last interglacial optimum (i.e., 5e) might have prepared finest materials in the source areas for the following periods. The coarsening trend towards end of the S1 is a result of overall climatic deterioration after 5e.

The third-order variations in <10 μm correspond well to the variations in frequency-dependent magnetic susceptibility, suggesting that pedogenically formed finer particles (i.e., <10 μm fraction) and the associated ultra-fine paramagnetic minerals as expressed by the frequency-dependent susceptibility (Maher et al., 1994) occurred only as a minor component superimposed upon the parenthetic trend (i.e., second order) of the <10 μm fraction. It should be particularly noted that the third-order variations seem to be obscured by soil welding and annexation at the Tianshui, Qingyang, Xunyi and Lantian Sections where the paleosols within the S1 pedocomplex were partially or completely welded. One more noticeable feature is that the <10 μm fraction peaks of the third order and observed clay coatings on ped-faces, as well as carbonate concentration, in the paleosols within the S1 indicate the occurrence of material translocation within these paleosols.

To sum up, our study suggests that both the first-order and second-order variations in particle size distribution are primarily controlled by predepositional weathering in the source areas, challenging the validity of particle size as a winter monsoon intensity proxy that was proposed and used by many researchers (e.g., Liu, 1985, 1987; An et al., 1991a, Ding et al., 1992). Our field-observed and laboratory analyzed data from these chosen two transects have pedogenically substantiated the geographic differentiation of the S1 pedocomplexes that was previously noticed by other researchers (e.g., Kemp et al., 1995, 1997; Evans and Rokosh, 2000; Zhu et al., 2001; Rokosh et al., 2002) and particularly documented the chronological discord between the S1 and its parent material. The pedogenic substantiation of the S1 geographic differentiation cautions us that the pedogenic meaning of the particle size distribution within the S1 and probably other pedocomplexes has to be thoroughly understood before a high-resolution climatic reconstruction is attempted.

Acknowledgement

This research was financially supported by a US National Science Foundation grant (BCS-0078557) and a Chinese Education Ministry grant (No. 2000-65). The comments by two anonymous reviewers considerably improved the paper.

References

Aitken, M.J., 1998. Introduction to Optical Dating. Oxford University Press, Oxford.

Almond, P., 1998. Up-building soil formation in loess in a high rainfall environment, Westland, New Zealand. In: Busacca, A.J. (Ed.), International Symposium on Dust Aerosols, Loess Soil and Global Change. Washington State University College of Agriculture and Home Economics Miscellaneous Publication no. MISC0190, Pullman, pp. 207-211.

An, Z.S., Porter, S.C., 1997. Millennial-scale climatic oscillations during the last interglaciation in central China. Geology 25 (7), 603- 606.

An, Z.S., Kukla, G., Porter, S.C., Xiao, J., 1991. Late Quaternary dust flux on the Chinese Loess Plateau. Catena 18, 125-132.

An, Z.S., Kukla, G., Porter, S.C., Xiao, J.L., 1991. Magnetic susceptibility evidence of monsoon aeration on the Loess Plateau of China during the last 130,000 years. Quaternary Research 36, 29–36.

Assallay, A.M., Rogers, C.D.F., Smalley, I.J., Jefferson, I.F., 1998. Silt, 2– 62 μm, 9–4A. Earth Science Reviews 45, 61–88.

Birkeland, P.W., 1999. Soils and Geomorphology, 3rd edition. Oxford University Press, New York.

Buol, S.W., Hole, F.D., McCracken, R.J., 1973. Soil Genesis and Classification. The Iowa State University Press, Ames, Iowa.

Catt, J.A., 1986. Soils and Quaternary Geology, Monographs on Soil and Resource Survey, vol. 11. Clarendon Press, Oxford.

Chen, F.H., Boemandel, J., Wang, J.M., Li, J.J., Oldfield, F., 1997a. High-resolution multiproxy climatic records from Chinese loess: evidence for rapid climatic changes over the last 75 kyr. Palaeogeography, Palaeoclimatology, Palaeoecology 130, 323–335.

Chen, J., Ji, J.F., Qiu, G., Lu, H.Y., Zhu, H.B., 1997b. Geochemical studies of the leaching processes in the Luochuan loess/paleosol section. Sciences in China (D) 27 (6), 531–536.

Chen, F.H., Boemandel, J., Feng, Z.–D., Wang, J.M., Gou, Z.T., Park, E., Shi, Q., 1999. East Asian monsoon variations during oxygen isotope stage 5: evidence from the northwestern margin of the Chinese Loess Plateau. Quaternary Science Reviews 18, 1127–1135.

Chen, F.H., Feng, Z.–D., Zhang, J.W., 2000. Loess particle size data indicative of stable winter monsoon during the last interglacial in the western part of the Chinese Loess Plateau. Catena 39, 233–244.

Dansgaard, W., Johnsen, S.J., Clausen, H.B., Dahl–Jensen, D., Gundestrup, N.S., Hammer, C. U., Hvidberg, C.S., Steffensen, S.J., Sveinbirnsdottir, A.E., Jouzel, J., Bond, G., 1993. Evidence for general instability of past climate from a 250 kyr ice-core record. Nature 364, 218–220.

Derbyshire, E., Keen, D.H., Kemp, R.A., Rolph, T.A., Shaw, J., Meng, X.M., 1995. Loess - paleosol sequences as recorders of paleoclimatic variations during the last glacial interglacial cycle: some problems of correlation in north - central China. Quaternary Proceedings 4, 7–18.

Derbyshire, E., Kemp, R.A., Meng, X.M., 1997. Climate change, loess and paleosols: proxy and resolution in North China. Journal of the Geological Society (London) 154, 793–805.

Ding, Z.L., Rutter, N.W., Han, J.M., Liu, T.S., 1992. A coupled environmental system formed at about 2.5Ma over eastern Asia. Palaeogeography Palaeoclimatology Palaeoecology 94, 223–

224.

Ding, Z.L., Sun, J.M., Rutter, N.W., Rokosh, D., Liu, T.S., 1999. Changes in sand content of loess deposits along a North - South transect of the Chinese Loess Plateau and the implications for desert variations. Quaternary Research 52, 56–62.

Dixon, J.C., Thorn, C.E., Darmody, R.G., 1984. Chemical weathering processes on the Vantage Peak Nunatak, Juneau Icefield, Southern Alaska. Physical Geography 5, 111–131.

Evans, M.E., Rokosh, C.D., 2000. The last interglacial in the Chinese Loess Plateau: a petromagnetic investigation of samples from a north - south transect. Quaternary International 68–71, 77–82.

Feng, Z.–D., 1996. Climatic implications of magnetic susceptibility and Be–10 flux in Chinese loess. Catena 27, 143–147.

Feng, Z.– D., 1997. Geochemical characteristics of a loess - soil sequence in central Kansas, USA. Soil Science Society of America Journal 61, 534–541.

Feng, Z.– D., Chen, F.H., 1999. Problems of magnetic susceptibility signature as the summer monsoon proxy in Chinese loess sequences. Chinese Science Bulletin 44 (Suppl. 1), 97–104.

Feng, Z.–D., Johnson, W.C., 1995. Factors affecting the magnetic susceptibility of a loess - soil sequence, Barton County, Kansas, USA. Catena 24, 25–37.

Feng, Z.–D., Johnson, W.C., Diffendal, R.F., 1994a. Environment of eolian deposition in south - central Nebraska during the last glacial maximum. Physical Geography 15 (3), 250–258.

Feng, Z.– D., Johnson, W.C., Sprowl, D.R., Lu, Y.C., 1994b. Loess accumulation and soil formation in central Kansas, USA, during the past 400,000years. Earth Surface Processes and Landforms 19, 55–67.

Feng, Z.–D., Johnson, W.C., Sprowl, D.R., Lu, Y.C., Ward, P.A., 1994c. Climatic signals from loess - soil sequences in the central Great Plains, USA. Palaeogeography, Palaeoecology, Palaeoclimatology 110, 345–358.

Feng, Z.–D., Wang, H.B., Olson, C.G., Pope, G.A., Chen, F.H., Zhang, J.W., An, C.B., 2004a. Chronological discord between the last interglacial paleosol (S1) and its parent material in the Chinese Loess Plateau. Quaternary International 117, 17–26.

Feng, Z.–D., Wang, H.B., Olson, C.G., 2004b. Pedogenic factors affecting magnetic susceptibility of the last interglacial paleosol S1 in the Chinese Loess Plateau. Earth Surface and Landforms 29, 1389–1402.

Feng, Z.– D., Wang, H.B., 2005. Pedostratigraphy and carbonate accumulation in the last interglacial pedocomplex of the Chinese Loess Plateau. Soil Science Society of America

Journal 69, 1094–1101.

Forman, S.L., 1991. Late Pleistocene chronology of loess deposition near Luochuan, China. Quaternary Research 36, 19–28.

Foth, H.D., 1978. Fundamentals of Soil Science, 6th edition. John Wiley and Sons Inc, New York.

Gile, L.H., 1979. Holocene soils in eolian sediments of Bailey County, Texas. Soil Science Society of America Journal 49, 994–1005.

Goudie, A.S., Cooke, R.U., Doornkamp, J.C., 1979. The formation of silt from quartz dune sand by salt weathering processes in deserts. Journal of Arid Environments 2, 105–112.

GRIP Members, 1993. Climate instability during the last interglacial period recorded in the GRIP ice core. Nature 364, 203–207.

Guo, Z.T., Fedoroff, N., An, Z.S., Liu, T.S., 1993. Interglacial dustfall and origin of iron oxides-hydroxides in the paleosols of the Xifeng loess section, China. Scientia Geologica Sinica 2, 91–100 (in Chinese).

Guo, Z.T., Liu, T.S., An, Z.S., 1994. Paleosols and their forming environments during the past 150,000 years in Weinan. Quaternary Sciences 3, 256–269 (in Chinese).

Guo, Z.T., Fedoroff, N., Liu, T.S., 1996a. The micromorphology of the loess-paleosol last 130 ka in China and paleoclimatic events. Science in China (B) 39 (5), 468–477.

Guo, Z.T., Liu, T.S., Guiot, J., Wu, N.Q., Lu, H., Han, J.M., Liu, J., Gu, Z., 1996b. High frequency pulses of East Asian monsoon climate in the last two glaciations: link with the North Atlantic. Climate Dynamics 12, 701–709.

Guo, Z.T., Peng, S.Z., Wei, L.Y., 1999. Weathering signals of millennial-scale oscillations of the East Asian summer monsoon over the last 220,000 years. Chinese Science Bulletin 44 (Suppl. 1), 20–25.

Hao, Q.Z., Guo, Z.T., 2001. Quantitative analysis of weathering and pedogenesis of the Chinese loess-paleosol sequence over the last 1.2 Ma and their implications for reconstructing the East Asian summer monsoon history. Science in China (D) 31 (6), 520–528 (in Chinese).

Heller, F., Liu, T.S., 1982. Magnetostratigraphical dating of loess deposits in China. Nature 300, 431–433.

Heller, F., Liu, T.S., 1984. Magnetism of Chinese loess deposits. Geophysical Journal of the Royal Astronomical Society 77, 125–141.

Janitzky, P., 1987. Particle size analysis. In: Singer, M., Janitzky, P. (Eds.), Field and Laboratory Procedures used in Soil Chronosequence Study, U.S. Geological Survey Bulletin, vol. 1648. Government Printing Office, Washington, DC, pp. 1–16.

Kemp, R.A., Derbyshire, E., Meng, X.M., Chen, F.H., Pan, B.T., 1995. Pedosedimentary reconstruction of a thick loess - paleosol sequence near Lanzhou in North - Central China. Quaternary Research 43, 30–45.

Kemp, R.A., Derbyshire, E., Meng, X.M., 1997. Micromorphological variations of the S1 paleosol across northwestern China. Catena 31, 77–90.

Kukla, G., An, Z.S., 1989. Loess stratigraphy in central China. Palaeogeography, Palaeoclimatology, Palaeoecology 72, 203–225.

Kukla, G., Heller, F., Liu, X.M., Xu, T.C., Liu, T.S., An, Z.S., 1988. Pleistocene climates in China dated by magnetic susceptibility. Geology 16, 811–814.

Li, J.J., Feng, Z.–D., Tang, L.Y., 1988. Late Quaternary monsoon patterns on the Loess Plateau of China. Earth Surface Processes and Landforms 13, 125–135.

Li, L., Sun, Y.B., Lu, H.Y., Lai, Z.P., An, Z.S., 1998. Comparison between North Atlantic cooling events and dust events in the Chinese Loess Plateau during the last interglacial. Chinese Science Bulletin 43 (1), 90–93 (in Chinese).

Liu, T.S. (Ed.), 1985. Loess and Environments. Ocean Press, Beijing.

Liu, T.S. (Ed.), 1987. New Aspects of Loess Research. Ocean Press, Beijing.

Liu, J.Q., Chen, T.M., Nie, G.Z., Song, C.Y., Guo, Z.T., Li, K., Gao, S.J., Qiao, Y.L., Ma, Z.B., 1994. Dating and reconstruction of the high resolution time series in the Weinan loess section of the last 150 000 years. Quaternary Sciences 3, 193– 202 (in Chinese).

Lu, H.Y., An, Z.S., 1997. Particle size distribution and the climatic implications in the Luochuan loess-soil sequence. Chinese Science Bulletin 42 (1), 66– 69 (in Chinese).

Lu, H.Y., An, H.Y., 1998. Particle size distribution and the climatic implications in the Chinese Loess Plateau. Science in China (B) 28 (3), 278– 283 (in Chinese).

Lu, Y.C., Zhang, J.Z., Xie, J., 1988. Thermoluninescence dating of loess and paleosol from the Lantian Section, Shanxi Province, China. Quaternary Research 7, 245– 250.

Machette, M., 1986. Calcium and magnesium carbonates. In: Singer, M.J., Janitzky, P. (Eds.), Field and Laboratory Procedures Used in a Soil Chronosequence Study, U.S. Geological Survey Bulletin, vol. 1648. U.S. Government Printing Office, Washington, DC, pp. 30– 33.

Mack, G.H., James, W.C., Monger, H.C., 1993. Classification of paleosols. Geological Society of America Bulletin 105, 129– 136.

Maher, B.A., Thompson, R., Zhou, L.P., 1994. Spatial and temporal reconstruction of changes in the Asian paleomonsoon: a new mineral magnetic approach. Earth and Planetary Science Letters 125, 461–471.

McManus, J.F., Bond, G.C., Broecker, W.S., Johnsen, S., Labeyrie, L., Higgins, S., 1994. High-resolution climate records from the North Atlantic during the last interglacial. Nature 371,

326- 329.

Moore, T.R., 1978. Soil formation in northeastern Canada. Annals of the Association of American Geographers 68, 518- 537.

Murray, A.S., Wintle, A.G., 2000. Luminescence dating of quartz using an improved single - aliquot regenerative-dose protocol. Radiation Measurements 32 (1), 57- 73.

Nettleton, W.D., Olson, C.G., Wysocki, D.A., 2000. Paleosol classification: problems and solutions. Catena 41, 61- 92.

Oches, E.A., Banerjee, S.K., Soheid, P.A., Frechen, M., 1998. High - resolution proxies of climate variability in the Alaska loess record. In: Busacca, A.J. (Ed.), International Symposium on Dust Aerosols, Loess Soil and Global Change. Washington State University' s CAHE MISC0190, Pullman, WA, pp. 167–170.

Olson, C.G., Nettleton, W.D., 1998. Paleosols and the effects of alteration. Quaternary International 51- 52, 185–194.

Pope, G.A., 1995. Internal weathering of quartz grains. Physical Geography 16, 315–338.

Porter, S.C., An, Z.S., 1995. Correlation between climate events in the North–Atlantic and China during the last glaciation. Nature 375, 305- 308.

Rokosh, C.D., Rutter, N.W., Ding, Z.L., Sun, J.M., 2002. Regional lithofacies and pedofacies variations along a north-south climatic gradient during the last glacial period in the central Loess Plateau, China. Quaternary Science Reviews 21, 811- 817.

Ruhe, R.V., 1973. Background of model for loess - derived soils in the upper Mississippi River Basin. Soil Science 115 (3), 250- 253.

Ruhe, R.V., 1983. Depositional environment of late Wisconsin loess in the midcontinental United States. In: Porter, S.C. (Ed.), Later Quaternary Environments of the United States. University of Minnesota Press, pp. 130- 137.

Ruhe, R.V., 1984. Soil - climate system across the prairies in Midwestern USA. Geoderma 34, 201- 219.

Ruhe, R.V., Olson, C.G., 1979. Estimate of clay content: additions of proportions of soil clay to constant standard. Clay Mineralogy 27, 322- 326.

Ruhe, R.V., Olson, C.G., 1980. Soil welding. Soil Science 130, 132- 139.

Ruhe, R.V., Prill, R.C., Piecken, F.F., 1955. Profile characteristics of some loess - derived soils and soil aeration. Soil Science Society of American Journal 19, 345- 348.

Schaetzl, R.J., Sorenson, C.J., 1987. The concept of "buried" versus "isolated" paleosols: examples from northeastern Kansas. Soil Science 143 (6), 426- 435.

Sun, J.M., Ding, Z.L., 1998. Deposits and soils of the past 130,000years at the desert - loess transition in the Northern China. Quaternary Research 50, 148- 156.

Sun, Y.B., Lu, H.Y., An, Z.S., 2000. Quartz particle size distribution in loess - paleosol sequence. Chinese Science Bulletin 45 (19), 2094- 2097.

Thompson, R., Oldfield, F., 1986. Environmental Magnetism. Allen and Oldwin, London.

Wang, W.Y., Liu, J.Q., Pan, M., Liu, T.S., 2000. Thermoluminescent dating of the loess sequence of the last Quaternary — the comparison study on the Weinan and Huining sections. Marine Geology & Quaternary Geology 20 (3), 67- 72 (in Chinese).

Wright, J.T., 2001. "Desert" loess versus "glacial" loess: quartz silt formation, source areas and sediment pathways in the formation of loess deposits. Geomorphology 36, 231- 256.

Zhang, Z.H., Chen, Y., 1995. New development in the loess in China. Episodes 18, 58-60.

Zhao, J.B., 1994. Quaternary Paleosols and the Environments in the Northwestern China. Shaanxi Science and Technology Press (in Chinese).

Zhu, R.X., Deng, C.L., Jackson, M.J., 2001. A magnetic investigation along a NW-SE transect of the Chinese Loess Plateau and its implications. Physics and Chemistry of the Earth (A) 6 (11-12), 867- 872.

（注：参考文献为原杂志格式。）

Spatiotemporal variations of Zr/Rb ratio in three last interglacial paleosol profiles across the Chinese Loess Plateau and its implications for climatic interpretation*

WANG HaiBin, LIU LianYou, FENG ZhaoDong

Abstract: The ratio of Zirconium to Rubidium (Zr/Rb) is suggested to be a better proxy for the East Asian winter monsoon strength than the widely - used grain size distribution. The rationale for the Zr/Rb proxy relies on the following assumptions: (1) Grain size fractionating characteristics during eolian dust transport should be archived in the Zr/Rb ratio records and this assumption is based on the premise that Zr is preferentially enriched in coarser grain size fraction while Rb tend to be enriched in finer grain size fraction; and (2) post - depositional weathering does not change the Zr/Rb ratio due to the immobility of these two elements. To examine these two assumptions, three last interglacial paleosols (S1) from Dingxi, Tianshui and Lantian, along a NW–SE transect across the Chinese Loess Plateau, were geochemically investigated. Our results show that the Rb concentration exhibits an increasing trend along the NW–SE transect both in the paleosol (S1) and the measured portions of the loess units (L1 and L2), being supportive to the assumption that Rb is enriched in the fine particles. But we also found that Rb loss did occur to some extent in the three profiles, contradicting to the presumption of Rb immobility during pedogenic processes. The Zr concentration exhibits an expected decreasing trend in the measured portions of the loess units and an unexpected increasing trend in the paleosol along the NW–SE transect. Moreover, the ratios of Zirconium to Hafnium (Zr/Hf) show different variation patterns between interglacial and glacial, implying that Zr - bearing minerals and their resident grain size fractions are probably not identical during interglacial and glacial. Thus, the assumption that Zr is enriched in coarse grain size fraction can no longer hold. We conclude that the final Zr/Rb value is not only dependent on grain size sorting processes but also on post - depositional alteration and source provenance. Under enhanced chemical weathering, especially when chemical index of alteration (CIA) is greater than 65, the Zr/Rb value loses its validity to be a reliable proxy for the winter monsoon

*本文发表于:Chinese Science Bulletin, 2008, 53(9): 1413–1422.

strength. In addition, all the Zr/Rb value is constrained above 1.7, a minimum which is definitely modulated by all the three aforementioned factors.

Key words: Zr; Rb; transportation sorting; weathering; provenance

It is well demonstrated that the Chinese loess is of wind-blown origin and the northerly East Asia winter monsoon is responsible for loess transportation and deposition[1]. The grain size has thus been utilized as a proxy for winter monsoon strength[2]. However, the bulk grain size may be greatly skewed by post-depositional weathering processes, especially during interglacial and interstadial periods when pedogenesis dominated the landscape. Subsequently, Xiao et al.[3] and Porter and An[4] argued that quartz and its coarse fraction can be a better candidate for winter monsoon strength because quartz is much more resistant to weathering than most of common minerals. Nevertheless, there exists evidence that quartz is vulnerable to organic acid dissolution[5]. More recently, Liu et al.[6] and Chen et al.[7] proposed that Zr/Rb is a more reliable indicator of winter monsoon strength.

The chemical composition of clastic sedimentary rocks is governed by many complex factors, including the average composition of source rocks, weathering processes, transportation processes, diagenesis and metamorphism[8,9]. The proposal for Zr/Rb being an indicator of winter monsoon mainly lies at the following assumptions[6,7]: (1) Grain size sorting process during eolian dust transport dominates the Zr and Rb abundance because Zr is preferentially enriched in coarser grain size fraction while Rb tends to be enriched in finer grain size fraction. Thus the grain size fractionating characteristics may be archived in the Zr/Rb ratio. (2) Post-depositional chemical weathering does not change the Zr/Rb ratio due to the immobility of these two elements. To test the first assumption, Liu et al. used least weathered (judged from magnetic susceptibility) loess (last glacial) samples from central part of Chinese Loess Plateau and their results show that Zr has highest relative abundance in >32 μm size fraction (unit μg/g or ppm) while Rb has its highest concentration in <2 μm size fraction, validating the first assumption[6]. But, the spatiotemporal patterns of Zr concentration cast doubt on the assumption on Zr enrichment grain-size fraction. Specifically, Zr concentration exhibits a decreasing trend along the N-S transect during last glacial, whereas there is an increasing trend during last interglacial (refer to Table 1 in ref. [6]). Therefore this leaves us an open question on whether Zr shared the identical grain size fractionating portion or not at different periods. To test the second assumption, Chen et al. conducted an acetic-acid leaching experiment (for 6 hours each sample) and concluded that Zr/Rb was little affected by leaching, supporting the second assumption. Nonetheless, contrary evidence has also been published by others from other regions. For example, Hodson [10] did a Soxhlet extraction experiment of granitic podzol (over a period of 27 days) and showed that Rb is much more mobile than Zr. A study on a weathering profile of the Toorongo Granodiorite (Australia) also revealed that Rb loss tends to be more evident than Zr loss when the chemical index of alteration (CIA) is greater than 65 (see Table 2 in ref. [11]). Generally speaking, Zr is immobile during chemical weathering because most Zr-bearing minerals (e.g., Zircon) are quite resistant to weathering and it is usually taken as a denominator (i.e., the most immobile element) to estimate the mobilities of other elements[12]. This means that the implication of Zr/Rb ratio is not straightforward and needs to be further investigated.

The main aims of this paper are: (1) to further investigate the spatiotemporal variation pattern of Zr concentration and to assess the effect of transporting processes on Zr concentration, (2) to estimate the Rb change relative to the Zr with reference to upper continental crust (UCC) average composition in hope that weathering and transporting effects on Rb concentration can be assessed, and (3) to evaluate the potential effect of provenance on Zr/Rb ratio.

1 Material and methods

There is a modern NW–SE climatic gradient in the Chinese Loess Plateau. In this study, we select three loess sections along NW–SE transect. They are located at Lantian (34°10′N, 109°19′E), Tianshui (34°34′N, 105°46′E) and Dingxi (35°35′N, 104°37′E) (see Figure 1). Lantian is situated in the broad–deciduous forest zone, the mean annual temperature (MAT) is about 12.5 ℃ and the mean annual precipitation (MAP) is about 668 mm in this area. Tianshui is situated in the forest–steppe zone, the MAT is about 10.7 ℃ and the MAP is about 540 mm in this area. Dingxi is situated in the steppe zone, the MAT is about 6.4 ℃ and the MAP is about 413 mm in this area. Samples were collected at 2 cm intervals except for the 0.5 m thick basal part of Lantian section in which the sampling intervals were 10 cm. All of the three sampled sections include the entire last interglacial paleosol (S1), the top portion of penultimate glacial loess (L2) and the bottom portion of last glacial loess (L1). The Lantian section (5.5 m thick) consists of 0.4 m L1, 4.1 m S1 and 1 m L2. The alfisol-like S1 of Lantian section is made up of 0.4-m-thick A horizon, 2.6-m-thick Bt horizon and 1.1-m-thick Bc horizon. Northwestward to the Tianshui section, the 5-m-thick section consists of 0.3 m L1, 4.5 m S1 and 0.2 m L2. The mollisol-like S1 here is made up of 0.8-m-thick A horizon, 2.5-m-thick Bt horizon and 1.2-m-thick Bk horizon. Farther northwest to the Dingxi section, the 6-m-thick section consists of 0.7 m L1, 4.9 m S1 and 0.4 m L2. The S1 here is a pedocomplex which consists of three subsoil units (S1S1, S1S2, S1S3) and two intercalating loess layers (S1L1, S1L2). The S1S1 and S1S2 are entisol-like A horizons and S1S3 is composed of A and Bk horizons.

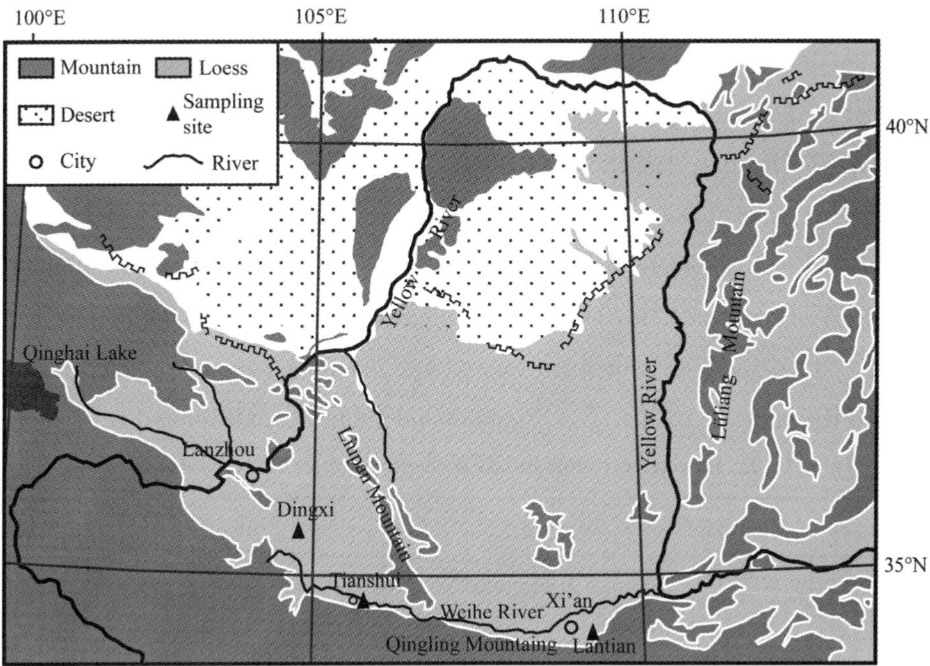

Figure 1 Map showing sampling locations.

Chemical composition was determined using Panalytical Magix PW2403 (a XRF spectrometer) in Key Laboratory of Western China's Environmental System, Ministry of Education, Lanzhou University. Sample preparation procedure for XRF analysis is as the following: first, the bulk samples were dried at about 105 ℃ for about 3 hours, then each bulk sample was ground to less than 75 μm in agate mortar, and finally about 4 gram of powder of each sample was made into a pellet with borate coating (40 mm in diameter and 8 mm in depth) using semiautomatic oil-hydraulic laboratory press, model YYJ-40. The uncertainty for measurement is ±2%.

2 Results

2.1 Rb and Zr spatiotemporal distribution

The following two trends can be observed with regard to the spatiotemporal variations in Rb concentration. First, Rb concentration increases from northwest to southeast in all of the three studied units (i.e., L1, S1, L2). Second, Rb concentration is higher in the paleosol (S1) than in the measured portions of the loess units (L1 and L2) at all of three studied sections (Lantian, Tianshui and Dingxi). Our observed trends are similar to those observed from a N-S transect across the central part of the Chinese Loess Plateau [6]. It should be noted that carbonate is an easily leachable component in loess. To eliminate the dilution effect of carbonate, we made a rectification by applying a coefficient of 1/(1-carbonate%) to originally measured Rb values. And the aforementioned trends still exist in the rectified Rb values (i.e., Rb) (see Figure 2 and Table 1), indicating that Rb is indeed

Table 1 Zr, Rb concentration and their rectified values in three loess sections

Section	Stratigraphy	Zr ($\mu g \cdot g^{-1}$)	Zr*($\mu g \cdot g^{-1}$)	Rb ($\mu g \cdot g^{-1}$)	Rb*($\mu g \cdot g^{-1}$)
Dingxi	L1	214.6	246.1	96.3	110.4
	S1	196.2	231.1	99.9	117.7
	L2	205.1	246.3	93.7	112.5
	Total	199.0	233.8	99.1	116.5
Tianshui	L1	196.6	232.3	100.6	118.8
	S1	211.3	237.3	111.6	125.3
	L2	190.7	231.5	96.1	116.7
	Total	209.5	236.8	110.3	124.5
Lantian	L1	193.4	225.1	100.8	117.5
	S1	252.3	259.6	119.1	122.8
	L2	197.7	232.2	101.1	118.8
	Total	241.8	254.0	115.7	122.0

Zr* and Rb* are rectified values on carbonate - free basis: Rectified value = Measured value/(1-carbonate%).

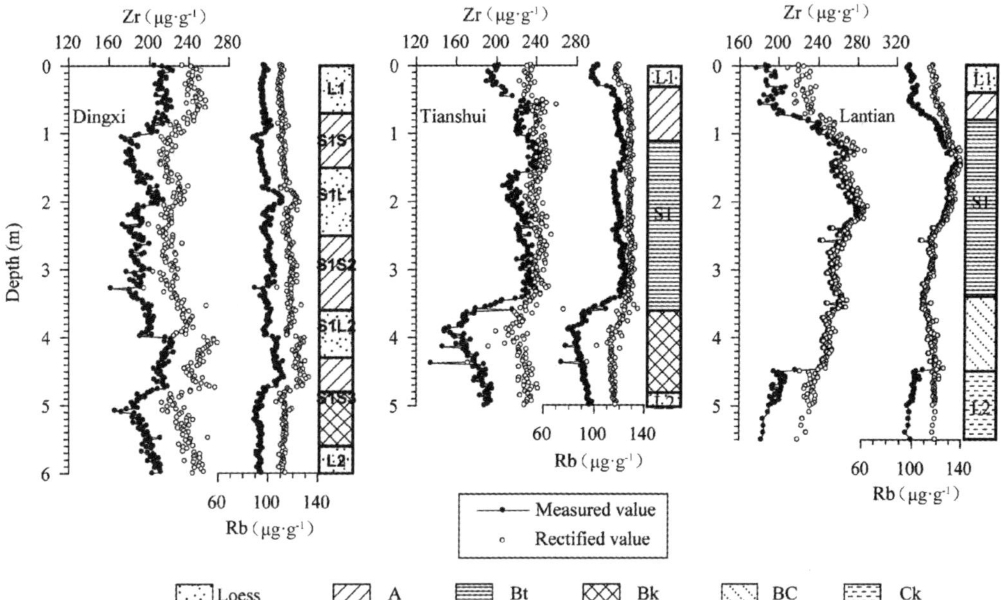

Figure 2 Variations of Zr, Rb and their rectified values (see text for details) along the profiles

enriched in finer grain size fraction during both interglacial and glacial. This is consistent with the experimental observation on Rb distribution in both L1 (last glacial) and S1 (last interglacial) samples as reported by Yang et al.[13].

Our data show that the variation of Zr concentration is more complicated than that of Rb concentration. But, several general observations can be readily made. First, Zr exhibits a decreasing trend in the measured portions of the loess units (both L1 and L2) and an increasing trend in the paleosol (S1) from northwest to southeast. Second, the average Zr concentration is lower in the paleosol (S1) than in the measured portions of the loess units (L1 and L2) at the Dingxi section, whereas the average Zr concentration is higher in the paleosol (S1) than in the measured portions of the loess units (L1 or L2) at Tianshui and Lantian sections. These two features are identical to the previous study from the Huanxian, Xifeng and Luochuan sections along the N-S transect[6]. The decreasing trend of Zr in the loess units along the NW-SE transect and the higher Zr values in the loess units (L1 and L2) at the Dingxi section seem supportive to the well - accepted notion that Zr is more enriched in coarser fractions and that finer fractions with lower Zr values were transported to longer distance. The observed increasing trend of Zr in the paleosol (S1) along the transect and higher Zr values in the paleosols than in loess units at the Tianshui and Lantian sections, where chemical weathering is significantly stronger than at the Dingxi section, might be attributed to pedogenic processes in which unstable elements was leached away to elevate the relative abundance of Zr. However, the pedogenic processes seem not to totally account for the southeastward enrichment of Zr in S1 because the rectified Zr concentration (Zr*) still exhibits southeastward enrichment trend. This leads us to speculate that Zr is enriched in coarser grain size fraction (especially in coarse silt and beyond) during the glacial, but possibly tends to be enriched in finer grain size fraction (medium to fine silt) during the last interglacial. Firstly, the enrichment of Zr in finer grain size fraction may benefit from increase of the percentage of finer Zircon grains held in source area due to enhanced chemical weathering during warmer interglacial. Also, there is a possibility that the Zr - bearing minerals and/or their percentage in last interglacial paleosol might be different from those in glacial loess. The later issue will be further discussed later in section 3.1(on Zr/Hf ratio).

2.2 Rb change relative to UCC

We adopted a mass - balance approach to assess the potential chemical weathering effect on Rb. This approach is accomplished by normalizing Rb concentration to the concentration of an immobile element and comparing it with the concentration of Rb in the parent material or unweathered C horizon of the soil. Here, we estimated the mass balance of Rb by using the average composition of UCC for composition of parent material and by assumption of immobility of Zr, for any given layer:

$$\Delta Rb\%=(Rb\times Zr_{UCC}/Zr-Rb_{UCC})/Rb_{UCC}\times 100\%, \quad (1)$$

then

$$\Delta Rb\%=[(Zr_{UCC}/Rb_{UCC})/(Zr/Rb)-1]\times 100\%, \quad (2)$$

where ΔRb represents Rb change, Rb and Zr denote measured values of Rb, Zr respectively, Rb_{UCC} and Zr_{UCC} denote average concentrations of Rb and Zr of UCC. If $\Delta Rb>0$, then Rb concentration in a given layer has gain over UCC; If $\Delta Rb<0$, then Rb concentration in a given layer has loss relative to UCC. Assuming Zr concentration decreases with increasing transporting distance while Rb concentration increases with transporting distance (from NW to SE) primarily due to eolian sorting processes, the Zr/Rb ratio of originally deposited material (i.e., parent material) should decrease along the NW- SE transect. Thereby we adopt two serials of average composition of UCC as references representing the chemical composition of the parent materials. One is from Wedepohl in which Zr and Rb are 237 μg/g, 110 μg/g respectively, and $Zr_{UCC}/Rb_{UCC}=2.15$[14] and the other is from Taylor and McLennan in which Zr and Rb are 190 μg/g, 112 μg/g respectively, and $Zr_{UCC}/Rb_{UCC} = 1.70$[9]. Our mass-balance approach further confirms the assumption that the eolian sorting processes are overwhelming factor controlling Rb concentration during glacial times. However, the assumption of eolian sorting does not hold for the last interglacial S1 in which ΔRb decreases southeastward, indicating that leaching of Rb by pedogenesis within more weathered soils counteracts the enrichment of Rb by sorting process to some extent. If $Zr_{UCC}/Rb_{UCC}=1.70$ [2] is taken as Zr/Rb ratio of originally deposited sediment at Lantian section, Rb loss in the paleosol S1 (shaded portion in Figure 3) is quite substantial. The mass balance of Rb at the northwestern section, Dingxi, is positive, suggesting a net accumulation of Rb within the S1 paleosol profile. Here, we have to admit that we are facing an awkward dilemma in assessing the mass balance of Rb and other elements in relation to Zr concentration simply because Zr is not a constant across the Chinese Loess Plateau due to eolian sorting - resulted southeastward enrichment. In other words, if the eolian sorting factor can be quantitatively defined, the aforementioned mass balance approach can be more confidently used not only for assessing Rb changes but probably also for estimating the weathering effects (e.g., dilution and enhancement) on other widely - used climatic proxies (e.g., grain size and magnetic susceptibility).

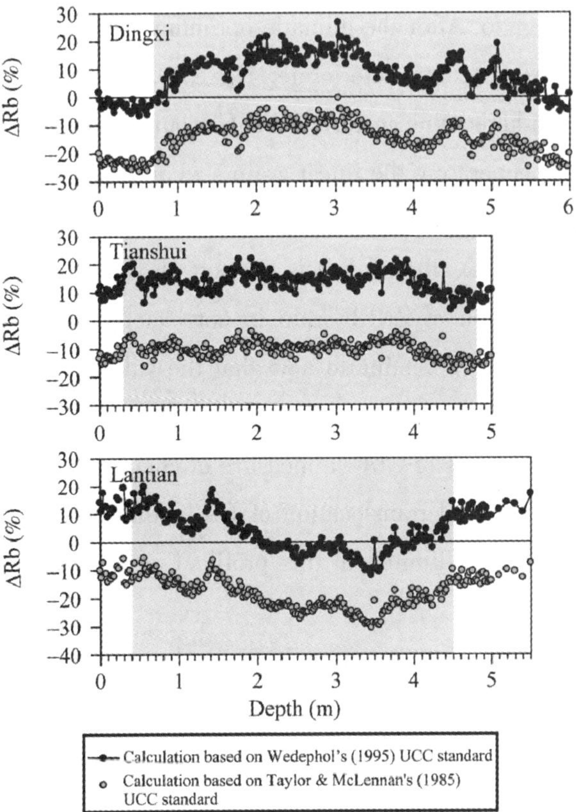

Figure 3 Rb changes relative to UCC

2.3 Spatiotemporal variation of Zr/Rb

At the Dingxi section which is located in the northwestern part of the Loess Plateau, the correlation coefficient between Zr/Rb ratio and mean grain size (Ms) is as high as 0.785 (P<0.001). The dependence of Zr/Rb on grain size is so high that the observed three orders of grain size variations[15] are nearly exactly mirrored by Zr/Rb ratio variations. The first order of Zr/Rb variations distinguishes the S1 from the underlying L2 and overlying L1 (Figure 4(a)). The average Zr/Rb ratios of L2 and L1 are 2.19 and 2.23 respectively, while the average Zr/Rb ratio of S1 is 1.97. This implies that the source material was considerably finer or/and the proximity to the source areas was farther during interglacial period than during the preceding (L2) and following (L1) glacial periods[15-17]. The second order refers to the bow-shaped curve within the last interglacial paleosol S1. That is, Zr/Rb ratio values in the middle portion are generally lower than those in the upper and lower portions within the S1. The bow-shaped curve of Zr/Rb ratio might result from the same processes that formed the bow-shaped curve of the grain size distribution[15]. Specifically, as the climate ameliorated gradually at the beginning of last interglacial, grain size became finer, resulting in a decrease in Zr/Rb ratio. After the climatic optimum (corresponding to Marine Isotope Stage 5e), the climate started to deteriorate. However, the climatic optimum (i.e., 5e) prepared abundant weathered fine materials in the source areas for the following periods (i.e., 5d and 5c), thus generating the finest grain size and the corresponding lowest Zr/Rb ratio in the middle portion of the S1. The coarsening trend of grain size or increasing trend of Zr/Rb in later periods (i.e., 5b and 5a) is a result of overall climatic deterioration after 5e. The third order variation of Zr/Rb ratio is not exactly in-phase with third-order variation of grain size. It is interesting to note that the valleys or lows of Zr/Rb ratio that are superimposed on the bow-shaped curve (e.g., va1, va2 and va3 in Figure 4(a)) have a slight lead relative to the peaks of CIA (a measure of chemical weathering intensity), This may be indicative of downward translocation of Rb in the S1S3 and S1S2. However, the leaching depth of Rb is quite limited in this profile (see the vertical arrows in Figure 4 (a)).

Southeastward to the Tianshui section, Zr/Rb is also dependent on grain size variation although the correlation coefficient between the two is lower (r=0.525, P<0.001) than that at the Dingxi section. It is apparent that the first-order variation of grain size was mirrored by Zr/Rb variation. That is, the Zr/Rb ratios within S1 are distinguishable from those in L1 and L2. The average Zr/Rb value for S1 is 1.90, the average Zr/Rb values for L2 and L1 are

1.98, 1.96 respectively. It is worthy to note that the difference of Zr/Rb between the paleosol S1 and loess units (L1 and L2) is reduced, probably implying that sorting-induced Rb enrichment was offset by leaching-induced Rb loss in more humid area. It appears that the second order variation of Zr/Rb in S1 is ambiguous at the Tianshui section, probably due to enhanced weathering and soil welding[15]. The enhanced weathering might have also contributed to the emergence of the third-order variation of Zr/Rb. That is, the troughs of Zr/Rb, such as vb1 at the top of Bk and vb2 at the bottom of Bt, may be indicative of Rb downward translocation from the upper layers (shaded zone Ⅰ and zone Ⅱ in Figure 4(b)). Interestingly, the Zr/Rb values in zone Ⅰ are not as low as those in zone Ⅱ though the CIA is higher in zone Ⅰ than in zone Ⅱ. This is probably because Rb translocation from upper horizon to zone Ⅱ is less due to weakened weathering in the following period and it didn't depress Zr/Rb as much as it did in zone Ⅰ. Consequently, the implication of Zr/Rb was complicated by weathering and pedogenic processes (including soil welding)[15,18]. Compared to Dingxi section, leaching depth of Rb in Tianshui is deeper (see arrows in Figure 4(b)).

At Lantian section in the southeastern margin of the Chinese Loess Plateau, though the correlation between mean grain size and Zr/Rb is still significant (r = 0.523, P < 0.001), the average Zr/Rb of S1 (2.12) is higher than those of L2 (1.95) and L1 (1.92), being opposite to the first-order variation of grain size observed in the other two sites (Dingxi and Tianshui). The positive correlation between Zr/Rb and CIA (r = 0.382, P<0.001) further confirmed our earlier speculation that the original Zr/Rb value was greatly altered by intense chemical weathering. It is notable that a plateau of Zr/Rb corresponds well to a plateau of grain size (Ms) in shaded zone Ⅰ (see Figure 4(c)), being supportive to the eolian-sorting assumption. However, the fact that the Zr/Rb values in zone Ⅰ (Figure 4(c)) are even higher than those in last glacial loess L1 at two sites (the Tianshui section and Baoji section[7] which are closer to source area) challenges the eolian-sorting assumption. Therefore we interpret this Zr/Rb peak in zone Ⅰ as a result of strong leaching of Rb. The Zr/Rb curve in shaded zone Ⅱ displays as a minor peak in S1 except for the presence of a trough (vc1) which is probably caused by Rb translocation from upper horizon (Figure 4(c)). Undoubtedly, the minor peak should also be related to significant Rb loss caused by strong weathering (CIA>70). Unlike at northwestern site (i.e., the Dingxi section), both the first-order and second-order variations in Zr/Rb ratio are absent at the Lantian section mainly due to pedogenic annexation and welding under warm and wet climate.

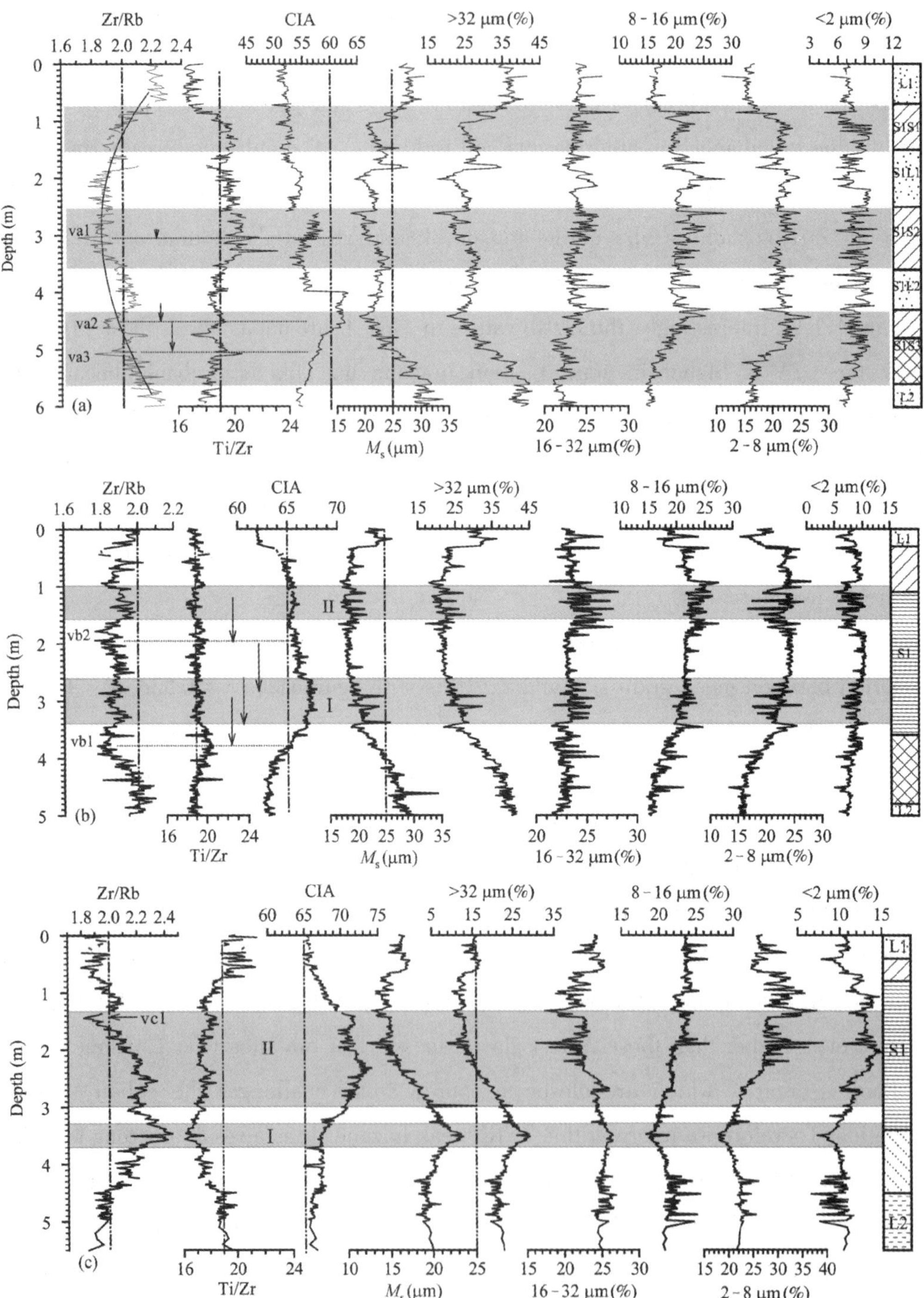

Figure 4 (a) Dingxi section: Zr/Rb, Ti/Zr, CIA and grain size parameters; (b) Tianshui section: Zr/Rb, Ti/Zr, CIA and Grain size parameters; (c) Lantian section: Zr/Rb, Ti/Zr, CIA and grain size parameters

3 Discussion

3.1 Zr/Hf ratio

The increasing trend of Zr concentration and the decreasing trend of grain size along the NW–SE transect for the last interglacial S1 contradict the assumption that Zr or Zr-bearing minerals are enriched in coarser grain size fraction. We have made one speculation in section 2.1 that the Zr-bearing minerals during last interglacial are possibly different from those during glacial periods. This needs to be further examined. The ratio of Zr to Hf (Zr/Hf) provides the potential to examine this speculation. Zr, Hf belongs to high-field-strength elements (HFSE). They are tetravalent metals that show broadly similar behavior[19] in various geochemical processes owing to their high valence, relatively small and similar ionic radii (8.4 nm for Zr, 8.3 nm for Hf) and intermediate electronegativity values[20]. Zr/Hf fractionation in oceanic island basalts (OIB) is mainly controlled by clinopyroxene crystallization during petrogenetic processes[21,22]. The Zr/Hf ratio in OIB is usually higher than Zr/Hf in mid-ocean ridge basalts (MORB) and Zr/Hf in continental crust[21]. Zr/Hf in continental crust is quite constant and generally displays the same range of variation for Zr/Hf ratios with average values close to chondrites (e.g. Zr/Hf=34.2±0.3 by Weaver[23]). As for Zr-bearing minerals, they have distinguishable Zr/Hf distribution ranges[24]. In this study, the average value of Zr/Hf at Dingxi, Tianshui and Lantian is 32.04, 32.71 and 33.95 respectively, all of which are close to Zr/Hf in UCC (32.76), indicating that the loess material is highly recycled and homogenously mixed. Figure 5 shows Zr/Hf ratios in loess and paleosol at the Dingxi section are relatively constant, while Zr/Hf ratios are higher in S1 than in loess layers at both the Tianshui section and the Lantian section. Assuming Zr/Hf ratio is constant in zircon which is a very common Zr-bearing mineral in loess, two reasons could probably account for the higher Zr/Hf ratio in last interglacial paleosols at the Tianshui section and the Lantian section: (1) ascent of concentrating effect by other Zr-bearing minerals (in finer grain size) with higher Zr/Hf ratio, and/or (2) descent of diluting effect by other Zr-bearing minerals (in coarser grain size) with lower Zr/Hf ratio. In thinking of the increasing trend of Zr in the last interglacial along NW–SE transect, we prefer the first explanation in which Zr-bearing minerals, with higher Zr concentration and higher Zr/Hf ratio, fractionated along NW–SE transect. If the Zr concentration (190 μg/g) in UCC is taken as a start point for the Zr-bearing minerals with higher Zr concentration and higher Zr/Hf ratio, we proposed that the most possible such minerals should at least include ilmenite. That is to say, the production of ilmenite released by weathering in source area was probably more during the last interglacial than during glacial periods.

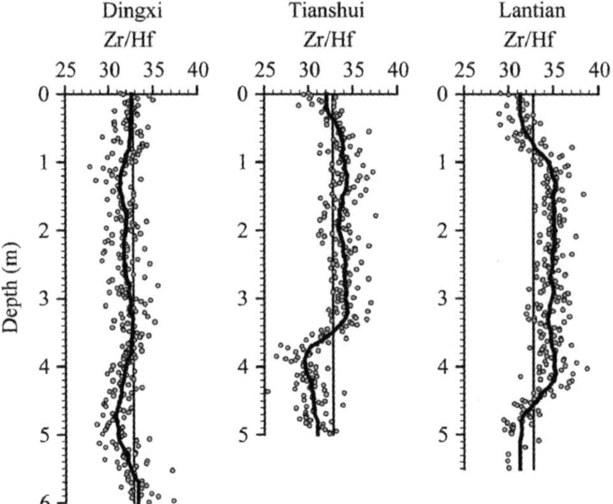

Figure 5 Zr/Hf variations in Dingxi, Tianshui and Lantian profiles. The vertical reference line represents Zr/Hf of UCC (32.76)[9]. The bold solid line represents 5-point running average of Zr/Hf.

3.2 Problem with comparison between Zr/Rb in loess record and eolian dust flux in deep sea core V21–146

The Northwest Pacific core V21–146 lies under the prevailing Northern Hemisphere westerlies and downwind from China - Mongolia dust source area. This core is situated within the latitudinal range with the maximum dust supply during either interglacial or glacial. Thus, the eolian flux recorded in core V21–146 has been suggested as an indicator of aridity in continental Asia[25]. But changes in Asian aridity as recorded in core V21–146 are inconsistent with other records, e.g., from core KK75–02[26]. Also, the records of eolian dust deposition in six Northwest Pacific cores during the last 30000 years are in conflict with loess records in China[27]. Therefore, a more plausible interpretation, as proposed by Pye and Zhou[28], is that fluctuations of eolian flux to Northwest Pacific reflects changes in the frequency and/or the intensity of vertical dust uplifting events, and the latitudinal position of westerlies, rather than changes in aridity of the source area. Liu et al. correlated the Zr/Rb in loess records to eolian flux in core V21– 146 and concluded that winter monsoon strength during MIS 3 is comparable to MIS 5[6]. We argued that the correlation and the conclusion are unwarranted for the following reasons: (1) the latitudinal position of westerlies must be different during glacial and interglacial [29]; and (2) the Zr - bearing minerals and their enrichment grain size fraction might be different during glacial and interglacial.

3.3 The significance of provenance and post-depositional weathering

It is well accepted that provenance, weathering, transportation and deposition, diagenesis and metamorphism are the most important factors affecting the chemical composition of clastic sedimentary rocks [8,9]. The importance of transportation on fractionating Zr and Rb was fully assessed in early studies [6,7,30]. As the heat and pressure conditions in S1, L1 and L2 are insufficient for diagenesis and metamorphism, so their affect on Zr/Rb ratio can be precluded. However, we argued that the effects of provenance and post-depositional weathering or pedogenesis on Zr/Rb should be addressed though they were ignored in early studies. Firstly, the fates of Rb and Zr are differentiated during soil formation processes, thus the initial Zr/Rb may be altered by subsequent weathering or pedogenesis. Secondly, the expansion and retraction of sandy desert area and dynamic evolution of Gobi desert occurred frequently during ancient periods [16,17,31,32]. This implies that the extent and location of source areas and even the weathering intensity of source material might fluctuate frequently.

Our results have shown that post-depositional weathering can more or less alter the original Zr/Rb. Thus, it is necessary to watch a CIA boundary for qualification of Zr/Rb as an indicator of winter monsoon strength. The bulk composition and mineralogy of the Toorongo Granodiorite, Australia, are similar to the average UCC. Nesbitt and Markovics studied the weathering characteristics of Toorongo profile and their results showed that Rb, Zr release is evident when CIA>65 [11]. This provides an insight into weathering of loess material which is an excellent starting point for estimating the average composition of UCC [33,34]. It seems that CIA=65 is a boundary in our profiles too. Thus caution must be exercised in using Zr/Rb ratio to reflect winter monsoon strength when CIA>65.

With regard to the provenance factors affecting Zr/Rb fluctuation, firstly, the proximity to source area has been demonstrated to play an important role in grain size distributions of loess in the desert–loess transitional zone, though it may play a lesser role in the middle and southern parts of the Loess Plateau [35]. Hence, the proximity to desert margin should also play a role in modulating Zr/Rb variation. Secondly, the Zr-bearing minerals and their enrichment grain size fraction are probably different during interglacial and during glacial. Specifically, during glacial periods, the Zr-bearing minerals are mostly enriched in coarser grain size fraction due to moderate weathering in source area; while during interglacial time, the Zr - bearing minerals tend to be enriched in finer grain size fraction owing to increased weathering in source area. It is worthy to note that the Zr/Rb ratios of S1 in this study as well as from other studies[7] are all constrained above 1.7, a value accidentaly equivalent to the Zr/Rb ratio of UCC[9]. Given an uncertainty of 5%, 1.7 is proposed to be the minimum value of Zr/Rb even in the Quaternary loess - paleosol sequence based on a long record of Zr/Rb variations presented by Chen et al.[7]. But it is worthy to note that the Zr/Rb minimum of red clay since late Miocene is less than 1.7[7]. All these suggest that the Zr/Rb minimum is shaped by transportation sorting and weathering in deposition area on the background of the Zr/Rb of source material (Figure 6), and only significant shift in location and weathering regime of source area[31,36] could lead to significant change of the Zr/Rb minima.

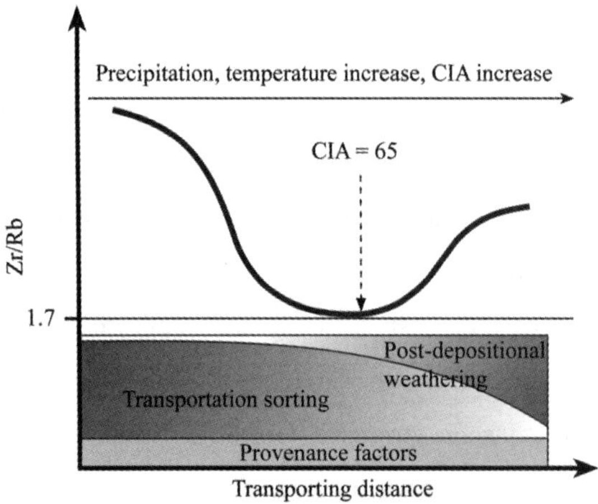

Figure 6 Schematic model showing spatial distribution pattern of Zr/Rb (The provenance factors, transportation sorting and post - depositional weathering may play different roles in shaping Zr/Rb curve along the dust input pathway)

4 Conclusion

The present study of spatiotemporal variations of Zr, Rb and Zr/Rb along the NW–SE loess transect leads to the following conclusions:

(1) Being consistent with previous studies, Rb is enriched in finer grain size fraction during either interglacial or glacial. However, the Zr - enriched grain size fractions are probably not identical during different periods: Zr is enriched in coarser grain size fraction during glacial periods while tends to be enriched in finer grain size fraction during last

interglacial. The differentiation of enrichment fraction might be attributed to diverse chemical weathering regime and/or different Zr - bearing minerals prepared in source area during interglacial and glacial periods.

(2) Transportation sorting definitely plays a significant role in regulating Zr/Rb. But the provenance factors, including the chemical composition of source sediments, location changes and weathering regime of source area, should play a predetermined role in Zr/Rb. Weathering and pedogenesis caused redistribution of Rb within soil, hence, the post - depositional weathering, superimposed on the provenance factors and sorting processes, also plays an evident role in modulating Zr/Rb. When CIA>65, the post - depositional weathering will significantly skew original Zr/Rb ratio, thus the Zr/Rb ratio loses its fidelity to follow grain size variation and caution must be observed on using Zr/Rb as an indicator of winter monsoon strength.

(3) The provenance factors, transportation sorting as well as post - depositional weathering constrain the Zr/Rb ratio of S1 above 1.7.

We are indebted to Ms. Duan Yindi for preparing XRF samples, and to Dr. Sun Aizhi, Dr. Pan Meihui and Mr. Li Shoubo for their assistance in laboratory analysis. We are also grateful to Prof. Sun Jimin and an anonymous reviewer for their constructive comments which greatly improved the manuscript.

1 Liu T S, Ding Z L. Chinese loess and the palaeomonsoon. Ann Rev Earth Planetary Sci, 1998, 26: 111–145.

2 An Z S, Liu T S, Lu Y C, et al. The long-term paleomonsoon variation recorded by the loess–paleosol sequence in central China. Quat Int, 1990, (7–8): 91–95.

3 Xiao J L, Porter S C, An Z S, et al. Grain Size of Quartz as an Indicator of Winter Monsoon Strength on the Loess Plateau of Central China during the Last 130000 Years. Quat Res, 1995, 43: 22–29.

4 Porter S C, An Z S. Correlation between climate events in the North Atlantic and China during the last glaciation. Nature, 1995, 375: 305–308.

5 Pope G A. Internal weathering of quartz grains. Phys Geogr, 1995, 16: 315–338.

6 Liu L, Chen J, Chen Y, et al. Variation of Zr/Rb ratios on the Loess Plateau of Central China during the last 130000 years and its implications for winter monsoon, Chin Sci Bull, 2002, 47(15): 1298–1302.

7 Chen J, Chen Y, Liu L W, et al. Zr/Rb ratio in the Chinese loess sequences and its implication

for changes in the East Asian winter monsoon strength. Geochim Cosmochim Acta, 2006, 70: 1471–1482.

8 Condie K C, Dengate J, Cullers R L. Behavior of rare earth elements in a paleoweathering profile on granodiorite in the Front Range, Colorado, USA. Geochim Cosmochim Acta, 1995, 59(2): 279–294.

9 Taylor S R, McLennan SM. The Continental Crust: Its Composition and Evolution. Oxford: Blackwell, 1985: 9–49.

10 Hodson M E. Experimental evidence for mobility of Zr and other trace elements in soils. Geochim Cosmochim Acta, 2002, 66(5): 819–828.

11 Nesbitt H W, Markovics G. Weathering of granodioritic crust, long-term storage of elements in weathering profiles, and petrogenesis of siliciclastic sediments. Geochim Cosmochim Acta, 1997, 61(8): 1653–1670.

12 Hutton J T. Titanium and zirconium minerals // Dixon J B, Weed S B. Minerals in Soil Environment. Madison: Soil Science Society of America, 1977: 673.

13 Yang S L, Ding F, Ding Z L. Pleistocene chemical weathering history of Asian arid and semi-arid regions recorded in loess deposits of China and Tajikistan. Geochim Cosmochim Acta, 2006, 70:1695–1709.

14 Wedephol K H. The composition of the continental crust. Geochim Cosmochim Acta, 1995, 59(7): 1217–1232.

15 Feng Z D, Wang H B. Geographic variations in particle size distribution of the last interglacial pedocomplex S1 across the Chinese Loess Plateau: Their chronological and pedogenic implications. Catena,2006, 65(3): 315–328.

16 Sun J M, Yin G M, Ding Z L. et al. Thermoluminescence chronology of sand profiles in the Mu Us Desert, China. Palaeogeog Palaeoclimatol Palaeoecol, 1998, 144: 225–233.

17 Sun J M, Ding Z L, Liu T S, et al. 580,000-year environmental reconstruction from aeolian deposits at the Mu Us Desert margin, China. Quat Sci Rev, 1999, 18: 1351–1364.

18 Feng Z D, Wang H B, Olson C G, et al. Chronological discord between the last interglacial paleosol (S1) and its parent material in the Chinese Loess Plateau. Quat Int, 2004, 117: 17–26.

19 Jochum K P, Seufert H M, Spettel B, et al. The solar-system abundances of Nb, Ta and Y, and the relative abundances of refractory lithophile elements in differentiated planetary bodies. Geochim Cosmochim Acta, 1986, 50: 1173–1183.

20 Shannon R D. Revised effective ionic radii and systematic studies of interatomic distances in halides and chalcogenides. Acta Crystallogr, 1976, A32: 751–767.

21 David K, Schiano P, Allègre C J. Assessment of the Zr/Hf fractionation in oceanic basalts

and continental materials during petrogenetic processes. Earth Planet Sci Lett, 2000, 178: 285–301.

22 Linnen R L, Keppler H. Melt composition control of Zr/Hf fractionation in magmatic processes. Geochim Cosmochim Acta, 2002, 66(18): 3293–3301.

23 Weyer S, Münker C, Rehkämper M, et al. Determination of ultra-low Nb, Ta, Zr and Hf concentrations and the chondritic Zr/Hf and Nb/Ta ratios by isotope dilution analyses with multiple collector ICP–MS. Chem Geol, 2002, 187: 295–313.

24 Bea F, Montero P, Ortega M. A LA–ICP–MS evaluation of Zr reservoirs in common crustal rocks: implications for Zr and Hf geochemistry, and zircon-forming processes. Cana Mineralogist, 2006, 44(3): 693–714.

25 Hovan S A, Rea D K, Pisias N G. Late Pleistocene continental climate and oceanic variability recorded in northwest Pacific sediments. Paleoceanography, 1991, 6: 349–370.

26 Janecek T R, Rea D K. Quaternary fluctuations in the Northern Hemisphere trade winds and westerlies. Quat Res, 1985, 24(2): 150–163.

27 Rea D K, Leinen M. Asian aridity and the zonal westerlies: Late Pleistocene and Holocene record of eolian deposition in the northwest Pacific Ocean. Palaeogeogr Palaeoclimatol Palaeoecol, 1988, 66: 1–8.

28 Pye K, Zhou L P. Late Pleistocene and Holocene aeolian dust deposition in North China and the northwest Pacific Ocean. Palaeogeogr Palaeoclimatol Palaeoecol, 1989, 73: 11–23.

29 Rea D K. The paleoclimatic record provided by eolian deposition in the deep sea: The geologic history of wind. Rev Geophy, 1994, 32: 159–195.

30 Dypvik H, Harris N B. Geochemical facies analysis of fine-grained siliciclastics using Th/U, Zr/Rb and (Zr+Rb)/Sr ratios. Chem Geol, 2001, 181: 131–146.

31 Ding Z L, Derbyshire E, Yang S L, et al. Stepwise expansion of desert environment across northern China in the past 3.5 Ma and implications for monsoon evolution. Earth Planet Sci Lett, 2005, 237: 45–55.

32 Feng Z D, Zhai X W, Ma Y Z, et al. Eolian environmental changes in the Northern Mongolian Plateau during the past 35,000 years. Palaeogeogr Palaeoclimatol Palaeoecol, 2007, 245: 505–517.

33 Taylor S R, McLennan S M, McCulloch M T. Geochemistry of loess, continental crustal composition and crustal model ages. Geochim Cosmochim Acta, 1983, 47: 1897–1905.

34 Gallet S, Jahn B M, Torii M. Geochemical characterization of loess-paleosol sequence from the Luochuan section, China, and its paleoclimatic implications. Chem Geol, 1996, 133: 67–88.

35 Ding Z L, Sun J M, Rutter N W et al. Changes in sand content of loess deposits along a north-

south transect of the Chinese Loess Plateau and the implications for desert variations. Quat Res, 1999, 52: 56–62.

36 Sun J M. Nd and Sr isotopic variations in Chinese eolian deposits during the past 8 Ma: Implications for provenance change. Earth Planet Sci Lett, 2005, 240(2): 454–466.

后　记

4年的博士求学生活是我人生中最为艰苦卓绝的一段历程。在博士论文结稿之际，心情释然，令我对周围的一切都充满了感激之心。

首先我要感谢导师冯兆东教授，感谢他多年来对我在物质和精神上持续的支持，对我在土壤发生学方面的训练。Professional（专业）、Paradigm（按规范行事）、Perfect（在力所能及的范围内求得完美）、Humorous（幽默）、Diligent（勤勉）是冯老师的几个特性，这些品质或许也是一个理学博士所应具备的品质吧。

我也十分感谢张家武博士，他是一位我最乐意寻求帮助并能得到帮助的朋友。攻读硕士之初我便跟着这位热心、仁厚的师兄学习实验技能，受到他的影响我的英语水平也不断获得提高。

野外的样品采集得到了陈发虎教授、张家武博士、安成邦博士等人的帮助，感谢他们的辛苦工作。另外，美国土壤调查局的土壤学家Carolyn Olson教授就天水、秦安、定西、庆阳、蓝田等土壤剖面的描述对我们进行了现场指导，受益匪浅。实验室的样品测量工作大部分是在段引弟女士、张开兰女士的协助下完成的，在此我向他们表示深深的谢意。美国蒙特克莱尔州立大学Gregory Pope教授对野外地层描述进行了指导并提供了定西剖面的地球化学资料；孙爱芝博士帮助测量了土壤样品的地球化学元素浓度，她还与韩惠博士、王维先生为我修改论文稿的文字和参考文献错误，在此亦向他们致以谢意。我还以处于一个和谐的学习、研究小组而深感荣幸。这绝对是一个欢乐制造小组，小组成员包括：俄有浩博士、张永忠博士、李常斌博士、韩惠博士、张小文博士、邹松兵博士、翟新伟博士、郭兰兰女士、王丽霞女士、王一博博士、李守波先生。

深深地感谢我的父母、妻子、女儿，家人的期望和支持是我前进的动力！

汪海斌

2005年5月

我的家庭

在别的同学眼里，我很可怜，可我不觉得，不就是单亲吗？我和妈妈一样可以挺过去。

那次妈妈过生日，我和爸爸、妈妈一起开开心心地过完，爸爸就要出野外了，我总有一种不好的预感，我和妈妈一起送爸爸出门，然后我就上学去了。放学回到家，写完家庭作业，妈妈让我学习英语，学完后已经九点了，妈妈就让我洗洗睡了。凌晨四点多的时候，我被一阵急促的手机铃声吵醒了，妈妈接完电话就急忙叫我穿衣服，我穿衣服的时候，妈妈在翻箱倒柜地找衣服，收拾完，拽着我就跑去了小区门口，一辆黑色的车停在门口，车后座上坐着爸爸的同事张东菊阿姨，我被一把推了上去，紧接着妈妈也坐上来。等车开动了，妈妈才告诉我爸爸出事了，我的预感是对的，我的心悬在空中，感觉很不安。

匆匆忙忙赶到了西宁，我们直奔医院的手术室。门口的医生说爸爸的头部受到了重创，刚做完手术，待会要送去重症监护室。我和妈妈焦急地等待着，时间在一分一秒地过去，我的心揪成了一团。突然，手术室的门开了，一辆推车急速地被推进了电梯，我扫了一眼，竟然认不出那是爸爸。等我和妈妈坐另一部电梯赶到爸爸的病房，走到爸爸的病床边，我吓了一跳：爸爸的额头上缠绕着厚厚的纱布，两只眼睛紧闭着，眼睛是紫色的，高高地肿起来，护士说我们不能待太久，所以我在懵懂之间和妈妈走出了重症监护室。等在外面的张冬菊阿姨问了一句，妈妈就哭了。随后，我被送去了附近的一家宾馆，我睡了一大觉醒来已是第二天早上，我和陪我的张东菊阿姨吃完饭，去了医院，妈妈说我不能耽误太多功课让我和张东菊阿姨先回兰州。晚上的时候，我正在同学家玩，妈妈却打电话让我回家。在路上的时候，我已经猜到，爸爸已经去了另一个世界了。

我知道有一天，我还会和爸爸见面的，每当我看到天上的星星，我知道，最亮的那颗星星是属于爸爸的。

汪悦扬

2013年4月

（本文2014年3月获得第十四届华人少年作文比赛二等奖）

写在海斌论文出版之前

冯兆东教授在2013年5月份的时候请杨晓燕老师转达了想要出版海斌的博士论文的建议，当时因为忙，更因为我自己的状态不好，提起海斌就会心痛，本能地想要逃避这种痛苦，所以耽搁到冯老师委托李常斌老师转来一封亲笔书信。从我本心来讲，冯老师的想法和我的是不谋而合的，我曾听海斌说起过想出版博士论文的想法，但因为他太忙了，一直都没顾上。冯老师很懂海斌的心思，海斌博士期间在学术方面的成就、野外经验的积累与冯老师的言传身教密不可分，冯老师科研资金的支持也为海斌学术上的发展提供了很大的发展空间，师生之间良好的沟通曾让海斌对我说过“冯老师是他的半个知音”这样的话，这次冯老师先提出发表海斌的博士论文就是他们师生之间心意相通的明证。海斌的心愿也是我的心愿，出版他的博士论文是我能为海斌做的一件有意义的事，也是我和女儿对海斌永久的纪念。

一直隐忍，一直坚持，想用更客观的语气来讲述这本书的出版，而不是煽情，但我此刻眼泪已决堤……想起海斌，想起英年早逝的爱人，我真的无法做到平静与坦然。同学7年，夫妻10年，我们两个外地人在兰州共同学习、生活了17年，从相识相知到相爱相随，从相依为命到一家3口，从负债累累到略有转机……我生命中将近半数的时间是与海斌在一起度过的，他的音容笑貌不仅刻在我的脑海里，他的名字、他的一切更融化在我的生命里。他一贯挺直的脊背、略微昂着的头颅、似笑非笑的眼睛、凝神屏息的神态经常浮现于我的眼前，他的执着、刻苦和追求完美的性格常常让我在记忆深处驻足，流连于往事。

从小学到博士后，海斌都是班上的优秀学生，他的刻苦和勤奋铸就了他学业上的成功。或许他不是最聪明的人，但在教过他的老师眼里，在他的同学眼里，他是最刻苦、最勤奋的学生。在我的眼里，他是没有周末、没有节假日的。除了出野外的时间，他不是在办公室就是在家里的电脑上工作，经常一坐就是半天。或许这就是搞学术的人的必修课，他的心里、眼里只有工作。虽然我有时会抱怨他不顾家，但唠叨归唠叨，心里对他的敬佩却与日俱增。

海斌的执着表现在他对所学专业的持之以恒和不懈努力。从就业角度来说，自然地理学是理科专业中较为冷僻的专业之一，但我从没听海斌说过任何抱怨专业的话，而是从进入大学的第一天开始就把这个专业作为自己的职业，并付出全部的努力，直至付出生命！

海斌是处女座的，追求完美的特质在他身上表现得淋漓尽致。任何事他都追求尽善尽美：他的钢笔字字体丰满，苍劲有力，一直让我引以为傲；他做的图细节完美，让导师无可挑剔；他做实验严谨认真，实验数据真实可靠……

老师、同学、朋友、家人的喜爱和信任是对海斌人品的充分肯定，他虽然不善言谈，但他用自己的实际行动向身边的人证实了自己，并获得了尊重和认可。可是天妒英才，他才35岁就离开了人世，离开了他所热爱的事业和家庭。海斌走后的一段时间内，我几乎天天凝视着他的遗像，望着他淡然的微笑和温热的双眸，心里一遍又一遍地问：海斌，你舍得离开我们吗？你舍得走吗？……

海斌的一生是短暂的，也是辉煌灿烂的，这离不开他个人的努力奋斗、家庭的大力支持，更离不开关心、爱护他的师长、朋友们。首先感谢海斌的硕士导师陈发虎教授，在陈老师的谆谆教导下，海斌夯实了专业基础，获取了宝贵的野外经验，并发表了他的第一篇学术论文；北师大的刘连友、马玉珍等教授、青海盐湖所的赖忠平研究员，还有杨石岭老师、陆珊年老师等对海斌的指导让他受益匪浅；张家武、吴海斌、张小文、郭兰兰等师兄弟姐妹与海斌在求学期间建立了深厚的情谊；上官冬辉、南卓铜、吴立宗、曹学诚、何春阳等同学的关心如一缕阳光温暖着海斌；海斌在美国做访问学者期间得到了Mary Ann Montana的无私帮助……借海斌博士论文出版的契机，我谨代表海斌向各位关心、爱护他的老师、长辈、同学、朋友致以最衷心的感谢，谢谢你们多年来对海斌的教导、帮助、支持和鼓励，才使他有了今天的成就；正是有了你们的关爱，才有了今天的海斌，谢谢你们！

最后，再次感谢冯兆东老师经济上和精神上的大力支持，才有了这本书的出版，在他的坚持和倡议下，我终于从萎靡不振的苦闷状态下走出来，让我把自己消极的、单纯的对海斌的思念转化为有意义的行动。在交付出版之前，我仔仔细细地读了三遍海斌的博士论文，认真修改、润色自认为不够完美的地方，既为完成海斌的遗愿，也为表达自己的思念。

李世萍

2014年2月